Law of Obligations

Law of Obligations

Geoffrey Samuel

Professor of Law, Kent Law School, UK

Edward Elgar
Cheltenham, UK • Northampton, MA, USA

© Geoffrey Samuel 2010

All rights reserved. No part of this publication may be reproduced, stored in a retrieval system or transmitted in any form or by any means, electronic, mechanical or photocopying, recording, or otherwise without the prior permission of the publisher.

Published by
Edward Elgar Publishing Limited
The Lypiatts
15 Lansdown Road
Cheltenham
Glos GL50 2JA
UK

Edward Elgar Publishing, Inc.
William Pratt House
9 Dewey Court
Northampton
Massachusetts 01060
USA

A catalogue record for this book is available from the British Library

Library of Congress Control Number: 2009937778

Mixed Sources
Product group from well-managed forests and other controlled sources
www.fsc.org Cert no. SA-COC-1565
© 1996 Forest Stewardship Council

ISBN 978 1 84844 764 6 (cased)

Printed and bound by MPG Books Group, UK

Contents

Preface	x
List of abbreviations	xii
Introductory remarks	xiii
List of cases	xvii
List of statutes and texts	xxxiv

1	**Theory and method: background to the law of obligations**	**1**
	The epistemological dilemma	1
	Institutional plan	2
	Codes and method	3
	English legal mentality	4
	Institutional system and the common law	8
2	**History and structure of the law of obligations**	**10**
	Real and personal remedies and rights	10
	Divisions and subdivisions of private law	12
	Public law	14
	Contract	15
	Delict	18
	Quasi delict (and liability without fault)	21
	Quasi-contract (and unjust enrichment)	23
	Alternative approaches	25
3	**General theory of obligations**	**27**
	Formation of an obligation	27
	Content of an obligation	29
	Content and rescission	31
	Level of obligational duty	32
	Obligations and the role of fault	33
	Debt and damages actions	36
	Extra-contractual liability	38
	Obligations as rights	40
	Abuse of rights	41
	Obligations as property	44
	Transfer of obligation rights	46

	Extinction of an obligation	46
4	**Obligations and the common law**	**48**
	Personal actions at common law (forms of action)	48
	Causes of action	51
	Contract and tort	53
	Restitution (unjust enrichment)	55
	Remedies	57
	Injunctions	59
	Specific performance in equity	60
	Damages	61
	Debt and account	63
	Restitutionary interest	65
	Rescission	66
5	**Contractual obligations: general provisions**	**69**
	General considerations	69
	Definition of contract	70
	Contract and remedies	73
	Contract and rights	77
	Classification of contracts	78
	Bailment and contract	82
	Public and private law contracts	83
	Commercial and consumer contracts	84
	Freedom of contract	85
	Good faith	86
	Domain of contract	88
6	**Enforcing contracts**	**90**
	Contract and methodology	90
	Formation models	93
	Cause (*causa*)	94
	Agreement (*conventio*)	94
	Promise (*promissio*)	95
	Promise and agreement	97
	Enforceable promises	99
	Difficult cases	101
	Absence of clarity	104
	Absence of consensus	105
	Intention to create legal relations	106
	Revocation of an offer	107
	Acceptance	108

	Consideration	110
	Variation of existing contracts	112
	Consideration and third parties	114
	Deed of covenant	116
7	**Escaping from contracts**	**117**
	Defective contracts	117
	Defective contracts and remedies	120
	Implied condition	122
	European approach	123
	Property problems	123
	Fraud and duress	125
	Capacity	128
	Illegality	129
	Cancelled contracts	131
	Non-performance of a contract	132
8	**Unperformed contracts and appropriate remedies**	**133**
	Interpretation and liability	133
	Differences of approach	135
	Terms	136
	Conditions and warranites	137
	Implied terms	139
	Unfair terms	141
	Performance and non-performance of the contract	142
	Onerous performance	144
	Non-performance and exclusion clauses	145
	Performance and third parties	148
	Non-performance and termination	149
	Non-performance and agreement	150
9	**Tortious obligations: general provisions**	**152**
	Civilian approach	152
	English approach	154
	Definitional considerations	156
	Purpose and policy of tort	158
	Actions for damages	159
	Aims of the law of tort	160
	Tort and methodology	163
	Policy and functionalism	166
	Interests and rights	168
	Axiology and argumentation	169

	Statutory interpretation	170
	Methodology: concluding remarks	172

10 Liability and intentional harm — 174

Liability and fault	174
Liability for individual acts: general elements	176
Intentional harm	179
Intentional torts	181
Intentional torts and methodology	191

11 Liability for unintentional harm — 193

Tort of negligence	193
Breach of duty	194
Duty of care	197
Extension of duty of care	200
Methodological approach to duty	201
Economic loss	203
Psychological damage (nervous shock)	206
Omissions	209
Public bodies	210
Human rights	212
Comparative reflections	213
Unlawful acts	216

12 Liability for things — 219

Liability for moveable things	219
Dangerous products	220
Defective equipment	222
Animals	223
Motor vehicles	224
Aircraft	225
Land and buildings: harm on the premises	225
Land and buildings: harm off the premises	229
Liability for dangerous things	234
Occupier's liability: methodological considerations	236

13 Liability for people — 239

Vicarious liability	239
Theory of vicarious liability	242
Non-delegable duty	244
Owners of motor vehicles	247
Publishers	248

14 Liability for words — 249
Deceit and negligence — 249
Defamation — 251
Beyond defamation — 253
Intellectual property rights — 255
Privacy — 256
Professional liability — 258

15 Escaping liability — 263
Causation: introduction — 263
Theories of causation — 265
Level 1: actionability — 269
Level 2: cause in fact — 272
Loss of a chance — 273
Overlapping causes and overlapping damage — 278
Novus actus interveniens — 280
Level 3: remoteness of damage — 283
Untypical damage — 287
Level 4: causation and remedies — 288
Measure of damages — 290

16 Beyond contract and tort: restitution — 295
Liability for gain — 295
Enrichment — 297
Expense of another — 299
'Unjust' (*sans cause*) — 300
Remedies and unjust enrichment — 301
Equitable remedies — 305
Tracing — 307
Present status of restitution — 309

17 Transnational law of obligations? — 312
Possibility of harmonisation — 313
Harmonisation through science and system — 314
Harmonisation through casuistic methods — 318
Obstacles to harmonisation — 322
Role of comparative law — 325
Obligations and property — 327
Spirit of non-codification — 330
Conclusion: abandoning the obligations category — 331

Bibliography — 334
Index — 341

Preface

This book is in part a second and expanded edition of my *Understanding Contractual and Non-Contractual Obligations* published by LawMatters in 2005. However certain parts of the book have been substantially rewritten and several new chapters added. Some of this rewriting has drawn on my other published books and contributions, but this new book does have its own aims and objectives. It is designed primarily to give students of English law and jurists from outside the common law an overview of contract and tort, including also a brief overview of the law of restitution. Another, and important, purpose is to give students of English law (and others) an introduction to the law of obligations in the civil (or continental) law tradition. Thus the book can be described as an introduction to the Western Law of Obligations, but with an emphasis (in terms of detail) on English law.

The author would like to thank Professors Franz Werro and Pascal Pichonnaz for their kind invitation to become a temporary member of their law faculty at Fribourg in 2008 (and at other times). Teaching on their intensive comparative contract programme has helped me to appreciate just how important it is to look at contract and tort in a comparative way. Whether one is in favour of harmonisation of private law or against it, the point remains that there is a hugely rich 2,000-year legal tradition in Europe and it seems intellectually criminal that many law students graduate from law faculties knowing little or nothing about this tradition. A quite recent publication by the Law Society has, sadly, revealed a depth of ignorance both among today's practitioners and some Lord Chancellors about the civil law tradition.

Thanks are due to other faculties and colleagues as well. Pierre Legrand and Horatia Muir Watt welcome me each year into their Paris faculties, as does Professor Jean-Pierre Duprat into his public law research and teaching institute in the law faculty at Bordeaux IV and Professor Christophe Jamin into Sciences-Po (Paris). These visiting posts are immensely stimulating and rewarding and have given me access not just to civil law research facilities but to the civilian outlook in general. Indeed looking at contract and tort from a strictly public law perspective in Bordeaux is always an interesting challenge for a common lawyer. My weekly Paris dinners with Pierre Legrand have helped me shape and develop comparative law theory and I thus owe him an enormous debt. Finally I must again thank my wife Jennifer and my sister Gillian for their constant family support.

Geoffrey Samuel
Kent Law School
May 2009

Abbreviations

BGB	Bürgerliches Gesetzbuch (German Civil Code)
C	Code of Justinian
CA	Court of Appeal
CC	Code civil (French Civil Code)
D	Digest of Justinian (also Dalloz)
G	Institutes of Gaius
HL	House of Lords
J	Institutes of Justinian (also Justice of the High Court)
JCP	Jurisclasseur périodique (La Semaine Juridique)
LJ	Lord Justice (Court of Appeal)
NBW	Nieuw Burgerlijk Wetboek (New Dutch Civil Code)
PC	Privy Council
PECL	Principles of European Contract Law
PETL	Principles of European Tort Law

Introductory remarks

The law of obligations is now a common term in English law both in professional practice and in academic writing. It is an import from the civil (Roman) law tradition and thus represents a concrete link, at least at the level of language, between English and continental private law. Some, no doubt, see its adoption as an early step in a journey towards the complete harmonisation of private law among the member states of the European Union. Indeed, there are now codes for both the law of contractual and non-contractual obligations. These codes, in particular the *Principles of European Contract Law* (PECL) (and see now the *Common Frame of Reference*) and the *Principles of European Tort Law* (PETL), will be important reference points in the chapters that follow since, even if they do not reflect current English positive law, they can help foster an understanding of how a law of obligations is structured. Nevertheless the use of the term 'obligations' in this present work and the references to European codes are not to be taken as implying that harmonisation of the common law and civil law is a foregone conclusion (see Chapter 17). In fact the adoption of the civilian category of a law of obligations does not come without a number of serious conceptual problems. Some of these problems will be dealt with in more depth in the chapters that follow.

In England the term 'law of obligations' is a generic category embracing three areas of law. These are: the law of contract; tort; and restitution (unjust enrichment). It is not entirely clear if trusts belong within the law of obligations since they tend to be more closely associated with the law of property. However they could have just as valid a claim to be included as, say, the law of restitution because trustees can be held liable for breach of a legal duty. Both the liability and the duty can be very similar to liabilities and duties within the law of obligations.[1] Indeed certain trust liabilities are actually classed within the law of restitution. It should thus already be apparent that the category of the law of obligations is not necessarily one that fits easily into the contours of the common law: for, on the continent property and obligations are alternative and not cumulative categories. Common lawyers have historically used a classification model very

---

[1] See eg *Royal Brunei Airlines v Tan* [1995] 2 AC 378.

different from the Roman one, even if both systems once thought in terms of a collection of forms of action.

This history of English law, among other things, will reveal that the present categories of contract and tort are a relatively recent way of classifying liability cases. This is not to say that contract was unknown to common lawyers before the 19th century, but it was often hidden behind a set of forms of action that had little or no connection with Roman law thinking. Trespass and debt were once more familiar categories than contract and tort.[2] The modern categories emerged and were consolidated in their definitive forms only over the last two centuries and restitution has gained its independence only very recently (see Chapter 16). The modern categories have, now, become detailed if not complex, yet the chapters that follow will not attempt to outline all the main principles of contract and tort (or restitution). Instead, with respect to the chapters on English law, the emphasis will be on how it approaches liability for breach of (or failure to perform) contractual and tortious obligations. In other words the tendency will be to look at what happens when things go wrong between the parties to an obligation.

In truth, the law of tort can be approached only from a liability point of view because, unlike contract, the subject is not one, even in the civil law, that thinks comprehensively in terms of a pre-existing binding duty between persons. The obligation to compensate arises out of the accident or the wrongful act itself. Nevertheless there are exceptions to this obligation point. Participating in certain activities such as driving and manufacturing, or occupying land, can be seen to carry with them duties or obligations towards others affected by these activities; and the existence of such an obligation is recognised by the various actors (or in some situations imposed by public law) in the recourse to liability insurance. Given this idea that an obligation can attach to activities, where damage has been caused by a person or thing under the control of another the present work will treat this as a liability for persons and for things (Chapters 12–13). This is rather French in its approach in the way it echoes a liability arising out of article 1384 of the *Code civil*; yet it is adopted here not so much to show harmonisation solidarity with civil law but simply because it is a most valuable approach to problem analysis. Distinguishing between harm arising out of an individual act and harm arising out of a thing is a factual distinction that is often useful to make when reflecting upon the legal concepts and rules that might be applicable. Indeed some things like dangerous premises, products or animals attract their own specific con-

---

[2] See generally Ibbetson (1999).

tract and (or) tort rules. Harm caused by one person connected by way of contract to another person can create causation and (or) duty problems and thus the idea of a liability for people is another useful analytical tool.

After an examination of the historical and conceptual foundations of the notion of a law of obligations, this work will focus primarily on contract and tort since these are foundational subjects in the law schools. Yet the law of restitution cannot be completely ignored since its main principles form part of the Obligations I and II syllabus and, anyway, both contract and tort problems can give rise to restitution issues.[3] The main structure underpinning liability arising out of the principle of unjust enrichment will thus be surveyed, but with reference to a draft statute which could act as something of an unofficial code and to the main remedies (Chapter 16). However this survey will be brief and will by no means attempt to do the law of restitution justice even in the context of an introductory book. The law of restitution is as detailed and rich as either contract or tort, but it tends to be studied in depth only at postgraduate level.

An introductory comment must also be made about legal method and reasoning because this is an aspect of legal knowledge that is as vital to understanding liability in any system of law. The official view of legal method in the law of obligations, especially in the continental (civil law) tradition, is that judges apply pre-existing contract and tort (delict) rules to sets of litigation facts as they present themselves before the courts (see Chapter 1). This view is not wrong, especially with respect to contract which is a subject that has many more rules than tort (see for example the *Code civil*). But such a view, at least with regard to English law, is only part of a larger methodological framework in which judges arrive at their solutions to cases using concepts, arguments and justifications drawn from sources not just from within the law but also from outside it. This is an aspect of English law that has a long history.[4] Policy and morality have their role to play in judgments and even where judges reason from within the law they might well draw some of their ideas and concepts from areas beyond contract or tort.[5] If contract and tort are to be properly understood, the methodology of the judges cannot be ignored as something 'outside' legal knowledge.

Finally this examination of the law of obligations will – by necessity – have a comparative dimension which will take several forms. First, the historical development of the law of obligations will be treated in some

---

[3] See eg *Att-Gen v Blake* [2001] 1 AC 268.
[4] See eg Lobban (1991).
[5] See in particular Waddams (2003).

detail since this is the intellectual source of the whole category (Chapter 2). Secondly, frequent references will be made to Roman law and to the law of some of the UK's partners in the European Union. Often this comparison will be at what might be termed the structural level, that is to say at the level of abstract relations between persons and persons and persons and things (together with the various categories and concepts associated with these relations), for this is the starting point of legal thinking in the civilian tradition.[6] However some more detailed comparative references will be made on occasions.

There are a number of advantages attached to this comparative approach for the English obligations student. Not only, for example, will it permit the problem-solver to reflect upon the various possible relations between the institutional focal points of a law problem (persons and things), but it will also allow the lawyer to reflect on alternative conceptual possibilities. Take for instance the problem of a person injured by a dangerous thing (say an exploding shell in a munitions factory). What relations should be emphasised? Should one put the emphasis on the land where the accident takes place and ask what duties should an occupier owe a visitor? Or should one put the emphasis on the exploding thing and ask who should bear the risk of injury caused by such a dangerous thing? Again, could one put the emphasis simply on the owner or occupier of the land, asking questions about his, her or its behaviour? More generally, with respect to this and to other problems, one could ask whether the emphasis should be put on acts or activities. Different legal systems will ask different questions.

Thirdly, in the final chapter, there will be a discussion of the current debate between comparative lawyers in Europe on the possibility, or impossibility, of developing a transnational law of obligations designed, ultimately, to eclipse national systems.

---

[6] Civil lawyers have never really been influenced by American Realism: see eg Jestaz and Jamin (2004).

Cases

COMMON LAW CASES

A v National Blood Authority
[2001] 3 All ER 289   **221**
Adams v Richard & Starling Ltd
[1969] 1 WLR 1645   **136**
Addis v Gramophone Co Ltd [1909]
AC 488   **255**
*Aerial Advertising Co v Batchelor's
Peas Ltd* [1938] 2 All ER
788   **139, 150**
Agip (Africa) Ltd v Jackson [1990]
Ch 265 (ChD); [1991] Ch 547
(CA)   **301, 307**
*Agnew v Länsförsäkringsbolagens
AB* [2001] 1 AC 223   **119**
Albazero (the) [1977] AC
774   **291, 305**
*Alcock v Chief Constable of South
Yorkshire* [1992] 1 AC 310   **206,
207–8, 209, 293**
*Allied Maples Group Ltd v
Simmons & Simmons* [1995] 1
WLR 1602   **274**
Allen v Flood [1898] AC 1   **187**
Alton v Midland Railway Co (1865)
34 LJCP 292   **9**
*Anchor Brewhouse Developments
Ltd v Berkley House (Docklands
Developments) Ltd* (1987)
38 BLR 82; (1987) 2 EGLR
172   **59, 231**
Anns v Merton LBC [1978] AC
728   **202, 205**

Aris v Orchard (1861) 30 LJ Exch
21   **54**
*Ashington Piggeries Ltd v C. Hill
Ltd* [1972] AC 441   **80**
*Ashmore, Benson, Pease & Co Ltd
v A. V. Dawson Ltd* [1973] 1
WLR 828   **129**
Att-Gen v Blake [2001] 1 AC
268   **xv, 49, 58, 65, 76, 296, 299,
302, 305**
*Att-Gen v Guardian Newspapers
(No 2)* [1990] AC 109   **302**
Att-Gen v PYA Quarries Ltd [1957]
2 QB 169   **190, 232, 233, 237**
Att-Gen v Times Newspapers Ltd
[1874] AC 273   **319**
Attia v British Gas Plc [1988] QB
304   **207, 293**
*Attica Sea Carriers Corporation
v Ferrostaal* [1976] 1 Ll Rep
250   **63–4**
Avon Finance Co Ltd v Bridger
[1985] 2 All ER 281   **125**

Bailey v Ayr Engineering Co Ltd
[1958] 2 All ER 222   **273**
Baker v Willoughby [1970] AC
467   **279**
Balfour v Balfour [1919] 2 KB
571   **107**
Bamford v Turnley (1862) 3 B & S
62; 122 ER 27   **237, 238**

Banks v Goodfellow (1870) 39 LJQB 237 **8**
Banque Bruxelles Lambert SA v Eagle Star Insurance Co Ltd [1997] AC 191 **267**
Banque Keyser Ullmann v Skandia Insurance [1990] 1 QB 665 (CA); [1991] AC 249 **67**
Barclays Bank Plc v Fairclough Building Ltd [1995] QB 214 **261, 289**
Barclays Bank Plc v O'Brien [1994] 1 AC 180 **127**
Barker v Corus UK Ltd [2006] 2 AC 572 **268, 276**
Barnett v Chelsea and Kensington Hospital Management Committee [1969] 1 QB 428 **272–3**
Barrett v Enfield LBC [2001] 2 AC 550 **200, 211, 212**
Barrett v Ministry of Defence [1995] 1 WLR 1217 **209**
Barry v Davies [2000] 1 WLR 1962 **102**
Barton v Armstrong [1975] 2 All ER 465 **67, 126**
Batthyany v Walford (1886) 33 Ch D 624 **9**
Bell v Lever Brothers [1932] AC 161 **99, 121, 123**
Benjamin v Storr (1874) LR 9 CP 400 **53, 220**
Berkoff v Burchill [1996] 4 All ER 1008 **251**
Bernstein v Skyviews & General Ltd [1978] QB 497 **231**
Best v Samuel Fox & Co Ltd [1952] AC 716 **206**
Beswick v Beswick [1966] Ch 538 (CA); [1968] AC 58 **58, 78, 114, 115**

Bird v Jones (1845) 115 ER 668 **191**
Birmingham CC v Oakley [2001] 1 AC 617 **171, 172**
Birse Construction Ltd v Haiste Ltd [1996] 2 All ER 1 **199**
Blackmore v Bristol & Exeter Railway Co (1858) 27 LJQB 167 **8**
Blackpool & Fylde Aero Club Ltd v Blackpool BC [1990] 1 WLR 1195 **70, 72, 105**
Blackshaw v Lord [1984] QB 1 **252**
Blake v Galloway [2004] 1 WLR 2844 **191, 270**
Blyth v Birmingham Waterworks Co (1856) 11 Exch 781; 156 ER 1047 **193–4**
Blyth v Fladgate [1891] 1 Ch 337 **9**
Bolam v Friern Hospital Management Committee [1957] 1 WLR 582 **196, 259**
Bolitho v City and Hackney Health Authority [1998] AC 232 **197, 259**
Bolton v Mahadeva [1972] 1 WLR 1009 **76, 132, 143, 297, 298, 301**
Bolton v Stone [1951] AC 850 **196, 230, 284**
Borag (the) [1981] 1 WLR 274 **290**
Boscawen v Bajwa [1996] 1 WLR 328 **306, 307**
Bourhill v Young [1943] AC 92 **207**
Bowmakers Ltd v Barnet Instruments Ltd [1945] KB 65 **130, 308**
Bradford Corporation v Pickles

[1895] AC 587 **43, 44, 55, 154, 178, 180**
Brew Brothers Ltd v Snax (Ross) Ltd [1970] 1 QB 612 **229**
Brinkibon Ltd v Stahag Stahl [1983] 2 AC 34 **110**
British Columbia Saw-Mill Co v Nettleship (1868) LR 3 CP 499 **8**
British Steel Corporation v Cleveland Bridge & Engineering Co Ltd [1984] 1 All ER 504 **300**
British Telecommunications Plc v James Thompson & Sons [1999] 1 WLR 9 **251**
Brook's Wharf & Bull Wharf Ltd v Goodman Brothers [1937] 1 KB 534 **303**
Broome v Cassell & Co Ltd [1972] AC 1027 **91, 163, 175**
Bryant v Herbert (1877) 3 CPD 389 **8, 9**
Buckley v Gross (1863) 32 LJQB 129 **54**
Building and Civil Engineering Holidays Scheme Management Ltd v Post Office [1966] 1 QB 247 **82**
Bunge Corpn v Tradax Export [1981] 1 WLR 711 **139**
Burris v Azadani [1995] 1 WLR 1372 **59, 168–9, 186**
Burton v Winters [1993] 1 WLR 1077 **231**
Butler Machine Tool Co Ltd v Ex-Cell-O Corporation [1979] 1 WLR 401 **103**
Byrne v Schiller (1871) 6 Exch 319 **8**
Byrne v Van Tienhoven (1880) 5 CPD 344 **8**

Cadbury Schweppes v Pub Squash Co [1981] 1 All ER 213 **256**
Cambridge Water Co v Eastern Counties Leather Plc [1994] 2 AC 264 **234, 272**
Canham v Barry (1855) 24 LJCP 100 **35, 96**
Caparo Industries plc v Dickman [1990] 2 AC 605 **166, 199, 202, 204, 259**
Car & Universal Finance Co Ltd v Caldwell [1965] 1 QB 525 **67**
Carlill v Carbolic Smoke Ball Co [1893] 1 QB 256 **54, 73–4, 101–2, 110, 137**
Carslogie SS Co v Royal Norwegian Government [1952] AC 292 **279**
Carmarthenshire CC v Lewis [1955] AC 549 **247**
Cassidy v Ministry of Health [1951] 2 KB 343 **240**
CBS Songs Ltd v Amstrad Plc [1988] AC 1013 **270**
Central London Property Trust Ltd v High Trees House Ltd [1947] 1 KB 130 **113**
Chadwick v British Railways Board [1967] 1 WLR 912 **207, 209**
Chaplin v Hicks [1911] 2 KB 786 **274**
Chapman v Honig [1963] 2 QB 502 **43, 77**
Chappell & Co v Nestle Ltd [1960] AC 87 **111**
Cherry v Tompson (1872) LR 7 QB 573 **9**
Chester v Afshar [2005] 1 AC 134 **277–8, 282**
Chikuma (the) [1981] 1 WLR 314 **135**

Christie v Davey [1893] 1 Ch
316 **180**
Clarke v Dunraven [1897] AC
59 **157**
Clarke v Kato [1998] 1 WLR
1647 **172**
Collier v P & MJ Wright
(Holdings) Ltd [2008] 1 WLR
643 **113**
Coltman v Bibby Tankers Ltd
[1988] AC 276 **222**
Constantine (Joseph) SS Ltd v
Imperial Smelting Corporation
[1942] AC 154 **92–3**
Co-operative Insurance Society Ltd
v Argyll Stores Ltd [1998] AC
1 **60–61, 305**
Copeland v Smith [2000] 1 All ER
457 **169**
Corby Group Litigation (in re)
[2009] QB 335 **175, 233, 235**
Cornwell v Myskow [1987] 2 All
ER 504 **251**
Corr v IBC Vehicles Ltd [2007] QB
46 (CA); [2008] AC 884 **281,
282, 283, 284**
Coxall v Goodyear GB Ltd [2003] 1
WLR 536 **196**
Courtney & Fairbairn v Tolani
Brothers (Hotels) Ltd [1975] 1
WLR 297 **104**
Crabb v Arun DC [1976] Ch
179 **80**
Craven-Ellis v Canons Ltd [1936] 2
KB 403 **304**
Credit Lyonnais Bank Nederland v
Burch [1997] 1 All ER 144 **127**
Cressman v Coys of Kensington
(Sales) Ltd [2004] 1 WLR
2775 **296**
CTN Cash & Carry Ltd v Gallaher
Ltd [1994] 4 All ER 714 **127**

Currie v Misa (1875) LR 10 Ex
153 **110**
Curtis v Betts [1990] 1 WLR
459 **224**
Customs and Excise Commissioners
v Barclays Bank plc [2007] 1 AC
181 **203, 204, 205, 210, 259**
Cutler v United Dairies (London)
Ltd [1933] 2 KB 297 **281**
Cutler v Wandsworth Stadium Ltd
[1949] AC 398 **217**

D v East Berkshire Community
NHS Trust [2005] 2 AC
373 **212, 262**
D & C Builders Ltd v Rees [1966] 2
QB 617 **113, 126, 127, 150**
Darbishire v Warran [1963] 1 WLR
1067 **290**
Darlington BC v Wiltshier Northern
Ltd [1995] 1 WLR 68 **114**
Davie v New Merton Board Mills
Ltd [1959] AC 604 **222**
Davis Contractors Ltd v Fareham
UDC [1956] AC 696 **1444**
Decro-Wall v Practitioners in
Marketing Ltd [1971] 2 All ER
216 **149**
Delaware Mansions Ltd v
Westminster CC [2002] 1 AC
321 **232, 237**
Dennis v MOD [2003] EWHC
793 **215, 225, 237, 272**
Derbyshire CC v Times Newspapers
[1993] AC 534 **192, 252**
Derry v Peek (1887) 37 Ch D
541 (CA); (1889) 14 App Cas
337 **201, 250**
Dick Bentley Productions Ltd v
Harold Smith (Motors) Ltd
[1965] 1 WLR 623 **138**
Dimskal Shipping Co v ITWF

(The Evia Luck) [1992] 2 AC 152 **126**
Director General of Fair Trading v First National Bank plc [2002] 1 AC 481 **86, 147**
Donoghue v Stevenson [1932] AC 562 **115–16, 156, 197–200, 201, 202, 203, 204, 205, 212, 220**
Dooley v Cammell Laird & Co Ltd [1951] 1 Ll Rep 271 **207**
Doughty v Turner Manufacturing Co Ltd [1964] 1 QB 518 **287**
Douglas v Hello! Ltd (No 3) [2008] 1 AC 1 **59, 162, 256, 257, 258, 332**
Downs v Chappell [1997] 1 WLR 426 **185**
Dunne v NW Gas Board [1964] 2 QB 806 **215**
Dymond v Pearce [1972] 1 QB 496 **233, 264**

East Suffolk Rivers Catchment Board v Kent [1941] AC 74 **209, 270**
Edwards v Railway Executive [1952] AC 737 **227**
Elguzouli-Daf v Commissioner of Police of the Metropolis [1995] QB 335 **210, 215–16, 244**
English v Dedham Vale Properties Ltd [1978] 1 WLR 93 **644, 305**
Entores Ltd v Miles Far East Corporation [1955] 2 QB 327 **109**
Erven Warnink BV v J Townend & Sons [1979] AC 731 **189**
Esso Petroleum Ltd v Commissioners of Custom and Excise [1976] 1 WLR 1 **112**
Esso Petroleum Ltd v Southport Corporation [1953] 3 WLR 773 (QBD); [1954] 2 QB 182 (CA); [1956] AC 218 **52, 155, 166, 173, 190, 230, 231, 270**
Evia Luck (the) see *Dimskal Shipping Co v ITWF*

F (In re) [1990] 2 AC 1 **191, 271, 303**
FA & AB Ltd v Lupton see *Lupton v FA & AB Ltd*
Fagan v Metropolitan Police Commissioner [1969] 1 QB 439 **180**
Fairchild v Glenhaven Funeral Services Ltd [2003] 1 AC 32 **169, 268, 274, 275–6, 277, 279, 282**
Falcke v Scottish Imperial Insurance Co (1886) 34 Ch D 234 **303**
Farley v Skinner [2002] 2 AC 732 **287, 293**
Femis-Bank Ltd v Lazar [1991] Ch 391 **59**
Ferguson v John Dawson & Partners (Contractors) Ltd [1976] 1 WLR 1213 **241**
Fibrosa etc v Fairbairn etc [1943] AC 32 **309**
Financings Ltd v Stimson [1962] 1 WLR 1184 **108**
Finlay v Chirney (1888) 20 QBD 494 **9**
Firstpost Homes Ltd v Johnson [1995] 1 WLR 1184 **104**
Fisher v Bell [1961] 1 QB 394 **100**
Foster v Wheeler (1887) 36 Ch D 695 **8, 51**
Freeman v Home Office (No 2) [1984] QB 524 **199**
Frost v Aylesbury Dairy Co Ltd [1905] 1 KB 608 **81, 198**

Frost v Chief Constable of South Yorkshire Police [1999] 2 AC 455 **208, 209, 281**
Fullalove v Parker (1869) 31 LJCP 239 **9**

Geismar v Sun Alliance Insurance [1978] QB 383 **130**
General Capinpin (the) [1991] 1 Ll Rep 1 **135**
Genossenschaftsbank v Burnhope [1995] 1 WLR 1580 **135**
Gibbs v Rea [1998] AC 786 **178, 182**
Gibson v Manchester City Council [1978] 1 WLR 520 (CA); [1979] 1 WLR 294 (HL) **97–8**
Ginty v Belmont Building Supplies Ltd [1959] 1 All ER 414 **281**
Gleaner Co Ltd (The) v Abrahams [2004] 1 AC 628 (PC) **163**
Glynn Mills Curie & Co v East & West India Dock Co (1882) 7 App Cas 591 **87**
Goldman v Hargrave [1967] 1 AC 645 **232, 235**
Goodwill v British Pregnancy Advisory Service [1996] 1 WLR 1397 **166, 202, 259**
Gorringe v Calderdale MBC [2004] 1 WLR 1057 **262**
Gorris v Scott (1874) LR 9 Ex 125 **273**
Grant v Australian Knitting Mills Ltd [1936] AC 85 **198**
Gray v Thames Trains Ltd [2009] 3 WLR 167 (HL) **272, 279, 281, 282**
Great Peace (the) [2003] QB 679 **66, 122, 123, 144**
Great Peace Shipping Ltd v Tsavliris Salvage (International) Ltd see Great Peace (the)
Great Western Railway Co v Sutton (1869) LR 4 App Cas 226 **9**
Greaves & Co v Baynham Meikle & Partners [1975] 1 WLR 1095 **261**
Gregg v Scott [2005] 2 AC 176 **275, 278**
Groves v Wimborne [1898] 2 QB 402 **176, 183, 217**
Gulf Oil (GB) Ltd v Page [1987] Ch 327 **181**
Gwilliam v West Hertfordshire Hospital NHS Trust [2003] QB 443 **226, 236, 245**

Hadley v Baxendale (1854) 9 Ex 341; 156 ER 145 **77, 286**
Haigh v Charles W Ireland [1973] 3 All ER 1137 **171, 222**
Haley v London Electricity Board [1965] AC 778 **196**
Hall v Wright (1858) 27 LJQB 345; (1860) 29 LJQB 43 **8, 96**
Hall (Arthur JS) & Co v Simons (a firm) [2002] 1 AC 615 **201, 260**
Hall (Inspector of Taxes) v Lorimer [1992] 1 WLR 939 (QBD); [1994] 1 All ER 250 (CA) **241**
Halsey v Esso Petroleum & Co Ltd [1961] 1 WLR 683 **232**
Halsey v Milton Keynes General NHS Trust [2004] 1 WLR 3002 **279**
Hannah Blumenthal (the) see Paal Wilson & Co A/S v Partenreederei Hannah Blumenthal
Harbutts Plasticine Ltd v Wayne

Tank and Pump Co Ltd [1970] 1 QB 447 **149**
Harnett v Bond [1925] AC 669 **191, 269**
Hart v O'Connor [1985] AC 1000 (PC) **128**
Hartley v Hymans [1920] 3 KB 475 **151**
Haynes v Harwood & Son [1935] 1 KB 146 **281**
Hazell v Hammersmith and Fulham LBC [1992] 2 AC 1 **128**
Hector v A G of Antigua & Barbuda [1990] 2 AC 312 (PC) **252**
Hedley Byrne & Co v Heller & Partners Ltd [1964] AC 465 **71, 200–201, 204, 205, 250, 254, 260–61**
Heil v Hedges [1951] 1 TLR 512 **221**
Heil v Rankin [2001] QB 272 **206, 292**
Henderson v HE Jenkins & Sons [1970] AC 282 **197, 224**
Henderson v Merrett Syndicates Ltd [1995] 2 AC 145 **8, 159, 205, 250, 251**
Heron II (the) see *Koufas v C Czarnikow Ltd*
Herrington v British Railways Board [1972] AC 877 **227**
Hewitson v Sherwin (1870) LR 10 Eq 53 **9**
Hill v Chief Constable of West Yorkshire [1989] AC 53 **167, 206, 260**
Hislop v Leckie (1881) 6 App Cas 560 **9**
Hoenig v Isaacs [1952] 2 All ER 176 **144**
Holbeck Hall Hotel Ltd v Scarborough CC [2000] QB 836 **232**
Hollier v Rambler Motors Ltd [1972] 2 QB 71 **145**
Hollywood Silver Fox Farm v Emmett [1936] 2 KB 468 **44, 190, 232**
Holmes v Mather (1875) LR 10 Ex 261 **53**
Home Office v Dorset Yacht Co [1970] AC 1004 **166, 200, 202, 210, 245–6**
Honeywill & Stein v Larkin Brothers [1934] 1 KB 191 **244**
Hong Kong Fir Shipping Co Ltd v Kawasaki Kisen Kaisha Ltd [1962] 2 QB 26 **76, 139, 142**
Hopkins v Tanqueray (1854) 15 CB 130; 139 ER 369 **75, 134**
Hotson v East Berks Area Health Authority [1987] AC 750 **274**
Houghland v RR Low (Luxury Coaches) Ltd [1962] 1 QB 694 **83**
Houghton v Trafalgar Insurance Co Ltd [1954] 1 QB 247 **136**
Hounslow LBC v Twickenham Garden Developments Ltd [1971] Ch 233 **78**
Household Fire Insurance Co v Grant (1879) LR 4 Ex D 216 **109**
Howe v Smith (1884) 27 Ch D 89 **8**
Holwell Securities Ltd v Hughes [1974] 1 WLR 155 **109**
Hughes v Lord Advocate [1963] AC 837 **288**
Hunt v Severs [1994] 2 AC 350 **292**
Hunter v Canary Wharf Ltd [1997] AC 655 **155, 231, 232**

Hussain v Lancaster CC [2000] 1 QB 1 **245**
Hussain v New Taplow Paper Mills Ltd [1988] AC 514 **292**

IBL Ltd v Coussens [1991] 2 All ER 133 **49**
Ingham v Emes [1955] 2 QB 366 **221**
Ingram v Little [1961] 1 QB 31 **124**
Ingram v IRC [2000] 1 AC 293 **329**
Interfoto Picture Library Ltd v Stiletto Visual Programmes Ltd [1989] QB 443 **88, 106**
Inverugie Investments Ltd v Hackett [1995] 1 WLR 713 (PC) **65**
Investors Compensation Scheme Ltd v West Bromwich Building Society [1998] 1 WLR 896 (HL) **136**
Island Records (Ex p) [1978] Ch 122 **46, 59**
Islington LBC v Uckac [2006] 1 WLR 1303 **118, 119**

Jackson v Horizon Holidays Ltd [1975] 1 WLR 1468 **58, 78, 115, 293**
Jacobs v LCC [1950] AC 361 **155**
Jaggard v Sawyer [1995] 1 WLR 269 **67, 305**
Jameel (Mohammed) v Wall Street Journal Europe Sprl [2007] 1 AC 359 **252, 253**
Janson v Ralli (1856) 25 LJQB 300 **8**
Jarvis v Swan's Tours [1973] QB 233 **206**

Jervis v Harris [1996] Ch 195 **49**
Jobling v Associated Dairies Ltd [1982] AC 794 **279**
Jobson v Johnson [1989] 1 WLR 1026 **142**
John v MGN Ltd [1997] QB 586 **251, 291**
John Summers & Sons Ltd v Frost [1955] AC 740 **222**
Jolley v Sutton LBC [2000] 1 WLR 1082 (HL) **227, 288**
Jones & Sons v Jones [1997] Ch 159 **309**
Jones v Padavatton [1969] 1 WLR 328 **112**
Jones v Vernon's Pools Ltd [1938] 2 All ER 626 **107**
Joyce v Sengupta [1993] 1 WLR 337 **188**
Junior Books Ltd v Veitchi Co Ltd [1983] AC 520 **203**

Keegan v Chief Constable of Merseyside Police [2003] 1 WLR 2187 **159, 180, 182**
Kelsen v Imperial Tobacco Co [1957] 2 QB 334 **59**
Kemp v Halliday (1865) 34 LJQB 233 **8**
Kent v Griffiths [2001] QB 36 **260, 262**
Keown v Coventry Healthcare NHS Trust [2006] 1 WLR 953 **227, 228, 229**
Keppel Bus Co v Sa'ad bin Ahmad [1974] 2 All ER 700 **242**
Khodaparast v Shad [2000] 1 WLR 618 **188**
Khorasandjian v Bush [1993] QB 727 **155**
Kite (the) [1933] P 154 **240**
Kleinwort Benson Ltd v

Birmingham CC [1997] QB 380 **331**
Kleinwort Benson Ltd v Glasgow CC [1999] 1 AC 153 **296, 310**
Kleinwort Benson Ltd v Lincoln CC [1999] 2 AC 349 **120, 302, 311**
Koufas v C Czarnikow Ltd (The Heron II) [1969] 1 AC 350 **287**
Krell v Henry [1903] 2 KB 740 **132**
Kuddus v Chief Constable of Leicestershire [2002] 2 AC 122 **161, 291**
Kuwait Airways Corpn v Iraqi Airways Co (Nos 4 & 5) [2002] 2 AC 883 **185, 264**

Latimer v AEC Ltd [1953] AC 643 **196**
Latter v Braddell (1881) 50 LJQB 448 **271**
Launchbury v Morgans see *Morgans v Launchbury*
Laurie v Scholefield (1869) LR 4 CP 622 **9**
Law Debenture Corporation v Ural Caspian Ltd [1993] 1 WLR 138 **59**
Lawrence v Metropolitan Police Commissioner [1972] AC 626 **109**
Lazenby Garages Ltd v Wright [1976] 1 WLR 459 **77**
Leaf v International Galleries [1950] 2 KB 86 **67**
League Against Cruel Sports v Scott [1986] 1 QB 240 **231**
Lennon v Comr of Police of the Metropolis [2004] 1 WLR 2594 **70, 71, 201**
Letang v Cooper [1965] 1 QB 232 **52, 173, 200**

Lewis v Averay [1972] 1 QB 198 **124**
Lewis v Daily Telegraph [1964] AC 234 **251**
Liesbosch (the) [1933] AC 449 **289, 293**
Lipkin Gorman v Karpnale Ltd [1991] 2 AC 548 **14, 131, 301, 302, 304, 310, 331**
Lippiatt v South Gloucestershire Council [2000] 1 QB 51 **245**
Lister v Hesley Hall Ltd [2002] 1 AC 215 **242, 243**
Lister v Romford Ice & Cold Storage Co Ltd [1957] AC 555 **140, 243, 298**
Liverpool City Council v Irwin [1977] AC 239 **140**
Lloyd v Guibert (1865) 35 LJQB 74 **8**
Lloyds Bank Ltd v Bundy [1975] QB 326 **127**
London & South Western Bank v Wentworth (1880) 5 Ex D 96 **8**
London, Chatham & Dover Railway Co v S.E. Railway Co [1892] 1 Ch 120 **49**
Lonrho v Shell Petroleum Co Ltd (No 2) [1982] AC 173 **181, 217**
Lumley v Gye (1853) 2 E & B 216; 118 ER 749 **187**
Lupton v FA & AB Ltd [1972] AC 634 **165–6, 318**
Luxor (Eastbourne) Ltd v Cooper [1941] AC 108 **80, 140**

Mackenzie v Whiteworth (1875) 44 LJ Ex 81 **8**
Mahmud v BCCI [1998] AC 20 **254–5**
Majrowski v Guy's & St Thomas's

NHS Trust [2007] 1 AC 224 **186, 240, 243**
Manchester Airport Plc v Dutton [2000] 1 QB 133 **78**
Mannai Investment Co v Eagle Star Life Assurance [1997] AC 749 **136**
Mansfield v Weetabix Ltd [1998] 1 WLR 1263 **224**
Marc Rich & Co v Bishop Rock Marine Co Ltd [1996] 1 AC 211 **199, 204, 251, 259, 260**
Marcic v Thames Water Utilities Ltd [2004] 2 AC 42 **225, 232, 237**
Maritime National Fish Ltd v Ocean Trawlers Ltd [1935] AC 524 **92**
Market Investigations Ltd v Minister of Social Security [1969] 2 QB 173 **241**
Martin v Watson [1996] AC 74 **180, 188**
Mason v Levy Auto Parts [1967] 2 QB 530 **235**
Mattis v Pollock [2003] 1 WLR 2158 **242**
McCance v L & N W Ry (1861) 31 LJ Exch 65 **96**
McCauley v Bristol CC [1991] 1 All ER 749 **229**
McDermid v Nash Dredging and Reclamation Co [1987] AC 906 **246**
McFarlane v Tayside Health Board [2000] 2 AC 59 **169, 172, 295**
McGhee v National Coal Board [1973] 1 WLR 1 **274**
McKew v Holland & Hannen & Cubitts [1969] 3 All ER 1621 **281**
McLoughlin v O'Brian [1983] 1 AC 410 **207**
McWilliams v Sir William Arrol [1962] 1 WLR 295 **273, 289**
Mediana (the) [1900] AC 113 **66, 293**
Mercedes Benz AG v Leiduck [1996] 1 AC 284 (PC) **57**
Merlin v British Nuclear Fuels plc [1990] 2 QB 557 **171, 203**
Mersey Docks & Harbour Board v Coggins & Griffiths (Liverpool) Ltd & McFarlane [1947] AC 1 **240**
Metcalfe v Britannia Ironworks Co (1876) 1 QBD 613 **8**
Midland Railway Co v Withington Local Board (1883) 11 QBD 613 **9**
Miliangos v George Frank (Textiles) Ltd [1976] AC 443 **172**
Millard v Serck Tubes Ltd [1969] 1 WLR 211 **222**
Miller v Jackson [1977] QB 966 **58–9, 232, 331**
Millet v Coleman (1875) 44 LJQB 194 **54**
Ministry of Housing and Local Government v Sharp [1970] 2 QB 223 **210**
Mint v Good [1951] 1 KB 517 **229, 233, 236**
Mirvahedy v Henley [2003] 2 AC 491 **172, 223**
Mitchell v Glasgow City Council [2009] 1 AC 874 **160, 202, 209, 211, 270**
Mitchell (George) (Chesterfield) Ltd v Finney Lock Seeds [1983] QB 284 (CA); [1983] 2 AC 803 **146**

Mogul SS Co v McGregor, Gow & Co [1892] AC 25   **43, 180, 183**
Moorcock (the) (1889) 14 PD 64   **72, 140**
Morgan Crucible Co Plc v Hill Samuel & Co Ltd [1991] Ch 295   **259**
Morgan v Odhams Press [1971] 1 WLR 1239   **251**
Morgans v Launchbury [1973] AC 127   **247**
Morris v C W Martin & Sons Ltd [1966] 1 QB 716   **82, 91, 114, 242**
Morris v Ford Motor Co Ltd [1973] 1 QB 792   **242, 298**
Morris v KLM Royal Dutch Airlines [2002] 2 AC 628   **171**
Morris v National Coal Board [1963] 1 WLR 1382   **222**
Murphy v Brentwood DC [1991] 1 AC 398   **204, 206**
Murray v Ministry of Defence [1988] 1 WLR 692   **191**
Mutual Life & Citizens Assurance Co Ltd v Evatt [1971] AC 793   **204**

National Carriers Ltd v Panalpina (Northern) Ltd [1981] AC 675   **144–5**
National Telephone Co v Baker [1893] 2 Ch 186   **165**
Nettleship v Weston [1971] 2 QB 691   **178, 195**
Nichols v Marsland (1876) 2 Ex.D 1   **235, 272**
Nocton v Lord Ashburton [1914] AC 932   **250**
Norweb Plc v Dixon [1995] 1 WLR 636   **107**

Norwich CC v Harvey [1989] 1 WLR 828   **205**
Notara v Henderson (1872) LR 7 QB 225   **8**
Nottingham v Aldridge [1971] 2 QB 739   **247**

OBG Ltd v Allan [2008] 1 AC 587   **178, 181, 187**
Orakpo v Manson Investments Ltd [1978] AC 95   **304**
Oropesa (the) [1943] P 32   **281**
Osman v Ferguson [1993] 4 All ER 344   **212–13**
Overseas Tankship (UK) Ltd v Morts Dock & Engineering Co Ltd see *The Wagon Mound*
Owen v Tate [1975] 2 All ER 129   **303**

Page v Smith [1996] 1 AC 155; [1995] 2 WLR 644   **206, 208, 270, 293**
Paal Wilson & Co A/S v Partenreederei Hannah Blumenthal [1982] 3 WLR 49 (CA); [1983] 1 AC 854   **105–6**
Palmer v Wick & Pulteneytown SS Co [1894] AC 318   **9**
Paris v Stepney BC [1951] AC 367   **195**
Parkinson v College of Ambulance Ltd [1925] 2 KB 1   **130**
Parry v Cleaver [1970] AC 1   **292**
Parsons (Livestock) Ltd v Uttley Ingham & Co [1978] QB 791   **286, 287**
Pau On v Lau Yiu Long [1980] AC 614   **126**
Pearce v Brooks (1866) LR 1 Ex 213   **129**
Peek v Derry see *Derry v Peek*

Pepper v Hart [1993] AC 593   **171**
Performance Cars Ltd v Abraham [1962] 1 QB 33   **268, 279**
Perry v Kendricks Transport Ltd [1956] 1 WLR 85   **235, 272**
Pharmaceutical Society of G.B. v Boots [1953] 1 QB 401   **99**
Phelps v Hillingdon LBC [2001] 2 AC 619   **212, 246, 260**
Phillips v Britannia Hygienic Laundry Co [1923] 2 KB 832   **176, 224**
Phipps v Rochester Corporation [1955] 1 QB 450   **227**
Photo Production Ltd v Securicor [1980] AC 827   **77, 86, 146, 148, 235, 242, 244**
Pickett v British Rail Engineering Ltd [1980] AC 126   **293**
Pigney v Pointers Transport Services Ltd [1957] 1 WLR 1121   **281**
Pinard v Klockman (1863) 32 LJQB 82   **8**
Pitts v Hunt [1991] 1 QB 24   **272**
Platform Funding Ltd v Bank of Scotland [2009] QB 426   **140, 261**
Polemis (In re) [1921] 3 KB 560   **284, 285**
President of India v Jebsens (UK) Ltd see *General Capinpin (the)*
Printing and Numerical Registering Co. v Sampson (1875) LR 19 Eq 462   **85**

Qualcast (Wolverhampton) Ltd v Haynes [1959] AC 743   **195**

R & B Customs Brokers Co Ltd v UDT Ltd [1988] 1 WLR 321   **86, 147**

R (European Roma Rights Centre) v Immigration Officer at Prague Airport [2005] 2 AC 1   **87**
R (Greenfield) v Secretary of State for the Home Department [2005] 1 WLR 673   **162, 187**
R v Lewisham LBC, ex p. Shell (UK) [1988] 1 All ER 938   **84**
R v Rimmington [2006] 1 AC 459   **233**
R v Tower Hamlets LBC, Ex p. Chetnik Ltd [1988] AC 858   **304**
Raffles v Wichelhaus (1864) 159 ER 375   **118**
Rahman v Arearose Ltd [2001] QB 351   **268–9, 280, 306**
Randall v Newsom (1876) 45 LJQB 364   **8**
Rantzen v Mirror Group Newspapers [1994] QB 670   **252**
Ratcliff v McConnell [1999] 1 WLR 670   **227**
Ratcliffe v Evans [1892] 2 QB 524   **180**
Read v Coker (1853) 138 ER 1437   **180**
Read v J Lyons & Co [1947] AC 156   **4, 172, 175, 215, 234, 235, 244, 318**
Readhead v Midland Railway Co (1869) LR 4 QB 379   **286**
Reading v Att.Gen. [1951] AC 507   **302**
Ready Mixed Concrete v Minister of Pensions [1968] 2 QB 497   **241**
Reckitt & Colman Properties Ltd v Borden Inc [1990] 1 WLR 491   **256**
Reed v Dean [1949] 1 KB 188   **93**
Reeves v Commissioner of Police

for the Metropolis [2000] 1 AC
360   **175, 209, 266, 281, 282**
*Regalian Properties Plc v London
Docklands Development Corpn*
[1995] 1 WLR 212   **300**
Reid v Rush & Tompkins Plc [1990]
1 WLR 212   **88, 140**
*Revenue and Customs
Commissioners v Total Network
SL* [2008] 2 WLR 711   **184**
Revill v Newbery [1996] QB
567   **76, 227**
Reynolds v Times Newspapers Ltd
[2001] 2 AC 127   **186, 252, 253**
*Rickards Ltd (Charles) v
Oppenheim* [1950] 1 KB
616   **151**
*Rigby v Chief Constable of
Northamptonshire* [1985] 1 WLR
1242   **214, 271**
*Riverstone Meat Co v Lancashire
Shipping Co* [1961] AC 807
244
Robinson v Post Office [1974] 1
WLR 1176   **288**
Roe v Minister of Health [1954] 2
QB 66   **197, 240, 259, 261**
Rogers v Night Riders (a firm)
[1983] RTR 324   **247–8**
Roles v Nathan [1963] 1 WLR
1117   **226**
Rookes v Barnard [1964] AC
1129   **188**
Rouquette v Overmann (1875) 44
LJQB 221   **8**
*Rothwell v Chemical & Insulating
Co* [2008] 1 AC 281   **293**
Rowe v Herman [1997] 1 WLR
1390   **240, 245**
Rowland (Re) [1963] Ch 1   **165**
Rowland v Divall [1923] 2 KB
500   **75, 137, 297**

*Royal Bank of Scotland v Etridge
(No 2)* [2002] 2 AC 773   **127**
Royal Brunei Airlines v Tan [1995]
2 AC 378   **xiii**
Ruxley Electronics Ltd v Forsyth
[1996] 1 AC 344   **62–3, 72, 77,
88, 144, 287**
Rylands v Fletcher (1866) LR 1 Ex
265 (Ex); (1868) LR 3 HL 330
(HL)   **165, 179, 190, 220, 230,
233–5, 237, 238, 244, 272**

Salsbury v Woodland [1970] 1 QB
324   **242**
Saunders v Anglia Building Society
[1971] AC 1004   **125**
*Schuler v Wickman Machine Tool
Sales Ltd* [1974] AC 235   **138**
Scott v Shepherd (1773) 96 ER
525   **50, 270**
*Scruttons Ltd v Midland Silicones
Ltd* [1962] AC 446   **115**
Searle v Laverick (1874) LR 9 QB
122   **8**
Selectmove Ltd (in re) [1995] 1
WLR 474   **113**
*Shell UK Ltd v Lostock Garages
Ltd* [1976] 1 WLR 1187   **131**
Shogun Finance Ltd v Hudson
[2004] 1 AC 919   **82, 85, 99,
105, 120, 124**
Sidaway v Bethlem Royal Hospital
[1985] 1 AC 871   **197, 259, 260**
Simkins v Pays [1955] 1 WLR
975   **107**
Sinclair v Brougham [1914] AC
398   **56, 307–8, 309**
*Sirius International Insurance Co
v FAI General Insurance Ltd*
[2004] 1 WLR 3251 (HL)   **136**
Smeed v Foord (1859) 28 LJQB
178   **8**

Smith v Baker & Sons [1891] AC 325 **271**
Smith v Eric Bush [1990] 1 AC 831 **146, 204, 205, 250**
Smith v Hughes (1871) LR 6 QB 597 **123**
Smith v Leech Brain & Co [1962] 2 QB 405 **288**
Smith v Littlewoods Organisation Ltd [1987] AC 241 **235**
Smith v London & South Western Railway Co (1870) LR 6 CP 14 **283**
Smith New Court Securities Ltd v Scrimgeour Vickers Ltd [1997] AC 254 **160, 161, 169, 250, 265, 291**
Solholt (the) [1983] 1 Ll Rep 605 **290**
Solle v Butcher [1950] 1 KB 671 **121**
Spain (Kingdom of) v Christie Ltd [1986] 1 WLR 1120 **52, 59, 155**
Spartan Steel & Alloys Ltd v Martin & Co [1973] 1 QB 27 **167–8, 170, 203, 286, 289**
Speed Seal Products v Paddington [1985] 1 WLR 1327 **182**
Spence v Crawford [1939] 3 All ER 271 **67**
Spring v Guardian Assurance Plc [1995] 2 AC 296 **189, 201, 204, 205, 254, 255**
St Aubyn v Att-Gen [1952] AC 15 **171**
Staffs Area Health Authority v South Staffs Waterworks Co [1978] 1 WLR 1387 **81, 134, 145**
Stansbie v Troman [1948] 2 KB 48 **281**

Staveley Iron & Chemical Co v Jones [1956] AC 627 **240**
Stevenson v Beverley Bentinck Ltd [1976] 1 WLR 483 **13, 85, 162, 328, 331**
Stevenson v Rogers [1999] QB 1028 **147**
Stilk v Myrick (1809) 170 ER 1168 **113**
Stooke v Taylor (1880) 5 QBD 569 **9**
Stovin v Wise [1996] AC 923 **209, 212, 262**
Strand Electric Co Ltd v Brisford Entertainments Ltd [1952] 2 QB 246 **299**
Stonedale (No 1) (the) [1956] AC 1 **160**
Stubbings v Webb [1993] AC 498 **156**
Sturges v Bridgman (1879) 11 Ch D 852 **60**
Suisse Atlantique etc v Rotterdamsche etc [1967] 1 AC 361 **146**
Sumpter v Hedges [1898] 1 QB 673 **303**
Supply of Ready Mixed Concrete (No 2) (in re) [1995] 1 AC 456 **239, 245**
Surrey County Council v Bredero Homes Ltd [1993] 1 WLR 1361 **62, 65, 310**
Sutcliffe v Pressdram Ltd [1991] 1 QB 153 **252**

Tarry v Ashton (1876) 1 QBD 314 **233, 244**
Tate & Lyle v GLC [1983] 2 AC 509 **233**
Taylor v Caldwell (1863) 122 ER 309 **8**

Tesco Supermarkets Ltd v Nattrass
[1972] AC 153   **149**
Thake v Maurice [1986] QB
644   **81, 261**
Thomas v Countryside Council for Wales [1994] 4 All ER 853   **290**
Thompson v Commissioner of Police for the Metropolis [1998] QB 498   **294**
Thompson v T Lohan (Plant) Ltd [1987] 1 WLR 649   **146**
Thompson-Schwab v Costaki [1956] 1 WLR 335   **191**
Thorne v Motor Trade Association [1937] AC 797   **181**
Thornton v Shoe Lane Parking Ltd [1971] 2 QB 163   **73, 100, 145**
Three Rivers DC v Bank of England (No 3) [2003] 2 AC 1   **183**
Tinsley v Milligan [1994] 1 AC 340   **130–31**
Tolley v Fry & Sons Ltd [1931] AC 333   **252**
Tomlinson v Congleton BC [2004] 1 AC 46   **175, 227, 228, 229, 265, 270, 284**
Total Gas v Arco British [1998] 2 Lloyd's Rep 209 (HL)   **137**
Transfield Shipping INC v Mercator Shipping INC [2009] 1 AC 61   **286, 287, 291**
Transco plc v Stockport MBC [2004] 2 AC 1   **55, 170, 175, 179, 193, 220, 232, 234, 235, 238, 285**
Tremain v Pike [1969] 3 All ER 1303   **287**
Trollope & Colls Ltd v Atomic Power Constructions Ltd [1963] 1 WLR 333   **103**
TSB Bank plc v Camfield [1995] 1 WLR 430   **67**

UDT v Eagle Aircraft Services Ltd [1968] 1 WLR 74   **80**
United Australia Ltd v Barclays Bank Ltd [1941] AC 1   **56, 295, 309**
United Overseas Bank v Jiwani [1977] 1 All ER 733   **302**
Universe Tankships v International Transport Workers' Federation [1983] 1 AC 366   **128**
University of Nottingham v Eyett [1999] 2 All ER 437   **88**

Van Colle v Chief Constable of the Hertfordshire Police [2009] 1 AC 225   **210, 211, 216, 260**
Veritas (the) [1901] P 304   **9**
Viasystems (Tynside) Ltd v Thermal Transfer (Northern) Ltd [2006] QB 510   **241**
Vigers v Cook [1919] 2 KB 475   **143**

W v Essex CC [1999] Fam 90 (CA); cf [2001] 2 AC 592   **70**
Wagon Mound (no 1) (the) [1961] AC 388   **267, 284**
Wainwright v Home Office [2004] 2 AC 406   **55, 159, 180, 182, 186, 187, 192, 256, 257, 258**
Walford v Miles [1992] 2 AC 128   **43, 88, 104**
Ward v Byham [1956] 2 All ER 318   **112**
Ward v James [1966] 1 QB 273   **195**
Ward v Tesco Stores Ltd [1976] 1 WLR 810   **99, 197, 237, 246**
Warner Brothers Pictures Inc v Nelson [1937] 1 KB 209   **74**
Watkins v Home Office [2006] 2 AC 395   **183, 258, 333**

Watt v Hertfordshire CC [1954] 1 WLR 835   **196, 215**
Watt v Longsdon [1930] 1 KB 130   **253**
Waverley BC v Fletcher [1996] QB 334   **328**
Wells v Cooper [1958] 2 QB 265   **195**
Wells v Wells [1999] 1 AC 345   **291–2**
West (H) & Son Ltd v Shephard [1964] AC 326   **292**
Westdeutsche Landesbank Girozentrale v Islington LBC [1996] AC 669   **302, 308**
Wheat v E Lacon & Co Ltd [1966] AC 552   **226**
Wheeler v JJ Saunders Ltd [1996] Ch 19   **232**
White v Blackmore [1972] 1 QB 651   **229**
White v Jones [1995] 2 AC 207   **70, 161, 163, 166, 170, 201, 204, 205, 251**
White & Carter (Councils) Ltd v McGregor [1962] AC 413   **149, 150, 290**
Whittaker v Campbell [1984] QB 318   **67, 89, 99, 120**
Wilkinson v Downton [1897] 2 QB 57   **180**
William Sindall Plc v Cambridgeshire CC [1994] 1 WLR 1016   **122**
Williams v Roffey Bros & Nicholls (Contractors) Ltd [1991] 1 QB 1   **112–13, 127–8, 150, 151**
Willis & Son (RH) v British Car Auctions [1978] 2 All ER 392   **185**
Willmore v SE Electricity Board [1957] 2 Ll Rep 375   **107**

Wilsher v Essex Area Health Authority [1988] AC 1074   **274**
Wilson v Best Travel Ltd [1993] 1 All ER 353   **148**
Wilson v First County Trust Ltd (No 2) [2004] 1 AC 816   **298**
Wilson v Pringle [1987] QB 237   **191**
Winson (the) [1982] AC 939   **303**
Withers v Perry Chain [1961] 1 WLR 1314   **196**
Wong Mee Wan v Kwan Kin Travel Services Ltd [1996] 1 WLR 38 (PC)   **148, 244**
Wookey v Wookey [1991] 3 WLR 135   **59**
Wringe v Cohen [1940] 1 KB 229   **233, 236**

X (Minors) v Bedfordshire County Council [1995] 2 AC 633   **183, 213, 216–17**

Young v Sun Alliance and London Insurance Ltd [1977] 1 WLR 104   **171**
Young & Co v Mayor of Royal Leamington Spa (1883) 8 App Cas 517   **9**

EUROPEAN LAW CASES

European Commission v United Kingdom [1997] CMLR 923   **222**
Hatton v United Kingdom (2003) 37 EHRR 611   **225, 230**
Osman v United Kingdom [1999] 1 FLR 193   **213**
Wainwright v United Kingdom (2007) 44 EHRR 40   **258**

Z v United Kingdom [2001] 2 FLR 612 **200**

FRENCH LAW CASES

Cas. civ 6 mars 1876, DP. 1876, 1, 193 **30**

Cas. req 15 juin 1892, D. 1892, 1, 596 **2**

CE 30 mars 1916, D. 1916, 3, 25 **30**, **145**

Cas. Ch réun 13 février 1930, DP. 1930, 1, 57 **219**

Cas. civ 19 février 1997, JCP 28, 5, 97, 22848 **153**, **176**, **246**

Statutes and texts

COMMON LAW STATUTES AND REGULATIONS

Animals Act 1971 **155, 247**
  s 2 **171, 223**
  s 3 **224**
  s 4 **224**
Anti-Social Behaviour Act 2003
  s 40 **230**
Civil Aviation Act 1982
  s 76 **225**
  s 77 **225**
Civil Liability (Contribution) Act 1978 **243, 269, 280**
  s 1 **306**
Common Law Procedure Act 1852 **9, 51**
Compensation Act 2006
  s 1 **196**
  s 3 **276**
Consumer Protection Act 1987 **198, 223**
  s 1 **222**
  s 2 **99, 220**
  s 3 **220**
  s 4 **221**
  s 5 **168, 199, 221**
Consumer Protection (Distance Selling) Regulations 2000 **72, 84**
  reg 10 **75, 131**
Contracts (Rights of Third Parties) Act 1999 **148, 198, 251**

s 1 **115**
s 6 **115**
County Courts Act 1984
  s 15 **55**
Courts Act 2003
  s 100 **291, 292**
  s 101 **291, 292**
Courts and Legal Services Act 1990
  s 8 **252**
Damages Act 1996 **170**
Defamation Act 1952
  s 3 **188, 256**
  s 5 **253**
  s 6 **253**
Defamation Act 1996
  s 1 **248**
  s 2 **253**
  s 3 **253**
  s 4 **253**
Defective Premises Act 1972
  s 4 **228–9, 233**
Employers' Liability (Defective Equipment) Act 1969 **222–3**
Environmental Protection Act 1990
  s 79 **230**
  s 80 **230, 231**
Fatal Accidents Act 1976 **170, 292**
  s 1A **206, 209, 293**
Fires Protection (Metropolis) Act 1774
  s 86 **235**

Gambling Act 2005
  s 335 **131**
Human Rights Act 1998 **159, 162, 185, 187, 212, 215, 225, 238, 252, 253, 257, 272**
  s 3 **172**
  s 6 **186**
  s 8 **186**
Law Reform (Contributory Negligence) Act 1945 **265, 289**
Law Reform (Frustrated Contracts) Act 1943 **297**
Law Reform (Miscellaneous Provisions) Act 1989 **96**
  s 1 **110, 116**
Limitation Act 1980 **260**
Local Government Act 1972
  s 222 **233**
Local Government Act 1988
  s 17 **84**
Marine Insurance Act 1906 **138, 140**
Mental Capacity Act 2005
  s 7 **129**
Minors' Contracts Act 1987
  s 3 **129**
Misrepresentation Act 1967
  s 2 **120, 185, 249, 250**
Occupiers' Liability 1957 **237, 238**
  s 2 **226, 227, 229, 236, 271**
Occupiers' Liability Act 1984 **228, 237**
  s 1 **227, 229**
Proceeds of Crime Act 2002 **295, 299, 301**
  s 316 **301**
Protection From Harassment Act 1997 **162**
  s 3 **186**
Sale of Goods Act 1979 **71, 80, 140**
  s 3 **129**
  s 8 **104**
  s 11 **138**
  s 13 **140**
  s 14 **81, 85, 91, 116, 141, 198, 220**
  s 16 **82, 111**
  s 17 **82, 111**
  s 18 **82, 111**
  s 23 **124**
Social Security (Recovery of Benefits) Act 1997 **170**
Supply of Goods and Services Act 1982
  s 13 **73, 81, 91, 194, 201, 258, 260**
  s 15 **104**
Torts (Interference with Goods) Act 1977 **50, 159, 184, 308**
  s 7(4) **310**
Unfair Contract Terms Act 1977 **100**
  s 1 **229**
  s 2 **142, 146, 229**
  s 3 **141, 146**
  s 5 **146**
  s 6 **146**
  s 10 **146**
  s 11 **146**
  s 12 **141, 147**
Unfair Terms in Consumer Contracts Regulations 1999 **84, 100, 146**
  reg 3 **141, 147**
  reg 4 **147**
  reg 5 **141, 147**
  reg 6 **141**
  reg 8 **147**
  reg 12 **147**
  schedule 1 **147**

EUROPEAN AND INTERNATIONAL CODES

Bürgerliches Gesetzbuch **13, 14**
  § 226 **42**
  § 323 **34**
  § 812 **24, 296**
  § 823 **20, 21, 39, 153, 200**
  § 831 **23**
  § 833 **23**
  § 836–838 **23**
Code civil **12, 13, 14, 15, 25, 26, 134**
  art 16 **257**
  art 544 **44, 45, 308, 328**
  art 1101 **95**
  art 1102–1107 **79**
  art 1108 **93, 95, 128**
  art 1109 **117, 125**
  art 1124 **128**
  art 1128 **129**
  art 1131 **129**
  art 1133 **129**
  art 1134 **17, 70, 85, 87**
  art 1147–1148 **33, 34, 92, 144**
  art 1150 **264, 286**
  art 1153 **37**
  art 1156 **135**
  art 1184 **31**
  art 1371 **24, 296**
  art 1372–1381 **24, 296**
  art 1382 **20, 21, 27, 33, 39, 44, 152, 153, 166, 176, 200**
  art 1384 **xiv, 22, 33, 39, 153, 176, 178, 219, 234, 239, 246**
  art 1386 **23**
  art 1582 **94**
  art 1713 **94**
  art 1927 **32**
  art 2279 **124**

Código civil **14**
Principles of European Contract Law **xiii, 69, 90, 134, 286, 312, 324**
  art 1:102 **85**
  art 1:201 **87**
  art 1:202 **87**
  art 2:101 **17, 95, 98**
  art 2:102 **21**
  art 2:201 **17**
  art 2:202 **108**
  art 2:204 **17, 108–9**
  art 2:205 **101**
  art 2:208 **103**
  art 2:209 **103**
  art 2:301 **88**
  art 4:103 **123**
  art 4:108 **126**
  art 4:110 **86, 141, 147**
  art 5:101 **135**
  art 5:102 **136**
  art 5:103 **136**
  art 6:101 **123**
  art 6:102 **123**
  art 6:107 **36**
  art 6:108 **36, 82, 143**
  art 6:111 **30, 81, 145**
  art 8:101 **77, 92, 143, 144**
  art 8:103 **139**
  art 8:107 **148**
  art 8:108 **33, 92, 144**
  art 9:101 **37**
  art 9:201 **31**
  art 9:301 **31, 138**
  art 9:501 **33**
  art 9:502 **77, 291**
  art 9:503 **36, 77**
  art 9:504 **36**
  art 9:505 **36, 289**
  art 14:101 **47**
  art 14:501 **28, 47**
  art 16:101 **30, 137**

art 16:103   **137, 138**
Principles of European Tort
  Law   **xiii, 21, 266, 269, 282,
  312**
art1:101   **174, 176, 179, 192,
  282**
art 2:101   **177, 192**
art 2:102   **160, 168, 177, 200,
  203, 282, 285–6, 288, 321**
art 3:101   **179, 267**
art 3:102   **179**
art 3: 103   **179, 268, 275**
art 3:104   **179, 268, 278**
art 3:105   **179, 268**
art 3:106   **179**
art 3:201   **267, 283**
art 4:101   **177, 200**
art 4:102   **194, 196**
art 4:201   **178, 197**
art 5:101   **23, 178**
art 5:102   **219**
art 6:102   **23, 179**
art 7:101   **270**
art 7:102   **272**
art 10:101   **77, 291**
art 10:103   **292**
art 10:203   **293**
art 10:301   **291**
Nieuw Nederlands Burgerlijk
  Wetboek
  Bk 6   art 1   **17**
  Bk 6   art 166   **154**
Polish Civil Code
  art 725   **79**
  art 903   **79**
Quebec Civil Code
  art 1385   **17**
  art 1400   **99**
  art 1508   **30**
  art 2389   **79**
Swiss Code of Obligations
  art 373   **74**

art 380   **79**
Unidroit Principles of
  International Commercial
  Contracts   **69, 90, 286**
art 1.1   **85**
art 1.7   **87**
art 2.1   **95, 98**
art 2.20   **106**
art 2.22   **103**
art 3.2   **98, 114**
art 3.5   **123**
art 3.7   **123**
art 3.9   **126**
art 3.18   **123**
art 5.1.4   **33**
art 5.2   **125, 140**
art 5.4   **81, 141**
art 5.6   **143**
art 6.2.1   **145**
art 6.2.2   **145**
art 6.2.3   **145**
art 6.6.2   **30**
art 7.1.1   **143**
art 7.1.6   **141**
art 7.1.7   **144**
art 7.2.1   **37**
art 7.4.1   **33, 144**

EUROPEAN AND INTERNATIONAL STATUTES AND OTHER TEXTS

Common Frame of
  Reference   **312**
Draft Rules on Unjustified
  Enrichment (Scottish Law
  Com DP No 99)
  r 1   **297**
  r 2   **297**
  r 3   **297, 299**

xxxviii　　　　　　　*Law of obligations*

　　r 4　**300**
　　r 5　**300**
　　r 6　**300**
EU Directive 25 July 1985 (85/374/
　　EEC)　**220**
　　art 7　**221**
EU Directive 5 April 1993 (19/13/
　　EEC; L95/29)　**86, 146**
European Convention of Human
　　Rights and Fundamental
　　Freedoms　**55**
　　art 3　**213**
　　art 6　**213**
　　art 8　**225, 231, 256**
　　art 10　**252**
　　art 13　**213**
Loi du 5 juilliet 1985　**176**

ROMAN LAW TEXTS

Digest of Justinian
　　1.1.1.2　**15**
　　1.5.1　**2**
　　2.14.1.2　**95**
　　2.14.1.3　**16, 95**
　　2.14.7.1　**79**
　　2.14.7.2　**16**
　　2.14.7.4　**16, 94**
　　2.14.7.5　**94**
　　3.3.42.2　**154**
　　3.5.6.3　**298, 300**
　　3.5.10.1　**298**
　　3.5.22　**298**
　　4.2.14.1　**120**
　　4.4.16.4　**87**
　　4.9.3.1　**29, 35**
　　5.1.20　**28**
　　6.1.38　**38, 42**
　　7.5.5.1　**11**
　　8.5.8.5　**42**
　　9.1.3　**20**
　　9.2.2pr　**18**
　　9.2.8.1　**178**
　　9.2.11pr　**179, 266**
　　9.2.13pr　**19, 44**
　　9.2.27.5　**18**
　　9.2.27.13　**19**
　　9.2.31　**19**
　　9.2.44pr　**152, 177**
　　9.2.51.2　**154**
　　9.2.52.2　**38**
　　9.3.1　**21**
　　9.3.1.1　**152**
　　12.1.2pr　**38**
　　12.1.3　**11**
　　12.1.9pr　**26, 37, 38**
　　12.4.5pr　**40**
　　12.6.1.1　**40**
　　12.6.14　**24**
　　12.6.54　**39**
　　12.6.66　**40**
　　13.6.18pr　**11**
　　13.6.5　**174**
　　13.6.5.2　**32**
　　13.6.5.4　**33**
　　13.6.5.7　**34, 39**
　　13.6.18pr　**34**
　　16.3.1.6　**16**
　　16.3.31pr　**87**
　　18.1　**26**
　　18.1.1.2　**95**
　　18.1.2.1　**104**
　　18.1.11.1　**36**
　　18.1.17　**36**
　　18.3.6pr　**31**
　　19.1　**26**
　　19.1.2pr　**36**
　　19.1.11.2　**26**
　　19.1.13.19　**26**
　　19.1.13.8　**31**
　　19.1.42　**36**
　　19.2.19.1　**37**
　　19.2.22.3　**87**

Statutes

19.5.1 **16**
21.1.18 **36**
22.6.2 **318**
29.3.37 **44**
39.3.1.12 **42**
39.3.2.9 **42**
41.2.3pr **44**
46.2.1pr **46**
46.3.80 **46**
47.2.21.9 **154**
44.7 **3, 27**
44.7.1pr **295**
44.7.1.4 **34**
44.7.1.7 **95**
44.7.2.1 **95**
44.7.4 **18**
47.7.25pr **28, 37, 41**
44.7.25.1 **28**
44.7.44 **29**
44.7.52pr **27, 28**
44.7.53pr **29, 154**
44.7.54 **28**

45.1.1 **96**
45.1.83pr **29**
45.1.134.2 **95**
46.3.85 **35**
46.3.95.4 **28**
46.8.25.1 **28, 47**
47.10.1pr **174**
50.17.1 **333**
50.17.23 **34**
50.17.35 **46**
50.17.55 **42**
50.17.151 **42**
50.17.185 **35**
50.17.206 **13, 24, 296**

Institutes of Gaius
2.14 **14, 38, 40, 44**
3.90 **11**
3.91 **295**

Institutes of Justinian
3.13 **10**
3.13.2 **21**
3.27.1 **24**

1. Theory and method: background to the law of obligations

The law of obligations occupies a central part of what a jurist from the Romano-Germanic tradition would call private law (itself to be distinguished from public law). The first task of a book devoted to the law of obligations would, therefore, appear to be to examine exactly what is meant by the notion of a 'law of obligations'. Now describing and defining such a domain might seem at first sight easy enough. One looks at the various authoritative sources of legal rules and at the categories within which these rules are classified and fashions a definition in relation to these two focal points. Yet, as obvious as this exercise might appear, defining what is meant by the law of obligations – or indeed any other domain of the law – is dependent upon the epistemological (that is to say a theory of knowledge) model deemed appropriate. Defining the law of obligations from, for example, a *functional* viewpoint – what does the law of obligations *do*? – is likely to lead to a rather different analysis than defining it from, say, a *formalist* and conceptual perspective.

THE EPISTEMOLOGICAL DILEMMA

The epistemological dilemma does not stop with this dichotomy in that it cannot be assumed that all legal systems share the same epistemological starting point. For example, at the beginning of the 19th century, the expression 'law of obligations' would probably have meant little to an English lawyer, for the categories of legal thought used within the common law were not at that time taken from Roman law.[1] Indeed even today the idea of a 'private law' is by no means without its problems. Thus, while it is possible to assert that the law of obligations is part of a coherent *system* of legal institutions and relations whose foundation is to be found in Roman legal thought, such an assertion is always contingent and relative. There are other ways of looking at the substantive material which has found itself in the obligations category.

---

[1] Waddams (2003), at 5–6.

The truth is that when one talks of a 'law of obligations' it has to be remembered that one is likely to be appealing – indeed conceptually one can only appeal – to a Roman model of law and to the epistemological implications, fashioned and refined over many subsequent centuries, lying behind the model. Now this model is extremely powerful – so powerful in fact that there is a movement calling for a European Code of Obligations – that an approach other than one that starts with Roman legal thought is almost unthinkable. This book will be no exception. Yet it must always be borne in mind that the notion of a law of obligations is not just a relatively new idea for common lawyers but one that comes from a particular way of thinking about legal knowledge. One might reflect, then, on whether it will still have validity in a century from now.

INSTITUTIONAL PLAN

The basis of a coherent law of obligations was to be found in the *Institutes of Justinian* (published 533AD), an introductory textbook for students known to be based on an earlier *Institutiones* written by the jurist Gaius and published around 160AD. An extract from Gaius in the *Digest* reproduced this plan: 'All law . . . relates either to persons (*personae*), things (*res*) or actions (*actiones*)' (D.1.5.1). What was so valuable about this plan – aptly named by Peter Stein as the 'institutional system' – was that it had the capacity to organise any body of laws (even those that are not Roman) and thus it was viewed by the later civil lawyers as transcending time and place.[2] It was the foundation for *scientia iuris*, another expression to be found in the Roman sources.

With the development of a scientific approach to law in the 16th century, this institutional scheme was subjected by humanist jurists to a much greater rigour. Moreover law itself moved from being an objective 'thing' to a subjective 'right'. In other words law became a matter of individual rights. This development impacted upon taxonomy in law in as much as jurists started to reconfigure the Gaian/Justinian scheme in terms of the individual. Law was now a matter of *rights* with the result that the Law of Things became a category containing two types of fundamentally different rights, namely rights *in rem* and rights *in personam*. As a result the Law of Actions category no longer made sense – for law was now about subjective rights – and thus remedies got removed to the separate category of procedure and the 'actions' category itself became the Law of Obligations

---

[2] Stein (1984), at 125–9.

(in Justinian's *Digest* obligations and actions were put together in the same book and section: D.44.7). Thus the new institutional scheme, the one that is to be found underpinning all of the European civil codes, is the threefold division of persons, property (things) and obligations. Each of these high level categories was in turn graded into sub-categories themselves, in their turn, divided into sub-sub-categories (and so on). Consequently knowledge of the law of obligations is, from this conceptual and scientific perspective, a matter of establishing a hierarchy of categories within this class; for example different types of contract make up the generic category of 'contract' and this category, along with the other types of obligation, make up the category of 'obligation' which itself forms one of the three categories, along with persons and property, of private law.

CODES AND METHOD

It is this model that dominates knowledge of the 'law of obligations', for the model seemingly provides a coherent and rational foundation from which solutions to factual disputes falling within its domain can be inferred using deductive logic.[3] The science of law dictates that contradiction and confusion in its rules cannot be tolerated and thus concepts, notions and norms need to be structured. The law is a matter of conceptual structuralism since this structure provides the security that citizens need when arranging their affairs. This conceptual and structural aspect of the law of obligations remains the fundamental starting point of legal knowledge in the civil law world.

This does not mean that empirical reality cannot influence the law – so for example the statistical impact of work and road accidents has generated specific statutory regimes within the civil law countries. What it means is that knowledge of the law of obligations in the civil law tradition remains a matter of rational categories based on a system – the institutional plan – inherited from Roman law. Indeed such a system of categories *is* the law in as much as it has been imposed on national states within the civilian tradition by the legislative act of codification. This structural and coherent approach to legal knowledge is justified on the ground not just of rationality – of science – but equally of legal certainty. Law reform, then, tends to be seen as a matter of reforming the codes or, as Sir Henry Maine once put it, reform of the law means reform of the law books.[4] But

---

[3] Mathieu-Izorche (2001).
[4] Maine (1890), 363.

these law books – codes – play a particular role in understanding how law functions in that, for a start, all of the main legal actors, that is to say judges, practitioners and academics, obtain their knowledge from the same book, that is, from the code. In addition, behind these law books, is a whole legal culture, history and methodological approach that needs to be appreciated before one can properly understand what is meant by the 'law of obligations'. The expression hides a methodology as well as a set of abstract rules organised into rationalised categories.

ENGLISH LEGAL MENTALITY

This scientific rationality is largely, although by no means completely, absent from the English common law tradition. As one Law Lord famously asserted, Your 'Lordships' task in this House is to decide particular cases between litigants and your Lordships are not called upon to rationalise the law of England.' Such an 'attractive if perilous field may well be left to others to cultivate' since arguments 'based on legal consistency are apt to mislead for the common law is a practical code adapted to deal with the manifold diversities of human life, and as a great American judge has reminded us, "the life of the law has not been logic; it has been experience."'[5] There are, of course, reasons for this difference of mentality.

The first reason is to be found in the historical procedure of the common law courts. In contrast to the Romano-canonical model in the civil law tradition, the English courts adopted almost from the start an 'unprofessional' element, namely the jury. There were juries in every common law case up until the end of the 19th century and they rendered their verdicts without reason or explanation. Moreover the whole procedure of the early courts was centred on the jury: cases had to be reduced to a set of facts amenable not to the application of a rationalised taxonomical model applied by professionals trained for the most part in Roman law but to a series of questions capable of giving rise to a verdict by a group of laymen who were likely to be illiterate. This in turn engendered an approach to law that was argumentative – or dialectical – in its form. The common law was not to be discovered through scientific methods but through debate and through decisions on facts.

A second reason was the classification structure upon which the common law was based. This structure was not bequeathed by a book like the *Institutes* (itself the product of several centuries of legal thought) but by

---

[5] Lord Macmillan in *Read v J Lyons & Co* [1947] AC 156, at 175.

an administrative structure that was fashioned, first, by the common pleas for the time (12th–13th centuries) and, secondly, by a desire to restrict the cases that could be brought before the royal courts. Moreover this administrative scheme was not founded on rights but on remedies; it was a law of actions in which the form of the action determined the jurisdiction, the procedure applicable and by ricochet the substantive 'rights' of the parties. Thus even as late as the 18th century, an historian of the common law is able to assert that 'most common lawyers did not seek to put their law into a rational form.' For 'most legal texts were written not in a systematic way, but as lists' and thus the 'literature of the common law built from the bottom up, describing what law existed and assuming that it had an internal rationality'.[6] 'Rationalising' this law of actions was not really an option because such actions were not amenable to the kind of scientific reductionism to be found in the *Institutiones*. Forms of claim such as trespass, debt, detinue, covenant, replevin, trover, deceit, assumpsit and so on were categories with insufficient or no common denominators that would make it possible to include groups of them in a scheme of hierarchical taxonomy. They were not, in other words, amenable to a genus and species analysis.

Had there been a thriving academic community of lawyers no doubt things would have been different.[7] However a third reason why the English legal mentality developed in the way it did was because, in complete contrast to the civil law countries, there were no university faculties in which English law could be studied and rationalised. There was, in short, no institutional means until the 19th century for encouraging a 'science of law'.[8] The common law, then, was until relatively recently a practitioners' law. It was a law of actions, a law of procedure, a law of pleas and writs, a law whose literature consisted mainly of lists organised according to the alphabet.[9] Even its vocabulary was usually quite alien to that of Roman law. In addition, of course, the absence of law faculties meant that there was no formal means of legal education which in turn meant that there was no real market for common law versions of the *Institutiones*. This was, admittedly, to change with the publication, at the end of the 18th century of Sir William Blackstone's *Commentaries of the Law of England* – a work that attempted to map English law along the lines of the Roman institutional scheme.[10] And in the 19th century there was a major call for the reform of legal education in England.

---

[6] Lobban (1991), at 9.
[7] Baker (2003), at 12.
[8] See Baker (2003), at 4–13.
[9] Lobban (1991), at 80.
[10] Cairns (1984).

In fact the 19th century as a whole was an era of reform and transition. At the end of the 18th century English law found itself with three courts of common law with almost concurrent jurisdiction, a separate Court of Chancery with its own procedure and remedies, a rigid system of forms of action (which did not apply to Chancery), juries (again absent from Chancery), no proper appeal courts, no legal education, few textbooks setting out law in terms of organised rules and principles and no system of small claims or local courts. Practitioners, judges and politicians, or some of them at least, tended to agree that English law was a mess and largely unfit for the post-Industrial revolution society. Consequently Parliament embarked upon a series of reforms. These reforms were largely procedural: the creation of appeal courts, some fusion of common law and equity and, most importantly perhaps, the abolition of the forms of action. Yet they had an enormous impact on the substantive law. They created a new structure within which practitioners and judges – and later academic lawyers – could think about law. In addition to this new structure, a Parliamentary commission report into the state of English legal education concluded in 1846 that there was no legal education and recommended that England develop a culture of legal science.[11] In Reacting to that report the universities and the Inns of Court took steps to provide such a legal education and for a century (until 1970) the teaching of Roman law became part of the academic and Bar syllabus in England. With the subsequent development of these university law departments, there equally developed a body of textbook doctrine which may well have gone some way to achieve for English law what codification did for continental law.[12] Law was being perceived less as a list of actions and remedies and more as a body of coherent rules. There was, as we shall see (below), a partial reception of civil law.[13]

Nevertheless this progression towards a body of law informed and organised by a legal science (itself informed by Roman and 19th century German thinking), was to experience during the 20th century a major counter-movement, namely American Realism. Although this movement is generally perceived as one of legal philosophy and theory, its main practical importance lay in the methodological change that it provoked. German legal science, founded on Roman law, was highly abstract and conceptual; its architects and builders had striven to create an abstract and axiomatic structural model of norms so coherent that the solu-

---

[11] Stein (1980), at 78–9.
[12] Hedley (1999).
[13] Samuel (2007).

tion to any litigation problem could be obtained purely and simply by deduction.[14] The methodology, then, was one that might be described as logical causality. Realism, in contrast, treated such thinking as transcendental nonsense and advocated in its place a functional approach to legal problem-solving.[15] The importance of law – particularly case law – is in what it *does*.

Such new thinking, which in fact reflected current developments in sociological thought, took time to reach English shores and when it did the impact was not immediate. However the legal science approach that had been informing the working of precedent and the writing of textbooks gradually gave way to a more functional attitude. The courts abandoned attempts (perhaps half-hearted anyway on the part of some if not many judges) to construct through precedent highly coherent models of law from which solutions could be logically inferred and became increasingly more sensitive to the social outcomes of what they were doing.[16] This is not to say that the influence of Roman and German legal science, and of the rigid rule-model, have been completely eradicated; they have not. But facts, remedies and functionalism remain important fundamental elements within judicial reasoning.

Today, then, the common law might be characterised in two ways. First, the boundary between law and the social sciences in general is much less distinct than is the case in the civil law world. In France, for example, doctrinal or 'black-letter' law remains isolated from history, from economics and from sociology.[17] In England, on the other hand, the majority of legal academics consider themselves to be, to a greater or lesser extent, socio-legal in outlook.[18] Secondly, legal reasoning is seen as being inherently complex and not dependent upon a highly systematised model of legal rights organised according to the institutional taxonomy that underpins civilian thinking. As Stephen Waddams notes, a 'single-minded search for precision in private law tends to be self-defeating as new terminology is devised, and concepts and sub-concepts are multiplied and then further refined, in an attempt to accommodate awkward cases.'[19] And he concludes that although the 'result has not been perfect order . . . it does not follow that it has been chaos.'[20]

---

[14] See generally Jouanjan (2005).
[15] Cohen (1935).
[16] Gray and Gray (2003).
[17] See generally Jestaz and Jamin (2004).
[18] Cownie (2004); McCrudden (2006).
[19] Waddams (2003), at 231.
[20] *Ibid*, at 233.

INSTITUTIONAL SYSTEM AND THE COMMON LAW

Despite this difference of history and mentality between the civil law and common law, it would nevertheless be a mistake to think that the institutional system has no relevance for English lawyers. Certainly the history of English law before the 18th century is little more than a commentary on the various writs (forms of action) and these writs were entirely different from anything to be found in Roman law.[21] However with the abolition of the writs in 1852 the common law found itself without any internal structure and thus was open to the influence of civilian legal science. Actions for debt and trespass gave way to categories taken from Roman law.

This development can be traced to some extent in the words of the common law judges themselves.[22] When in the middle of the 19th century the forms of action were formally abolished and the legal fraternity began to put its mind towards remedying the deplorable lack of legal education in England, the judges and teachers turned to the civil law for help.[23] During a period of about 30 years from the 1850s until the end of 1870s English judgments began to move away from the procedural mechanism approach towards one that saw liability more in the language of a Romanist.[24] This

---

[21] Although things began to change in the 16th century when the jury verdict moved from being the focal point of the whole litigation to being just an important procedural step: see generally Baker (2003).

[22] See eg Bramwell LJ in *Bryant v Herbert* (1877) 3 CPD 389, at 390 and Lord Goff in *Henderson v Merrett Syndicates Ltd* [1995] 2 AC 145, at 184.

[23] See eg, *Janson v Ralli* (1856) 25 LJQB 300, 309; *Blackmore v Bristol & Exeter Railway Co* (1858) 27 LJQB 167, 172; *Hall v Wright* (1858) 27 LJQB 345, 354; *Smeed v Foord* (1859) 28 LJQB 178, 181–2; *Pinard v Klockman* (1863) 32 LJQB 82, 84; *Kemp v Halliday* (1865) 34 LJQB 233, 236, 237, 240; *Lloyd v Guibert* (1865) 35 LJQB 74; *British Columbia Saw-Mill Co v Nettleship* (1868) LR 3 CP 499, 508; *Banks v Goodfellow* (1870) 39 LJQB 237, 243ff; *Byrne v Schiller* (1871) 6 Exch 319, 320–2, 325–6; *Notara v Henderson* (1872) LR 7 QB 225, 233–4; *Searle v Laverick* (1874) LR 9 QB 122, 128–9; *Rouquette v Overmann* (1875) 44 LJQB 221, 232; *Mackenzie v Whitworth* (1875) 44 LJ Ex 81, 84; *Metcalfe v Britannia Ironworks Co* (1876) 1 QBD 613, 626; *Byrne v Van Tienhoven* (1880) 5 CPD 344, 346; *London & South Western Bank v Wentworth* (1880) 5 Ex D 96, 106–107; *Howe v Smith* (1884) 27 Ch D 89, 101–02; *Foster v Wheeler* (1887) 36 Ch D 695, 697. See also, of course, *Taylor v Caldwell* (1863) 122 ER 309. In *Randall v Newsom* (1876) 45 LJQB 364 counsel cited Pothier, but the judges decided the case with reference only to English law. A range of introductory textbooks on the civil law also appeared just before, and during, this period: see eg Bower (1848).

[24] 'I am aware that there may be causes of action for which a party may seek redress either in the form *ex contractu* or *ex delicto*; and there are instances in which advantages can be obtained in the procedure by suing in the form *ex delicto*

was not a sudden shift of emphasis as such since the development of more substantive ideas, particularly with respect to a law of contract, can be traced back to the 18th century, if not before.[25] Indeed an appeal to legal maxims (*regulae iuris*) as a tool of reasoning was in evidence long before the great procedural changes of the 19th century. Moreover academic commentators such as Jeremy Bentham and John Austin acted as vehicles for the importation of the deductive and axiomatic systematics of the post-Enlightenment continental jurisprudence. And while one must not over-emphasise the influence of these two writers on everyday case law, Austin's work on legal thought, which had been heavily influenced by the German Pandectists, set the scene for the rise of the textbook era of English law. This, in turn, was to provide the necessary conceptual basis for English legal reasoning in the century following the abolition of the forms of action.[26]

No doubt it would be a gross exaggeration to say that there was an actual reception of Roman law into the English common law in the second half of the 19th century. All the same, both the judges and the growing band of legal academics looked to the civil law for inspiration. And although this direct use of civilian material lasted only for a few decades until English law had built up its own sources of substantive rules, indirectly the continental influence has continued in various ways. It is, then, (just) possible to talk of an English 'law of obligations'. Nevertheless it must be stressed that there remain problems with respect to this category within the context of the common law and these problems will be investigated in subsequent chapters. The use of the expression does not, in other words, come without difficulties.

---

instead of *ex contractu*' per Erle CJ in *Alton v Midland Railway* (1865) 34 LJCP 292, 296. '[S]ince the *Common Law Procedure Act* . . . the form of action is out of the question. But I must say I have always understood that when a man pays more than he is bound to do by law . . . he is entitled to recover the excess by *condictio indebiti*, or action for money had and received' per Willes J in *GWR v Sutton* (1869) LR 4 App Cas 226, 249. See also *Fullalove v Parker* (1869) 31 LJCP 239, 240; *Laurie v Scholefield* (1869) LR 4 CP 622, 627; *Hewitson v Sherwin* (1870) LR 10 Eq 53, 55; *Cherry v Thompson* (1872) LR 7 QB 573, 577; *Bryant v Herbert* (1877) 3 CPD 389, 391; *Stooke v Taylor* (1880) 5 QBD 569, 572, 581; *Hislop v Leckie* (1881) 6 App Cas 560, 581; *Young & Co v Mayor of Royal Leamington Spa* (1883) 8 App Cas 517, 522; *Midland Ry Co v Withington Local Board* (1883) 11 QBD 788, 796; *Batthyany v Walford* (1886) 33 Ch D 624, 629; *Finlay v Chirney* (1888) 20 QBD 494, 504, 506; *Blyth v Fladgate* [1891] 1 Ch 337, 366; *Palmer v Wick & Pulteneytown SS Co* [1894] AC 318, 327 (note also the use of the expression '*ex quasi delicto*'); *The Veritas* [1901] P 304, 312–14.

[25] cf Baker (2003).
[26] See generally Lobban (1991).

2. History and structure of the law of obligations

The notion of a law of obligations comes from Roman law where an obligation was defined as 'a legal bond (*vinculum iuris*) whereby we are constrained to do something according to the law of our state' (J.3.13). This definition is, evidently, rather meaningless as a proposition. However the metaphorical image of a *vinculum iuris* binding two persons has proved extraordinarily powerful and lies at the heart of all modern definitions of a law of obligations. Thus in French law an obligation is still defined as a *lien juridique*.

In addition to this idea of a legal bond between two people, the law of obligations has to be understood as an area of law occupying a central part of what a continental jurist would call private law. This category is given its shape and meaning from an external and an internal viewpoint. Externally private law is that part of the law that does not fall within the category of public law and public law is about public entities and the interests of the state. Internally private law is concerned with individuals and their private interests and is defined, structurally, in relation to the 'institutional system' – that is to say, persons, things and actions (obligations) – inherited from Gaius. This system, as we have seen (Chapter 1), has its origins in a Roman work called the *Institutiones* and the law of obligations forms a central part of its structure. In other words, a knowledge of continental law is essential if one is properly to understand the law of obligations as a generic category.

REAL AND PERSONAL REMEDIES AND RIGHTS

Another way of understanding the law of obligations is from the position of legal remedies and legal rights. In Roman law two fundamental types of remedy underpinned private law. An action *in rem* was a claim used to vindicate ownership or some lesser property right in a thing; it was a remedy aimed at the thing itself. The substantive area of law concerned with these real remedies was (and remains in modern continental law) the law of property. The other type of remedy was an action *in personam*; these personal actions were aimed not at things but another person and the substantive area of law dealing with these claims was the law of obligations. Accordingly the law of obligations is in part to be understood in contrast to the law of property. This contrast is today one of rights: real rights (*iura in rem*) are contrasted with personal rights (*iura in personam*) and the law of obligations is that area of law concerned with personal rights. Perhaps this property and obligations dichotomy can be put another way: the law of obligations is about 'owing' while the law of property is about 'owning' (and its associated lesser rights and interests).

The importance of the distinction can be illustrated in relation to factual reality. If A lends B a book and fails to return the object, A can recover the book by asserting his legal relation in the thing itself. In practical terms this could mean that should A find the book lying in the corridor outside B's room he can in principle simply retake possession of the object. If the book remained in the possession of B, and B refused to return it to A, the latter could bring a vindication action, that is to say an *actio in rem* aimed at the book itself. In short, the book remains his in the strict sense of an actual and direct *dominion* between *persona* and *res*.

However if A 'lends' B a loaf of bread the ownership (*dominium*) relationship must come to an end the moment when B eats the thing. In fact, Roman law took the view that the *dominium* relationship came to an end the moment A transferred consumable goods like wine, flour or oil to another (unless perhaps A did this only for their safe-keeping) (G.3.90). The sole legal relation that existed from the moment of the disappearance of the ownership relationship was an obligation to return an equivalent amount of the property (D.12.1.3). If A therefore found a loaf of bread lying in the corridor outside B's room he would not be entitled to take it. This property distinction reflected itself equally in the law of obligations. If A lent B a book and the book was destroyed in some accident for which B was in no way responsible B may well have a defence to any contractual claim brought by A against him (D.13.6.18pr). However such a defence would never be available in the case of goods to be consumed: *genera non pereunt* (generic goods do not perish).

What if A lent B a sum of money: is this property to be treated as consumable or non-consumable? The Romans gave a clear answer to this question: money was property to be consumed and so when one person lent a sum of money to another it could be recovered only via an *actio in personam* (D.7.5.5.1). Thus if A lent B a sum of money for the weekend and on Monday found the money lying on the table in the communal kitchen, A would not be entitled to retake it even if the sum consisted of the same coins or notes (unless again the notes and coins were transferred only for their safe-keeping). This is one reason why Roman lawyers found it necessary to develop a third category of obligations alongside contract and delict. If A paid money to B by mistake, perhaps thinking B was C, the payment could not be recovered by an *actio in rem* since money, like flour or wine, was a consumable item; ownership passed to the payee on payment. However the payee could not keep the value of the money since there was no cause to justify the payment; he would be obliged to reconvey an equivalent amount on the basis that no one should be unjustly enriched at the expense of another.

As we shall see, English law more or less conforms to this pattern of legal relations at the level of fact. However there are exceptions, one of the most important being the equitable remedy of tracing (see Chapter 16). The Court of Chancery took the view that money might *not* be a consumable on occasions and thus could be reclaimed from another's patrimony on the basis of an *in rem* relation.

DIVISIONS AND SUBDIVISIONS OF PRIVATE LAW

We have already seen (in Chapter 1) that the structure of all the modern codes is largely based upon what Peter Stein has called the institutional system of Roman law. There is, however, another important aspect to the system developed by Gaius. Each 'institution', that is to say each person, thing and action, represents a focal point at one and the same time in the world of social fact and the world of law. Persons and things exist both as social realities and as legal concepts thus providing a means by which one can move from fact to law and from law to fact. The same is largely true of actions. Consequently the institutional system is more than just a taxonomical scheme; it actually integrates itself into social fact and thus plays a role not just in the way facts are categorised but also in the way lawyers reason.[1]

The first major division in private law is, accordingly, the law of persons. In the later civil law this became the category encapsulating all rights that were non-patrimonial in nature, that is to say rights which are in principle devoid of any monetary value. They are not, in other words, treated as property rights in the broad sense of the term 'property'; they are rights which depend strictly on the person and are thus referred to as rights of personality. Perhaps the two most striking personality rights – at least if one takes the French *Code civil* as the paradigm map of private law – are privacy and dignity; yet in the larger plan of human rights these are simply

---

[1] See generally Samuel (1994).

two among many. Now, personality and human rights would appear by definition to be outside of the law of obligations, a point seemingly confirmed by their location within the law of persons in the French *Code civil*. However they cannot be ignored by the obligations lawyer for several reasons. First, despite being extra-patrimonial in nature, they tend to be protected by the law of obligations and thus each time there is an actionable invasion of dignity or privacy the victim may well receive damages founded upon extra-contractual liability. Secondly, personality rights can be the object of a contract; a sports personality may contract with a commercial enterprise to exploit his or her image. Thirdly, in English law, many 'personality rights' are defined and protected – as far as they are protected – only by the law of tort. Indeed in English law even ownership itself can be dependent upon status, that is to say upon a rule belonging to the law of persons.[2]

The distinction between patrimonial and non-patrimonial rights is not the only fundamental distinction to be made by civil lawyers.[3] As has already been mentioned, rights *in rem* have to be distinguished from *rights in personam*. The distinction is said to have come from Roman law, but a close reading of the sources will soon reveal that the dichotomy was one that found expression at the level of actions rather than rights (*iura*). Even the *Institutes* do not clearly assert that the law of property is quite separate from the law of obligations, although it is fair to say that this can be implied. Nevertheless the Romans constructed the foundation for the distinction in suggesting that there were two kinds of legal relations: one flowing between *persona* and *res* (*in rem*) and one flowing between person and person (*in personam*). A right *in rem* attaches to a thing, while a right *in personam* lies only against another named person.

The law of obligations is thus concerned with personal (not *personality*) rights. In Roman law the sources of such 'rights' (*iura*) were originally contracts and delicts, but this was extended to quasi-contracts and quasi-delicts by Justinian (J.3.13.2). These four categories are to be found in the French *Code civil*, but the German Civil Code (BGB) has rejected quasi-contract as a contradiction in terms and adopted unjust enrichment instead, a principle equally to be found in the Roman sources (D.50.17.206). All the modern codes tend to treat, to a greater or lesser extent, contract as the paradigm obligation and thus the majority of the paragraphs are devoted to contractual rules. However the case law tells a rather different story. The Industrial Revolution created a social situation in which the empirical

---

[2] *Stevenson v Beverley Bentinck Ltd* [1976] 1 WLR 483.
[3] See generally Beignier (2003).

source of non-contractual obligations (road and industrial accidents) grew to such a proportion that it changed the litigation symmetry that formerly existed between contractual and extra-contractual liability. What is different is that there seems to be far fewer 'rules' in the area of non-contractual obligations, although this perhaps is being modified by an ever-increasing body of EU law.

In Gaius the law of obligations was part of the 'law of things' because an obligation was a form of property (G.2.14). Thus, despite the fundamental distinction made by later civilians between real and personal rights, it has to be remembered that an obligation is an intangible thing, a *res incorporalis*. Property and obligations, in other words, merge once one thinks in terms of patrimonial rights. One might note, also, that in the *Code civil* the law of obligations still forms part of the law of property in that obligations are classified alongside succession and gifts in Book III entitled *Des différentes manières dont on acquiert la propriété*. In the *Código civil* obligations are elevated into their own Book IV under the title of *De las obligaciones y contractos*. The BGB makes a fundamental distinction between property and obligations.

This property point needs to be developed because it is the source of both the strength and the weakness of the whole institutional scheme. It is a source of strength in as much as the idea of a legal relation, or right, attaching to a thing allows the system to construct a conceptual foundation both for secure property rights and for real security; the owner or secured creditor simply follows the thing. There is a weakness, however, in that once one treats a debt as a 'thing' it would seem to follow that the debt itself can be 'owned'.[4] Perhaps, in the civil law system, these paradoxes do not really matter since the institutional systems seem to work well enough in commercial practice, although the point has been made many times that contract is a new form of property. However in the common law world the concepts of owning and owing – that is to say property rights and obligation rights – can and do become confused on occasions, especially in the area of the law of restitution.

PUBLIC LAW

Mention must also be made of a category that does not form part of private law in the civil law tradition but which can nevertheless impact upon the law of obligations. This is the category of public law. The

---

[4] See eg *Lipkin Gorman v Karpnale Ltd* [1991] 2 AC 548.

persona, *res* and *actio* structure was a model of private law, that is to say, it was a structure primarily concerned with the interests of private individuals. The Romano-Germanic tradition has also recognised a category of public law (*ius publicum*) which, according to the Roman sources, was concerned with the interests of the state (D.1.1.1.2). This division between public and private law is one of the distinctive features of the civil law tradition and, in France, it is so fundamental that there are two sets of courts each with its own jurisdiction. Public law matters are heard in public law courts, while private law matters are dealt with in the private system. The law of obligations is not generally seen as having a place in public law, save to the extent that a public authority is permitted to enter into private law contracts or sue and be sued for acts or facts giving rise to a private law liability.

This is not to say that, from the historical viewpoint, there has been no interrelation between the two areas. The Post-Glossators of the 14th century plundered Roman private law in order to develop constitutional structures and early administrative law was closely interwoven with appeal procedures.[5] Moreover administrative liability in France has developed largely in parallel to structural ideas to be found in the *Code civil*. Yet the difference of relationship – *imperium* (sovereignty) as opposed to *dominium* (ownership) – has permitted the French supreme court in administrative law matters, the *Conseil d'État*, to move beyond private law, particularly in the field of liability without fault. 'Private law' as an independent and discrete field of law underpins much legal thinking in the civilian mind and knowledge of the law of obligations is traditionally regarded as one of the key requirements for a true *privatist*. The question, of course, is whether this kind of thinking belongs to a past age given the increasing importance of EU and human rights law. One ought perhaps to note, as well, that the distinction between public and private law has little place, formally speaking, in the common law of obligations, although, as will be seen, it is not irrelevant.[6]

CONTRACT

Returning to the law of obligations, the first sub-category is that of contract. The notion of contract is Roman in origin in the sense of a *vinculum iuris* based upon agreement, but the fashioning of a general theory of

---

[5] See generally Mestre (1985).
[6] Allison (1996).

contract is post-Roman. The Romans themselves developed a detailed set of contractual ideas around a range of transactions such as sale, hire, partnership, loan and deposit; and each of these transactions had their own particular *actio*, that is to say legal remedy.[7] The Romans did not stop with these transactional forms, for they equally developed some more general ideas of contracting. For example, formal promises (stipulations) were enforceable at law provided they were spoken in a particular form and pacts and innominate (unnamed) contracts were also given legal enforceability where justice required (D.19.5.1). What the Romans did not do was to fashion a general theory of contract based upon promise or agreement. Indeed Ulpian famously asserted that '*nuda pacta obligationem non parit*' ('no obligation arises from a bare pact') (D.2.14.7.4). This said they nevertheless recognised that all the different contracts shared the common denominator of agreement (*conventio*) (D.2.14.1.3) and they were accordingly able to categorise them within the single classification of actions *ex contractu*. Indeed Ulpian suggests that if there was a sufficient ground (*causa*) this might be the basis for a 'synallagmatic' obligation (D.2.14.7.2), for contracts arise out of agreements (D.16.3.1.6).

In the later civil law the medieval doctors of law and the canon lawyers began to develop the common denominator of *conventio* and *consensus* (also found in Roman law) into a general theory of contract. This was not achieved without difficulty, for the early medieval Roman lawyers felt very constrained by the authority of the Roman texts and thus 'bare pacts' seemed unenforceable. The canonists, in contrast, were more independent in that the Church had other moral priorities than those inherent in Roman law. To break a promise was, in the Church's eyes, a sin, even if the promise amounted to a bare pact and thus the canon lawyers tended to assert that a bare pact could nevertheless give rise to a legal action.[8] However the later medieval Roman lawyers (the Post-Glossators) were more ambiguous in their approach; they searched for 'clothing' in order to make the pact enforceable. In other words formalism still had something of a role simply because the Roman texts had such great authority. Yet gradually the idea of a *nudum pactum* was by-passed, at first with the help of the stipulation, and later by ideas from customary and mercantile law, with the result that by the 17th century lawyers on the Continent recognised a general common principle that all consensually-formed contracts should be kept (*pacta sunt servanda*).[9] *Consensus* had become the norma-

---

[7] Weir (1992).
[8] Deroussin (2007), at 155.
[9] Rampelberg (2005), at 68–9; Zimmermann (2004), at 28–9.

tive foundation of the contractual obligation and there was no longer a need for a law of contracts based on a set of empirical transactions and associated legal actions (although these specific contracts and their rules never disappeared and are to be found in all the modern codes). There was a general theory of contract which was to find its most perfect expression in the French *Code civil* (CC) of 1804: '*Les conventions légalement formées tiennent lieu de loi à ceux qui les ont faits*' ('Agreements legally made have the force of legislation between those that have made them') (art 1134).

In some ways, this early 19th century axiom proved to be the high point of contractual theory in that many subsequent codes did not subscribe to the private legislation thesis. Indeed the New Dutch Code of 1992 makes it very clear that obligations arise from legislation and not vice versa (NBW Book 6 art 1). However what has survived is the principle of *consensus* as the normative trigger for a contractual relationship and so the *Principles of European Contract Law* (PECL), one of the latest codes, asserts that a contract is formed, provided the parties intend to be legally bound, if there is 'sufficient agreement' (art 2.101). The new Civil Code of Québec states that a 'contract is formed by the sole exchange of consents' (art 1385), although, echoing both the old *Code civil* and Ulpian, it continues to insist on the presence of an object and a cause (unlike the PECL). Most of these new codes recognise, however, that consent is not something that can be objectively gauged and thus it finds its formal expression through offer and acceptance (PECL arts 2.201 and 2.204). Yet this analysis model is much less empirical than it might at first seem and so one is often forced back to the transactional categories – sale, hire, deposit, insurance, carriage and so on – that were typical of the old Roman approach. The result is that in the modern civil law the starting point for contract is not actually the general theory but the particular type of transaction in play. As Professor Rampelberg notes, the civilian jurist tends to start out 'from the list of "named" contracts, the unnamed contract playing only a marginal role'. Indeed the 'civilian jurists practically never work within the general category of contract; in particular they never worry about knowing if a new agreement can or cannot be considered as a contract.' For, 'when faced with a new form of agreement, they deal with it either by combining existing agreements or adapting a quite different one'.[10]

Professor Rampelberg continues by contrasting this civilian attitude with that of the common lawyers. As we shall see, English lawyers did not develop a general theory of contract until the 19th century – since their thinking before then was dominated by the forms of action – but when

---

[10] Rampelberg (2005), at 35.

they did they used this general theory as their starting point. Thus, according to Professor Rampelberg, the common lawyers 'are not familiar with types of contractual agreement'; and from 'the very moment an agreement has a patrimonial content, the English judge has to determine if there is a contract in starting out from the general notion of unnamed contract, the only category on which he can base himself'. The professor interestingly warns that 'when the civilians wish to convince the common lawyers to abandon the requirement of consideration they run the risk of doing away with the one authentic unifying element . . . in exchange for a mutilated general notion of contract'.[11] The foundation of contract in the civil law would appear to be, then, the named transaction which acts as the *causa*; in the common law, by way of contrast, it is consideration which acts as the *causa*, operating within the general category of contract.

DELICT

In terms of theory, then, the history of contract in the civil law tradition is one of a movement from the descriptive towards the 'axiomatic'. It is a movement from induction to deduction. A similar story is to be found in the history of delictual liability. In Roman law a number of legal actions had been developed to deal with harm arising outside of contractual transactions and the general foundational idea, according to Gaius, was the notion of wrongfulness (*ex maleficio*) (D.44.7.4). Thus obligations arose from theft (*ex furto*), damage (*ex damno*), robbery (*ex rapina*) and insult (*ex injuria*) (D.44.7.4). In order to be actionable the harm suffered had to fall within one of these categories and although Gaius tells us that they share the common denominator of wrongfulness the Romans did not fashion any general theory of delictual liability at the level of the generic category itself. What the Romans did do, however, was to lay the foundations for a claim for wrongful damage based upon fault (*culpa*).

The action for wrongful damage was originally established by an old statute called the *Lex Aquilia* (287BC?) which provided in its first chapter a claim for damages against anyone who unlawfully killed a slave or four-footed beast (D.9.2.2pr). A third chapter went on to give an action in respect of the wrongful burning, breaking or spoiling of other property (D.9.2.27.5). From these two chapters generations of Roman jurists were able to construct, through discussion of practical examples, a whole area of delictual liability in respect of almost any physical damage to property

---

[11] *Ibid.*

caused by the intention or negligence of the defendant. Such an extension was achieved in three ways. First, of course, by interpretation of the words in the statutory texts itself; and so for example the word '*ruperit*' (break) was understood to mean '*corruperit*' (destroy) and this allowed the jurists to grant a claim where damage was caused in a more indirect manner (D.9.2.27.13ff). Secondly, through the use of reasoning by analogy; thus in a famous text involving a wagon that rolled backwards on a hill killing a slave boy, the jurist Alfenus asserted that, with respect to the men who were holding up the tilted wagon, an action might be available. For 'if someone who steers an ass does not restrain it, he would do wrongful damage in the same way as if he had discharged a spear or anything else from his hand' (D.9.2.52.2). Seemingly descriptive cases could, accordingly, prove to be more normative than they might first appear in that the jurists were using analogy to construct a causal model around specific empirical focal points (damage, cause, thing, carelessness) that could then transcend these specific facts. In this way, the *Lex Aquilia* was extended across the whole range of commercial and social activities of Roman life. A third way by which the action was expanded was through the formulation of principle. This inductive method was perhaps less common than analogy, but it is to be found, as indeed one has seen with *conventio* and contract. Perhaps the most celebrated example is the case of a pruner who throws down branches, one of which kills a passer-by; the jurist Paul, affirming that there would be a claim if there was negligence, went on to assert that there is fault when a person fails to foresee what a diligent man would have foreseen (D.9.2.31).

What the later European jurists found, then, in the Roman sources, in addition to agreement and consensus in the contract titles, were several key delictual ideas, namely fault (*culpa*), damage, cause and foreseeability. Yet it is not just these ideas that make the work of the Roman jurists so fertile. The methodology – hermeneutics, causal reasoning, structural analogies framed around casuistic extensions from concrete examples and inductive analysis – are equally important in the formation of the law of liability arising out of the violation of a legal obligation.[12] However, as with contract, there were also some quite serious limitations which were to constrain the Glossators and Post-Glossators. The most serious was the fact that the *Lex Aquilia* prima facie applied only to damage to property and this meant that when a freeman was injured there could in principle be no claim since a person is not deemed to be the owner of his own body (D.9.2.13pr). As Ulpian makes clear, the Roman jurists had managed to

---

[12] See further Samuel (2003), at 98–104.

by-pass this restriction and allow a claim for medical expenses, but in classical law there was no general principle of personal injury liability because a free individual, not being property, could not be valued (D.9.1.3). The medieval lawyers were reluctant to depart from these texts. One might add to this limitation the absence, as has been mentioned, of any general theory of non-contractual liability for damage; liability was determined in relation to the existence of a number of independent delicts.

It was the jurists and practitioners of the later *jus commune* who undertook the work of extending and adapting the Aquilian action. The key concept was that of *culpa* and these jurists gradually managed to detach this notion not just from its foundation in actions for wrongful damage to property but from the Aquilian category itself. Thus by the 17th century Grotius (1583–1645) recognised the general principle that any person who does culpable damage ought to make good such harm.[13] And, later in the century, Domat (1625–96) asserted that: '*Toutes les pertes, tous les dommages qui peuvent arriver par le fait de quelque personne . . . doivent être réparées par celui dont la faute y a donné lieu*' ('All losses and all damage which has happened through the act of someone . . . must be made good by the person whose fault has given rise to it').[14] This formula was taken to an even higher level of abstraction by the drafters of the *Code civil* with the result that article 1382 declares, simply, that any act which causes damage must be compensated by the person whose fault it was that caused the damage.

Now there is no doubt that this French code provision reflected what was to become an axiomatic truth during the 19th century: there could be liability for damage only if there was fault. As Zimmermann observes, this principle had a number of very real advantages – moral, economic and historical – which can be summed up in the idea that 'it was seen to provide adequate protection without unduly restricting the freedom of the individual will or hampering entrepreneurial activities'.[15] However, such a wide liability, which encompassed all types of physical and economic harm, did not appeal to the 19th century German jurists (Pandectists) and so the provision in paragraph 823 of the BGB is more limited. Whereas the French provision requires only damage, fault and causation, the German text adds a list of particular interests that must be invaded before there can be liability (life, body, health, freedom, property or other right).

---

[13] Zimmerman (1996), at 1032.
[14] Domat, J (1735), *Les lois civiles dans leur ordre naturel* (Nouvelle édition, 1735), Book II, Title VIII, Section IV, para I.
[15] Zimmerman (1996), at 1035.

This idea of balancing fault with protected interests proved to be an important focal point for debate during the 20th century. Certain types of harm, in particular pure economic loss, was not recoverable in principle under the German model because such damage was not a protected interest. The fear amongst German lawyers was that liability should not be indeterminate and that 'damage' itself should be, in addition to the requirement of fault, a means of limiting the scope of the action for damages. This idea has also found expression, a century later, in the European Tort Law Group's *Principles of European Tort Law* (PETL) which, between the two poles of CC art 1382 and BGB paragraph 823, has opted more for the German approach. In article 2:102(1) it is stated that the 'scope of protection of an interest depends on its nature; the higher its value, the precision of its definition and its obviousness, the more extensive is its protection.' Thus life, bodily or mental integrity, human dignity and liberty are given the most extensive protection in article 2:102(2), while a slightly lower level of 'extensive protection' is granted to property rights, including those in intangible property, in article 2:102(3). However in sub-paragraph (4) protection 'of pure economic interests or contractual relationships may be more limited in scope'. And in 'such cases, due regard must be had especially to the proximity between the actor and the endangered person, or to the fact that the actor is aware of the fact that he will cause damage even though his interests are necessarily valued lower than those of the victim.' If the defendant intended the damage, then an interest may receive more extensive protection (sub-paragraph (5)) and, of course, the public interest may also be a factor (sub-paragraph (6)). This code provision by no means gives expression to a consensual view amongst European tort lawyers, but what it does indicate that liability for wrongful damage, even today, is not simply a matter of fault. There remains a debate about the exact balance between the four focal points of damage, fault, cause and interest.

QUASI DELICT (AND LIABILITY WITHOUT FAULT)

One reason why the fault principle can give the impression of being trapped within 19th century thinking is that it has to some extent been outflanked by developments in non-fault liability. The foundations of such liability are once again Roman in origin in that the *Corpus Iuris* contains examples of certain actions based on ideas other than fault. Some of these actions were said to arise *quasi ex maleficio* (J.3.13.2). The occupier of a house, for example, was liable without proof of fault for things thrown or falling from his house onto the public way (see D.9.3.1) and innkeepers and certain others were strictly liable for property lost or stolen while in their custody.

Other actions such as the liability for harm done by animals suggest the notion of a liability for damage done by things. These latter claims were not actually classified under quasi-delict, but even if they had been, it would still be difficult to determine what the common-denominator of this category was and thus it cannot be asserted with any certainty that quasi-delict is a term that gives expression to no-fault liability. All that one can say was that the category of quasi-delict in Roman law included a number of actions dealing with particular liabilities (liability of occupiers to those on the street, together with the liability of judges, carriers, innkeepers and stablekeepers) and it is the most problematic of all the sub-divisions of the law of obligations because to 'find a common denominator for what has been lumped together here, is not at all easy'.[16]

The result is that the category of quasi-delict was never properly developed in the later civil law, although it did not disappear completely. French legal theorists used the term to give expression to non-intentional harm and thus in the *Code civil* the dichotomy between delict and quasi-delict reflects the distinction between intention and negligence.[17] Of course, this thesis had no basis whatsoever in Roman law itself. Yet given that in Rome the category did contain certain actions that could be described as no-fault claims, it is permissible, if only for the sake of symmetry, to use this category as a space for explaining that the French jurists, in respect of non-contractual liability claims, went further than the induction of a single principle based on *culpa*. They also continued to develop the forms of stricter liability established by the Romans with respect to slaves, buildings and animals. And so, for example, Pothier (1699–1772) declared that a master was generally liable for delicts committed by his servant. Now, before the 19th century, it would be misleading to state that these forms of stricter liability were seen as harbouring some general principle of strict (no fault) liability, if only because *culpa* carried with it such a moral force leading in turn to the principle of justice, especially in Germany, that there should be no liability without fault. Accordingly most strict liability cases up into the 20th century were often rationalised in terms of fault on behalf of, say, an employer in his appointment or surveillance of the employee who caused the damage. Nevertheless in CC art 1384 there is the opening declaration that '*On est responsable non seulement du dommage que l'on cause par son propre fait, mais encore de celui qui est causé par le fait des personnes dont on doit répondre, ou des choses que l'on a sous sa guard*' ('one is liable not only for damage caused by one's own act but equally

---

[16] Zimmerman (1996), at 16.
[17] Deroussin (2007), at 87–8.

for damage caused by persons for whom one must answer or by things in one's keeping').

This statement in the code was originally regarded only as an article of transition linking the general fault liability with various specific liabilities placed on one person for damage caused by another (in particular employers and parents) and for damage resulting from dangerous things (notably buildings and animals).[18] Indeed, as we have just mentioned, these specific liabilities were themselves originally seen as forms of *culpa in vigilando* and *culpa in custodiendo*. However, at the end of the 19th century, the *Cour de cassation* elevated the transitional article into a general principle with its own independent normative force thus opening up the way for an area of strict liability to rival that of fault. *Ubi emolumentum ibi onus* became the basis for making the employer liable for the delicts of his employees and 'collective solidarity' based upon the idea of risk and insurance ensured an ever-increasing liability without fault for damage done by things.[19] These developments prompted the legislator to intervene with specific statutes to ameliorate the position of victims from the two main empirical sources of personal injury, namely work and traffic accidents.

Germany, by contrast, never developed a general non-contractual principle of strict liability for things or for persons and even liability in respect of animals and buildings has a certain fault dimension (BGB §§ 833, 836–8). However legislation outside the code has gone further and there are special regimes covering traffic accidents, dangerous products (and see also the new French CC art 1386), railways and the environment. Not surprisingly, then, the *Principles of European Tort Law* (European Tort Law Group) has reached a compromise and recognises a liability arising out of abnormally dangerous activities (art 5:101). The liability of an employer for delicts committed by employees, or 'auxiliaries', acting within the scope of their employment is also now universally recognised in civilian thinking (see art 6:102), although in the BGB the absence of fault would appear to allow the employer to escape liability (§ 831).

QUASI-CONTRACT (AND UNJUST ENRICHMENT)

Quasi-delict itself may not have had much of a history in the later civil law, but the same cannot be said of the other Justinian category of quasi-contract. In fact, in substance, the need for such a category was recognised

---

[18] Lévy and Castaldo (2002), at 919–22.
[19] Gazzaniga (1992), at 264–7.

by Gaius who dealt with a number of claims, classed under 'various causes', which could not actually be treated as arising out of a contract nor could they be seen as delicts. They could be regarded as being founded only upon an obligation 'as if there had been a contract' ('*quasi ex contractu teneri*'). These remedies had been developed to deal, for example, with situations where money had been paid under a contract that turned out to be defective or where there never had been such a relationship in the first place. As we have seen, these situations were logically problematic in Roman law because money was treated as a consumable item and thus ownership passed with the payment of the money. This meant that the payer could not reclaim the sum using an *actio in rem*.

Perhaps the two most important actions within the quasi-contract category were the *condictio*, an *actio in personam* for a sum of money or for a thing, and the *actio negotiorum gestorum contraria* which was a means by which someone who had reasonably intervened into the affairs of another in the sole interests of that other could recover his expenses (J.3.27.1). These two actions, as has been stated, were independent of any contractual relationship between the parties and thus the question arose as to what the normative basis of the remedies might be. It could not be *conventio* and *consensus* because there was no such agreement and consent; equally it could not be a wrong because there was no wrong. The Romans suggested that these claims might be motivated by the principle that no one should be allowed unjustly to enrich himself at the expense of another (D.12.6.14; D.50.17.206). However, they never really developed this idea and as a result the category of quasi-contract on the one hand and the principle of unjust enrichment on the other remained rather separate conceptual focal points.

This separation was largely maintained in the early part of the second life of Roman law with the result that, until recent times, the two notions have attracted their own interpretation and developments. Thus in the *Code civil* there is no reference to the principle of unjust enrichment as a source of obligations but there is a section on quasi-contracts (arts 1371–81). In the BGB, by contrast, there is no section on quasi-contracts but the unjust enrichment principle finds expression in paragraph 812(1). French jurisprudence has, however, modified the position in as much as unjust enrichment was recognised as a general principle of law lying behind the action *de in rem verso* (art 1371) and thus, to this extent, it is a normative force which is independent of the code.[20] In addition, the whole notion of a 'quasi-contract' came in for criticism, above all on the basis that it

---

[20] *Arrêt Boudier*: *Cas.req*.15 juin 1892, Dalloz.1892.1.596.

was a contradiction in terms; either there is agreement, and thus contract, or there is no agreement and thus no (not even an 'as if') contract.[21] The result is that the unjust enrichment principle has largely become the starting point for analysing problems where money, property or services have been transferred to another in situations where the facts disclose neither a contractual nor a delictual obligation. Yet despite the criticisms, the category of quasi-contract has by no means been suppressed: it remains not just as a formal category within the *Code civil* but as a practical starting point for the remedies available for reversing enrichments.

As for the principle itself, it does give expression to a certain symmetry in the law of obligations. Whereas delictual liability arises from physical or patrimonial damage and thus tends to generate the compensatory remedy of damages, unjust enrichment liability looks to patrimonial benefit and asks whether a cause for it exists in law. If no such legal cause can be established the person whose patrimony has diminished because of the other's enrichment might well have a remedy. There is therefore a dichotomy between liability *ex delicto* and liability *quasi ex contractu* that does make sense at the level both of fact and of law. Furthermore the principle itself contains the conditions of liability in as much as there must be (i) an enrichment (ii) at the expense of another which is (iii) unjust, that is to say *sans cause*. Of course each of these three conditions have given rise to difficulty – indeed there are several celebrated real and hypothetical examples that generate pages of discussion – but at least they provide a structural starting point and will no doubt be used as the basis for a European code.

ALTERNATIVE APPROACHES

The threefold classification of the law of obligations into contract, delict and unjust enrichment (or quasi-contract) continues to dominate legal thinking in the civil law world, if only because it has been formalised for so long in the *Institutiones* and then in the civil codes. Nevertheless this tripartite approach is not the only possibility. One can approach obligations

---

[21] Zimmermann (1996a), at 20–24. In Roman law itself it has to be remembered that there was no general theory of contract based upon *conventio* and *consensus*; liability was a matter of established transactions. Accordingly, the idea of a 'quasi-contract' made sense since one was not looking for agreement but for a transactional analogy. In French law the term 'quasi-contract' continued to attract criticism in the two centuries following codification: Lévy and Castaldo (2002), at 805–6; Deroussin (2007), at 94–6.

at an empirical level, distinguishing between legal acts (wills, agreements, contracts) and legal facts (damage, enrichment), or at a source of law level, distinguishing between private will and legislation (*volonté/loi*).[22] Some writers have introduced more complex schemes. However one theme that runs through the whole history of obligations taxonomy is the central place accorded to the law of contract. Indeed, contract and obligation are sometimes treated as being almost synonymous and this helps explain why there are nearly 900 articles devoted to it in the French *Code civil* (against five devoted to delict)[23] and why French jurists are often captivated by the dichotomy of contractual and non-contractual liability.

In the same period in England (end of the 18th century), the law of contract hardly figured in Blackstone's scheme.[24] However one of the earliest common law writs was the action for debt, that is to say an action for a specific sum of money. In the history of the law of obligations in the civil law world such a claim barely receives a mention, despite the fact that it has probably been the most common of contractual claims (as the existence of the *condictio* action in Roman law seems to indicate: D.12.1.9pr). Perhaps, then, there is nothing inevitable about contract. Yet once it is expressly formulated it becomes extremely persuasive, as indeed 19th common lawyers discovered. Even if Western lawyers will one day be able to abandon the idea of a law of obligations, it is difficult to imagine that they will ever be able to dispense with a general theory of contract: for so many transactions enticingly seem to fall within its general theory. Nevertheless, one should not lose sight of the fact that common commercial transactions such as sale can equally be seen in terms of the remedies (*actiones*) they generate. Thus in Roman law the practical essence of the legal obligation was that the seller could obtain the price (D.19.1.13.19) and the buyer the thing (D.19.1.11.2). It is not unthinkable, therefore, that a legal system might actually start out from such remedies rather than from a refined theory of substantive contractual obligations. Roman law mixed both approaches of course (compare D.18.1 with D.19.1); but the common law was a law of remedies (debt and detinue) before it became a law of substantive rights and duties (contract and tort).

---

[22] Deroussin (2007), at 91–102.
[23] *Ibid*, at 104.
[24] Waddams (2003), at 5.

3. General theory of obligations

The notion of a 'law of obligations' is not just a generic category but also an independent concept in itself. As such it has attracted attention at the level of general theory: how are obligations formed, what are their content and how are they discharged? Such rules and theories are given attention in themselves in the civil law world. In addition, something should perhaps be said of the relationship between obligations and actions since not only were the two seen as having an intimate relationship in Roman law itself (they were treated together in the *Digest*: D.44.7) but the tension between obligations on the one hand and liability on the other – a tension mediated by the *actio* – continues to find expression in the modern civil law (and as we shall see in the common law).

FORMATION OF AN OBLIGATION

We have already seen that according to Justinian, obligations arise out of four sources, three of which – contract, quasi-contract (or unjust enrichment) and delict – remain as formal sources today in the civilian tradition. Thus the question of the formation of an obligation is one that is usually studied within particular source categories (D.44.7.52pr). Indeed the formation of the contractual obligation takes up a considerable part of any code or university course devoted to contract law.

There are, nevertheless, a number of general points about formation that merit attention at a more abstract level of which, perhaps, the dichotomy between legal acts and legal facts is the most important. A contractual obligation is said to have its empirical source in the conscious act of an individual whereas an extra-contractual obligation is created by a set of objective facts. In contract, therefore, one searches for subjective factors such as agreement and consent; and while these cannot easily be judged by external facts – save perhaps by 'offer' and 'acceptance' – it is not, in civil law, the facts that actually create the obligation but the *consensus ad idem*. As for extra-contractual obligations, these are created by the coming together of certain objective facts such as damage, cause and fault (CC art 1382) or of an enrichment *sans cause* which has depleted the patrimony of another. An interesting question, then, is whether the source of liability for damage caused by negligence in, say, French law is the existence of certain facts or existence of the normative linguistic proposition in the code. Or, put another way, are all obligations created either by voluntary agreements or by the law? In fact if one looks at the origins of delictual liability one finds that in the very ancient Roman law the obligation was created neither by the facts nor by the law but by a pact on the part of the victim to renounce vengeance.[1] There was a time, then, when all obligations might be said to be 'contracted' and although delicts were subsequently seen by the Romans as a domain independent of contract – delicts arose from facts (*ex facto*) (D.44.7.25.1) – it is possible that contract nevertheless remained the paradigm obligation (D.5.1.20).

This said, the Romans never really developed any general theory about the formation of an obligation over and above the various ways in which specific obligations were created (see D.44.7.52pr). Indeed at first sight they seemed interested only in isolating the law of obligations by ricochet through the law of actions and thus *obligationes* could be seen as simply a category for explaining how certain types of claim might arise. Actions against another person (*in personam*) had to be distinguished from actions against a thing (*in rem*) (D.44.7.25pr). It is thus tempting to suggest that the importance of the law of obligations as a category was more procedural than substantial. Yet the Romans recognised that an obligation could be created by 'nature', as opposed to the *ius civile*, and this suggests a social relationship that had more than a merely procedural meaning. Normally, then, the expression *iuris vinculum* was a means of indicating a legal bond arising out of all the various contracts and delicts (D.44.7.54), but the 'legal chain' could have an existence detached from the various species of obligation. A *vinculum aequitatis* (D.46.3.95.4) could be created by certain social circumstances.

This idea of a natural obligation was, not surprisingly, taken up and developed by the later civilians since it seemingly confirmed the existence of a duality in law, namely between the *ius civile* and the *ius naturale*. Even with the disappearance of dualism in legal thought as a result of legal positivism the natural obligation survived and thus it still has a role in the modern civil law. For example, one who pays a statute-barred debt cannot recover the payment (PECL art 14.501(2)), although this rule does not appear to be Roman in origin (D.46.8.25.1). Yet the main strength of the natural obligation is at the level of general theory in that the idea appears to confirm the existence of a separation between obligational duty

---

[1] Deroussin (2007), at 81.

and legal remedy (see also D.44.7.53pr). Roman law has bequeathed a structure in which it is possible to begin to think in terms of the formation of an obligation over and above the positive methods set out in the four categories enumerated by Justinian.

CONTENT OF AN OBLIGATION

Once created, the next issue is the actual content of an obligation. Again, this is, for the most part, a matter for the various sub-categories of obligations rather than for a general regime. Nevertheless there are some issues that could be said to function at a general theory level and, as we shall see later in this chapter, one is the role of fault. Is the obligation one that is measured in terms of some objective result or set of facts or is it one measured in relation to the behaviour of the parties? In fact this question is normally tackled under the heading of liability for non-performance (or breach) of the obligation rather than as one of content but the question of liability and non-liability is, logically speaking, measured in turn by reference to the actual content of the *iuris vinculum*. In fact the Roman jurists often did not approach the question in such a logical way because, in classical times, the starting point was one of actions (remedies) rather than rights. Thus for example when discussing the liability of seamen, innkeepers and stablekeepers a jurist ponders as to why the praetor introduced a separate action against such people given that there were other contractual actions available. The jurist concludes that it is because the praetor wished to make such people liable without fault for the loss of another's property (D.4.9.3.1). One can say, then, that the content of the obligation of such people is by ricochet different from the content of the obligation in the contract of hire or deposit. Indeed, this can be tested by reflecting upon the nature of a promissory obligation: a promisor can directly promise to achieve a specific result and if the result is not achieved he will automatically be liable (D.45.1.83pr).

In fact when talking of the content of obligations the Roman jurists did not always distinguish between the *iuris vinculum* as a general notion and the contractual obligation. In other words, because the Romans had a law of contracts rather than contract, when they did talk in terms of a contractual obligation in the abstract they tended to treat such an obligation as a general one. The result is that much of the learning devoted to the content is focused on the contractual obligation. For example, in the Roman sources there are said to be four types of content (*causae*), namely: the term (*dies*), the condition (*conditio*), the alternative object (*modus*) and the alternative subject (*accessio*) (D.44.7.44). All of these *causae* have entered into the modern law in one form or another, but the two most immediate are the term and the condition. The term is a future event which is certain and upon which depends the enforceability or the extinction of the obligation; it may be certain or uncertain in the sense that the date of the future event can be determinable or undeterminable (for example the death of a person) (see for example Québec CC art 1508). The condition is a future event that is uncertain in that it may or may not occur. And thus a 'contractual obligation may be made conditional upon the occurrence of an uncertain future event, so that the obligation takes effect only if the event occurs (suspensive condition) or comes to an end if the event occurs (resolutive condition)' (PECL art 16:101).

This notion of a condition can be of particular conceptual importance in situations where an unexpected event occurs which destabilises a contractual obligation for one or both of the parties. Can the court imply into the contract a condition that the obligation is dependent upon events remaining the same (*rebus sic stantibus*)? The canonists and Post-Glossators were prepared to recognise such an implied condition and this was to be taken up by the subsequent schools of civil law with the result that the idea found acceptance in German and Italian law.[2] In France the position was different. In private law the theory of *imprévision* was rejected by the *Cour de cassation* in a case where monetary inflation had undermined the commercial viability of a contract, although the *Conseil d'État* took a different view for an administrative contract where inflation threatened to destroy the company that supplied gas to Bordeaux.[3] In this latter situation it was in the public interest that the company should be kept commercially viable. The contemporary *lex mercatoria* has adopted the more liberal approach and thus while the *Principles of European Contract Law* (PECL) reaffirm the importance of the binding nature of contractual obligations 'even if performance has become more onerous' because of increased costs or devaluation (art 6.111(1)), there is a duty to renegotiate where performance has become 'excessively onerous' (art 6.111(2)). A similar duty to renegotiate is to be found in the *Unidroit Principles for International Commercial Contracts* where a subsequent event 'alters the equilibrium' of the contract (art 6.6.2). These international provisions seem now conceptually to be divorced from the implied condition theory, but the power of the court to grant remedies where a party unreasonably fails to renegotiate is historically rooted in the implied agreement of the parties which found its expression in the condition.

---

[2] Lévy and Castaldo (2002), at 930–31.
[3] Deroussin (2007), at 489–90.

CONTENT AND RESCISSION

The implied condition is important in respect of two other contractual remedies, namely the right either to withhold performance until the other party performs (*exceptio non adimpleti contractus*) or to rescind the obligation for failure of performance by the other party (*si fides servetur*). The first remedy arose out of the synallagmatic nature of contracts such as sale: one party's undertaking was seen to be conditionally dependent on the other party's undertaking and so if one party seemed reluctant to perform this gave the other party the right to withhold his performance. In Roman law itself this particular remedy was very limited – indeed there was no general theory in Roman law about reciprocal obligations[4] – and thus it is to be found only in the contract of sale. As a matter of *bona fides*, a seller was not under an obligation to deliver the goods until the buyer indicated that he was ready to pay (D.19.1.13.8). In the later civil law the idea was developed that each obligation was conditional upon the other and in modern contract law the right to withhold performance is expressed simply as a remedy (see for example PECL art 9:201).

The self-help remedy to rescind equally did not exist as such in Roman law except where such a clause had been expressly inserted into a contract (D.18.3.6pr). However the medieval canonists developed the idea that a synallagmatic (bilateral) contract was dependent upon each party keeping his promise (*frangenti fidem non est fides servanda*)[5] and this was taken up by the late medieval jurisprudence if not by the Post-Glossators.[6] In the later civil law Dumoulin and Pothier reconciled the canonist learning with the jurisprudence in basing the remedy on the notion of an implied resolutive condition and this analysis found its way into the *Code civil*.[7] According to article 1184, a resolutory condition is always implied in a synallagmatic contract where one of the two parties does not satisfy his undertaking. However the condition does not automatically destroy the contract; the innocent party has the choice either to force the other to perform the undertaking when it is possible or to claim the rescission with damages. In the modern *lex mercatoria* a party may terminate the contract if the other party's non-performance is fundamental (PECL art 9:301).

---

[4] Lévy and Castaldo (2002), at 695.
[5] *Ibid*, at 833.
[6] *Ibid*, at 696.
[7] *Ibid*, at 833–4.

LEVEL OF OBLIGATIONAL DUTY

Another, rather different, aspect of obligational content is the level of the duty as measured by the acts and behaviour of the parties. A doctor undertakes to treat an ill patient but, despite her best efforts, fails to save the patient: is the doctor in breach of her obligation? A hotel takes into its custody a valuable item belonging to a guest, but when the latter asks for its return the hotel is unable to find the item despite having what many would consider an excellent security system: is the hotel in breach of its obligation to the client? A purchaser of a product discovers that it has a hidden defect: is the seller of the product in breach of his obligation to the buyer even if it was impossible for him to discover the defect before the sale? These kinds of problem, it must be said at once, are usually seen as questions of liability rather than obligation and as such the tendency is to start out from the harm suffered by the victim within the context of the transaction or facts in issue. However liability problems also logically bring into play the content, or level, of the obligational duty. What did a contractor actually undertake to do? For example, did the doctor undertake to cure the patient or just to use her reasonable professional skills? Did the hotel guarantee that the valuable item would not be lost or stolen?

In order to answer these kinds of question civil lawyers from Roman to modern times have had recourse to two kinds of analysis. The first is to focus on the notion of fault itself and to distinguish between different kinds of *culpa*, demanding for example gross negligence (*culpa lata*), or perhaps even fraud (*dol*), in some situations and the slightest negligence (*culpa levissima*) in others. Between these two poles an intermediate level of fault was identified (*culpa levis*). In contractual obligations, of course, as Ulpian notes (D.13.6.5.2), the parties themselves are free to determine the level, but in other situations it is the nature of the transaction that is of importance. Accordingly there was a tendency in later Roman law to grade the level of fault required in relation to the intensity of the interest of the responsible person in the contract itself.[8] These different types of negligence have now largely disappeared – although not completely among the different types of contract (see for example CC art 1927) – leaving only the important distinction between negligent and intentional harm (including fraud).

The second approach is to distinguish between means and ends. Some obligations are undertakings to achieve a particular result while others are undertakings only to use one's best efforts. Thus the doctor

---

[8] Ourliac and De Malafosse (1969), at 184.

does not undertake to cure the patient, only to apply her reasonable skill and care. From a liability point of view, this translates into liability without fault (strict liability) and liability for fault, the doctor being liable to the patient only if she was negligent. The seller of a product, in contrast, will be strictly liable if the product itself proves defective. This distinction between *obligation de moyens* (best efforts) and *obligation de résultat* is fundamental in French law even though it finds no expression in the *Code civil* itself; it was fashioned by doctrine and adopted by *la jurisprudence*. However the distinction does find formal expression in the *Unidroit Principles* (art 5.1.4) and it is now being proposed that the distinction should be formally inserted into the French *Code civil*. One should add that the dichotomy between fault and no fault (strict) liability is equally to be found in extra-contractual obligations and so it could be said for example that the distinction between articles 1382 and 1384 of the *Code civil* is one of content or level of the duty imposed by these provisions.

OBLIGATIONS AND THE ROLE OF FAULT

The distinction between an obligation to use one's best means and an obligation to achieve a result suggests that actual contractual liability can be a matter of fault liability or liability without fault. The same can be said of non-contractual obligations. However the position turns out to be more complex when one actually examines the modern codes. Thus article 9.501 of the PECL states that an 'aggrieved party is entitled to damages for loss caused by the other party's non-performance which is not excused under Article 8:108'. And when one turns to this latter article one finds that a 'party's non-performance is excused if it proves that it is due to an impediment beyond its control and that it could not reasonably have been expected to take the impediment into account at the time of the conclusion of the contract, or to have avoided or overcome the impediment or its consequences.' In other words, according to these provisions – which substantially mirror provisions not just in the *Unidroit Principles* (art 7.4.1) but also in the *Code civil* (arts 1147–8) – a non-performing party is not to be liable in damages if he can prove he was not at fault.

This emphasis on fault in contractual liability probably has its roots in the text of Ulpian who discusses in depth the range of possible liabilities in a contract for the loan of a *res*. No liability will be incurred by the borrower of a thing 'if a fire or collapse of a building happens or some similar fateful damage'. The borrower 'is not liable, unless by chance he might have saved the things borrowed, he preferred to save his own' (D.13.6.5.4).

And he went on to give further examples about the loan of a slave making the point that if the slave was killed by falling from scaffolding the risk would normally be with the lender unless 'the scaffolding is faulty through having been tied together, not by him [the slave], with lack of care or with old ropes or poles' (D.13.6.5.7). This casuistic analysis was gradually refined over the centuries into a set of axiomatic principles and thus in the *Code civil* one finds that a 'debtor is judged liable, the case arising, to the payment of damages, either by reason of the non-performance of the obligation or by reason of delay in the performance at all times when he does not prove that the non-performance came from an outside cause which cannot be imputed to him, and further that there was no bad faith on his part' (art 1147). And that, therefore, no 'damages arise when, as result of an act of God or of a fortuitous event, the Debtor was prevented from giving or doing that for which he had bound himself, or did what was forbidden to him' (art 1148). Similar approaches are to be found in some of the other civil codes.

Several questions arise out of this emphasis on fault in contractual liability. The first concerns the nature of the *force majeure* that will allow the non-performer to escape liability and this brings into play the content of the obligation discussed earlier. What kind of event will amount to a *force majeure* and what will not? According to the Roman jurists it must be an event that a normal person is unable to resist (D.44.7.1.4), an inevitable accident in other words (D.4.9.3.1). Moreover such an accident must occur within the terms of the contract and thus if a *force majeure* occurs while a borrower of property is using it in a situation outside of what the contract permits the defence will not be available (D.13.6.18pr). Questions of liability and fault need to be related, then, to the content of the obligation.

This gives rise to a second question. Does the *force majeure* act simply as a defence or does it go further and actually destroy the obligation? Some Roman texts suggest that the obligation itself disappears (see for example D.50.17.23) and this idea finds expression in the modern civil law under the heading of impossibility of performance (see for example BGB § 323). In fact this question takes us back not only to the content of the obligation – is there an implied condition that things remain the same (*clausula rebus sic stantibus*)? – but also to the nature of the intervening event. Is serious inflation, for example, an outside event capable either of providing the non-performer with a defence or of discharging the whole obligation? According to French private law, as we have seen, it will provide neither a defence nor a discharge of the obligation (*imprévision*). However German law takes a different attitude if the event is of such a nature that it actually undermines the commercial basis of the contract

(*Wegfall der Geschäftsgrundlage*).[9] In the modern international codes the dichotomy between defence and disappearance is no longer to be found as such. Instead, the emphasis is on the duality between the defence for non-performance and the possibility of modification for change of circumstances or hardship.

A further question with respect to fault in contract relates to how the role of fault in liability is to be reconciled with the idea of liability without fault in contract. In other words, what is the role of fault in relation to an *obligation de résultat*? One answer, seemingly adopted by French law, perhaps following Roman law (D.4.9.3.1), is to say that a *force majeure* is a defence even where liability is strict. In other words, the issue can be seen as one of causation: the damage is caused not by the defective or non-performance of the contract but by the outside event. Another possibility is to assert that there is no such thing as liability without fault in contract and that the apparently strict legal obligation to achieve a result arises from a procedural or defence rule. There is a presumption of fault if the result is not achieved and such a presumption can be rebutted only by proving a *force majeure*. Such an approach appealed to some of the early modern civilians of the *ius commune*[10] and it has a certain logic if one subscribes to the view, clearly expressed in Roman law, that no one can be subjected to an obligation to achieve the impossible (D.50.17.185). However it might be worth noting here that English contract law does not subscribe to this view: if a person contractually promises that it will rain tomorrow he will be held to this promise.[11]

Yet another question revolves around the whole notion of performance and non-performance. Where is the line between the two to be drawn? One response is to say that this is a question of fact and thus not subject to expression in terms of a legal norm, other than the assertion that performance must be full and on time (D.46.3.85). Indeed what amounts to performance will vary not just with respect to the nature of the contract but also with regard to the type of damage arising out of any allegedly defective performance. Where a personal service has seemingly caused damage to the other contracting party the quality of performance question might well focus upon whether or not the actor was at fault in some way. Was he actually negligent? Equally it might be a question of the quality of the work itself. Has the contractor actually done what he contracted to do? Some Roman texts indirectly suggest that quality does not have to be

---

[9] Zimmermann (1996a), at 582.
[10] *Ibid*, at 524–6.
[11] *Canham v Barry* (1855) 24 LJCP 100, at 106.

perfectly in accord with the contract; what matters is whether or not there has been substantial performance (see for example D.18.1.11.1). However it is likely that the seller may have to make up for the defect by accepting a lower price (D.18.1.17). If goods are clearly below the quantity specified in the contract the buyer would have an action (D.19.1.2pr); but what if the difference between the two was minimal? Much would depend upon the nature of the defect – was it superficial? – and the damage, if any, to the buyer (see D.19.1.42). And so for example if the performance does not accord exactly with the contract specifications but the buyer both loses and gains from these differences of specification the buyer himself ought not to act unreasonably (D.19.1.42). Generally speaking, a contractor was probably under an obligation to furnish a performance of average quality (see for example D.21.1.18) and this is the rule that is now to be found in the civil law. Thus the PECL state that if 'the contract does not specify the quality, a party must tender performance of at least average quality' (art 6:108). Moreover they also make clear that a 'party who entrusts performance of the contract to another person remains responsible for performance' (art 8:107).

DEBT AND DAMAGES ACTIONS

The emphasis on fault in contractual liability is in truth very misleading in that it is probably irrelevant in the majority of non-performance actions brought before the courts. For most contract claims, at least if English statistics are to be believed, are claims for a specific sum of money in which fault has no role. Such actions in English law are called debt claims and these are remedies that are different from damages actions in a number of ways.

A claim for debt is a claim for a pre-determined and specific sum of money that is not subject to rules of causation. Either a defendant is liable to pay the whole sum or he is not liable at all. Damages, in contrast, have been described as claims that are compensatory and are awarded where certain recognised interests have been invaded.[12] The sums are not specific or definitively pre-determinable as such since the amounts awarded depend not just upon assessing in terms of money the interests invaded but upon other principles such as foreseeablity and other causal rules (see for example PECL arts 9:503–05). The remedy of damages is notable, of course, because it transcends contract to become the main remedy in delictual actions;

---

[12] Treitel (1988), at 76.

indeed, in Roman law, the remedy was inspired more by the notion of *culpa* than by reference to the actual source of the obligation in issue.[13] Damages, in other words, is a remedy largely inspired by the behaviour of the person (*persona*) in issue whereas debt, as we shall see, responds more to ideas of property, that is to say to the notion of a thing in action (*res*).

Secondly, unlike damages, debt is not, at least in contract, a secondary or substitutionary remedy. It is a form of enforced performance in that the court is ordering a contractor to perform his primary contractual undertaking, namely to pay the price agreed (usually for goods supplied or services rendered). In this sense it is a form of liability without fault.[14] Indeed, it is this strict liability aspect to the remedy of debt that underpins a relationship between quasi-contract (unjust enrichment or restitution) and contract: a restitutionary remedy in respect of a benefit *sans cause* is similar in form to a claim for a specific sum owing under a contractual obligation. In short, wrongs give rise to damages actions, while enrichments give rise to debt claims.

In the codes the remedy of debt is not given much, if any, formal prominence. It is mentioned in passing in the *Code civil* (art 1153); and in the PECL (art 9:101) and UNIDROIT (art 7.2.1) the strict liability nature of the remedy appears to receive some formal recognition. In all the codes the main emphasis, instead, seems to be on damage suffered by the innocent party as a result of non-performance by the other contractor. That is to say the codes are more preoccupied with damages rather than debt. Yet it seems clear from the Roman law texts that the paradigm claim in the law of obligations was an action for a fixed sum, so much so in fact that such actions often eclipsed the remedy of damages when it came to general description (see for example D.44.7.25pr). Indeed, not only did Roman law clearly distinguish an action for the price from one of compensation (see for example D.19.2.19.1), but it had a specific remedy in the law of obligations in respect of a 'fixed claim' (*certum petitur*) (either a specific thing or a specific sum of money) and this action, the *condictio*, existed in addition to all those available in contract and delict (D.12.1.9pr).

The need for such a specific claim arose as a result of the distinction between property and obligations. An *actio in rem* (*vindicatio*) used for asserting ownership in a specific thing could not be employed in respect of a sum of money since this was a *res fungibilis*, that is to say a consumable item (although the two terms are not in fact synonymous). When money was transferred from one person to another, as a loan or even by mistake,

---

[13] Deroussin (2007), at 582.
[14] Treitel (1988), at 13.

ownership was equally transferred and all that remained was the obligation to repay. Nevertheless such a claim had a 'proprietary' flavour in that even if one was not claiming back the specific item of property one was demanding something of the same kind and quality (D.12.1.2pr). Thus the action for a debt had another characteristic which distinguished it from a claim in damages: it was very much a form of property in itself, that is to say a *res incorporalis* (G.2.14). However the property was generic rather than specific and thus the rules that applied to specific items – for example rules regarding accidents and *force majeure* – were not applicable to consumable items since they were always replaceable. In other words generic items were incapable of being destroyed (*genera non pereunt*). This is what helps give debt its proprietary and no-fault flavour; a defendant who no longer has the claimant's on-loan valuable book can plead that it was destroyed or stolen without any fault on his part but he cannot plead this with respect to money or food borrowed. They are never destroyed as such and so will always be capable of being owed and delivered.

The *condictio* was not, however, just a remedy associated with contract. It was a general action for the return of property or money from someone who was not entitled to keep the thing or the sum (D.12.1.9pr). Debt thus transcends contract in that it is the primary remedy in quasi-contract and unjust enrichment claims. Debt is, in other words, a kind of restitution action and its close relationship with quasi-contractual claim lies in the fact that it is aimed at a specific sum of money – an enrichment – in another's patrimony. One might note, also, how such a restitution claim transcends the frontier between obligations and property (D.6.1.38). Damages, in contrast, are concerned with a claimant's loss. Is the gap between contract and restitution, then, so wide? If one considers that contract is a form of justified enrichment, a law dealing with unjustified enrichment is, unless it can be linked to the law of property (and, anyway, it must not be forgotten that debt obligation was a *res incorporalis*), bound to have close ties to standard transactions. A good many transfers of money or property *sans cause* probably resulted, then, from defective contracts and this is one reason why perhaps the Romans were perfectly content to treat many restitution actions 'as if' they were contractual.

EXTRA-CONTRACTUAL LIABILITY

The role of fault beyond the contractual obligation is in many ways just as central as it is in contractual liability. Even in Roman law one might note, for example, how the analysis of a wrongful damage case in a famous text dealing with an action under the *Lex Aquilia* (D.9.2.52.2) is almost identical to Ulpian's analysis of the problems arising under the contract for the loan of a slave (D.13.6.5.7). In the later civil law the notion of *culpa* was to transcend the category of the *Lex Aquilia* to become the basis for delictual liability in general; not only did it conform to the prevailing moral idea that one should pay only for one's sins[15] but with the Industrial Revolution it proved a means of reconciling commercial freedom of action with the need to compensate the victims of such activities.[16] Accordingly, although delictual and quasi-delictual liability under the *Code civil* is today seen in terms of a dichotomy between fault (art 1382) and no-fault liability (art 1384), this is uniquely a 20th century French development. In the 19th century the central article was 1382 and all the others in this domain were regarded as applications of it.[17] The fault principle was central to the other European codes as well; indeed the German code even restricted its scope by requiring, in addition, the invasion of a stated interest (BGB § 823). What changed was the emphasis on the individual, for statistics revealed that the number of victims of industrial and road accidents were fairly constant year-by-year indicating that the problem is one attaching more to activities rather than to acts. The growth of liability insurance only confirmed the shortcomings of an all-pervasive fault principle and in its place a new moral vision developed based on the idea of risk.[18] It would, however, be a mistake to think that the fault principle no longer plays a central role in civil liability.

More difficult, of course, is the role of fault in the area of unjust enrichment since this area of the law of obligations has something of a proprietary flavour. The good neighbour who intervenes at his own expense to preserve the property of another is conferring a benefit, but his loss does not as such arise from any fault of the person whose patrimony is enriched. The same is true of the mistaken payment: it may be that neither party is morally blameworthy and thus the problem becomes one of restitution in the property sense rather than responsibility in the damage sense (D.12.6.54). Put simply, benefit and damage are not symmetrically perfect since the former can be conferred without there necessarily being a single individual who suffers loss as a result (insider dealing being a modern example). Nevertheless, where a person profits from his wrongful behaviour the 'unjust' aspect can be seen in terms of fault, yet in these situations, of course, it may well be that a delictual claim will be available. One does not really need a theory of unjust enrichment in order to make a fraudster

---

[15] Deroussin (2007), at 698–9.
[16] Zimmermann (1996a), at 1034–5.
[17] Lévy and Castaldo (2002), at 919.
[18] *Ibid*, at 921.

liable in damages if not debt. Equally, it is unlikely that a window cleaner who cleans the windows of the wrong house in error will be able to claim for the benefit he has mistakenly conferred on another, for his own negligence might well be seen as one obstacle to such a restitutionary action. However if the owner of the mistaken house, aware of the error, deliberately fails to warn the window cleaner of his mistake, he might be deemed to have accepted the service and be under a liability to pay for the improvement to his property. In short, then, unjust enrichment is not an area based directly on fault since the notion of 'unjust', in the civil law world, has been interpreted in the sense of 'without just cause' (*sine causa*) (D.12.6.66). Nevertheless fault can re-enter by the back door so to speak in that it may have a role in the defence to a claim in quasi-contract (see for example D.12.4.5pr; D.12.6.1.1).

OBLIGATIONS AS RIGHTS

Debt has another characteristic: it is a form of incorporeal property and that is why one can talk about 'having' money in the bank. Accordingly the fundamental point that needs to be made about an obligation is that it is a 'thing' (*res*) and thus finds expression in Roman law within the law of property (G.2.14), property and obligations themselves being classed under the 'law of things' (*ius rerum*). Of course, the *Institutes* do not clearly mark the frontier between the two areas of private law, as HF Jolowicz has remarked; and so 'we have to remember that "obligations" are themselves "things" of a sort, namely "incorporeal things"' and if 'we forget that (and we are not reminded of it where the relevant subdivision begins), we are likely to think that this important subject is not a subdivision of "things", but co-ordinate with it, and to take "things" in the more obvious sense of physical objects'.[19] This separation was to some extent to take place in the later civil law, partly because the Romans did seem to recognise an important difference between actions *in rem* and *in personam* but also because before the 19th century the civilians often had no real understanding of why the law of actions had its place in the institutional scheme. Accordingly, thanks to humanist legal science, actions were to be replaced by obligations and once this had become the third institution it was bound to become the focus of intense theorising.[20]

---

[19] Jolowicz (1957), at 62.

[20] A leading figure in this transformation was the humanist jurist Hugues Doneau (Donellus) (1527–91) and his work *Commentarii de iure civili*.

The proprietary dimension to an obligation was reinforced with the development of *le droit subjectif* which had the effect of introducing property talk across the whole of private law. It becomes difficult, in other words, to distinguish between a property right and a contractual right since both rights are assets within a person's patrimony. The New Dutch code recognises this development in as much as it has an independent book devoted to both kinds of rights. The position becomes even more confused, as we shall see, when one starts to reflect upon the relationship between property and property rights: are ownership, possession and *iura in re aliena* all simply 'rights' or is ownership, and maybe possession, something different? If they are all 'rights', why, then, distinguish between money in a bank account (personal rights) and other forms of incorporeal property (for example rights of way)? These problems did not trouble the Romans, of course, for they conceived claims through the medium of actions rather than rights; one enforced a debt through a *condictio* and an ownership 'right' through a *vindicatio* or other form of *actio in rem* (D.44.7.25pr). In the contemporary world, however, the notion of a right is the basis of a general theory in itself.

ABUSE OF RIGHTS

The shift from remedies towards rights has had another impact at the level of general theory of obligations. What if one uses one's right intentionally to inflict damage on another? For example, what if one digs holes on one's own land with the specific intention of interrupting the supply of water to a neighbour? In contemporary civil law such a problem might well be seen as an abuse of a right; that is to say that the landowner would be condemned to pay damages to the person he had harmed provided that it could be shown that he had exercised his right with the intention of causing harm to the victim, without any legitimate interest on his part, and that this exercise caused damage.

The theory of abuse of rights as a specific theory was developed primarily by French doctrinal writers at the end of the 19th century, yet as a debate it has textual roots going back to Roman law.[21] However in order to understand this debate and the theory itself it is first important to distinguish between the concept of a 'right' and the notion of 'abuse'. Now texts can be found in Roman law where abuses by, for example, landowners have been sanctioned for what a common lawyer would call nuisances, for

---

[21] Deroussin (2007), at 755–69.

example pollution by smoke, smell, water and the like (D.8.5.8.5). What is more it would seem that someone who dug holes on his land to divert water might, exceptionally, be liable to an action if he acted with the malicious intention of harming a neighbour (D.39.3.1.12; D.39.3.2.9). In addition there are texts suggesting that malicious behaviour (*animo nocendi*) in a range of other situations might be sanctioned directly or indirectly (see for example D.6.1.38). Yet none of these texts are linked as such to the idea of an abuse of a general legal relationship (*ius*); in fact there are texts suggesting that if one causes damage while acting in conformity with one's *ius* this will not be actionable (D.50.17.55). More generally it can be said that actionability depended upon there being an *actio* available to meet the facts in question; if there was no action relevant to the situation then there could be no liability (D.8.2.9). In other words because the Romans did not think in terms of subjective rights, the idea of directly linking abuse with a right was outside their scope of analysis. No doubt the Roman legal system wanted to sanction abusive behaviour where it could and indeed it developed the idea of good faith as one general weapon. Yet equally there was the view that if one acted within the law this should not be sanctioned even if the act did cause harm to others (D.50.17.151).

With the development of more individualistic thinking and the subjective right after the end of the Middle Ages, it gradually became feasible to shift the emphasis off the *actio* and onto the *ius*. Any kind of abusive behaviour that gave rise to harm could be seen as prima facie delictual – wrongful damage based on *dolus* or *culpa* – and the idea that one had a lawful 'right' to so behave could be relegated to the level of a defence. Again, this is not a theory of abuse of rights as such, but at least the structural foundation was more or less in place. All that was now needed was a functional theory of rights and this is what civilian jurists provided at the end of the 19th century.[22] Rights have as their source legislation and in granting them to individuals the legislator would have in mind a social function. Should a right-holder exercise a right in a way that did not conform to this perceived social function, to a legitimate interest, this could give rise to a delictual claim (fault liability) on behalf of any person suffering harm (see for example BGB § 226). What, then, are the key elements of liability? Four have been identified. There must be (1) an intention to injure which (2) is achieved through an act that can be qualified as fault without (3) there being any legitimate economic interest on the part of the actor and (4) involving the diverting or misappropriation of a right from its social function.[23]

---

[22] *Ibid*, at 764.
[23] *Ibid*, at 765.

These four elements are worth reflecting upon since abuse of rights, like good faith, is a topic that has attracted the attention of comparative lawyers. It is sometimes claimed that one of the differences between common lawyers and civil lawyers is that the former do not subscribe to any theory of abuse of rights and the case of *Bradford Corporation v Pickles* (1895)[24] is offered as evidence. Bradford Corporation brought an action for an injunction and damages against Mr Pickles who had allegedly dug holes on his land in order to interfere with the supply of water to the corporation's reservoir. Although the House of Lords were prepared to accept by way of argument that the defendant had acted 'maliciously' (see for example Lord Halsbury LC), they nevertheless held that the state of mind of the defendant – his motive – was 'immaterial' (Lord Macnaghten). Thus, however reprehensible the behaviour, there could be no liability since the defendant had the right to dig holes on his land. Certainly this case does not encourage the view that English law subscribes to a theory of abuse of rights – and the attitude displayed by the judges can be found in other tort cases of the late 19th century. Moreover it would certainly not be misplaced to argue that this case *might* have been decided differently in France under the abuse of rights doctrine.

Yet if one applies the four elements identified in the civil law it can be argued that they are not all actually present in *Bradford*. Mr Pickles and the Corporation were in fact involved in a long running dispute over the land and in acting the way he did it can be argued that Pickles was attempting to further his own economic interest. The same point can be made about another case of the same period when a shipping company lowered its freight rates to uneconomic levels with the motive of putting a rival out of business. Again the House of Lords held that there could be no liability.[25] The point to be made, therefore, is that in some ways it is unhelpful simply to focus on whether or not a legal system subscribes to a theory of abuse of rights (or even good faith in contract); what matters more is the role played by the interest element. Seemingly the common law takes the view that motive in a commercial context should not be an essential element if, objectively, it can be said that a party who takes full advantage of his rights chooses to do so 'for a good reason, a bad reason or no reason at all'.[26] Indeed one might even argue that the social function of legal rights in commercial law is to permit the advancement of

---

[24] [1895] AC 587.
[25] See eg *Mogul SS Co v McGregor, Gow and Co* [1892] AC 25.
[26] Pearson LJ in *Chapman v Honig* [1963] 2 QB 502, at 520; and see also *Walford v Miles* [1992] 2 AC 128.

economic interests free from the threat of liability. But none of this means that the common law is not prepared to sanction abusive behaviour where the commercial interest is not in play.[27] One might say that English law, in its approach, is very similar to the approach to be found in the writings of the Roman jurists.

OBLIGATIONS AS PROPERTY

The facts of a case like *Bradford* are interesting because they bring into play the relationship between the law of obligations and the law of property. Can the exercise of a property right ever give rise to liability under the law of obligations? In fact what is in play is the clash of two fundamental concepts in the civil law, namely ownership and fault, and this reveals that the system of the codes is not quite as coherent as perhaps the *mos geometricus* jurists might have hoped. In article 544 the *Code civil* announces that ownership is the right to enjoy and dispose of property in the 'most absolute manner' while article 1382 states that 'any act whatsoever by a man that causes harm to another obliges the one by whose fault it has happened to make reparation'. With such absolutes in direct conflict in the facts of cases like *Bradford* (there are similar ones in French law) one can understand why recourse to a theory of abuse of rights proved so attractive.

Yet in Roman law itself the availability of an action to compensate for damage caused by fault ought not to be seen as something capable of giving rise to a conceptual or taxonomical conflict with the law of property but as part and parcel of property law itself. Thus it has to be remembered that the delictual action for wrongful damage applied in origin only to property (including slaves) and not to injury to a freeman, for a freeman was not considered to be the owner of his own body (D.9.2.13pr). This, of course, is why both the law of property and the law of obligations are classified by Gaius within the same institutional category of the law of things (*ius rerum*). Obligations are a form of intangible property just like a right of way over another's land (G.2.14). This property dimension becomes even more evident in respect of contractual and restitutional debts; they are assets and thus things (*res*) (D.29.3.37) even if they are abstractions incapable of being possessed (D.41.2.3pr). Why, then, do jurists persist in formally distinguishing real rights from personal rights, the law of property from the law of obligations? Indeed, with the development of the notion of a subjective right (*ius*), is not all law, property rights and obliga-

---

[27] See eg *Hollywood Silver Fox Farm v Emmett* [1936] 2 KB 468.

tion rights, reduced to the same level? Is not the law about the vindication and the transfer of 'rights' (*iura*)?

The point of raising this question is not so much to demand an answer but to indicate that the civil codes give expression to what might be called the Roman model of law and that there is nothing necessarily inevitable about this model. It is perfectly feasible to construct other models of relations between persons and things.[28] Accordingly in a feudal model the major distinction is not between property and obligations as such but between land and other things. Moreover, within such a model, the concept of ownership, in the Roman model sense of the term (see CC art 544), has little meaning since the relationship between people and land is one based more on a 'right to possession' (holding and tenure), such rights being incorporeal in nature (*iura incorporales*).[29] In this model, then, the distinction between real and personal rights becomes, at one level, meaningless because all rights – whether 'property or 'obligation' – are 'things', that is to say *res incorporales*.[30] This feudal model of law was originally the dominant one in Europe but was gradually suppressed with the expansion of the Roman model via the *ius commune* from the 14th century onwards. The final obliteration came with the *Code civil* in 1804 of which article 544 was nothing less than a return to the Gaian notion of an exclusive relation between person and thing.[31]

However such an obliteration was never to occur in England with the result that after abolition of the forms of action in 1852 it might be said that the common law remains an arena in which the two models of law – the Roman and the feudal – still find themselves struggling for supremacy. In a way, therefore, history is to some extent repeating itself within Europe. When one talks of a new *ius commune* within the countries of the EU what is effectively happening is that advocates of the Roman model of law are, under the guise of a European Civil Code (or just under the guise of 'rationalising' the common law in terms of its taxonomy), attempting to force a rethink of some of its basic concepts and divisions.[32] This, of course, may be a good thing or a bad thing, but the important point to be stressed is that one should not necessarily expect to find within the history of the common law anything approaching a general theory of obligations. Much more likely (had common lawyers been interested in theorising) is something approaching a 'general theory' of incorporeal things confronting a 'general theory' of actionable wrongs. The result is that the common

---

[28] See Lawson (1951).
[29] Zenati and Revet (1997), at 58–9.
[30] *Ibid*, at 17.
[31] Patault (1989), at 219–20.
[32] See generally Hartkamp *et al* (2004).

law (including equity) has a much more flexible notion of property and this means that English lawyers find it much easier to move from obligations to property and from property to obligations – often via remedies – in their reasoning, for they are not hampered by any general theory that erects an impenetrable wall between the two.[33]

TRANSFER OF OBLIGATION RIGHTS

Nevertheless there is one technical area where the personal nature of an obligation right has always made itself felt: it cannot be transferred in the same way as a property right. Indeed in Roman law itself such transfer proved technically very difficult because the *vinculum iuris* was regarded as attaching to two named individuals. If the obligation was to be ceded from one living person to another this could be done only by formally extinguishing the first legal bond and then creating another with a different legal subject (D.46.2.1pr). Commercial reality, however, was to make itself felt in as much as a debt was, as has been seen, an asset to the creditor and as such had a real economic value which a creditor might wish to realise before the contractual date of payment. The primary difficulty resides in the fact that the source of the economic value is not a *res corporalis* but a *persona* whose permission for a transfer always seemed a reasonable requirement. The result is that in the modern *lex mercatoria* contractual claims are generally assignable (PECL art 11:102), but such transfers are subject to quite detailed rules as to requirements and effects.

EXTINCTION OF AN OBLIGATION

The final aspect of an obligation is the way it can be extinguished. The Romans regarded the extinction of the *vinculum iuris* as a matter of form analogous to the formation of the obligation. Thus if a contractual obligation has been created by the delivery of a thing then its extinction will occur only on redelivery and if it has been created by words then its extinction will be either by performance of what was promised or by words (D.46.3.80). Equally contracts formed by bare agreement can be ended by agreement (D.50.17.35). Two particular means of extinction emerge from this formality: an obligation can be extinguished either by performance or

---

[33] See eg *Ex p Island Records* [1978] Ch 122; and see generally Waddams (2003).

by agreement. Now the observer of city life will see that a vast number of contractual operations are entered into and completed without giving rise to any problem whatsoever. The sale of everyday articles, the use of public transport, the purchase of consumer services are the foundation of commercial life; equally, for the most part, traffic flows without too many accidents and pedestrians only rarely assault each other (relatively speaking). Even when transactions prove problematic, there is a good chance that they will be settled by agreement; many sellers simply replace the defective product without the purchaser demanding the cost of a bus fare and business people are usually reluctant to go to court. Equally small accidents might well be settled informally. Performance and agreement remain, in short, the most important ways of ending an obligation.

However Roman law also recognised that an obligation could be extinguished indirectly through rules that attach to the *actio*. A creditor who failed to enforce a claim at law would after a certain period of time lose the right to sue through a device known as prescription. The flow of time presumed the extinction of the debt.[34] In Roman law itself this flow of time actually extinguished the obligation itself and thus if one paid a debt after the period it might well have been recoverable via a *condictio* (D.46.8.25.1). But in the later civil law the obligation itself did not completely disappear because even after the period of prescription a natural obligation continued to exist; what was extinguished was the *civil* obligation.[35] Accordingly the modern civil law talks in terms of the extinction of a 'right to performance' of the obligation (PECL art 14.101) and so if one actually does pay a debt after the prescribed period it cannot be reclaimed (PECL art 14.501(2)).

In situations where the *actio* has not been extinguished by time, the effect of legal proceedings is to put an end to an obligation either through enforced performance or through the payment of damages. Of course it may be that a defendant will be able to resist a claim for damages on the basis of a *force majeure*, in which case it could be said that an obligation is extinguished as a result of an outside event. However, as has been seen, one traditional explanation of such an extinction is through the notion of a condition and thus it could be said that the obligation is ended by implied agreement. Assignment, already mentioned, is yet another means of putting an end to an obligation as far as one of the parties is concerned. Perhaps, then, one comes back to Roman law: obligations are ended either by performance (prescription being a negative form of performance) or by agreement (construed widely).

---

[34] Lévy and Castaldo (2002), at 1031.
[35] *Ibid*, at 1035.

4. Obligations and the common law

We saw in an earlier chapter (Chapter 1) that common lawyers did not really begin to think in terms of the Roman institutional model of law until the 19th century and this meant that there was no notion of a 'law of obligations' before this period. English lawyers had traditionally classified their law according to the forms of action. Thinking undoubtedly changed during this century of reform and today the expression 'law of obligations' is to be found in both academic and judicial writing.

PERSONAL ACTIONS AT COMMON LAW (FORMS OF ACTION)

The main formal distinction to be found in the early days of the common law was the one between real and personal actions. Real actions were those brought for the specific recovery of land, tenements or hereditaments, whereas personal actions were those brought for the specific recovery of moveable goods, of a debt, of damages or for other redress. By the end of the 14th century real actions had largely fallen into disuse as a result not just of the decline of feudalism but also of unpopularity owing to their excessive procedural technicalities.[1] The history of common law remedies is, therefore, largely a history of personal actions. In the early days of the common law courts, the court which supposedly had exclusive jurisdiction over personal actions was the Court of Common Pleas. However this arrangement 'was departed from at the expense of the Court of Common Pleas, for the other two courts, while retaining each its own exclusive jurisdiction, succeeded in encroaching upon the jurisdiction of the Common Pleas over personal actions, with the result that in modern times any personal action could be brought in any one of the three Courts of Common Law.'[2]

The personal actions at common law were very different from the *actiones* to be found in Roman law and were based on the system of writs.

---

[1] Baker (2002), at 236–7.
[2] Sutton (1929), at 36.

The original formulation of each action was a response to an empirical problem that existed in English society at the time of formulation.[3] However some of the actions subsequently became enlarged, if not deformed, through development by lawyers and courts, often as a result of the use of fictions. The main actions of relevance to the law of obligations which were to survive into the 19th century (if not later) are account, debt, detinue and various forms of trespass on the case such as nuisance, assumpsit and deceit.

The action of account was a writ ordering the defendant to render an account of the plaintiff's money.[4] The action was less an actual claim than an accounting process aimed at identifying money in the defendant's possession 'belonging' to the plaintiff. It 'was not therefore primarily concerned with the obligation to pay [a] sum, which sounded in debt, but with the antecedent obligation to enter into an account in order to discover what, if anything, was owing'.[5] By the 16th century the common law action for an account had declined into oblivion, but in form the remedy survived in the Court of Chancery and by the 19th century account was regarded as an equitable, rather than common law, claim.[6] Often mistaken as a kind of damages action, account is actually closer to debt and thus is now proving useful as a means of reversing an unjustified enrichment.[7]

Debt itself was a claim for a specific sum of money alleged to be due to the plaintiff and generally arising out of some 'contract' between the parties.[8] However the action was not limited to contractual situations and was thus also a restitutionary remedy; when combined with its sister writ detinue the two joint writs resemble quite closely the Roman law *condictio*. In the 17th century debt got eclipsed to a certain extent by a special form of assumpsit called *indebitatus assumpsit*, but it nevertheless survived as a remedy into the modern law and must therefore be distinguished from an action for damages.[9] If debt was a claim for a specific sum of money, detinue was an action for a specific moveable thing; it was accordingly the nearest action that the common law had to an *in rem* claim.[10] It survived as

---

[3] Baker (2002), at 55; Milsom (1981), at 36.
[4] Milsom (1981), at 275–82.
[5] Baker (2002), at 363.
[6] See *London, Chatham & Dover Railway Co v SE Railway Co* [1892] 1 Ch 120, at 140.
[7] *Att-Gen v Blake* [2001] 1 AC 268.
[8] Milsom (1981), 250–62.
[9] See Millett LJ in *Jervis v Harris* [1996] Ch 195.
[10] *IBL Ltd v Coussens* [1991] 2 All ER 133, at 137.

a cause of action until 1977 when it was abolished by statute, the gap being filled by another similar action once called trover but today known as the tort of conversion.[11] Trover was an action for damages brought against a defendant who had 'converted' to his own use the plaintiff's goods and chattels.

The most important original writ was trespass which was a claim for damages against a person who had harmed the plaintiff in breach of the king's peace (*contra pacem nostram*) and by a forcible wrong (*vi et armis*). 'The word "trespass"', notes Ibbetson, 'meant no more than "wrong", and its legal use had no predetermined boundaries.'[12] Three distinct varieties of trespass developed – trespass to the person (*vi et armis*), to goods (*de bonis asportatis*) and to land (*quare clausum fregit*) – and these three varieties have survived into the modern law of tort. There was, in addition, a more general form of trespass known as an 'action on the case' where the facts did not disclose a forcible wrong and thus fell outside the Writ of Trespass (direct action). There is some debate over why actions on the case developed, the traditional learning being that when the Register of Writs became closed statute authorised Chancery to issue writs on an analogy with trespass (*in consimili casu*).[13] Whatever the situation, the action on the case became the means by which 'trespass' was transformed, from the 14th century onwards, into a more general liability action through the development of 'special cases'.[14] 'Case' thus became both general and particular at the same time in that it consisted of a series of actions based on model special facts which later became particular types of actionable wrongs such as assumpsit, trover, public nuisance, negligence and so on. However one oddity of case was that trespass and trespass on the case remained independent personal actions whose difference was rationalised, in the 17th century, on the basis of direct (trespass) and indirect (case) damage.[15] The action of assumpsit was a development of trespass on the case and was used as a means of claiming damages for a breach of promise.[16] Viewed from a modern perspective, it can be seen as the remedial basis for a theory of contractual liability.[17]

---

[11] Torts (Interference with Goods) Act 1977, s 2(1).
[12] Ibbetson (1999), at 14.
[13] Baker (2002), at 61–2.
[14] Ibbetson (1999), at 48–56; and see Baker (2002), at 62.
[15] *Scott v Shepherd* (1773) 96 ER 525.
[16] Ibbetson (1999), at 95–6.
[17] *Ibid*, at 126–51.

CAUSES OF ACTION

Even after many centuries of personal actions it was still not easy to conceive of the common law as a coherent system of abstract rules or principles (see Chapter 1). The law was still a matter of plea precedents in which the emphasis was on procedural form; the job of the lawyer was to make sure that the right form had been chosen and to present correctly the case to the jury.[18] From the 16th century onwards more substantive ideas slowly began to emerge[19] with the result that in the 19th century, in the grip of course of the Industrial Revolution, the old system was seen to be quite inadequate and in need of fundamental reform. When this reform was undertaken, however, it was not at the level of substantive law: it was almost exclusively procedural. Nevertheless these reforms were to impact on the law in general and one in particular, the abolition of the forms of action, was to free the 'law of obligations' from its procedural straightjacket.

Reform came with the Common Law Procedure Act of 1852 which did away with having to name the form of the action and this was subsequently followed by a more wholesale reform of the English legal system in 1873–75. A claimant was, according to this new legislation, only required to state the material facts of his case. The effect was momentous in that the common law, freed from the procedural grip of the old personal actions, could now give expression to a theory of contract which had been slowly taking shape over the previous century or so.[20] This theory had been partly shaped by the influence of the civil lawyers, in particular Pothier; partly by the fact that the role of the judge in shaping the law was becoming more prominent as the emphasis began to shift away from the jury; and partly by the development of a body of doctrinal works on contract during the 19th century.[21]

The starting point for civil liability in the common law is now to be found in the existence or non-existence of a cause of action. These causes of action were developed out of the old common law forms of action which were, as we have mentioned, really different methods of procedure adapted to different kinds of cases. However the procedural aspects have gradually receded and today a cause of action is 'simply a factual situation the existence of which entitles one person to obtain from the court a

---

[18] Lobban (1991), at 9–10.
[19] Baker (2003), at 48–52.
[20] Ibbetson (1999), at 215.
[21] See eg *Foster v Wheeler* (1887) 36 Ch D 695, at 698.

remedy against another person' which, historically, 'varied with the nature of the factual situation and causes of action were divided into categories according to the "form of action" by which the remedy was obtained in the particular kind of factual situation which constituted the cause of action.' Accordingly 'it is essential to realise that when, since 1873, the name of a form of action is used to identify a cause of action, it is used as a convenient and succinct description of a particular category of factual situation which entitles one person to obtain from the court a remedy against another person.'[22]

Despite the growth of ideas such as 'obligations', the causes of action remain the key to the factual situations since a cause of action is the means by which one organises the facts in terms of the law and the law in terms of the facts.[23] It is the means by which one discovers within the facts whether or not a remedy exists. The point is well illustrated in the approach of Denning LJ in *Esso Petroleum v Southport Corporation* (1954).[24] The defendants' ship had become stranded on a sandbank and, fearing for the lives of his crew, the captain ordered the discharge of its cargo of crude oil which several days later ended up on the claimant's beach. The latter incurred much expense in clearing up the pollution and sought to reclaim the money, in an action for damages in tort, from the owners of the ship. In order to assess whether or not the owners would be liable, Denning LJ worked his way through the various causes of action in tort advanced by the claimants. He started with trespass, then moved on to private nuisance before finally finding the defendants liable in public nuisance. In fact Denning LJ's conclusion was not the final word. The defendants appealed to the House of Lords at which point the claimants attempted to add a new cause of action to their pleadings. One of the heads of liability they had advanced was the tort of negligence, but they had only pleaded that the captain had been negligent; if his act had indeed been careless, then the defendants, as the employer of the captain, would have been automatically liable under the principle of vicarious liability (see Chapter 13). In the Court of Appeal, Denning LJ had used public nuisance to get around the problem; this tort had put the burden of disproving fault onto Esso itself. But in the House of Lords they took a different approach. The claimants had not pleaded a direct duty between Esso and the claimant and thus they were not to be permitted at this late stage to add this new cause of action.

---

[22] Diplock LJ in *Letang v Cooper* [1965] 1 QB 232, at 242–3.
[23] *Kingdom of Spain v Christie, Manson & Woods Ltd* [1986] 1 WLR 1120, at 1129.
[24] [1954] 2 QB 182; but cf [1956] AC 218 (HL).

Two points emerge from this final decision. The first is that legal reasoning and decision-making based on precedents often depends upon which set of fact constructions appeal as the basis of an applicable analogy. Was *Esso* analogous to a traffic accident case where, since the 19th century, fault had to be proved before one could recover for personal injury or property damage (*Holmes v Mather*)?[25] Or was it analogous to the case of a café owner who had successfully claimed damages, without having to prove negligence, from a neighbour whose horses had polluted his café (*Benjamin v Storr*)?[26] This point will be investigated in more depth in a subsequent chapter (Chapter 9), but what needs to be noted here is that Denning LJ had seen the facts in terms of a public nuisance (pollution) whereas the House of Lords had constructed the facts around an individual act (the behaviour of the captain). Secondly, the decision of the House of Lords provokes the thought that despite the abolition of the forms of action the mentality that attached to them remains alive and well. If one fails to mention the right cause of action one's case is doomed despite its merits. In fairness, changes in procedural rules at the end of the 20th century might now encourage the court to be more flexible in its attitude, yet there is no reason to think that the importance of the cause of action in the English 'law of obligations' has diminished completely.

CONTRACT AND TORT

The forms of action thought in terms, then, of particular types of writ of which the most important dichotomy was that between trespass and debt. Trespass was a compensation (damages) action based upon a 'wrong', while debt (together with detinue) was a claim for a specific sum of money founded upon a 'right'. With the abolition of the forms of action the common law started to move away from thinking in terms of debt and damages and to adopt the Roman-inspired categories of contract and tort. Indeed, during the latter half of the 19th century there was a distinct romanisation of thinking in as much as one finds the judges not only referring to civilian doctrine but also employing terms such as *ex contractu* and *ex delicto* (see Chapter 1).

The importing of a Romanist category like contract[27] was not undertaken, however, within a context of any general attempt to systematise

---

[25] *Holmes v Mather* (1875) LR 10 Ex 261.
[26] *Benjamin v Storr* (1874) LR 9 CP 400.
[27] See Simpson (1975).

private law at an abstract level (cf Chapter 1). Instead it was a matter of inserting the idea through the linking of particular remedies with the notion of promise. The breach of a promise could give rise either to a 'trespass' (*assumpsit*) remedy in damages or to the 'proprietary' remedy of debt.[28] If there was no promise that could be breached but, nevertheless, there was an actionable remedy, the logic of the new contract and tort classification system dictated that the substance of the claim must be either tort or a matter for equity. There was no separate category to deal with property relations because the forms of action had never clearly distinguished ownership from possession; the remedies of trespass and detinue had been adequate enough to protect property – that is possessory – interests.[29]

Nevertheless the basic principle that people could make promises enforceable as substantive contracts was well established by 1850. Thus one finds a judge in 1861 asserting that there 'can be no contract until there is a final and mutual assent; an agreement of the minds of the parties, upon the same terms'. And when 'that assent has taken place . . . there is a contract; and a cause of action on that contract then and there arises'.[30] All that remained was for the courts, aided by the growing textbook tradition, to refine the theory in terms of a model of rules regarding formation (offer, acceptance, consideration and intention to create legal relations), content (condition, warranties and implied terms) and discharge (performance, agreement, breach and frustration). This model of rules was largely complete by the end of the 19th century as the foundational (and still leading) case of *Carlill v Carbolic Smoke Ball Co*[31] so clearly attests.

One might note, however, that contract was enforceable at common law not as a form of private legislation, despite the consistent emphasis during the 19th century of the doctrine of freedom of contract. A failure to perform a contractual obligation was actionable as a 'cause of action'. However this cause of action foundation to liability is much less evident in contract because the breach of a contractual promise is a cause of action in itself. Moreover, unlike the civil lawyer, common lawyers seem little interested in classifying contractual claims under different transactional categories, that is to say under sale, hire, loan and the like; they are happy

---

[28] Ibbetson (1999), at 147–51. And note: 'In the Courts of common law the party who had earned wages might either sue for the wages as a debt and recover the amount, or bring an action of *assumpsit* and recover the same sum as damages for the breach of contract in not paying them': per Blackburn J in *Millett v Coleman* (1875) 44 LJQB 194, at 201.

[29] See eg *Buckley v Gross* (1863) 32 LJQB 129.

[30] Wilde J in *Aris v Orchard* (1861) 30 LJ Exch 21, at 23.

[31] [1893] 1 QB 256.

to work with a general theory of enforceable promises.[32] The cause of action foundation becomes, in other words, eclipsed by the general theory of contract.

In tort, on the other hand, the individual causes of action remain fundamental because the common law has never developed a general principle of wrongful liability. Indeed, such an approach was specifically rejected in the famous case of *Bradford Corporation v Pickles*[33] (see Chapter 3) and the requirement of a cause of action has not, as such, been affected by the incorporation of the European Convention of Human Rights and Fundamental Freedoms into United Kingdom law.[34] Thus in order to establish liability in tort one must still have recourse to a list of actions.[35] A claimant is, as we have seen, obliged to show that the facts pleaded constitute trespass, public nuisance, private nuisance, negligence, misfeasance in public office, defamation or some other tort and failure to plead such a cause of action might jeopardise the whole action. As one leading tort lawyer has asserted, tort 'is what is in the tort books, and the only thing holding it together is the binding'.[36] This said, such fragmentation at the level of causes of action has not prevented more theory-orientated minds from advancing taxonomical possibilities other than the alphabetic list. And it is possible to discern since 1873 a shift towards general principle. In particular, the tort of negligence, established as an independent cause of action in 1932, has grown so rapidly that it is encroaching upon other, older established causes of action.[37] One result of this expansion is that the areas of liability without fault are becoming increasingly restricted.[38]

RESTITUTION (UNJUST ENRICHMENT)

The terms 'contract' and 'tort' were not restricted to the case law but were equally employed by the legislature with the result that they became formally embedded in legal thinking.[39] Of course, the judges could have developed a third category of liability after 1875, but a rigid adherence to the doctrine of precedent resulted in the contract and tort dichotomy

---

[32] Weir (1992).
[33] [1895] AC 587.
[34] *Wainwright v Home Office* [2004] 2 AC 406.
[35] Rudden (1991–2).
[36] Weir (2006), at ix.
[37] Weir (1998).
[38] See eg *Transco plc v Stockport MBC* [2004] 2 AC 1.
[39] See eg County Courts Act 1984 s 15.

being reconfirmed by the House of Lords in 1914 as a matter of law. Lord Haldane said that 'broadly speaking, so far as proceedings *in personam* are concerned, the common law of England really recognises (unlike the Roman law) only actions of two classes, those founded on contract and those founded on tort.'[40]

This duality was, of course, to prove problematic for common lawyers, just as it had done for Gaius, in that there were a number of claims that could not easily be accommodated either under wrongs (tort) or under agreements (contracts). The most difficult of these claims taxonomically speaking were several debt actions which were allowed where a defendant had received money from the plaintiff to which he was not entitled in situations where there was no actual contract. As Lord Atkin pointed out in 1941, 'it was necessary to create a fictitious contract: for there was no action possible other than debt or assumpsit on the one side and action for damages for tort on the other.'[41] In short, these quasi-contractual debt claims were rationalised under the principle of an implied contract. This rationalisation was, however, to prove logically problematic where money had been paid under a supposed contract that subsequently proved to be non-existent for reasons of *ultra vires*. Quasi-contractual debt claims could not be used to recover the money because all contracts, express or implied, were void. In addition, it was clear that the implied contract theory was a fiction. As a result both doctrine and the case law, in the second half of the 20th century, gradually moved towards a re-conceptualisation of these quasi-contractual claims under a third category generally called 'restitution' whose indirect normative basis was the principle of unjust enrichment (see Chapter 16).

The independence of restitution does not, however, come without a price. First, although it is independent of contract and tort, there are many contract and tort cases that seem equally to belong to restitution. For example, contract textbooks and casebooks contain a range of cases dealing with the recovery of money, either as debts or as damages, in situations where contracts have proved to be defective for misrepresentation, duress, illegality, frustration or whatever. Equally, in the law of tort, there are cases where damages have been measured less by the claimant's loss and more by the defendant's enrichment. Indeed, the property torts – in particular trespass to goods and conversion – are almost by definition 'restitutionary' in that the gist of the claim is the restoring of a benefit. Secondly, the category of restitution, together with the principle of unjust

---

[40] *Sinclair v Brougham* [1914] AC 398, at 415.
[41] *United Australia Ltd v Barclays Bank Ltd* [1941] AC 1, at 27.

enrichment, is wider than the old category of quasi-contract. There are a number of equitable (and common law) claims whose basis is more proprietary than obligational with the result that the category of restitution belongs just as much within the law of property as within the law of obligations.

Thirdly, it would probably be wrong to think that there is as yet a general unjust enrichment action in English law. In order to succeed a claimant must establish a cause of action and thus the rules attaching to the old quasi-contractual debt claims – and of course any equitable principles attaching to the various tracing, account or trust actions – remain of relevance.

Finally, the law of restitution has generated a mass of doctrinal literature far out of proportion to the social importance of the subject. This has resulted not just in wasted energy but also in the production of theories, with regard both to restitution itself and to taxonomy in general, that have little connection with practical reality. A more realistic dividing line would be a remedial one between debt (including account) and damages; and thus an independent category of quasi-contractual remedies (minus the implied contract theory), together of course with equitable remedies, would probably have been more suitable for the common law mind. But 'contract', 'tort' and 'other remedies' are an anathema to those who think that legal categories should be scientific and that legal solutions should have logic rather than the complexities of social reality as their source.

REMEDIES

The cause of action is not the only institutional focal point in 'law of obligation' cases. Another focal point is the remedy which continues to enjoy in English law a certain independence from the cause of action in issue. As Lord Nicholls once observed: 'practising lawyers tend to think in terms of established categories of causes of action, such as those in contract or tort or trust or arising under statute' but they 'do not always appreciate that the range of causes of action already extends very widely, into areas where identification of the underlying "right" may be elusive.'[42] The reason, says one specialist on civil justice, 'may be attributed to the vast number, variety, diversity and flexibility of its judicial remedies' whose 'categories . . . are not closed, and [thus] the judicial machinery . . . may devise and

---

[42] *Mercedes Benz AG v Leiduck* [1996] 1 AC 284, at 310.

operate new remedies, or variations of old remedies.'[43] These remedies – debt, damages, injunction, specific performance, rescission to name but some – can, then, not only give expression to existing 'rights' but on occasions play a creative role in helping to establish new 'rights'.

The way this is done is through the recognition at the law of actions level of certain 'interests' that are not themselves given direct protection by any cause of action. Thus in one case a claimant received in damages for breach of contract a sum that covered not just his own directly protected interest but also the interests of his family, these latter persons not actually having any direct contractual rights *vis-à-vis* the defendants.[44] A similar third party interest was protected in another case when the House of Lords granted the equitable remedy of specific performance in respect of a promise to pay a debt made by the defendant, not to the claimant herself, but to her late husband.[45] In this latter case the House of Lords were, perhaps, motivated to protect the widow's interest by the principle of unjust enrichment; if they had not enforced the debt the defendant would have obtained a benefit at a price less than he had promised to pay. This unjust enrichment principle was also in evidence when the House of Lords used the equitable remedy of account of profits in order to prevent a person from profiting from his breach of contract.[46] Again, there was no direct contractual right in play because the actual plaintiff had suffered no damage and thus was not entitled to the remedy of substantial damages; instead the judges simply switched from the law of contract to the law of actions. They focused their attention on the rules attaching to the equitable remedy of account.

One must not, of course, exaggerate the position. Remedies do not function in a legal world unrestrained by pre-existing rules and principles and so formally are linked to substantive law. They must normally be related to a right and not a mere interest. Nevertheless the remedy is capable of being creative at the rights level if the interest can be categorised as 'property' and once it has issued to protect a particular 'interest' that interest can harden into a 'right'. This is particularly true of equitable remedies which have, by definition, always been more flexible because Equity itself is motivated by the need to do justice and is thus more responsive to 'international' principles such as unjust enrichment and abuse of rights. In addition, Equity has as one of its missions the protection of property

---

[43] Jacob (1987), at 171–2.
[44] *Jackson v Horizon Holidays Ltd* [1975] 1 WLR 1468.
[45] *Beswick v Beswick* [1968] AC 58.
[46] *Attorney-Gen v Blake* [2001] 1 AC 268.

rights and in pursuing this mission it takes a wide view of what constitutes property.[47]

INJUNCTIONS

One particularly effective remedy in this respect is the injunction. An injunction is a discretionary remedy derived from the equitable jurisdiction of the courts[48] and although it is normally cast in negative form there exists a positive form called a mandatory injunction. A negative injunction directs the person to whom it is addressed not to do something (for example not to trespass on the applicant's land),[49] while a mandatory injunction actually requires that the person do something positive such as removing a trespassing sign from the plaintiff's land.[50] A court can also issue an emergency (interlocutory) injunction to protect an immediate interest even if such an interest does not seem to be based directly on a cause of action.[51] Sometimes a later court comes to accept that an injunction was, perhaps, not deserved in respect of the interest in issue.[52] But in the case of other interests such as confidential information the effect of the injunction is gradually to create a new and identifiable 'right' which may well then become an interest protected not just by Equity but also the common law.[53]

In contrast to this positive right-creating role an equitable remedy can be the vehicle for a more negative approach. In *Miller v Jackson*[54] the plaintiffs bought a newly constructed house that had been erected on a site close to a long established cricket ground. During the cricket season it became difficult for the plaintiffs to sit in their garden because of the danger of cricket balls being hit out of the ground; the club attempted to resolve the problem by erecting a high fence and offering to install unbreakable windows and a safety net. However the plaintiffs resorted to the legal remedy of an injunction and this was granted by the trial judge

---

[47] See eg *Ex p Island Records* [1978] Ch 122; *Spain (Kingdom of) v Christie Ltd* [1986] 1 WLR 1120.
[48] *Wookey v Wookey* [1991] 3 WLR 135.
[49] *Anchor Brewhouse Developments v Berkley House* [1987] EG 173. See also *Law Debenture Corpn v Ural Caspian Ltd* [1993] 1 WLR 138, 144–5.
[50] *Kelsen v Imperial Tobacco Co Ltd* [1957] 2 QB 334.
[51] See eg *Burris v Azadani* [1995] 1 WLR 1372.
[52] See eg *Femis-Bank Ltd v Lazar* [1991] Ch 391.
[53] See *Douglas v Hello! Ltd (No 3)* [2008] 1 AC 1.
[54] [1977] QB 966.

on the basis that the invasion of the plaintiffs' garden amounted to the tort of private nuisance. The fact that the cricket ground pre-dated the houses was no defence because legal precedent dictated that a defendant could not justify a nuisance by arguing that the plaintiff was the cause of his own misfortune in coming to live close to the defendant's activity.[55] In the Court of Appeal, however, the injunction was lifted as a result of the decision of two of the judges. Both Lord Denning MR and Cumming-Bruce LJ were of the view that an injunction should not issue, not because there was no nuisance as such (although Lord Denning himself was of the view that the club's activities should not be classed as a nuisance), but because an injunction was a discretionary remedy. Lord Denning MR saw the problem as one of a contest between the interest of the public at large and the interest of the private individual; and, in deciding this contest, what became crucial was the nature of the remedy. Accordingly, in situations where the plaintiff was bringing an action in damages for compensation for physical damage the public interest would, Lord Denning assumed, play a different role than when it was a question of an injunction.[56] The injunction brought into play an element of judicial discretion and this discretion was in turn to be determined by the interests in play.

SPECIFIC PERFORMANCE IN EQUITY

In addition to injunctions, the Court of Chancery could also order a contractor directly to perform a contractual promise. The granting of such an order was generally regarded as exceptional in that the court would not order specific performance if it considered that the common law remedy of damages would be an adequate remedy. Accordingly, in the case of sale contracts, the object being sold must be unique (land always is) before a purchaser will be granted specific performance. Again what is interesting about specific performance is that it can bring into play equitable principles that attach to the remedy rather than to the rights of the parties.

For example in *Co-operative Insurance Society Ltd v Argyll Stores Ltd*[57] a company wished to close one of its supermarkets situated in a shopping centre because it was losing money. However such a closure amounted to the breach of a term in the lease and the question arose as to whether the landlord could insist that the supermarket keep trading until the date stipu-

---

[55] *Sturges v Bridgman* (1879) 11 Ch D 852.
[56] [1977] QB at 981–2.
[57] [1998] AC 1.

lated in the contractual term. Reversing the Court of Appeal, the House of Lords held that the equitable remedy could not be used. The principal reason given by Lord Hoffmann was that the granting of specific performance would require constant supervision enforceable by the quasi-criminal procedure of contempt of court. Such a weapon would often 'be unsuitable as an instrument for adjudicating upon disputes which may arise over whether a business is being run in accordance with the terms of the court's order'.[58] In addition, there was the further objection that the granting of specific performance could cause injustice by allowing the plaintiff to enrich himself at the expense of the defendant. 'The loss which the defendant may suffer through having to comply with the order (for example, by running a business at a loss for an indefinite period)', said Lord Hoffmann, 'may be far greater than the plaintiff would suffer from the contract being broken'.[59] With respect to the question of whether or not the court was encouraging contractors to break their word, the Law Lord responded by saying that it was neither the purpose of the law of contract to punish wrongdoing nor the role of the courts to require someone to carry on a business at a loss if there was a plausible alternative remedy (damages at common law).

In terms of the creative role played by the remedy in this case, one might note that the reasoning of Lord Hoffmann seems to come close to accepting that some breaches of contract are simply commercial calculations which should attract no special condemnation by the courts (the 'efficient breach of contract').[60] In other words, there are some situations where it might be more economically justifiable to break a contract and pay the other party damages than to be forced to perform the contract. Such a 'principle' cannot of course be easily reflected in the substantive rules of contract itself since the whole point of these rules is to ensure that the contract is enforceable. But the economic principle can be given expression through the remedy and thus it remains important to appreciate that in common law systems a distinction still exists between a law of 'obligations' and a law of 'actions'.

DAMAGES

This idea of an efficient breach of contract can find expression not just through the equitable remedies (that is to say those remedies developed

---

[58] *Ibid*, at 12.
[59] *Ibid*, at 15.
[60] Waddams (2000).

by the old Court of Chancery) but also through the common law remedy of damages. Now the general principle behind the remedy of damages is *restitutio in integrum* but this hides as much as it reveals since the 'interests' protected can vary according to the cause of action in play. In contract the award of damages is supposed to protect what has been called an 'expectation interest', that is to say the sum awarded should put the claimant in the position he would have been in had the contract not been broken.[61] But this 'interest' is itself capable not just of being divided up into more specific interests (personal injury, psychological injury, mental distress, property injury, loss of profit and failure to receive a gain) but also of attaching itself either to the subject matter of an obligation (*res*) (for example the thing sold or service supplied) or to the contractor as a person (*persona*) (personal injury, mental distress, disappointment and the like). There is, in other words, much flexibility.

Thus, to return to the efficient breach point, the court has a certain 'discretion' when it comes to analysing the facts and the interests in play. In *Ruxley Electronics Ltd v Forsyth*[62] the claimant had contracted with the defendants to have a swimming pool built in his garden. The contract specified that the pool was to have a maximum depth of 7ft 6in, but when constructed the claimant discovered that the deepest point was only 6ft 9in. The trial judge found as a fact that the pool was perfectly safe to dive into and that there was no decrease in the actual value of the pool; it was, he said, a 'reasonable' pool. Ought, then, the claimant to be able to recover the full cost of demolishing the pool and having one built that conformed to the contract (£21,560) or must he be satisfied with damages for loss of pleasure and amenity (£2,500)? The trial judge awarded £2,500. A majority of the Court of Appeal replaced this award with the full £21,560, holding that this was the 'only way in which his interest [could] be served'.[63] However the House of Lords restored the amount awarded by the trial judge on the basis that the contractual objective had been substantially achieved and that it would be unreasonable to award the cost of reinstatement on these particular facts. According to Lord Lloyd, the analogy to be applied was the package holiday contract: the claimant damage in *Ruxley* was not damage that attached to the swimming pool as such (*res*) – he had received a perfectly good pool – but damage that was a form of mental distress. The damage, in other words, attached to the person (*persona*). He

---

[61] *Surrey County Council v Bredero Homes Ltd* [1993] 1 WLR 1361, at 1369 (Steyn LJ).
[62] [1996] 1 AC 344.
[63] [1994] 1 WLR 650, at 660 per Mann LJ.

had lost the pleasure of having a 7ft 6in swimming pool and he should be compensated only for that damage.

Of course the judges were not condoning as such the breach of contract. Nevertheless they were not actually awarding the full 'expectation interest' in terms of the subject matter of the contract, that is to say the pool. The consumer expected to have a pool that was 7ft 6in deep, but to put him in this position would require a completely new pool which would mean that all the resources put into building the 6ft 9in pool would be wasted. If the pool was seriously defective – for example if it leaked badly – one can imagine that the court would have been happy to condemn the constructor in full damages for a new pool. But the judge (assuming a role once held by the jury) decided that the pool was 'reasonable'; the constructor, it might be said, had substantially performed the contract. Should not, then, the buyer be forced to pay the full price less a sum for his disappointment? The House of Lords could not say that there was no breach of a contractual obligation because there clearly was. Yet what the remedy, as an independent legal institution, allowed the judges to do was to rethink the whole notion of 'damage'. And while the case will no doubt be welcomed by some (builders) and criticised by others (consumers), it should at least indicate how difficult it is to apply categories to the common law such as the 'law of obligations' since contract and tort (and now restitution) do not reveal the full complexity of how the law and legal reasoning operate. Or, put another way, the various interests in play in contract, tort and restitution cases can often be diffuse and distributed between different institutional elements in a way that means that they cannot be encapsulated within a single category such as 'contract' or even 'obligations'. Social, moral and economic facts and interests are complex and the law of remedies at least recognises this.

DEBT AND ACCOUNT

The theory of the efficient breach of contract has emerged equally in some debt cases. In *Attica Sea Carriers v Ferrostaal Poseidon*[64] the hirers were under a contractual duty to redeliver a ship in good repair, but, owing to engine trouble, to put the ship in good repair would cost over twice the actual value of the vessel. When the hirers tried to redeliver the ship without the repairs being done, the owners refused to accept redelivery and claimed the hire fees for the whole period during which the ship remained

---

[64] [1976] 1 Ll Rep 250.

un-repaired. The Court of Appeal held that the owners were not entitled to sue in debt, only to claim in damages, because the owners were in effect attempting to enforce specific performance of the contract in a situation where damages would be an adequate remedy. As Lord Denning MR said, to force the hirers to do the repairs would be a waste of money since the ship would then only be sold for scrap; equally to make the hirers liable in debt for a useless and idle ship would equally be a waste. By refusing to allow the owners to use the remedy of debt, such economic waste could be avoided. There is, of course, another aspect to this case in that the civil lawyer might be tempted to see here the operation of an abuse of rights theory. No such theory was alluded to in the judgments, but the owners' behaviour was deemed 'unreasonable' which is, in some ways, another name for abusive behaviour. The point to stress, however, is that flexibility at the level of remedies often means that formal theories such as abuse of rights or good faith are unnecessary.

Debt is a common law remedy. However Equity has developed its own type of debt claim called account of profits which can be used in situations to prevent a person from retaining an unjust profit as a result of behaviour which, although not necessarily wrongful at common law, might well be unconscionable in Chancery.[65] Or, put another way, Equity can prevent both an 'abuse of a right' and an unjustified enrichment by forcing a party to disgorge a profit. An excellent example is provided by *English v Dedham Vale Properties*[66] in which an elderly couple agreed to sell their bungalow and four acres to a property company. Between the signing of the contract and the conveyance of the property, the property company, without informing the couple but using their name, applied for planning permission in respect of the four acres and when this was granted the value of the land increased substantially. After the conveyance the couple discovered what had happened and brought an action for damages at common law based on misrepresentation and an action for an account of profits in equity. Slade J held that the damages claim had to fail because the property company's behaviour did not actually amount to a misrepresentation; however the claim for an account of the profit succeeded on the basis that there was a fiduciary relationship between the plaintiffs and defendants. The fiduciary relationship meant that the profit obtained by the property company could not in all conscience be retained and account was the remedy through which the equitable obligation was given expression.

---

[65] To be accurate account may have originally been a common law remedy: see Milsom (1981), at 275–82.
[66] [1978] 1 All ER 382.

RESTITUTIONARY INTEREST

Such a claim in account is often labelled as 'restitutionary' and has been described as an action that 'is analogous to property' in that 'it concerns wealth or advantage which ought to be returned or transferred by the defendant to the plaintiff'.[67] This is to be contrasted with a compensatory damages claim which is based on the claimant's loss. The relevance of the restitutionary label is to be found in the fact that it can transcend both debt and account to embrace equally an action for damages where the interest in play is the 'restitutionary interest'.[68] In the area of the law of contract, such a restitutionary claim may be available in equity through its remedy of account in situations where a contracting party has profited from a breach of contract that has not actually caused the other contracting party any damage.[69] In such a situation the remedy of damages is not normally available because damage must be proved.[70]

However in tort the restitutionary claim is given expression within the remedy of damages itself. Thus in *Invergie Investments Ltd v Hackett*[71] the defendants had been trespassers for 15 years on the claimant's property but the latter did not bring an account of profits action probably because the defendants' business was running at a loss. The defendant accepted that they were liable in damages for a reasonable rent, but the question to be decided was how this figure should be calculated. The Privy Council fell back on the 'user principle': the defendant is liable to pay a reasonable rent and this figure is to be calculated according to a daily rate. 'If a man hires a concrete mixer,' said Lord Lloyd, 'he must pay the daily hire, even though he may not in the event have been able to use the mixer because of rain'. And 'so also must a trespasser who takes the mixer without the owner's consent.' Such a trespasser 'must pay the going rate, even though in the event he has derived no benefit from the use of the mixer' and it 'makes no difference whether the trespasser is a professional builder or a do-it-yourself enthusiast.'[72] Lord Lloyd concluded that the same applied to residential property. If the claimant had sued for an account of profits, then the measure would have been any profits made; but if the claim is in damages the 'chance of making a profit from the use of the apartments is

---

[67] *Att-Gen v Blake* [2001] 1 AC 268, at 296 per Lord Hobhouse.
[68] *Surrey County Council v Bredero Homes Ltd* [1993] 1 WLR 1361, at 1369 (Steyn LJ).
[69] *Att-Gen v Blake* [2001] 1 AC 268.
[70] *Surrey County Council v Bredero Homes Ltd* [1993] 1 WLR 1361.
[71] [1995] 1 WLR 713.
[72] At 718.

not the correct test for arriving at a reasonable rent.' As the Privy Council itself admitted, the principle to be applied 'need not be characterised as exclusively compensatory, or exclusively restitutionary; it combines elements of both'.[73]

What needs to be noted here is the cause of action in trespass. It is part of the law of obligations in as much as it is a tort, yet it is equally part of the law of property in that trespass to land is a remedy protecting property rights. The starting point, then, is invasion of a 'right'. Thus the 'loss' is one that attaches to the *res* and what is being defined as the restitutionary interest is the deprivation of the thing during the period that it was in the trespasser's possession. In other words, the 'loss' is being partly constructed by the cause of action itself. If a trespasser deprives an owner of the use of one of his chairs it is, as the Privy Council, acknowledged, no answer to say that the owner suffered no empirical loss because he had so many chairs he would not notice the absence of one of them. The trespasser is liable for the owner's loss of the use of the chair.[74] The law of property 'constructs', so to speak, the 'loss', whatever the owner's actual mental state vis-à-vis the *res*. This, of course, is not problematic in itself. But it does indicate that attempting to draw hard and fast lines not just between property and obligations but also between tort and restitution is extremely precarious given the absence of Roman learning. The law of remedies cuts across these frontiers; moreover, in *Invergie*, the form of the action was damages. Yet in substance the claim was closer to debt.

RESCISSION

Another important remedy that transgresses the boundaries between contract, restitution and property is rescission. This is equitable in origin (although there may be a common law version today) and is used to order the setting aside of a contract (or other transaction) entered into under fraud, duress, undue influence, misrepresentation or mistake.[75] It is a remedy which cuts across the frontier of contract and restitution in that it is a means 'by which the unjust enrichment ... is prevented' and, 'though for historical and practical reasons [rescission is] treated in books on the law of contract, [it] is a straightforward remedy in restitution subject to

---

[73] At 718.
[74] *The Mediana* [1900] AC 113, at 117.
[75] The equitable remedy of rescission may no longer be available for contractual mistake: *The Great Peace* [2003] QB 679.

limits which are characteristic of that branch of the law'.[76] This remedy must, however, be distinguished from other, seemingly similar, remedies such as declaration – whereby for example a contractor asks the court to declare that a contract is void[77] – or termination at common law. This latter remedy in origin arises out of an implied condition within the contract itself and so is not really an independent '*actio*' so to speak. A contractor is simply exercising his contractual 'right'.[78] Where equity does order rescission – and it retains a discretion to withhold relief where damages would be a more suitable claim[79] – it will only do so where *restitutio in integrum* is possible.[80]

The gap between common law rights and equitable remedies is particularly evident with respect to equitable rescission. D makes a misrepresentation (a false statement which induces a contract) to C which results in C entering a contract with D and suffering financial loss. If C wants both to escape from the contract and to obtain compensation for his loss he will have to bring an action for rescission and an action for compensation. But what must C establish in order to succeed in both remedies? Can C simply allege that D is in breach of a 'duty' in order to trigger both the non-monetary and the monetary claim? Or must C establish breaches of duty in equity (rescission) and at common law (damages)? In *Banque Keyser Ullmann v Skandia Insurance*[81] the Court of Appeal held that the existence of a breach of an equitable duty giving rise to rescission in equity was not enough in itself to act as the basis for a damages claim as well. In order to succeed in the monetary action the plaintiff must establish a cause of action in tort or contract.

---

[76] Robert Goff J in *Whittaker v Campbell* [1984] QB 318, at 327.

[77] *Barton v Armstrong* [1975] 2 All ER 465.

[78] *Car & Universal Finance Co Ltd v Caldwell* [1965] 1 QB 525. In principle rescission in equity does require intervention of the court since the contract remains valid at common law. In practice, however, an innocent party can of course rescind leaving it to the other party to go to court if this party feels the self-help action to be unjustified. It has to be admitted that this analysis does not fully accord with recent judicial opinion. In *TSB Bank plc v Camfield* [1995] 1 WLR 430, 438 Roch LJ said that the 'right to set aside or rescind the transaction is that of the representee, not that of the court'. In other words the existence of the remedy of rescission has had the effect of creating a 'right' to rescission.

[79] *Leaf v International Galleries Ltd* [1950] 2 KB 86.

[80] But in order to achieve such restitution the court cannot make use of the remedy of damages in addition to rescission unless there is a separate right to damages at common law or under statute: cf *Jaggard v Sawyer* [1995] 2 All ER 189. However it can, via the remedy of account, order that an indemnity be paid so as to prevent unjust enrichment: *Spence v Crawford* [1939] 3 All ER 271, at 288–9.

[81] [1990] 1 QB 665 (CA). The analysis by the Court of Appeal was not actually disputed in the House of Lords: [1992] 2 AC 249 (HL).

This decision should serve as a warning, therefore, to those tempted to think that English law thinks in terms of a law of obligations. Certainly it is useful to have a general category into which one can place the common law and equitable claims; but this general category does not of itself provide a normative basis to the causes of action. The duties which provide such normative force are defined by categories (contract) or by causes of action (eg trespass, negligence, conversion) within categories (tort) and by remedies (rescission, injunctions etc.) functioning, on the whole, at a low level of abstraction. This 'complexity' may well annoy those who dream about rationalised taxonomies along the lines of a perfected Roman model. However the common law was formed within a feudal and not a Roman model.

5. Contractual obligations: general provisions

When one turns to look at the substantive detail of the English law of obligations, it is difficult not to start with contractual obligations. The subject is central to the codes and to English commercial law and it is contract that has been codified at an international and European level (see PECL and UNIDROIT). As these codes have a first chapter devoted to 'General Provisions', it would seem fitting to provide an overview of these provisions. In addition this chapter will set out a framework for understanding contract.

GENERAL CONSIDERATIONS

Contract requires a chapter on generalities for several reasons. First, because it is underpinned by a number of general principles which are relevant to the subject in its entirety. Secondly, because although there is a general theory of contract both in the civilian and in the common law traditions, there are nevertheless different types of contract; these different types need to be identified and classified at an early stage. Thirdly, because the scope and limits of the contractual obligation have to be identified. Such identification is necessary not just because it can be important, at a formal level, to know when one is moving from contractual to non-contractual rights, duties and (or) remedies but also because identification of the domain of contract is of importance for conceptual and policy reasons. Fourthly, a general section can be useful for a number of other reasons; for example it can contain some general definitions, some rules as to mandatory and non-mandatory provisions, articles about usage and custom and so on and so forth (see generally Chapter 1 in the PECL and in UNIDROIT). Finally, a chapter on contract generalities is important for setting out the methodology by which contract as an area of law and as a conceptual and practical concept can be understood (see also Chapter 6).

DEFINITION OF CONTRACT

Defining the law of contract is both simple and difficult depending on the scheme of analysis adopted. It is simple to the extent that it can be summed up, at the level of form, by expressions such as legally enforceable agreements or promises. Thus contract has been defined as 'a promise or set of promises that the law will enforce' (Pollock) or 'an agreement that is freely entered into on terms that are freely negotiated' (Stuart-Smith LJ).[1] Difficulties arise when one tries to match these definitions with the mass of factual situations to be found in the cases. There are many factual situations displaying the essential requirements of a contract which turn out not to support a contract.[2] Equally there are other facts which do not seemingly support a contract, yet the disappointed party still manages to secure a legal remedy if not always an actual contractual remedy.[3]

Another difficulty arises when one tries to approach contract and its definition from a functional perspective. What is the *purpose* of contract or what does it *do*? This perspective is difficult not just because contract has a whole range of different functions. It is difficult, first, because these functions are shared by other areas of the law; and, secondly, because it is not always clear that the identified functions actually require, or fully correspond to, a law of contract. Indeed it has been said that the 'classical model of contract, notwithstanding its formal perpetuation to the present day as a body of general principles, was a failure'.[4] The model simply does not accurately reflect social reality. In short, contract theory on the one hand and social and commercial reality on the other are not always reconcilable. Thus at the level of form it is by no means clear that terms such as 'promise' or 'agreement' adequately give expression to the substance of contract whether this substance is seen as a set of rules or facts that make up contractual situations. Sometimes the courts are quite open about this mismatch; and so for example the judges have indicated on a number of occasions that liability in tort is being imposed to fill a gap in the law of contract.[5] Academics have talked of contract as a remedy.

Perhaps the most challenging theory is the one to be found in article 1134 of the French *Code civil* which asserts that a contract has the force of

---

[1] *W v Essex CC* [1999] Fam 90, para 50.
[2] See eg *Lennon v Commissioner of Police of the Metropolis* [2004] 1 WLR 2594.
[3] See eg *Blackpool & Fylde Aero Club Ltd v Blackpool BC* [1990] 1 WLR 1195.
[4] Atiyah (1979), at 693.
[5] See eg *White v Jones* [1995] 2 AC 207.

legislation between the two parties. This is the starting point for the idea of contract as private legislation. There is no doubt that this thesis has some support in commercial reality in as much as contractual relationships are often reduced to texts and that these texts can attract the same methodological analysis as statutory interpretation. Accordingly, in civilian systems, the role of the courts is to give expression to the will of the parties just as it is to give expression to the will of the legislator when it is a matter of a statutory text. Similar statements can be found in the law reports of common law systems. One way of understanding contract, therefore, is to see them as privatised 'legislative' texts binding two persons. However this theory is plagued with difficulties. For a start there are many contractual situations that do not involve texts; the everyday transactions made by consumers with suppliers of goods and services do not consist of detailed negotiations to be reduced with great care to paper, although admittedly some of these transactions may involve contractual documents. Rather than legislating, parties are entering into different forms of transaction such as sale, carriage, parking and the like; and these forms can often involve rules laid down by objective law rather than subjective text (see for example Sale of Goods Act 1979). Of course, it is possible to re-conceptualise these objective rules as implied promises flowing between the parties. But a sociologist looking at consumer behaviour is unlikely to theorise it in terms of private legislation.

Another difficulty is that the line between contractual and non-contractual operations is often arbitrary depending upon the formation rules of the system in question. Thus in France a medical negligence case might well be a contractual problem while in England, if the defendant is the National Health Trust, it will be tort. Only if the hospital is private, will the relationship between hospital and patient be contractual. A similar difficulty can arise in other areas of professional negligence. A bank that gives 'gratuitous' advice is probably not acting within a contractual relationship.[6] Yet the relationship is very close to contract and in systems where the requirement consideration is unknown the bank's act might well be contractual. Some employment relationships, which at first sight look contractual, might not be so for reasons of public law; in these situations tort may have to play a 'contractual' role.[7]

The private legislation thesis is at best partial in its portrayal of contract. It undoubtedly reflects certain kinds of contractual behaviour, particularly in the commercial world where the drawing up of contracts

---

[6] *Hedley Byrne & Co v Heller & Partners Ltd* [1964] AC 465.
[7] *Lennon v Commissioner of Police of the Metropolis* [2004] 1 WLR 2594.

requires negotiation and professional skill, and there are similarities on occasions between cases involving the interpretation of contracts and those involving the interpretation of statutes. But the theory breaks down when faced with consumer transactions and with areas of commerce requiring detailed regulation (see in particular Consumer Protection (Distance Selling) Regulations 2000). Contract is less facultative here and, since at least the middle of the 20th century, much more regulatory. In other words, the idea that commercial and consumer transactions belong exclusively to a world of private law agreements is simply no longer true within the EU.

Perhaps another difficulty with the private legislation thesis is that it fails to emphasise what is now seen as an important distinction between the contractual *obligation* and contractual *liability*. In theory the distinction should be meaningless in that contractual liability is simply the logical outcome of a failure to perform a contractual obligation. Yet in practice the distinction is important in that many obligation issues become relevant only when the contract has gone wrong and when one party finds itself suffering damage seemingly caused by the other party. Damage and causation thus become the starting point for deciding whether or not the other party ought to compensate. And in deciding this issue of compensation, although the judges might in form refer to contractual promises (terms) contained in the obligation, in reasoning substance they could well base their decision on objective factors like the status of the parties and the allocation of risk.[8] Indeed, liability might well come down to 'reasonableness' rather than rights.[9]

This distinction between obligation and liability is of even greater importance in English law than in civil law countries where the rules of contract are set out in an abstract code. In the English system textbooks do, admittedly, try to state the rules in abstract and a short 'nutshell' may even look like a 'code' of principles if elegantly executed. But it has to be remembered that the rules of contract are for the most part induced out of cases and, as we shall see, no *ratio decidendi* of a precedent can ever be detached from the material facts of the case. There will always be some element of 'contract as remedy' in the common law system.[10] This is the reason why one way of understanding contract is to view the subject from a litigation and (or) remedy perspective.

---

[8] See eg *The Moorcock* (1889) 14 PD 64.
[9] See eg *Ruxley Electronics Ltd v Forsyth* [1996] 1 AC 344.
[10] See eg *Blackpool & Fylde Aero Club Ltd v Blackpool BC* [1990] 1 WLR 1195.

CONTRACT AND REMEDIES

When viewed from the position of liability and non-performance, contract can assume, therefore, a rather different shape and form. It can appear much less subjective and can even merge into other areas of the law of obligations, that is to say into tort or restitution (see Chapter 4). In fact many contract problems are shaped not just by the loss or damage suffered by a party but also the actual remedy pursued.

Take, first of all, damages. Where a victim of a breach of contract suffers damage a number of set focal points immediately emerge. The nature of the act complained of is one issue and the causal link between act and damage is another. Merely because one contracting party is in breach, this does not necessarily mean the party will be liable for the damage, or all the damage, suffered. Sufficient cause and connection must be shown and so if, for example, the victim has failed to mitigate a loss the other contracting party will not be liable for this part of the damage (see Chapter 15). Behaviour can become relevant in that causing damage is not always enough; the party causing the damage must be in breach of its promise and this may in effect mean that it will be liable only if at fault.[11] In this situation an action for damages in contract looks little different from an action for damages in the tort of negligence (or put another way it might be just as useful to class all the cases under the heading 'fault'). Where the contractual text can become of major importance in a damages claim is when the contract contains an exclusion or limitation clause. Such a contractual promise can isolate a party in breach from full liability in damages, provided, of course, it is actually incorporated into the contract.[12] Yet even here the approach is not necessarily that far removed from an action in tort, for consent to the damage (*volenti non fit injuria*) is a defence to most non-contractual claims (although rarely successful).

Yet not all contractual claims are actions for damages. Indeed, most are not. The most frequent complaint is that one contractual party has failed to perform his promise to pay a price for a service or for goods supplied. Here the claim is for debt rather than damages. A good example is *Carlill v Carbolic Smoke Ball Co*[13] where the claimant was not seeking compensation but a specific sum of money promised to her on the happening of a certain event. There was no question here of her having to mitigate or prove a causal link between her 'loss' and the defendant's

---

[11] Supply of Goods and Services Act 1982, s 13.
[12] See eg *Thornton v Shoe Lane Parking Ltd* [1971] 2 QB 163.
[13] [1893] 1 QB 256.

non-performance. The issue was one that focused entirely on the obligation: did the defendant promise to pay and was the promise a contractual one? If so, there is liability for the whole amount; if not, there is no liability whatsoever. In other words debt cases, unlike damages claims (where the claimant might get less than he claimed), are all or nothing (but see on this point Swiss CO art 373).

In substance, if not in form, debt is an action for specific performance in as much as a claimant is asking the court to force a contractor to do what he promised to do, namely pay a price for goods or services rendered. Where the promise is one other than to pay a sum of money the common law courts were helpless when it came to specifically enforcing the primary obligations. There was no form of action available and all the common law courts could do was order compensation (damages). The Court of Chancery, however, stepped in, as we have seen, to remedy this gap and provided its own action for specific performance. Yet this was only an exceptional remedy; Equity would not allow its use where damages would be adequate and this discretionary aspect to the remedy remains of vital importance in today's commercial world. A claimant might not be able to force a contractor to perform his contractual promise if such performance would, for example, be economically inefficient. This remedy, then, should give one an insight into one function of contract, which is economic efficiency and this function can be perceived in non-specific performance cases as well (see Chapter 4).

As we have seen (Chapter 4), Equity can also offer a negative remedy, that is to say it can issue an injunction to prevent a contractor from breaking his contractual obligation. Thus if an actress, who has contracted to work exclusively for the claimant studio, starts to work for another employer it may well be that the claimant will be able to obtain an injunction ordering the actress not to work for the other employer.[14] Injunctions can be used, in other words, to enforce contracts in a negative way, while specific performance is required if the non-performing party is to be forced to do something positive, such as convey property.

A quite different claim is one where a party wishes simply to escape from the contractual obligation and is asking the court to set aside the contract. In theory there is no question about the actual existence of the contract; what the claimant is arguing is that the other party has spoken, acted or failed to act in such a way that it would be unconscionable for the law to enforce the promises. The words or act complained of do not, as such, fall within the domain of the contractual obligation;

---

[14] *Warner Brothers Pictures Inc v Nelson* [1937] 1 KB 209.

indeed, in the case of misstatements, they often do not form contractual promises.[15] But in causing the victim to enter into a contract, a situation is arrived at where it would be unjust for the court to insist that the contract be enforced. In other words, a justified form of enrichment is rendered unjust by the pre-contractual behaviour of one of the parties. Rescission, then, provides yet another perspective from which to view contract.

Indeed, this perspective is so important that it acts in itself as one means of understanding an important aspect of contract law. When can a person escape from a contract? The equitable remedy itself will not, it must be said, provide anything like a complete answer to this question. The common law, for example, also allows a contractor to escape from a contract where the other party is in serious breach. Equally statute permits a consumer to escape from a distance selling contract within a statutory period; this statutory escape is not truly rescission since the contract is deemed never to have existed.[16] In addition a declaration that a contract is non-existent for mistake or frustration often looks similar to the granting of rescission in equity, even if from an internal position the positive rules governing the situation prove very different.

We have seen that another type of claim, loosely called restitution, is where the claimant is seeking either the return of money or property transferred, or even a service rendered, to another under a purported contractual relationship or the rendering of a profit made by the other party which the claimant believes should not be retained. There is in truth no such remedy as 'restitution', but the term is valuable in that it acts as a generic category for claims aimed at a specific sum of money or item of property. It includes the remedies of debt, account and damages in the tort of conversion or in the tort of trespass. Restitution claims may of course follow an action for rescission of a contract: a party seeks the return of money or property transferred under the contract before rescission. Or such claims may arise in situations where the contract turns out to be inexistent because of a mistake or because it has been frustrated. For example, in one case the claimant had been sold a car that turned out not to be owned by the seller; he successfully sued the seller in debt for the return of the purchase price.[17] In another case, an ex-government employee had secured a nice profit as a result of behaviour that amounted to a breach of contract; the government could not sue in damages as they had suffered

---

[15] *Hopkins v Tanqueray* (1854) 15 CB 130; 139 ER 369.
[16] Consumer Protection (Distance Selling) Regulations 2000, reg 10.
[17] *Rowland v Divall* [1923] 2 KB 500.

no actual damage from the breach, but they could sue in equity for an account of profits.[18]

The remedies discussed so far, with the exception of rescission, all involve going to court and even rescission may require (or result in) a court decision. However a contractor may decide to take matters into his own hands and use a self-help remedy. One of the most common in the area of contract is a refusal to perform a contractual obligation because the other party has failed adequately to perform his obligation. In short, this often comes down to a refusal to pay. Thus in one case a householder refused to pay a firm of heating engineers who had contracted to install a central heating system in his house; the firm certainly provided radiators, boiler and pipes but it could not get the system actually to heat the house. In the end, after the engineers appeared to have given up trying to get the system to function properly, the householder simply withheld payment of the agreed price. The Court of Appeal held that he was entitled to do this.[19]

It needs to be noted, however, that self-help can be a dangerous remedy. If a contractor unilaterally decides to abandon a contract because of the other party's non-performance, this self-help abandonment will be valid only if the non-performance (breach) of contract was serious. If it was not, then the self-help behaviour is not only unjustified, but amounts to a breach of contract entitling the other party to damages.[20] Here the situation is analogous to self-help in tort. A victim of some torts, such as trespass (assault for example) is permitted in certain situations to resort to self-defence. However if the victim uses more force than was reasonable in the circumstances, then the victim himself will become a trespasser allowing the original attacker to sue the victim for his injuries (this is the reason why some burglars can sue for damages having been assaulted by the house owner).[21]

One point that emerges from this remedy-orientated view of contract is that some remedies like debt and specific performance in Equity attach to the primary contractual promise itself. Debt forces a contractor to do what he has promised to do. Damages, in contrast, arise out of what Lord Diplock has called a secondary obligation. 'Every failure to perform a primary obligation is a breach of contract', said the Law Lord; and such a breach gives rise to a 'secondary obligation . . . to pay monetary compensation to the other party for the loss sustained by him in consequence

---

[18] *Att-Gen v Blake* [2001] 1 AC 268.
[19] *Bolton v Mahadeva* [1972] 1 WLR 1009.
[20] See eg *Hong Kong Fir Shipping Co Ltd v Kawasaki Kisen Kaisha Ltd* [1962] 2 QB 26.
[21] See eg *Revill v Newbery* [1996] QB 567.

of the breach'.[22] Here, then, is the link between the contractual obligation and contractual liability: contract creates promises (or obligations) at two different levels, the secondary level coming into play when a party fails to perform his obligation under the contract and this failure is not excused (see for example PECL art 8.101). Of course, if the innocent party suffers no actual loss than damages will not lie,[23] but this lack of damage does not necessarily mean that some other remedy might not be available.

The idea of a secondary obligation is equally useful in understanding that the remedy of damages attracts its own rules. The entitlement to damages for breach of contract will not of itself determine what actual interests will be protected. The general rule does try, in the abstract, to protect what is called the 'expectation interest', that is to say to compensate the victim of a breach of contract by reference to the position he would have been in had the contract been performed (PECL art 9.502). (In tort, in contrast, the general rule is restoration: that is, to be put back into the position the victim was in before the tort: PETL art 10:101.) However such an expectation will be the subject of compensation only if it was in the contemplation of the contract-breaker at the time of the making of the contract (PECL art 9.503).[24]. Moreover, the court has some leeway in the determination of what actually counts as damage. It would appear that a product that is defective to the extent that it does not conform to the primary obligation might not be defective from an objective point of view.[25]

CONTRACT AND RIGHTS

Contract can be approached from yet another perspective, that of rights. This is a perspective that emphasises entitlements and is perhaps summed up by the judicial observation that a 'person who has a right under a contract... is entitled to exercise it... for a good reason or a bad reason or no reason at all'.[26] Contract, or promise, is from this perspective to be viewed as a form of property. A legally enforceable promise, in other words, is an asset just like an item of property.

Now, as we have seen (Chapter 2), property, or 'real', rights are, in strict legal science, to be differentiated from contract, or personal, rights. Yet some contractual rights, in English law at least, are either property rights

---

[22] *Photo Production Ltd v Securicor* [1980] AC 827, at 849.
[23] *Lazenby Garages Ltd v Wright* [1976] 1 WLR 459.
[24] *Hadley v Baxendale* (1854) 9 Ex 341; 156 ER 145.
[25] *Ruxley Electronics Ltd v Forsyth* [1996] 1 AC 344.
[26] *Chapman v Honig* [1963] 2 QB 502, at 520.

in themselves – for example a right to a debt[27] – or are capable of creating indirectly rights in an item of property. Thus a contractual right to enter upon land belonging to another can of itself entitle the contractor to a proprietary remedy against a third party who is preventing the contractor from entering.[28] Normally, however, contract rights are 'weaker' than real property rights in that an owner of land can expel a contractor (for example a decorator) from his property. All that the expelled contractor can do in such circumstances is to rely upon his secondary obligation (or right) to sue for damages for breach of contract; he cannot re-enter the property, complete the contract, and sue for the price of his service.[29]

Yet not all contract 'rights' have the same status since some arise directly out of the contractual promise while others are created by ricochet from the existence of a contractual remedy. The householder who refuses to pay for the badly installed central heating system does not have a direct contractual right as such to free services and free heating equipment; it is an indirect right arising out of the failure of the heating engineers to perform their obligations under the contract. Sometimes the right is even more indirect. Thus the family of a contractor who indirectly received compensation for their ruined holiday via payment of damages to the actual contractor were not in theory being compensated for invasion of their contractual rights, for they had no contractual rights. All they had was an interest in the performance by the tour operator of its contractual obligations towards the father as contractor. Yet the law of damages, in recognising this interest, in effect bestowed an indirect contractual right on the family members.[30]

CLASSIFICATION OF CONTRACTS

That there exist different types of contract should be of no surprise since purchase and sale, employment, the hire of ships, renting rooms, transport, insurance and so on are in the real world all very different transactions. In other words the facts themselves would appear to determine difference and in Roman law these empirical distinctions between the various private and commercial operations gave rise to a law of contracts rather than contract. Yet with the development of a general theory of contract these differences

---

[27] On which see *Beswick v Beswick* [1966] Ch 538 (CA); cf [1968] AC 58.
[28] *Manchester Airport Plc v Dutton* [2000] 1 QB 133.
[29] *Hounslow LBC v Twickenham Garden Developments Ltd* [1971] Ch 233.
[30] *Jackson v Horizon Holidays Ltd* [1975] 1 WLR 1468.

between empirical transactions became subsumed under the abstract elements of agreement and promise with the result that contract today is rather 'as if medical students had a first year course entitled "Disease" and consequently came to believe that diseases were all much of a muchness'.[31] Classification of contracts ought, therefore, to pay some attention to reality. Yet even if all the different contractual transactions are 'much of a muchness', at the level of form, civil lawyers, and to some extent common lawyers, do recognise different kinds of contract.

Civil Law

The French *Code civil* has a list of the different kinds of contract and has whole sections devoted to specific (named) contracts reflecting the various Roman types. The classification operates at two levels. At the level of general theory there are three dichotomies set out in the general introduction to contractual obligations: synallagmatic (or bilateral) and unilateral contracts (arts 1102–3); *commutatif* and *aléatoire* (uncertain event) contracts (art 1104); and gratuitous (*à titre gratuit*) and advantageous (*à titre onéreux*) contracts (arts 1105–6). At a substantive level – that is to say at the level of transaction – the codes distinguish between named and unnamed contracts, the former being subject not just to the general rules of contract but also to specific rules devoted to these named contracts (CC art 1107). These named contracts are based on those to be found in the Roman sources – the main ones being sale, hire, partnership, deposit (D.2.14.7.1) – but the more modern codes often add transactions that appeared only in the modern world. The Québec Civil Code, for example, has a section on insurance and this class of contract is in turn subdivided into marine and non-marine (art 2389); and the Swiss Code of Obligations has articles devoted to publishing contracts (arts 380ff). The Polish Civil Code goes further: there are sections devoted to bank account (arts 725ff) and pension contracts (arts 903ff). The Lando Commission, which drafted the PECL, intends to produce further codes on specific contracts.

Common Law

Some of the civilian distinctions are to be found in the common law. Thus the distinction between unilateral and bilateral contracts is fundamental and certain specific contracts are governed by their own legislative regimes

---

[31] Weir (1992), at 1639–40.

of which the most important is perhaps sale of goods.[32] Even where there is no formal distinction, certain classes of contract do tend to attract their own rules (for example charterparties and bailment contracts). Moreover, although the civilian distinction between gratuitous and non-gratuitous contracts cannot in theory exist in the common law given the fundamental requirement of consideration in the general theory of contract, the equitable doctrine of estoppel can in practice result, on occasions, in a gratuitous promise being given legal effect.[33]

Unilateral and Bilateral Contracts

One distinction to be found in French and English law is that between a unilateral contract and a bilateral contract.[34] In the former only one party makes a promise while, in the latter, promises move from both parties. A unilateral contract is a promise for an act (performance); a bilateral contract is a promise for a promise. Accordingly in a unilateral contract the promisee can never be in breach. If, therefore, D declares, in a take-it-or-leave-it fashion, to C that he will pay £100 if C turns up and sings 'My Way' at his birthday party, C will not be in breach if he does not turn up. He will simply not be able to claim the £100. However if D makes a specific contract with C (or C's agent) for C to come and perform at a certain date and C agrees to turn up on that date, C could well find himself in breach of a bilateral contract if he fails to perform. Often it is easy to distinguish the unilateral from the bilateral contract – reward cases are usually unilateral – but as the two above examples suggest there may be situations where it is more difficult (for example estate agent contracts).[35]

Instantaneous and Long-term Contracts

Neither the civil law nor the common law makes a formal distinction between instantaneous and long-term contracts. Nevertheless the distinction is of importance in a number of ways. First, the relationship of the parties is likely to be so different as to generate different expectations. Thus a contractor will not have the same expectations of a shop owner from whom he occasionally buys a newspaper than of his employer for whom he has worked for many years. Secondly, a long-term contract is

---

[32] Sale of Goods Act 1979; *Ashington Piggeries Ltd v C. Hill Ltd* [1972] AC 441, at 501 per Lord Diplock.
[33] *Crabb v Arun DC* [1976] Ch 179.
[34] See Diplock LJ in *UDT v Eagle Aircraft Services Ltd* [1968] 1 WLR 74.
[35] See eg *Luxor (Eastbourne) Ltd v Cooper* [1941] AC 108.

always subject to the risk of changing circumstances. A contract to supply water at a fixed price in 1929 might appear a most reasonable bargain for both sides at the time of signing the deal; 50 years later, however, the fixed price, thanks to inflation, could prove economically ruinous for one of the parties.[36] Long-term contracts thus raise a question of whether parties should be under a contractual duty to renegotiate the terms where circumstances have changed to such an extent that it has given rise to hardship (see PECL art 6.111). A further reason for distinguishing the long-term contract from the instantaneous one is that such contracts may require more long-term planning. This can impact upon formation, upon terms and upon the general structure of the contractual arrangement.

Goods and Services

Another important distinction to be found in the common law is the one between a contract to supply a thing (sale and hire) and a contract to supply a service. This distinction is important when it comes to non- or defective performance. If the quality of goods supplied under a commercial sale or a hire contract turn out to be defective and cause damage (the exploding television that destroys a valuable vase or food that poisons the purchaser) the supplier of the goods will be strictly liable.[37] However if the quality of a service proves defective (the electrician who knocks over a valuable vase), the supplier will be liable only if he was negligent.[38] This distinction, as we have seen (Chapter 3), is to be found in civil law thinking but at a more abstract level. French lawyers distinguish between a contractual obligation to achieve a result (*obligation de résultat*) and an obligation of best efforts (*obligation de moyens*). According to this terminology – which has been adopted by UNIDROIT (art 5.4) – a sale of goods contract imposes an obligation of result in respect of the quality of the goods[39] while a contract of service contains an implied term only of best efforts. There are some difficult situations[40] and in French law the dichotomy has become increasingly complex with the development of various sub-categories and overlaying obligations (for example an obligation of safety). But on the whole the distinction is clear enough when applied to the dichotomy between goods and services. One might add, however, that problems can

---

[36] *Staffs Area Health Authority v South Staffs Waterworks Co* [1978] 1 WLR 1387.
[37] *Frost v Aylesbury Dairy Co Ltd* [1905] 1 KB 608.
[38] Supply of Goods and Services Act 1982, s 13.
[39] Sale of Goods Act 1979, s 14.
[40] See eg in English law *Thake v Maurice* [1986] QB 644.

arise over the quality itself. Normally goods must conform not just to the statutory implied terms but also to any express term about quality; if there is no such term the PECL stipulate that goods must be of 'average quality' (art 6.108).

Contract and Conveyance

A further reason why the distinction between supply of goods and supply of service contracts is of importance is that the former involve not just obligation rights (*in personam*) but also property rights (*in rem*). In a sale contract the seller promises to pass title (ownership) and usually possession in the goods. However, unlike Roman and German law, English law follows the French model in which it is the contract itself that acts as the conveyance of this title provided the goods are ascertained, although the seller can always reserve title.[41] Accordingly, sale of goods contracts are different from service contracts to the extent that they also form part of the law of personal property.[42] One should note here that land is different. Contract does not pass legal title in the property – a separate conveyance is necessary – although it can pass an equitable title which arises because Equity is prepared to force the seller of land to perform through an action for specific performance.

BAILMENT AND CONTRACT

Contracts which involve the transfer of possession (and not ownership) in goods also bring the law of personal property into play. This is because the transfer of possession in a chattel from one person (bailor) to another (bailee) gives rise to a legal relationship, independent of contract, called a bailment. The relationship is independent because bailment belongs to the law of property rather than the law of obligations and thus arises even if there has been a gratuitous transfer of a chattel.[43] Accordingly bailment contracts – that is to say contracts for the carriage of goods, contracts of hire and even some contracts of service like cleaning clothes – need to be distinguished from other contracts simply because bailment itself creates rights and duties.[44] These obligations may, of course, be modified by the

---

[41] Sale of Goods Act 1979, ss 16–18.
[42] See *Shogun Finance Ltd v Hudson* [2004] 1 AC 919.
[43] *Building and Civil Engineering Holidays Scheme Management Ltd v Post Office* [1966] 1 QB 247.
[44] *Morris v C W Martin & Sons Ltd* [1966] 1 QB 716.

contract itself. However if a coach company contracts to take C from one town to another and manages to lose C's suitcase on the way, having taken possession of it by putting it into the hold of the coach, C will be able to claim its value from the coach company. This claim will not be based on the contract of carriage to transport C, but on the bailment (property) relationship arising out of the transfer of possession of the suitcase, the remedy itself being, now, the tort of conversion.[45]

PUBLIC AND PRIVATE LAW CONTRACTS

The distinction between obligations and property is not the only fundamental distinction to be found in civilian thinking. The dichotomy between public and private law is another important division and it is reflected in French contract law in the difference of regime between public (administrative) and private contracts. In English law there is no such formal distinction. The ordinary law of contract applies equally to all persons and institutions whether they are in the public or private sectors. However in substance it may on occasions be important to distinguish between the two sectors in that public bodies are subject to rules and principles that are not necessarily applicable in the private sector.

In truth the whole public and private question is rather complex in English law for a range of reasons. First, because public bodies themselves differ; the Crown for example has a different status in the eyes of the law than local authorities and an organisation such as the BBC differs from governmental institutions. Secondly, many relations that appear at first sight as contractual may turn out not to be so. Thus the postal services and the supply of gas, electricity and water were not contractual relationships and privatisation has not necessarily altered this situation. Certain Crown servants may find, also, that their employment is not governed by contract but by a public law relationship. Thirdly, the capacity of local authorities to contract is governed quite rigidly by statute and if such an authority exceeds its powers any such contract will be void rather than voidable. Fourthly, many government contracts contain adjudication clauses which have the effect of keeping disputes out of the ordinary courts. As Rudden points out, a 'combination of this factor and the use of . . . standard terms over a long period means that English courts have been spared the task of fashioning a general law of public contracts.'[46]

---

[45] *Houghland v RR Low (Luxury Coaches) Ltd* [1962] 1 QB 694.
[46] Rudden (1989), at 103.

Another reason for complexity is that while a private body or individual is at liberty to refuse to contract with another without giving reasons or, indeed, because of non-commercial or personal reasons, a public body is not. In fact, were a public body to refuse to contract with a local firm because the authority did not approve of the firm's support of a particular political party or policy, this most probably would be regarded as an abuse of power and subject to judicial review.[47] Indeed, statute specifically restricts the pursuit of collateral policies via certain public works contracts by a local authority.[48] In substance, then, the distinction between public and private contracts is not completely devoid of meaning in English law.

COMMERCIAL AND CONSUMER CONTRACTS

Abuse of power is not confined to public servants: powerful corporations have on occasions proved quite capable of exploiting those with whom they contract. Such exploitation arose as a result of the principle that parties were deemed by the law always to be equal in terms of their bargaining power. However abuse of power in the private sector has been remedied to some extent through an increasingly formalised distinction between consumer and non-consumer contracts. The distinction is most evident in respect of two situations. First, unfair or abusive clauses inserted into contracts by commercial suppliers are unenforceable against consumers.[49] Secondly, consumers who have entered into a distance selling contract have a right of cancellation within a period of seven working days from the receipt of goods or services.[50] More generally the distinction probably manifests itself with respect to interpretation of contracts: it is unlikely that the courts will approach a written contract between a business and a consumer with the same attitude as they adopt with regard to charterparties.

More generally one can ask if, as in French law, a distinction can be made between civil and commercial law. In other words are commercial contracts to be distinguished from other 'civil' or 'private' transactions? The practical response is probably to say that such a distinction has been largely eclipsed by the consumer/commercial divide. Yet sometimes it can be important to ascertain either the status of one or more of the parties or

---

[47] *R v Lewisham LBC, ex p Shell (UK)* [1988] 1 All ER 938.
[48] Local Government Act 1988, s 17.
[49] Unfair Terms in Consumer Contracts Regulations 1999.
[50] Consumer Protection (Distance Selling) Regulations 2000.

the nature of the transaction itself. For example, the status of the purchaser of a car that turns out not to have belonged to the seller because it was on hire purchase will be vital since it will determine whether or not the buyer will get title to the vehicle.[51] The nature of the transaction can be important with respect to the quality of any item purchased, for legal recourse if goods prove defective will depend upon whether or not the goods were sold 'in the course of a business'.[52] A purely private deal negotiated at a car boot sale, although a contract, may turn out to be a different kind of sale of goods transaction than the sale agreed in a shop or a showroom. At an even more fundamental level the distinction between a commercial and a private transaction can be of relevance in deciding whether or not a contract between the parties actually exists. If the transaction is one that has taken place within the context of commerce, then there will always be a presumption the parties intended to enter into legal relations. If, however, the arrangement is a family one, things might be different.

FREEDOM OF CONTRACT

The distinction between consumer and non-consumer contracts results indirectly from a general principle that has underpinned contract at least since the early 19th century if not before. This is the principle of freedom of contract affirmed in both the PECL (art 1.102) and UNIDROIT (art 1.1), although perhaps finding its most perfect expression in the French assertion that contracts are a form of private legislation between the parties (CC art 1134). In its heyday this principle assumed not only that contractual parties were formally and substantially equal but that parties were free to make what a third party might consider unreasonable contracts. Contract, in other words, was a matter for the parties and not the courts.

This freedom of contract doctrine is perhaps well encapsulated by an English judge in 1875 who asserted that if 'there is one thing more than another which public policy requires, it is that men of full age and competent understanding shall have the utmost liberty of contracting and that their contracts, when entered into freely and voluntarily, shall be held sacred and shall be enforced by courts of justice'.[53] The ideology was to result in a paradox: a party had the freedom to insert in a contract a clause

---

[51] *Stevenson v Beverley Bentinck Ltd* [1976] 1 WLR 483; cf *Shogun Finance Ltd v Hudson* [2004] 1 AC 919.

[52] Sale of Goods Act 1979, s 14.

[53] *Printing and Numerical Registering Co. v Sampson* (1875) LR 19 Eq 462, at 465.

that stipulated whatever his behaviour he was in no circumstances to be contractually liable. Such freedom inevitably resulted in abuse where economically powerful parties were able to impose on weaker parties standard form contracts full of exclusion clauses.

Courts in the UK and continental Europe developed a number of tactics to deal with this abuse (strict interpretation, *contra proferentem* rule, good faith, abuse of rights, fundamental terms and the like), but it was only with legislative intervention in the 1970s that the problem became fully regulated. This legislation, on the whole, tackled the paradox of freedom and abuse by formally making a distinction between consumer and non-consumer contracts.[54] Freedom of contract was maintained as between commercial parties able to look after their own interests;[55] consumers, on the other hand, were given more or less full protection against abusive terms, although in England much will turn on what 'unfair' means to judges. Will this be judged from the consumer or the commercial perspective?[56]

In fact the control of unfair clauses is not confined to consumer contracts. Both in English law and at the European level (see PECL art 4.110) unfair clauses can be struck down in certain types of commercial contracts. Moreover there is authority to the effect that a small commercial concern might even be treated, in certain circumstances, as a consumer.[57] As is typical with English law, much will depend upon the facts. One might note in addition that Equity can have a role with respect to certain types of abusive clauses. If such a clause imposes on the other party a 'penalty' for any breaches of contract – that is to say a clause stipulating that the contractor must pay a fixed sum of money that is in excess of any damage suffered by the party not in breach – it will be unenforceable.

GOOD FAITH

One way in which abusive terms can be tackled in civil law systems is through the doctrine of good faith. To contract and not to contract at the same time, or indeed to contract on terms where one party is put under a significant disadvantage, could be seen as evidence of bad faith (cf PECL art 4.110).

The notion of *bona fides* has its origin in Roman law where it required

---

[54] See EU Directive 5 April 1993; 93/13/EEC: L 95/29.
[55] *Photo Production Ltd v Securicor* [1980] AC 827.
[56] cf *Director General of Fair Trading v First National Bank plc* [2002] 1 AC 481.
[57] *R & B Customs Brokers Co Ltd v UDT Ltd* [1988] 1 WLR 321.

equity in contract to the highest degree (D.16.3.31pr). Nevertheless this general statement must be seen in the context that contracting parties were also free to take advantage of each other (D.4.4.16.4; D.19.2.22.3) and thus the exact scope of the duty of good faith in the context of commerce has never been easy to gauge. One Scottish Law Lord has pointed out that good faith functioned at the level of the remedy rather than right and was not therefore 'a source of obligation in itself'.[58] Yet in modern civil law the requirement of good faith is to be found in all the codes; thus for example article 1134 of the French *Code civil* states that agreements 'must be performed in good faith' and it is a general duty to be found in both the PECL (art 1.201) and UNIDROIT (art 1.7) ('good faith and fair dealing'). The rule has been described as a means 'of inserting into positive law moral rules' and as such has 'given rise, because of its imprecision, to many questions'.[59]

Certainly the topic has attracted much literature. What makes the duty difficult is whether it is simply a passive duty – that is to say a duty not to act in positive bad faith – or does it go further and impose active duties on contracting parties? Traditionally, in France, good faith has translated itself into two main obligations: the duty of loyalty (*devoir de loyauté*) and a duty of co-operation. Both of these raise interesting questions in themselves. However more recently French doctrine and jurisprudence seems to have gone further and is imposing a duty to inform and to collaborate, this latter specifically appearing as an independent duty in the PECL (art 1.202). Good faith is, in other words, being used to construct a new philosophy of *solidarisme contractuel* in which a contracting party has to further not just his own interests but, to an extent, the interests of his co-party.[60]

Whether good faith is to be found in English law is a difficult question given that there are judicial dicta pointing in both directions. One writer has described it as an 'irritant',[61] while a Victorian Law Lord has claimed that it is a term implied in all mercantile contracts.[62] However what is clear is that English law is very sceptical about any notion of *solidarisme contractuel* and the case law itself demonstrates that parties are expected to look after their own interests and are not generally under a duty to

---

[58] *R (European Roma Rights Centre) v Immigration Officer at Prague Airport* [2005] 2 AC 1, at paras 59–60 per Lord Hope.
[59] Terré, Simler and Lequette (2002), at 434–5.
[60] *Ibid*, at 43–7, 434–40.
[61] Teubner (1998).
[62] Lord Watson in *Glynn Mills Curie & Co v East & West India Dock Co* (1882) 7 App Cas 591, at 615.

inform.[63] The only general duty is not positively to mislead (misrepresentation). Good faith has in some civilian systems extended itself beyond the contractual obligation and into the pre-contractual domain; this extension is reflected in the PECL in that negotiations broken off in bad faith may give rise to liability (art 2.301). But English law has seemingly rejected such a principle, although not without some dissent in the academic literature.[64] Perhaps the English position has best been summarised by Bingham LJ where he said of good faith that:

> English law has, characteristically, committed itself to no such overriding principle but has developed piecemeal solutions in response to demonstrated problems of unfairness. Many examples could be given. Thus equity has intervened to strike down unconscionable bargains. Parliament has stepped in to regulate the imposition of exemption clauses and the form of certain hire-purchase agreements. The common law also has made its contribution, by holding that certain classes of contract require the utmost good faith, by treating as irrecoverable what purport to be agreed estimates of damage but are in truth a disguised penalty for breach, and in many other ways.[65]

One might add to this list devices such as equitable estoppel and the (occasional) duty to behave as a reasonable contractor.[66]

DOMAIN OF CONTRACT

The discussion on administrative and ordinary contracts raised a question about the scope and extent – or perhaps one should say province – of the law of contract. Some relations that at first sight might appear contractual turn out not to be so and some rules which appear to be contractual prove on closer examination to fall outside contract. Thus for example an action for damages for misrepresentation belongs to the law of tort and money claims arising after the disappearance of a contract for, say, frustration belong now to the law of restitution (see Chapter 16). Indeed the whole topic of vitiating factors in contract is not really part of contract at all; for the remedy of rescission in Equity, which is often the vehicle for giving expression to such factors, is in reality founded on the principle of unjust

---

[63] See eg *Reid v Rush & Tompkins Plc* [1990] 1 WLR 212; *University of Nottingham v Eyett* [1999] 2 All ER 437.
[64] *Walford v Miles* [1992] 2 AC 128.
[65] *Interfoto Picture Library Ltd v Stiletto Visual Programmes Ltd* [1989] QB 433, at 439.
[66] See eg *Ruxley Electronics Ltd v Forsyth* [1996] 1 AC 344.

enrichment.[67] The distinction between contract and Equity proves important in the area of consideration as well. For example, while it remains perfectly true to say that a promise unsupported by consideration is incapable at common law of forming a contractual obligation, it does not follow that such a promise will be devoid of legal effect.

The important point to arise from these domain observations is that knowledge of contract law extends beyond the actual rules of contract law. Knowledge of certain equitable doctrines and remedies, familiarity with aspects of the law of tort and even an acquaintance with property and administrative law are required if one is to have what might be called a practical and functional view of contract. For example negligence cases such as *Hedley Byrne v Heller*[68] and *White v Jones*[69] are regarded even by the judges as filling certain gaps in contract law, these gaps resulting from the requirement of consideration or the rule of privity. This is, perhaps, the most compelling reason for importing the obligations category from civilian thinking. Obligations as a class provides a perspective which transcends the boundaries between contract, tort, restitution and equity, boundaries that often do more harm than good when it comes to solving litigation problems. Another approach is to switch to the substance of legal reasoning. Here it becomes evident that precise categories and boundaries are not things that necessarily act as reasoning premises for the English judiciary.[70]

---

[67] *Whittaker v Campbell* [1984] QB 318, at 326–7.
[68] [1964] AC 465.
[69] [1995] 2 AC 207.
[70] See generally Waddams (2003).

6. Enforcing contracts

Contract is normally approached from an external position. It is generally presented as a closed (or relatively closed) coherent model of inter-related rules waiting to be applied to factual situations as they arise. Both the PECL and UNIDROIT are excellent example of such models. These models broadly fall into two parts: rules concerning the formation of the obligation (including obstacles to formation or vitiating factors); and rules dealing with the dissolution or non-performance of the obligation, often with reference to the contents of the contract. Sometimes, it must be added, the content of a contract is dealt with as a third part falling between the other two parts. Yet there is another view of contract in which cases tell their own story. This is an alternative viewpoint because cases reveal concepts, principles and forms of reasoning that are not always fully exposed by the contract model. They give a view from the bottom-up so to speak. And this is why it is possible to argue that there is another way of understanding contract. This will be the approach of this chapter and the two that follow. They will not cover all the rules in the model – this is something that a standard contract textbook will do – but the bottom-up approach might facilitate understanding from a problem-solving position.

CONTRACT AND METHODOLOGY

If such a bottom-up approach is to be adopted, something must be said, first of all, about method. Some guidance has already been provided in the preceding chapters, but a reflection on methods is vital because, when contract cases are viewed from the position of the facts, complexities are revealed that are not always reflected in the standard abstract models.

A general theory of contract impacts upon methodology in two main ways. First, it makes the law of contract, in the common law world, something of an oddity when compared with the law of tort. Tort tends to operate via categories of liability closely linked to different types of factual situation. Yet, as we have seen, in contract, the hire of a super-tanker, the sale of an onion, the employment of a gardener and the taking out of a loan are all governed by the same legal principle. Secondly, a general theory tends to make problem solving both easy and complex. It is easy in that one can carry a model in one's head to be applied to this vast range of different transactions. Thus formation is a matter of invitation to treat, offer and acceptance, consideration and intention to create legal relations; this structure is then applied to transactions in shops, supermarkets, garages, buses, agencies, offices, factories, construction sites, ships and so on and so forth. The general theory is difficult, however, when things go wrong because it is tempting to think that it always results in the remedy of damages, unless perhaps a defendant is able to offer some convincing defence as to why he should not be liable. This in not helped by the judges. 'Of all the various remedies available at common law,' said Lord Hailsham, 'damages are the remedy of most general application at the present day, and they remain the prime remedy in actions for breach of contract and tort'.[1] This may be true of tort, but it is not actually true of contract since statistically the great majority of claims in contract are in debt (that is to say for money owing and not paid).[2]

This damages and debt point is made in respect of methodology because most contract cases get to court only because something has gone wrong and one party is claiming that the other is in breach of one or more of his contractual promises. Two important methodological questions thus arise when dealing with practical contract problems. What has the non-performing (or defective performing) contractor failed to do? What does the disappointed expectant contractor want in order to remedy the situation?

A general theory of contract tends, then, to mask transactional distinctions that, on occasions, might usefully be revealed. Sometimes these distinctions can be vital particularly when it comes to non-performance. As we saw in a previous chapter, in English law if a purchaser of a bottle of lemonade is injured after purchase he or she will be entitled to damages in contract without having to prove fault.[3] However, if after leaving a supermarket, a consumer is injured when the bus in which he or she is travelling crashes, the consumer will be able to get damages from the bus company only if fault is proved.[4] Again, if the consumer goes to the cleaners to recover her mink stole only to be told that it has gone missing she will be able to recover its value *unless* the firm of cleaners is able to prove they were not at fault (and that may not always be enough).[5]

Take another problem. Consumer A contracts to hire a standard van

---

[1] *Broome v Cassell & Co Ltd* [1972] AC 1027, at 1070.
[2] Zakrzewski, R (2005), at 108.
[3] Sale of Goods Act 1879, s 14.
[4] Supply of Goods and Services Act 1982, s 13.
[5] *Morris v C W Martin & Sons Ltd* [1966] 1 QB 716.

from a van hire firm; consumer B contracts to hire a *particular* van from the same hire firm and the firm only has one such van. After the contracts are signed but before either A or B collects the van there is a fire at the firm and B's particular van is destroyed; however just two or three of the standard vans are destroyed (and the firm has a dozen of them). Provided the fire is not due to the fault of the firm, it may well be able to say to B that the contract to supply a van no longer exists[6] while it will not be able to say the same thing to A.[7] One is not talking here of a different type of transaction (hire), yet one can and must distinguish between a contract to supply a *specific* thing from one to supply a *generic* thing. Method requires careful consideration of the type of transaction and the nature of the 'thing' promised.

Another way of deconstructing contract is, as we have seen in previous chapters, from the viewpoint of remedies. When a transaction goes wrong or proves unfortunate or defective, what does a disappointed contractor actually want or is entitled to? Take facts similar to those in *Constantine v Imperial Smelting*.[8] H hires a ship from O and before H can transport his cargo from one destination to another the ship explodes and sinks for some unexplained reason. H may well want compensation from O for failing to supply a ship, while O may want to know if H remains liable to pay the hire fee. These are two quite different claims: compensation is about *damages* while claiming hire fees is about *debt*. In a debt claim causation and fault are often irrelevant; the money is either owed or not owed. In damages claims, on the other hand, causation and fault become central. Thus, to go back to the exploding ship, if O is sued by H for non-performance (that is not supplying a ship as promised) can O say that the non-performance is not due to fault on his part and thus he is no longer under a contractual liability to supply the ship (and ought he be able to say this)? And if so, who must prove fault or its absence? In most civilian systems the burden would be on O to prove that the non-performance is due to an absence of fault (see for example CC arts 1147–8; PECL art 8.101, 8.108). However English law seemingly puts the burden on H (*Constantine* case). Yet this *Constantine* rule must be treated with some caution. Imagine that H hires a motor launch for a holiday on the river but for some unexplained reason the launch catches fire and he has to abandon ship losing all his possessions. Can it really be said that O could claim he is not liable unless H

---

[6] *Constantine (Joseph) SS Ltd v Imperial Smelting Corporation* [1942] AC 154.

[7] *Maritime National Fish Ltd v Ocean Trawlers Ltd* [1935] AC 524.

[8] [1942] AC 154.

proves fault? This seems most unlikely.[9] Does, then, *Constantine* lay down a 'rule' of contract or is it simply a liability case decided on its own particular facts themselves dependent to some extent on time and place?

FORMATION MODELS

If an obligation is a *vinculum iuris* binding two parties it must, evidently, have a beginning, a content and an end. These three aspects certainly act as focal points for legal rules and analysis, but, depending on the system under examination, they may not always be expressed in quite this way. All systems, however, have rules dealing with the formation of a contractual obligation and contracts everywhere in Europe are often regarded as agreements, this idea of agreement being a unifying factor. Yet it can hide as much as it can reveal since behind 'agreement' there are different models of contract. These different models disclose different theories about formation and thus enforceability.

If one surveys the whole Western legal tradition – Roman law, modern civil law and the common law – three foundational ideas can be identified for the formation of a contractual obligation and thus the possibility of legal enforcement. The first is *causa*, which acted as the basis for contract in Roman law; the second is *conventio* (together with *consensus*), which became the foundation for a general theory of contractual formation in the modern civil law; and the third is *promissio*. This latter notion is arguably the basis for contract in the common law.

However none of this is to say that these three foundational ideas have remained independent one from the other. In French law, for example, *conventio* and *causa* have both become foundational elements (CC art 1108) and there are those who would argue that contracts in the common law are based upon promise, consent and agreement (*conventio*). If one had to extract from these notions a single dichotomy it is that between the 'subjective' and the 'objective'. Thus French contract law is, in relation to English law, sometimes said to be more subjective in its approach to formation of contracts and to vitiating factors. Yet even this dichotomy is misleading in as much as any distinction between subjective legal 'acts' (making wills, entering a contract and the like) and objective legal 'facts' (causing of damage) can break down. How can one judge if a person has consented to something save in respect of his objective behaviour? As will be seen, acts and facts often merge.

---

[9] *Reed v Dean* [1949] 1 KB 188.

CAUSE (*CAUSA*)

Roman law did not develop a general theory of contract as such. What developed was a law of contracts, each with its own particular *actio* (remedy); and these contracts fell into a number of discrete categories based upon a 'cause' which in turn reflected a range of transactions typical of a commercial society. There were the real contracts (*re*) founded upon the transfer of a thing; consensual contracts based upon the main forms of consensual transactions, namely sale, hire, mandate and partnership; and verbal contracts arising out of a formal promise. Later Roman law did, it has to be said, develop more informal contracts such as pacts and innominate agreements but these never really escaped their own particular categories. In a sense, then, it can be said that the obligation arose out of a particular factual transaction and thus *causa* has an objective aspect; it represents particular categories of 'natural' operations (*naturam contractus* said Ulpian: D.2.14.7.5). If there was no cause there could be no contractual *actio* and no contractual obligation and thus no enforcement (D.2.14.7.4).

This idea of obligations arising from particular categories of transaction is still to be found in contractual thinking and, indeed, in the codes. Thus one can divide up one's daily ('natural') contracts into a limited range of operations such as purchase, carriage, hire and other services (including contracts *re*: dry cleaning for example, involving the handing over of a thing). Accordingly the codes have not just general rules of contract, but also rules with respect to those specific contracts to be found in the Roman sources (see for example CC arts, 1582ff, 1713ff), with perhaps the addition of post-Roman transactions such as insurance and banking in the more modern codes.

Common lawyers have not made use of *causa* as such, but no contract can be formed without 'consideration' and this does share a common feature with cause. Each promise has to be bargained for and thus each party must attract an economic detriment and benefit. Consideration thus provides a kind of objective economic 'clothing' to a 'pact'. It must be remembered, also, that bailment, although not as such a contract, does give rise to obligations between bailor (transferor) and bailee (transferee). These bailment obligations are very similar to a Roman real contract in that they arise simply as a result of the transfer of the thing.

AGREEMENT (*CONVENTIO*)

Despite this requirement of *causa*, the Romans observed that all the various contracts shared a common denominator, namely *conventio* (agreement) (D.2.14.1.3). Indeed, agreement was the direct basis of the consensual contracts such as sale, hire and partnership (D.18.1.1.2). Moreover, with respect to *pacta* and the consensual contracts, there was the further idea of *consensus* (D.2.14.1.2; D.44.7.2.1). These two ideas were used by the later civilians to develop a general theory of contract. Domat (17th century jurist) stated that 'agreements are engagements which are formed by mutual consent' and Pothier (18th century) developed the idea of *consensus* in saying that contract 'contains the coming together of the wills of two persons'.[10] These two ideas became the foundation of contract in the *Code civil*: a contract is 'an agreement' (*une convention*: art 1101) based upon 'consent' (*le consentement*: art 1108). The German Natural Lawyers equally thought in terms of agreement and consent but being more influenced by the Roman notion of *pactum* they came to the conclusion that there had to be, in addition to *Vertrag*, a declaration of intentions by the two parties (*Willenserklärungen*).[11] Today, *conventio* has transcended national systems to become the basis of contract in the PECL (art 2.101) and UNIDROIT (art 2.1); a contract is formed if there is 'sufficient agreement' (and note that there is no requirement of either cause or consideration).

PROMISE (*PROMISSIO*)

The Romans might not have developed a general theory of contract, but they did create a general form of contracting, the *stipulatio*, which fell within the class of verbal contracts. The source of the obligation was a promise expressed by set words in the form of a question and answer (D.44.7.1.7): 'Do you promise to do X?' 'Yes, I promise (*spondeo*)'. This, together with the informal *pacta* of later law, became the nearest the Romans got to a general form of contracting; and indeed the *stipulatio* subsequently moved from its oral basis to one where writing was sufficient (D.45.1.134.2).

Now it may seem that this form of contracting would become irrelevant with the development of a general theory based on *conventio* and *consensus*, yet it remains important for several reasons. First, the formality of the operation has left its mark on certain modern contracts which will be valid only if, in addition to agreement, they conform to certain formal requirements such as being in writing. Thus certain contracts are enforceable in

---

[10] Zimmermann (1996), at 566–7.
[11] *Ibid*, at 568–9.

English law only if they are evidenced in writing; and, indeed, a unilateral written promise will itself be enforceable, even in the absence of consideration, if set out in a certain form and properly witnessed.[12] Secondly, the modern penalty clause whereby a contracting party promises to pay a specific sum of money if he fails to perform can be traced back (in civil law) to the *stipulatio*. A party could formally promise to pay a certain sum if another contract was not properly performed.

Thirdly, it is feasible to argue that the formal means of determining agreement and consent, namely the rules of offer and acceptance, owes its form to the *stipulatio* (see for example D.45.1.1). It would be quite wrong to say that contract in English law developed out of the *stipulatio* since the forms of action meant that the building blocks of contract were rather different from those to be found in the Roman sources. The main early actions, and categories of thought, were, as we have seen, trespass and debt (together with covenant) rather than specific types of contracts. However, as the centuries progressed, certain 'contractual' ideas began to emerge 'with the defendant's "undertaking" and "faithful promise" as the central elements of the plaintiff's claim'.[13] In other words what emerges is the idea of a liability for breach of promise (*assumpsit*).[14] Accordingly in the 19th century, when a general theory of contract was imported and superimposed upon the old common law, the normative basis remained promise rather than *conventio* with the result that contract is arguably less a meeting of the minds and more an exchange of promises (or an exchange of promise for an act).

In fact a close look at the 19th century cases reveals that the English law of contract was, in its formative days at least, founded on two ideas. First there was a general principle that 'if a man has made a deliberate statement, and another has acted upon it, he cannot be at liberty to deny the truth of the statement'.[15] Secondly, there was the principle that any contractual promise was *prima facie* actionable even if it lacked an object and a cause in the French law sense of these terms. Accordingly if a person was contractually to promise that it shall rain the next day he would be liable on the basis not only that he ought not to be allowed to go back on his word[16] but also that he has assumed a risk and must bear the consequences.[17] These two ideas give rise to a law of contract in England which

---

[12] Law Reform (Miscellaneous Provisions) Act 1989.
[13] Ibbetson (1999), at 135–6.
[14] *Ibid*, at 137–8.
[15] Baron Bramwell in *McCance v L & N W Ry* (1861) 31 LJ Exch 65, 71.
[16] *Canham v Barry* (1855) 24 LJCP 100, 106.
[17] *Hall v Wright* (1860) 29 LJQB 43, 46.

is based, historically at least, more on the effect of words than upon the coming together of two wills. This is not to say that *consensus* is irrelevant; it is not. Nevertheless the cause of action for a breach of contract does not arise out of any agreement as such but out of the promise either to pay a debt or to perform some act; the language is one not of 'non-performance' but of 'breach'.

PROMISE AND AGREEMENT

English contract law is, then, built upon the notion of enforceable *promise* rather than agreement and this distinction is more than academic. In the civil law tradition the emphasis on consent (*consensus*) and agreement (*conventio*) has given rise to an idea of contract as essentially subjective. The contractual bond is based on the coming together of two wills. In the common law, in contrast, the idea of promise is much more objective; it is a 'thing' that once launched assumes a life of its own and upon which others might well rely.

There are a number of areas where the objective flavour to English contract law manifests itself. One of the most striking decisions where the distinction between promise and agreement had a practical effect in terms of enforcement is that of *Gibson v Manchester City Council*.[18] In this case a council house tenant brought an action for specific performance to enforce what he believed was a binding contract of sale to sell him the house in which he was living. The local authority had sent him a number of preliminary letters indicating a willingness to sell the house and stipulating the procedure to be followed. However half way through this process there was a change of political control and the incoming Labour group ordered a halt to council house sales except where there was a binding contract.

In the Court of Appeal, Lord Denning MR thought there was a binding contract on the basis of the correspondence between the local authority and tenant. 'If by their correspondence and their conduct you can see an agreement on all material terms, which was intended thenceforward to be binding,' said the Master of the Rolls, 'then there is a binding contract in law even though all the formalities have not been gone through'.[19] However this decision was overruled in the House of Lords. Lord Diplock asserted that the 'conventional approach' was to examine the actual correspondence itself in order to discover if there was a specific offer made

---

[18] [1978] 1 WLR 520 (CA); [1979] 1 WLR 294 (HL).
[19] [1978] 1 WLR 520, at 523–4.

by the council which had been accepted by the tenant.[20] On doing this he found that 'the words ... make it quite impossible to construe this letter as a contractual offer capable of being converted into a legally enforceable open contract'. For the 'words "may be prepared to sell" are fatal to this'.[21]

One is not asserting here that a civil law court would necessarily have arrived at the same decision as Lord Denning. But when one considers that the test of the existence of a contract in Romanist thinking is now 'sufficient agreement' (PECL art 2:101(1)(b)), it is perfectly feasible to argue that Lord Denning's analysis might well be acceptable to a civil lawyer. Lord Diplock, in contrast, is looking for a specific offer (promise) to sell and for him the word 'may' was objectively fatal, even if at the time the council sent the letter it fully intended to sell the house provided the tenant accepted to pay the asking price (which, after some hesitation, he did).

The distinction identified in *Gibson* between agreement and promise reflects itself in two principal ways with regard to contract formation. First, all Western systems, to a greater or less extent, determine contract formation through recourse to a search for an 'offer' and an 'acceptance'. However in civilian thinking a contract can be formed if there is 'sufficient agreement' even (presumably) in the absence of offer and acceptance (PECL arts 2.101 and 2.211; UNIDROIT arts 2.1 and 3.2). In English law, on the other hand, there normally has to be offer and acceptance before there can be a binding contract since one has to find a concrete promise. Offer and acceptance (rather than agreement) is, in other words, a matter of English substantive contract law. The distinction does of course have a practical aspect as *Gibson* indicates. The claimant was not seeking damages as such; he was trying specifically to force the owner of the house (the local authority) to do what he considered it had agreed to do, namely to transfer ownership of the property to him. His whole action (specific performance) depended on the existence of a binding contract. *Gibson* is an excellent example of the importance that formation rules can play on occasions.

Secondly, in a system based upon *conventio*, the existence of fraud, mistake or duress will logically act as an obstacle to the formation of a contract because they act as obstacles to the coming together of two minds. In a system based on promise, although the law might not be prepared to enforce (at the level of remedies) a contract tainted by a vitiating factor, such a factor does not, as a matter of conceptual logic, prevent the

---

[20] [1979] 1 WLR 294, at 297.
[21] *Ibid*, at 298.

formation of a contract. A promise can still have an objective existence even if it has been induced by fraud, error or duress. This explains why, as Robert Goff LJ once pointed out, fraud in English contract law does not vitiate consent.[22] Fraud is dealt with by remedies coming from outside contract (damages in tort and rescission in equity). As Lord Nicholls (dissenting) put it, fraud 'can destroy legal rights; it cannot destroy facts'.[23] It equally explains why there never really developed, within the common law (as opposed to equity), a general theory of mistake in contract. There is simply no principle at common law similar to the one to be found in the Québec Civil Code which states that error 'vitiates consent of the parties or one of them where it relates to the nature of the contract, the object of the prestation or anything that was essential in determining that consent' (art 1400). The result is that it is by no means easy for a party to escape from a contract, where the other party is guilty neither of fraud nor misrepresentation, on the basis that had he known of certain facts he would not have contracted.[24] This is a point to which we shall return in the next chapter.

ENFORCEABLE PROMISES

English contract law is thus based on the promise to do something. In many contract cases this promise is, as one might expect, to pay a specific amount of money. Thus the purchaser or hirer of goods and services normally promises to pay a price in return for receiving some benefit. If such a transaction displays three essential elements or conditions the promise to pay will be enforceable. These three conditions are: offer and acceptance: consideration; and intention to create legal relations.

With respect to a great many transactions there is, in English law, little problem with regard to formation since the factual situations are relatively settled. Thus in a supermarket the contract is formed, not when the product is taken from the shelf and put into the basket or trolley, but when the price is registered on the till at the cash desk.[25] Consequently, if a product explodes and injures a consumer before he or she arrives at the checkout any claim for injury will have to be brought in tort.[26] The idea

---

[22] *Whittaker v Campbell* [1984] QB 318, at 327.
[23] *Shogun Finance Ltd v Hudson* [2004] 1 AC 919, at para 7.
[24] *Bell v Lever Brothers* [1932] AC 161.
[25] *Pharmaceutical Society of GB v Boots* [1953] 1 QB 401.
[26] Consumer Protection Act 1987's 2; *Ward v Tesco Stores Ltd* [1976] 1 WLR 810.

that it is the customer who makes the offer – products on the shelf being an 'invitation to treat' (an invitation to make an offer) – applies equally to shops and so goods displayed in a shop-window are not offers. Even if they have a price label attached stating for example 'special offer', this display will not amount to a contractual offer[27] and so the customer cannot claim an enforceable contract with the seller.

In the days of bus conductors, the exact time when the contract of carriage formed between a person who jumped on the bus and the bus company could create difficulties in theory. But buses have, on the whole, now changed with the contract being formed via the driver or when one buys a pre-paid ticket. Taxis prove interesting from a comparative law viewpoint since some systems treat the 'offer' on the taxi as a legal offer accepted by the customer who hails the vehicle. But, again, in English law it is the customer who must make the offer. Small-scale service transactions are equally well settled in respect of the formation of the contract. Many such transactions are carried out in high street premises with the customer making the offer accepted by the person behind the counter. The handing over of any item for cleaning or servicing will, of course, create a bailment relationship, but here the customer needs to take some care since the seller of the service may well wish to modify the common law obligations. Such modifications will be incorporated in the contract, and thus enforceable, only if they are brought to the customer's attention *before* the formation of the contract.[28] This is normally done by a notice displayed, say, above the counter or in a ticket or other document supplied to the customer. The latter method is risky since one could argue that the contract had formed before the customer had had a chance to read the document; but if the client had used the same firm on many occasions he or she might be bound by reason of a course of dealing. If the clause modifying the contract turns out to be unfair or unreasonable it may not be enforceable thanks to legislation.[29]

Service transactions with small builders, plumbers and the like are usually negotiated through an estimate and in the case of a builder a written contractual document. The estimate possibly amounts to an offer accepted by the customer when he or she asks the builder or plumber to proceed. One might note here that it could be particularly important to determine if a written estimate amounts to an offer if the customer's

---

[27] *Fisher v Bell* [1961] 1 QB 394.
[28] *Thornton v Shoe Lane Parking Ltd* [1971] 2 QB 163.
[29] Unfair Contract Terms Act 1977; Unfair Terms in Consumer Contracts Regulations 1999.

acceptance is made by post; for, if it does, the offer will, in English law, be accepted the moment the client posts the letter of acceptance. This is the so-called posting rule, specifically rejected by the PECL (art 2.205(1)).

Window cleaners are more interesting from a contract point of view since nothing may be in writing, the window cleaner arriving every month or so and cleaning the windows without gaining the actual assent of the house owner. Usually the owner has specifically agreed with a particular window cleaner that the latter will maintain the windows and thus each time he arrives to do the cleaning it is implied that he is doing the work expecting to be paid. A similar situation will apply with respect to the family solicitor. Each time a client needs a service, he will no doubt telephone the solicitor with the request and this will be carried out, the solicitor then sending his bill. Given that the solicitor will have provided the service expecting to be paid, there is no question of 'past consideration', that is to say the rendering of consideration (the service) that does not connect with any actual promise to pay moving from the other party. The offer, acceptance and consideration are part of the ongoing relationship (family solicitor).

DIFFICULT CASES

There are, however, a number of difficult situations which could easily result in litigation if sufficient amounts of money are at stake or if a person faced with a bill decides not to pay. These difficult cases can arise out of a number of typical situations.

The first is the non-serious promise. Imagine the following situation: a potential restaurant customer sees a notice outside a pub stating that any person ordering a meal who has to wait more than 45 minutes for the food to arrive will be entitled to eat free of charge. The customer orders a meal, waits more than 45 minutes for the food to arrive, eats it, and then, when faced with the bill, refuses to pay. The contract question is of course this: can the customer refuse to pay the bill or can the pub owner claim that the promise is not to be taken seriously since it is simply an advertising gimmick? The foundational case is *Carlill v Carbolic Smoke Ball Co*[30] in which the defendants, manufacturers of a medical product, placed an advert for the product in a popular magazine. The advert stated that the defendants would pay a £100 reward to any person who purchased, and used as per directions, the medical product and who nevertheless caught

---

[30] [1893] 1 QB 256.

influenza. In addition there was a statement in the publicity that £1000 had been deposited with a bank in Regent Street 'showing our sincerity in the matter'. The claimant purchased and used the product and on contracting flu demanded her reward money. When the company refused to pay, she brought an action in debt for the £100 and the Court of Appeal upheld the decision of the trial judge that the defendants were to be liable for the sum. The case raised several fundamental points about contract formation. However with respect to offer and acceptance, the case is important because it confirmed that offers could be made to the world at large (as opposed to individuals) and that individuals accepting such an offer need not communicate an acceptance since the advertisement contained an implied waiver.

What is important about this precedent is that it can apply to so many contemporary situations. A pub or restaurant that states on a board outside its premises that customers who are kept waiting for more than a certain period of time before their food arrives will not have to pay for their meals, may well find that they have made a contractual offer which legally they will have to respect. The same is true for a manufacturer of a consumer product who promises free air tickets to the USA to any consumer who purchases one of their products. *Carlill* makes it very clear that such specific promises are not always mere advertising 'puffs' and this is one of the reasons why the case remains an important precedent. Another form of offer to the public is an auction sale without reserve. In this situation the auctioneer offers to sell the auction item to the highest bidder, this offer being accepted when the bid is made.[31] This contract is of course one that is collateral to the actual contract of sale between the seller of the auctioned item and the highest bidder (buyer). But of course *Carlill* itself was a collateral contract case in that Mrs Carlill did not actually buy the product directly from the Carbolic Smoke Ball Company.

Difficult formation problems can also arise where two contractors send out documentation to each other that contradict. This is not necessarily untypical in the commercial world where parties often contract using their own printed conditions of contract. B orders material from S using its standard contract form full of conditions; S does not read the conditions but delivers the requested material along with his own printed contractual document equally full of contractual conditions; a dispute subsequently arises, say, about the amount to be paid, after B has consumed the ordered material, and lawyers have to decide which

---

[31] *Barry v Davies* [2000] 1 WLR 1962.

set of conditions form the contract. Now strictly speaking it could be said that there is no contract between B and S because there was no actual offer and acceptance of each other's terms.[32] But this would be commercially inconvenient since S has delivered and B has consumed the requested material. There must, in other words, be some sort of contract. Indeed both the PECL (art 2:209) and UNIDROIT (art 2.22) lay down that there is in principle a contract founded on any common terms even if there is a conflict with regard to the exchange of contractual forms; a party unhappy with this situation must without delay inform the other party that he will not be bound.

English law seems not so generous. The Court of Appeal in *Butler Machine Tool Co v Ex-Cell-O-Corp*[33] approached this kind of problem from the position of the contractual documents themselves and reduced it to a 'battle of forms'. The battle is won by the last form which is sent and which is received without objection, for these are seen as the conditions and terms 'offered' and if the other party then performs the contract without raising an objection to these latest terms he is deemed to have 'accepted' them. Yet, as Lord Denning MR observed, there are other cases where 'the battle is won by the man who gets the blow in first' or 'where the battle depends on the shots fired on both sides'.[34]

These battle of form situations are complex because if an 'acceptance' does not accord with the offer it can amount to what is called a counter-offer. This has the effect of depriving the original offer of its legal force and so if the 'acceptance' (that is the counter-offer) is not accepted by the original offeror, the counter-offeror cannot then purport to accept the original offer. For example if S offers his car to B for £2,000 and B purports to 'accept' for £1,500, this latter 'acceptance' is no acceptance but a counter-offer which S can either accept or reject. If S rejects the counter-offer, B cannot then claim to accept the original offer to sell for £2,000. What if B purports to accept S's offer to sell the car for £2,000 by replying that he accepts for £1,995 since that is all the cash he has and he knows that S would like to be paid in cash? According to English law, where the foundation of contract is promise, the reply is no less a counter-offer than the £1,500 reply. But civil law, based on agreement, can be different since there may be a sufficient accord between the two parties (PECL art 2.208(2)).

---

[32] *Trollope & Colls Ltd v Atomic Power Constructions Ltd* [1962] 3 All ER 1035, at 1040.
[33] [1979] 1 WLR 401.
[34] [1979] 1 WLR 401, at 405.

ABSENCE OF CLARITY

Offer, acceptance and consideration will not be sufficient to create a contract if the subject matter itself is too uncertain to uphold such an obligation. Vague transactions will not, in other words, be treated as contracts. To be enforceable a contract 'must contain mutual obligations and a commitment by each party'[35] and so, for example, in a contract of sale there must normally be a commitment to pay a specific price for a specific object. For example, if B merely promises to buy S's car without anything being agreed as to price, it is doubtful if a contract would form. Indeed in Roman law there could be no contract if there was no price (D.18.1.2.1). However, this said, English law is prepared to be much more subtle in that it accepts that there can in certain circumstances be a binding contract even if no price is agreed. In such a situation the buyer is under an obligation to pay a reasonable price.[36] Accordingly in a commercial setting, where S periodically delivers raw material to B's factory and B consumes the material, there will, if only for practical reasons, be a contract. Should a dispute arise, the law will be that B must pay a reasonable price for any material delivered (although, as we have seen, there might in such a situation be a battle of forms problem). The same is true for a contract for the supply of a service.[37] A contract can equally form in situations where it is agreed that a price will be determined in the future; what the law looks for is a means by which the uncertain can be rendered certain. *Certum est quod certum reddi potest* (what can be rendered certain is certain), a maxim that is probably valid equally in Roman and in English law. Perhaps one should add here that there is a general principle (*favor contractus*) to be found in the civil law systems that contracts should, if at all possible, be upheld rather than declared non-existent.

The certainty rule has been held to apply to a contract to contract, that is to say a contract to negotiate.[38] Such a contract is too vague and, anyway, one might recall that there is a further general principle that a duty to negotiate in good faith is repugnant to the adversarial position of contractual parties.[39] There are however exceptions. Potential purchasers and sellers of real property can bind themselves in a lock-out agreement (not to sell to anyone else) and an invitation to tender has been held in one

---

[35] Peter Gibson LJ in *Firstpost Homes Ltd v Johnson* [1995] 1 WLR 1567, at 1573.
[36] Sale of Goods Act 1979, s 8.
[37] Supply of Goods and Services Act 1982, s 15.
[38] *Courtney & Fairbairn v Tolani Brothers* [1975] 1 WLR 297.
[39] *Walford v Miles* [1992] 2 AC 128.

rather exceptional case to be an offer capable of being accepted, to form a collateral contract, merely by the submission of a tender.[40]

ABSENCE OF CONSENSUS

The distinction between promise and agreement is also reflected in the role that subjective intentions play in the formation of a contract. Here it has to be said that it is not true that *consensus* has no role in the common law because offer and acceptance does have a subjective dimension. If by chance two offers, for example one to sell an item and one to buy this precise item, were to cross in the post and that the cross-offers were identical in terms of price and the like there would not be a contract. There has to be *consensus ad idem* between the parties.[41]

This *consensus* principle has two aspects. The subjective aspect is that of intention and the meeting of the minds. In the cross-offers example there is certainly an intention to sell and an intention to buy on identical terms, yet the minds themselves have not been brought into contact. On the other hand there is an objective dimension. An acceptance can be sufficient to create a contract even if the acceptor had no subjective intention to accept on the terms offered. As Lord Diplock has stated, 'what is necessary is that the intention of each *as it has been communicated to and understood by the other* (even though that which has been communicated does not represent the actual state of mind of the communicator) should coincide.' And he went on to say that this 'is what English lawyers mean when they resort to the Latin phrase *consensus ad idem* and the words . . . italicised are essential to the concept of *consensus ad idem*, the lack of which prevents the formation of a binding contract in English law'.[42] This approach has been reiterated more recently by Lord Phillips. 'Whether the parties have reached agreement on the terms is not determined by evidence of the subjective intention of each party', he said; it 'is, in large measure, determined by making an objective appraisal of the exchanges between the parties.'[43]

Returning to Lord Diplock, he went on to add this. He said that the 'rule that neither party can rely upon his own failure to communicate accurately to the other party his own real intention by what he wrote or said or did, as negativing the *consensus ad idem*, is an example of a general principle of

---

[40] *Blackpool & Fylde Aero Club Ltd v Blackpool BC* [1990] 1 WLR 1195.
[41] *Shogun Finance Ltd v Hudson* [2004] 1 AC 919, at para 123 per Lord Phillips.
[42] *The Hannah Blumenthal* [1983] 1 AC 854, at 915 (emphasis in original).
[43] *Shogun Finance Ltd v Hudson* [2004] 1 AC 919, at para 123.

English law that injurious reliance on what another person did may be a source of legal rights against him."[44] Here Lord Diplock is perhaps going further than the rules of contract and, possibly, into the realm of equity which has a general doctrine that one can be estopped from denying the legal force of a statement (representation) where another has relied upon it to his detriment. It would appear, therefore, that the equitable principle of estoppel can produce a binding contract even although there is no *consensus*. However care must be taken here because estoppel does not in fact create a 'contract'. What it does is to create a situation at the level of procedure and (or) remedies where a party who has led another by his acts or words to rely upon him is prevented from raising in court his own lack of intention. This may have the effect, objectively, of creating a contract, but it might be more helpful, as indeed Lord Diplock himself went on to suggest, to see it as creating an equitable 'obligation'.

The *consensus* rule might also have the effect on occasions of putting onto one contractual party a special obligation to bring to the attention of the other party any onerous terms (promises) that he is deemed to have accepted (or made) (UNIDROIT art 2.20). Thus in one case a contractor hired some photographic transparencies from an agency and, by an oversight, failed to return them on time. The agency then claimed an exorbitant sum of money as a debt from the hirers, pointing to a clause in the delivery note allowing them to charge such a sum. The Court of Appeal rejected the claimant debt claim on the basis that the hirer never agreed to the charge. To be enforceable the claimant would have had to bring to the hirer's attention the specific clause; merely inserting it into the written delivery note alongside other clauses was not enough.[45]

INTENTION TO CREATE LEGAL RELATIONS

Some promises may be treated as outside the law of contract on the basis that there is a lack of intention to create a legally binding contract. The courts take the view that any commercial agreement in which there is offer, acceptance and consideration is prima facie a legal contract. There is, in other words, a presumption of an intention to create legal relations if the agreement is a commercial one. This presumption can be displaced; and so for example a negotiation letter may specify that it will not be capable

---

[44] *The Hannah Blumenthal* [1983] 1 AC 854, at 916.
[45] *Interfoto Picture Library Ltd v Stiletto Visual Programmes Ltd* [1989] QB 433.

of giving rise to a contractual obligation. Or if a 'contract' contains a clause stating that it will not be enforceable at law the agreement will lack an intention to create legal relations and be unenforceable.[46] If the agreement is a non-commercial one – that is to say within the family or between friends – there is a presumption that it will not be legally binding.[47] Again, however, this presumption can be displaced by the evidence and there are therefore cases where family separation arrangements and agreements between friends have been held to be contracts. An informal agreement among friends to share a prize will probably be a contract if each member has contributed entrance money to the competition.[48]

One might add here that the essential condition of an intention to create legal relations can appear superfluous given the requirement of consideration, certainty and *consensus*. But it does have a practical role in as much as it can be used to remove from the law of contract a number of agreements that the courts consider, for policy reasons, to be unsuitable for contractual regulation. For example the courts have been most reluctant to see the supply of energy as contractual arrangements; gas, water and electricity are supplied pursuant to a statutory rather than a contractual duty and the difference between the two relationships was explained in terms of a lack of intention to create legal relations.[49] One way of viewing these statutory duty cases was in terms of the public and public divide; but the privatisation of energy would suggest that this explanation is no longer valid, although the courts continue to insist that even after privatisation the legal status of the supply relationship has not changed.[50]

REVOCATION OF AN OFFER

It is a rule of common law that an offer can be revoked at any time before acceptance and this remains true in principle even if the offeror has stated a fixed time for its duration or that it is 'irrevocable'. The reason why the offer always remains revocable is that there is no consideration to support this promise to keep the offer open.

In theory such a rule could create problems. In the case of a unilateral contract acceptance is complete only when the offeree has performed what is required of him and the revocation rule implies that in principle the

---

[46] *Jones v Vernon's Pools Ltd* [1938] 2 All ER 626.
[47] *Balfour v Balfour* [1919] 2 KB 571.
[48] *Simpkins v Pays* [1955] 1 WLR 975.
[49] *Willmore v SE Electricity Board* [1957] 2 Ll Rep 375.
[50] *Norweb Plc v Dixon* [1995] 1 WLR 636.

offeror could withdraw his offer even after the offeree has entered upon performance. The classic example is the offer to pay £100 to anyone who walks between London and York. The offeror can in theory revoke his offer even when the walker has reached the outskirts of York since acceptance would not at that point be complete. In fact English law would not allow the offeror to revoke until the offeree had been given a reasonable opportunity to complete and the conceptual basis of this rule is probably to be found in equity. At common law the offeror would have the right to revoke, but equity would regard this as an abuse of a 'right' and would hold that the offeror would be estopped from revoking until the offeree had had a reasonable opportunity to complete. This example possibly has a practical commercial application in the area of house sales. It may well be that the contract between the vendor of a house and an estate agent is unilateral (an interesting question), the latter being able to claim a fee only if they introduce a buyer. If a potential vendor agrees that a particular estate agent should handle the sale, it is possible, especially if the agent has invested time and money in advertising the property, that the owner will have to give the agent a reasonable opportunity to sell before the house can be withdrawn (unless perhaps there is a good reason for the withdrawal).

An offeror could no doubt be equally estopped from revoking an offer when he indicates that an offer is irrevocable or states a fixed time for its acceptance (PECL art 2.202(3)). Yet these rules can be ambiguous in that if a revocation reaches an offeree before he has actually accepted the offer, it is prima facie a valid revocation.[51] The equitable rule will come into play if the offeree has relied to his detriment upon the offer's statement that the offer will not be withdrawn. Much, however, will depend upon the facts and the contract in issue. A potential buyer of a house might well promise to keep an offer open for a stated period of time, yet if he does break this promise it is by no means clear that the potential seller of the house will have an action against the buyer (if only because contracts for the sale of land have to be in writing).

ACCEPTANCE

An offer must be accepted before there can be a binding contract. Yet it is probably true to say of English law that any 'form of statement or conduct by the offeree is an acceptance if it indicates assent to the offer' (PECL

---

[51] *Financings Ltd v Stimson* [1962] 1 WLR 1184.

art 2.204(1)). Thus in *Carlill v Carbolic Smoke Ball Co*[52] Mrs Carlill's purchase and use of the product during the stipulated period amounted to an act of acceptance; she did not have to contact the company and expressly accept its offer. Where problems can arise is in respect of reward cases in which a person performs the act of consideration (for example returning a lost cat) but is actually ignorant of the reward offer. In such a situation logic would dictate that there cannot be a contract because there is no *consensus ad idem*.

What must be stressed, however, is that silence does not amount to an acceptance. And so in situations where a company extracts money from a bank account of a consumer simply because the consumer has failed to respond to an 'offer' hidden in the small print of some other contract, it may be that the extraction amounts to theft.[53] One can take money only if there is a contractual entitlement to it. Such small print clauses might well be void, anyway, under consumer legislation, but, apart from this, there is a general principle of the common law that liabilities should not be forced upon people behind their backs.

A more curious exception to the communication of acceptance rule is where a contract is concluded by post. Provided that it is reasonable to use the post as a means of acceptance, the rule formulated last century is that an offer is accepted at the moment the letter of acceptance is posted.[54] Whether this rule has much of a future is now in some doubt,[55] but modern means of communication can still present problems with regard to the receipt of an acceptance. If for example an email or fax message of acceptance is not received by the offeror (for example he did not maintain his fax machine properly) then there will be no contract unless the offeree can show that the offeror was at fault in some way. However if fault on the part of the offeror can be shown, the reason why the acceptance will be effective is that the offeror will be estopped in equity from denying the existence of a contract.[56] This use of estoppel is interesting in that it seems to be getting close to an exception to the principle that estoppel is strictly a defence and not a cause of action. Yet the real cause of action is a claim that the offeror is contractually liable in damages. Normally the offeror would claim that such liability is non-existent given the non-existence of the contract; but his fault would preclude him from raising

---

[52] [1893] 1 QB 256.
[53] *Lawrence v Metropolitan Police Commissioner* [1972] AC 626.
[54] *Household Fire Insurance Co v Grant* (1879) LR 4 Ex D 216.
[55] *Holwell Securities Ltd v Hughes* [1974] 1 WLR 155; Kötz and Flessner (1997), at 26–7.
[56] *Entores Ltd v Miles Far East Corporation* [1955] 2 QB 327, at 333.

this 'defence' thus allowing the claimant to succeed at common law. All the same, this is a difficult and complex area and thus must be accompanied with a warning. 'No universal rule can cover all such cases', said Lord Wilberforce, 'they must be resolved by reference to the intentions of the parties, by sound business practice and in some cases by a judgment where the risks should lie'.[57]

CONSIDERATION

One of the main differences between civil and common law contracts is that consideration is a vital requirement for an enforceable promise at common law. A promise to pay a sum of money as a gift is enforceable only under 'property' legislation if the promise conforms to certain requirements.[58] It is not enforceable as an ordinary contractual 'obligation'. 'A valuable consideration', said Lush J, 'in the sense of the law, may consist either in some right, interest, profit, or benefit accruing to one party, or some forbearance, detriment, loss, or responsibility, given, suffered, or undertaken by the other.'[59] In short, a benefit and a detriment must attach to each contracting party in order that the contract is enforceable.

Take, once again, the case of *Carlill*. AL Smith LJ noted in his judgment that the defendants had argued that there was no consideration, but he responded in saying that there were two. One 'is the consideration of the inconvenience of having to use this carbolic smoke ball for two weeks three times a day; and the other more important consideration is the money gain likely to accrue to the defendants by the enhanced sale of the smoke balls, by reason of the plaintiff's user of them'.[60] Smith LJ's approach is indicative of the methodology. One takes each party and asks if there is a benefit and if there is a detriment. From the position of Mrs Carlill, there is the detriment of having to use the product, but the benefit of the possibility of a reward. From the position of the Carbolic Smoke Ball Co, there is the detriment of putting oneself under an obligation to pay a reward if the flu condition materialises; on the benefit side, however, there is the extra profit generated by the advertisement with its reward offer. Smith LJ was thus able to conclude that there was 'ample consideration to support this promise'.

---

[57] *Brinkibon Ltd v Stahag Stahl* [1983] 2 AC 34, at 42.
[58] Law of Property (Miscellaneous Provisions) Act 1989, s 1.
[59] *Currie v Misa* (1875) LR 10 Ex 153, at 162.
[60] *Carlill v Carbolic Smoke Ball Co* [1893] 1 QB 256, at 275.

However it is necessary to be clear as to what actually amounts to consideration in contract and several distinctions need to be made. The first is between the formation of a contract and its performance (or execution). The second is between bilateral and unilateral contracts. In a unilateral contract only one person makes a promise and the consideration rendered by the other party is the actual act of performance (D promises C to pay him £100 if he walks from London to York). In a bilateral contract, where both contracting parties make promises, what amounts to consideration is not actually the physical object that makes up the economic value. It is the promises themselves. Thus if S offers to sell his car to B for £2,000 and B accepts the offer, the consideration is not actually the car and the money. The contract is formed before delivery (and indeed B may well become owner of the car as a result of this contract)[61] and payment and what amounts to consideration are the promises moving from each party (promise for a promise). It is thus a mistake to think that when one goes into a shop to buy a newspaper the consideration consists of the handing over of the money and the paper. This handing over is the *performance* of the contract. In theory the contract is formed beforehand and the consideration consists of the promise to pay and the promise to convey title in the paper. Of course reality may telescope the two aspects of contract, but that does not mean that they should be telescoped at the level of contract theory. Unilateral contracts are different, for here only one party makes a promise (for example the Carbolic Smoke Ball Co) while the other party (Mrs Carlill) promises nothing. Consequently the consideration moving from the promisee can only be the performance.

A third distinction that is of importance is that between sufficient and adequate consideration. In order to support the existence of a contract the consideration must be sufficient, that is to say of some (however small) economic value. For example even three wrappers from a bar of chocolate can amount to sufficient consideration if they are required to claim a 'free' gift.[62] But promising something in return for 'love and affection' will probable not be sufficient. Consideration need not, however, be adequate. That is to say that a promise to sell a valuable painting for one penny will be sufficient and the court will not be concerned whether or not it is a fair price, save in circumstances where for example fraud or undue influence is in issue.

---

[61] Sale of Goods Act 1979, ss 16–18.
[62] *Chappell & Co v Nestle Ltd* [1960] AC 87.

VARIATION OF EXISTING CONTRACTS

Most consumer and commercial contracts do not give rise to consideration problems since goods and services are rarely supplied free.[63] Promises within the family can of course be problematic, but this is partly because the courts do not always wish to turn family arrangements into binding contracts.[64] Where problems can arise in the commercial world is in two situations, the first being the variation or modification of an existing set of promises and the second being the enforceability of debts. This can be difficult because one party may agree to a modification and the only way the English courts seemed to have been able to handle this is by treating the variation or modification as a new promise. Accordingly it must in theory be supported by consideration.

In *Ward v Byham*[65] Denning LJ thought that a promise to perform an existing duty ought to be regarded as good consideration because it is a benefit and this view seems now to have been accepted by the Court of Appeal. Or, at least, it seems to have been accepted in certain commercial circumstances. In *Williams v Roffey Brothers*[66] a carpenter brought an action for an extra sum of money promised to him by a building contractor. The sum had been promised in return for the carpenter completing within a particular time limit the refurbishment of 27 flats, a job that the carpenter had already been contracted to do, by the contractor, for an agreed price of £20,000 and on which he had completed about third of the total job. After the completion of some more flats, the carpenter claimed the extra sum promised but the defendant building contractor argued that the extra sum promised was not supported by consideration. The Court of Appeal allowed the carpenter's claim for the extra money to succeed on the basis that 'there was clearly a commercial advantage to both sides from a pragmatic point of view'[67]. And, with respect to the rule of consideration, 'the courts nowadays should be more ready to find its existence so as to reflect the intention of the parties to the contract where the bargaining powers are not unequal and where the finding of consideration reflect the true intention of the parties'.[68]

This case may be exceptional. For a start, the Court of Appeal did

---

[63] But cf *Esso Petroleum Ltd v Commissioners of Custom and Excise* [1976] 1 WLR 1.
[64] *Jones v Padavatton* [1969] 1 WLR 328.
[65] [1956] 2 All ER 318.
[66] [1991] 1 QB 1.
[67] [1991] 1 QB at 22 per Purchas LJ.
[68] [1991] 1 QB 1 at 18 per Russell LJ.

not discard either the necessity of consideration or the original case that established the existing duty rule.[69] It made a decision within a particular, and modern, commercial context. Furthermore, the facts disclosed no improper pressure on the part of the carpenter; he had genuinely underpriced the job and was not trying to blackmail the contractor into paying more.[70] In addition, *Roffey* is not authority for the proposition that a promise by a creditor to accept a sum less than the debt is enforceable as a contractual promise.[71] Nevertheless, despite these reservations, *Roffey* remains to date a leading consideration case and is a clear example of a commercial promise being held enforceable on the basis of the facts before the court.

Yet even if consideration is insufficient to support a contractual promise this does not necessarily mean that the promise is without legal effect. A promise is a specific form of representation (statement) and certain representations made by one party to another can have legal effects in equity if it has been relied upon to that person's detriment. Equity, using its doctrine of estoppel, will prevent in such circumstances a person going back on his promise. This doctrine of estoppel was extended to situations where one contractor promises not to enforce his full contractual rights and the other contractor relies upon this statement. For example where a landlord, in order to encourage a tenant to remain in one of his flats, informs the tenant that he need pay only half the rent stipulated in the lease, this promise, although not supported by consideration, will be effective in equity. The landlord will be estopped from enforcing his right to the full debt during the period he has indicated to the tenant that he need pay only the reduced amount.[72] This principle can be seen as an equitable intervention to prevent a contractor from abusing his common law (contract) right. However if the person seeking equity's aid is himself guilty of abusive behaviour the aid will be withheld under the principle that he who comes to equity must come with clean hands. This will allow the other contractor to enforce his full contractual right to the original debt.[73] What if a contractor subsequently promises more than the original sum? The Court of Appeal in *Williams v Roffey* has left open the question as to whether estoppel might apply; but it is generally considered that estoppel is a shield not a sword and this presents a difficulty. Estoppel is not a cause of action

---

69 *Stilk v Myrick* (1809) 2 Camp 317; 170 ER 1168.
70 cf *D & C Builders Ltd v Rees* [1966] 2 QB 617.
71 *In Re Selectmove Ltd* [1995] 1 WLR 474.
72 *Central London Property Trust Ltd v High Trees House Ltd* [1947] 1 KB 130; *Collier v P & M J Wright (Holdings) Ltd* [2008] 1 WLR 643.
73 *D & C Builders Ltd v Rees* [1966] 2 QB 617.

and functions only at the level of remedies. All the same, it could be used to prevent a defendant from raising in court the inexistence of a contract.

It should be evident from these cases that the common law does not have a theory of variation of contracts. In order to change an existing contract the old contract has to be extinguished and a new one created. This is in contrast to the civil law which, of course, tends to think in terms not just of a contract but also of a *iuris vinculum* between the parties itself governed by a general theory (see Chapter 3). Such a general theory level permits the possibility of variation of an existing contract without having to return to formation principles; once formed the consensus aspect remains active at the general level and contracts can be adjusted accordingly (see UNIDROIT art 3.2). English law cannot easily copy this approach for the simple reason that it does not conceive of any obligation which transcends the categories of contract, tort, restitution and equity. It can only think in terms of enforceable promises and thus gets trapped by the consideration requirement.

CONSIDERATION AND THIRD PARTIES

The second situation where consideration, or the lack of it, can cause problems is where it has not moved from the actual claimant or victim of the breach of promise. This rule is closely associated with another principle known as privity of contract and basically declares that only the actual parties to a contract can be bound within the contractual nexus.[74] Thus, at common law, if A promises B, in return for consideration supplied by B, that he will pay C a sum of money C cannot, in principle, according to the case law, sue to enforce the promise. This rule – or at least the rule of privity of contract – was confirmed by the House of Lords in the 1968 case of *Beswick v Beswick*.[75] Equally if A makes a contract with B containing a clause that neither B nor C will be able to sue A for damages should A be in breach, C will not in principle be bound by the clause.[76] The principle of privity arises out of the nature of an obligation itself: it is strictly *in personam* and thus cannot bind third parties (otherwise it would be effectively creating rights *in rem*). In civil law this rule is known as the relative effect of contract.

The principle of privity is, then, clear enough and it would be mislead-

---

[74] cf *Darlington BC v Wiltshier Northern Ltd* [1995] 1 WLR 68.
[75] [1968] AC 58.
[76] *Morris v C W Martin & Sons Ltd* [1966] 1 QB 716.

ing to suggest that the rule has not created difficulties for third parties harmed by another's breach of contract. Equally it has created problems for contracting parties hoping to limit their liabilities arising out of poor or non-performance of contracts. It would, however, be just as misleading to overstate the effects of the privity rule since the courts have developed a range of important exceptions. Moreover statute has now intervened in order to give a third party beneficiary a general right to sue, in certain circumstances, for a breach of a contractual promise.

The Contracts (Rights of Third Parties) Act 1999 permits a third party who is not a party to a contract to enforce in his own right a term of the contract in two situations. First if the contract expressly provides that he may (s (1)(a)) and, secondly, where a contract term purports to confer a benefit on him (s 1(1)(b)). The third party must be expressly identified in the contract by name, as a member of a class or as answering a particular description, although he need not be in existence at the time of the contract (s 1(3)). In the leading English privity case of *Beswick v Beswick* the wife of a dead contractor was not allowed to enforce the contract in her own name despite being specifically named as a promisee. Today she would probably be able directly to sue thanks to section 1 of the 1999 Act.

Some of the most troublesome cases have been in the area of carriage of goods by sea where contracts have purported to confer benefits on for example stevedores.[77] Although the new Act excludes carriage of goods contracts covered by their own international conventions, it expressly allows third parties in such contracts to take the benefit of exclusion or limitation clauses (s 6(5)). More generally it has to be said that the 1999 Act stands in stark contrast to the short provision in the PECL (art 6.110) since there are many restrictions and defences that make the 1999 statute rather long and complex. Moreover it is by no means clear, despite its length and complexity, that the 1999 Act has resolved all of the traditional problem areas in this part of the law of obligations. A father contracts with a tour operator for a holiday for himself and his family; the holiday, in breach of contract, proves a most unpleasant experience.[78] Does the 1999 Act allow the mother and children each to sue the tour operator for breach of its contractual promise to provide a reasonable holiday? Perhaps a more fundamental example is *Donoghue v Stevenson*.[79] Would Mrs Donoghue, who was made ill by a defective bottle of ginger beer purchased for her in a café by a friend, now have an action against the seller of the contami-

---

[77] See *Scruttons Ltd v Midland Silicones Ltd* [1962] AC 446.
[78] See *Jackson v Horizon Holidays Ltd* [1975] 1 WLR 1468.
[79] [1932] AC 562.

nated ginger beer for breach of section 14 of the Sale of Goods Act 1979 (assuming the facts arose in England)? Care must be taken, therefore, before asserting that the privity rule has been abolished in English law; it has not. What the Act does is to recognise the civilian notion that a contractor can stipulate for a third party; and it does this, not by abolishing the privity rule, but by granting a remedy, in certain circumstances, to the third party.

DEED OF COVENANT

Form can equally be important in ensuring that a promise is enforceable even in the absence of consideration. English law has for most of its history recognised that a promise made under seal is enforceable as a deed and what gives the promise its legal force is the form in which it is made (document plus seal). The theory in some ways echoes the one behind the Roman *stipulatio*, but the history of the deed is very different. It arises out of the tradition that the courts would never look behind the sealed document.[80] In 1989 the requirement of an actual seal was abolished and, in its place, Parliament has declared that a deed need only be described as such and should carry an attested signature.[81] The potential of this statutory form of contracting is rather interesting; it is a little like the *stipulatio* in as much as it is a method of pure form for creating a binding promissory obligation free of all the substantive necessities associated with the parole contract. But it seems that only those with a sense of history appreciate this potential.

---

[80] Ibbetson (1999), at 241.
[81] Law of Property (Miscellaneous Provisions) Act 1989, s 1.

7. Escaping from contracts

Few books on the law of contract have chapters on how to escape from the obligation because such a category does not really conform to what might be called the classical model. Contracts can of course be set aside or declared inexistent, but bringing together under one heading all of the different arguments that might be used by a party to evade its duties could be seen as somewhat cynical. Nevertheless such a 'cynical' category can reflect commercial reality, for the law reports are full of cases where parties simply want to escape from the *vinculum iuris*. At any rate, having examined how contracts are enforceable, it might be useful to look at the reverse side of the coin so to speak. Assuming that a person is a party to a contract or imagined contract, how might such a party go about freeing itself from the contractual obligation if such an obligation is no longer proving convenient? This question brings into focus a number of areas of the classical model contract, in particular vitiating factors and discharge of obligations.

DEFECTIVE CONTRACTS

The distinction between promise and agreement underpins a section of contract formation law known to a civil lawyer as 'defects' or 'obstacles to consent'. If contract is founded upon agreement and *consensus ad idem*, any obstacle that impedes the meeting of the two *volontés* (wills) must by definition threaten the coming into existence of the *vinculum iuris* and this is why French lawyers talk of *vices du consentement*. English law, in contrast, is based on promise and it does not necessarily follow that because a promise was given under conditions that might be seen as an 'obstacle' or *vice* that such an obstacle threatens the very existence of the promise. Objectively the promise may remain valid. However this does not mean that English contracts are not subject to vitiating factors which may generate, or open the way for, a remedy.

In the *Code civil* article 1109 declares that: 'There is no valid consent if the consent was given only by error, or was extorted by duress or obtained by fraud.' This provision is of course perfectly logical given the *conventio* basis of contract. Thus a person who consents, labouring under a mistake, is said not to consent at all ('*non videntur qui errant consentire*', as Pothier put it). Yet, even where the foundation of the contract is promise, duress and fraud must equally impact upon the normative force of the promise that results. Consequently the idea of *vices* or defects in formation is to be found, to a greater or lesser extent, in all Western contract systems, even if the idea itself is quite recent.[1]

However, as between the civilian and the common law traditions, there is an important difference of emphasis that in turn can be related to the subjective and objective approaches. Generally speaking, although this is not fully and reliably reflected in the whole of the case law, promise, being more formal than agreement, is less sensitive from an internal position to problems of *vices du consentement*. Now, this not to say that such *vices* will not impact upon the enforceability of the promise. The point to be made – particularly given the dichotomy in England between law and Equity – is that *vices* are approached more from an external position. In other words the law of equity and of tort impact upon the law of contract.

The dichotomy between an external and an internal approach to the problems of *vices* is also tied in with the different types of defect that can affect a contract in English law. A contract – or one should say 'contract'– can be defective in that it does not actually exist in law. Such contracts are said to be *void*. In truth, of course, a 'void contract is strictly a contradiction in terms, because if an agreement is truly void, it is not a contract'. However 'the term is a useful one and well understood by lawyers'.[2] For example, the possibility clearly exists that a contract may be fundamentally defective simply because there is no matching offer and acceptance. One leading case here is that of *Raffles v Wichelhaus*[3] which concerned a contract for a cargo on board a ship called the *Peerless*. In fact there were two ships of the same name and one of the parties was thinking of one while the other was thinking of the other ship. It was held that there was no binding contract. How is this case to be analysed given the ambiguity of the law report? One answer is to say that it is not a matter of 'mistake' as such; there is no contract simply because there is no offer and acceptance in respect of the same object (or person) and thus *no enforceable agreement or set of promises*. A similar analysis might be made in situations where there is extreme duress ('an offer he cannot refuse'); an acceptance in such circumstances is simply not an 'acceptance'. It is in these situations that a common lawyer would talk of a *void* contract, that is to say a contract that

---

[1] Lévy and Castaldo (2002), at 811.
[2] Dyson LJ in *Islington LBC v Uckac* [2006] 1 WLR 1303, at para 25.
[3] (1864) 159 ER 375.

never existed. And it never existed because there was a lack of proper offer and acceptance.

The expression 'void' contract needs to be distinguished from 'voidable' contract. 'A contract which is voidable', said an English judge a few years ago, 'exists until and unless it is set aside by an order of rescission made by the court at the instance of a party seeking to terminate it or bring it to an end.'[4] Accordingly a voidable contract cannot be described as never existing; it exists but is subject to one party's right to set the contract aside, normally for misrepresentation, duress or undue influence. If the party decides to exercise this right, the contract will come to an end. However this termination will not act retrospectively, unless it is rescission *ab initio*, and thus the expression voidable contract is not a contradiction in terms.

The right to rescind does not, as a matter of history, arise from internal contractual rules; it was granted by the Court of Chancery through the equitable remedy of rescission. One distinction, then, between void and voidable contracts is that the former usually involves rules of common law while the latter is a matter of Equity. The dichotomy is no longer perfect, it must be said, because there is now a right to rescind at common law, but from the historical perspective the dichotomy makes sense. The dichotomy remains of importance, however, in that it gives rise to an interesting question. If a party does have a right to rescind the contract in equity, does this mean that the other party is guilty of a breach of duty capable of giving rise, not just to rescission in equity, but also to an action for damages? A clear answer to this problem has been given by Lord Millet in the 2001 case of *Agnew v Länsförsäkringsbolagens AB*.[5] It gives no such right to damages. Nevertheless, what is intriguing about Lord Millett's analysis, is that he recognised that what counsel was trying to do was to turn the equitable 'duty' (giving rise to rescission) into a common law duty via the medium of an obligation of good faith. In rejecting this analysis, the Law Lord was, of course, reaffirming not just the distinction between common law and equity but also the absence of an independent doctrine of good faith.

Void and voidable contracts have in turn to be distinguished from an unenforceable one. This idea of an unenforceable contract arises as a result of English law traditionally distinguishing between rights and remedies: a contract might exist at the level of legal rights but the courts, perhaps because of the illegality of one or more of the promises, refuse to grant any remedy. The contract thus becomes unenforceable. This

---

[4] Dyson LJ in *Islington LBC v Uckac* [2006] 1 WLR 1303, at para 26.
[5] [2001] 1 AC 223.

situation may give the impression that the contract is in reality void (or has been rescinded), yet an unenforceable contract is different because it can, unlike a void contract, have some effects. It can for example act as a means of passing title in property.[6]

DEFECTIVE CONTRACTS AND REMEDIES

This distinction between right and remedy illustrates another external approach to the problem of error, duress or fraud: the law can provide remedies independent of contract for the innocent contracting party. This is the approach to be found in Roman law in respect of fraud and duress, for these were wrongs giving rise to delictual actions and thus were designed to protect victims against loss by allowing them to sue for damages. Another possibility was for the law to grant an action in restitution, which indeed, if available, would take precedence over an action for *dolus malus* (D.4.2.14.1).

This remedies approach is an important characteristic of the common law as well. It was the Court of Chancery that provided the remedy of equitable rescission to relieve a party who had been induced to enter a contract as a result of a false statement (misrepresentation) or duress (which includes undue influence). A misrepresentation is traditionally defined as an untrue statement of existing fact which induces the representee to enter into a contract with the representor. The word 'statement' is not confined literally to speech; various other kinds of acts and omissions can be construed on occasions as representations. And the word 'fact' now includes, as a result of a major House of Lords decision in the law of restitution, an untrue statement of law.[7] If the misrepresentation was made fraudulently this also gave rise to a damages action in tort for deceit and today this tort is available to a contracting party even in the absence of fraud.[8] One might note here how the emphasis is not on error or fraud as such, but on the words uttered by a party to induce a contract. This is why an English judge has observed that 'there is . . . no general principle of law that fraud vitiates consent'. The 'effect of fraud is simply to give the innocent party the right, subject to certain limits, to rescind the contract'.[9]

What if there is an error but no misrepresentation? The leading author-

---

[6] cf *Shogun Finance Ltd v Hudson* [2004] 1 AC 919.
[7] *Kleinwort Benson Ltd v Lincoln CC* [1999] 2 AC 349.
[8] Misrepresentation Act 1967, s 2(1).
[9] Goff LJ in *Whittaker v Campbell* [1984] QB 318, at 326–7; confirmed in *Shogun Finance Ltd v Hudson* [2004] 1 AC 919, at para 7.

ity on mistake is the House of Lords decision in *Bell v Lever Brothers*.[10] A company, which had made termination contracts with two of its directors, brought an action to have the contracts set aside after subsequently discovering that the directors had committed serious breaches of their contracts of employment while working for the claimant company. These breaches would have permitted the company to dismiss the directors without compensation. The company equally sought return of the compensation payments they had made in performance of the termination contracts. The jury returned a verdict that the two directors had not fraudulently concealed their breaches. The trial judge, the Court of Appeal and two Law Lords thought that the termination contracts were void for mistake, but the majority of the House of Lords thought that the contracts were valid. Lord Atkin stressed two fundamental points. First, that it was vital to keep in mind the jury verdict acquitting the directors of fraudulent misrepresentation or concealment; and, secondly, that the company got exactly what it bargained for, namely the retirement of the directors. 'It seems', said the Law Lord, 'immaterial that [the company] could have got the same result in another way'.[11]

Lord Atkin went on to give a number of analogous examples. Most of these involve buying something that either the buyer or both parties believed to be much better quality than it turned out to be; provided that the seller has made no representation or warranty the contract is not void. This may be unjust on the buyer, but, said the Law Lord, the example 'can be supported on the ground that it is of paramount importance that contracts should be observed, and that if parties honestly comply with the essentials of the formation of contracts – ie, agree in the same terms on the same subject-matter – they are bound, and must rely on the stipulations of the contract for protection from the effect of facts unknown to them'.[12] This mention of stipulations does, however, provide an insight into how the courts can declare a contract void for mistake even if there is no misrepresentation. If a fact is so fundamental to the whole transaction it is possible for a court to imply a condition into the contract to this effect.

The rigour of this common law position was, until recently, partly mitigated by the equitable remedy of rescission. According to a decision given in 1950 equity could set aside a contract for mistake,[13] but the Court of Appeal has recently ruled that this decision is wrong and that there is no

---

[10] [1932] AC 161.
[11] *Ibid*, at 224.
[12] *Ibid*, at 224.
[13] *Solle v Butcher* [1950] 1 KB 671.

such equitable jurisdiction.[14] It may well be, therefore, that the remedy of rescission in equity is no longer available for mistake. However equity is still not entirely excluded. Another important remedy for mistake is rectification and this is available to correct a written contractual document that wrongly records what was clearly agreed between the parties, for example a £200,000 price stated as £20,000. What the court does here is to order that the document itself be corrected. This remedy of rectification in equity is not one that strictly allows a party to escape from the contract, but it does allow him to escape from the contract as recorded in a contractual document.

IMPLIED CONDITION

One approach to mistake, as we have mentioned, is to imply a condition (promise) into the contract that if the object of the contract turns out to be quite different from the object promised then the contract is annulled. For example if S promises to sell to P a sterile cow but, before delivery, the cow proves to be fertile (and thus of much higher value), the contract could be said to be void on the basis that there was an implied condition precedent that the cow be sterile. It has to be said that the courts are very reluctant to do this since they tend to put the emphasis on the form rather than the substance, treating the latter as a question of risk.[15] And this reluctance might even have been strengthened by the knowledge that equity could always intervene (although even here the courts were not prepared to interfere with normal commercial risks). However it may be that the whole conceptual basis of mistake in English law has changed as a result of a recent Court of Appeal decision. For the Court has stated that it does 'not consider that the doctrine of common mistake can be satisfactorily explained by an implied term' even if 'an allegation that a contract is void for common mistake will often raise important issues of construction'.[16]

One might note here that the topic of implied terms in the common law covers what in civil law is often described as simply 'interpretation of contracts'. Accordingly mistake in English law might now be summed up as follows: 'Where it is possible to perform the letter of the contract, but it is alleged that there was a common mistake in relation to a fundamental assumption which renders performance of the essence of the obligation

---

[14] *The Great Peace* [2003] QB 679.
[15] *William Sindall Plc v Cambridgeshire CC* [1994] 1 WLR 1016.
[16] *The Great Peace* [2003] QB 679, at para 82.

impossible, it will be necessary, by *construing* the contract in the light of all the material circumstances, to decide whether this is indeed the case.'[17]

EUROPEAN APPROACH

The PECL and UNIDROIT have on the whole amalgamated the two approaches to *vices du consentement*. That is to say they have internalised the approach so that fraud, mistake and duress are now matters of validity (see PECL Chapter 4 and UNIDROIT Chapter 3) but, at the same time, have retained a trace of the English law of misrepresentation (PECL art 6.101) and the concept of an implied term (PECL art 6.102 and UNIDROIT art 5.2). There remain, also, traces of a remedies approach in as much as damages and avoidance of contract are retained as separate entitlements (PECL art 4.117; UNIDROIT art 3.18); and, under UNIDROIT, a party cannot avoid the contract for mistake if he has an alternative remedy for non-performance (art 3.7; but cf PECL art 4.119).

One important development in the PECL is that mistake has now been made the subject of good faith (PECL art 4.103(1)(a)(ii)), although in UNIDROIT there is the (lesser?) obligation of 'reasonable commercial standards of fair dealing' (art 3.5(1)(a)). Subjecting mistake to an obligation of good faith could have far-reaching consequences for the traditional English approach since it might put a contracting party under a positive obligation to inform. Thus two of the most fundamental English mistake cases, namely *Smith v Hughes*[18] and *Bell v Lever Brothers*,[19] might have been decided quite differently if the PECL had applied to their facts. It is, of course, unlikely that the PECL will replace English contract law in the foreseeable future,[20] but one might still reflect upon whether the interpretation (construction) approach asserted in *The Great Peace*[21] allows for the presumption of reasonableness or good faith.

PROPERTY PROBLEMS

The distinction between void and voidable contracts becomes vital in situations where a contractor is mistaken as to the identity of his co-contractor

---

[17] *Ibid*.
[18] (1871) LR 6 QB 597.
[19] [1932] AC 161.
[20] Ashton (Baroness) (2006).
[21] [2003] QB 679.

(*error in persona*). Most of these cases follow a common pattern and give rise to a similar property problem: a rogue (R) assumes the identity of a famous celebrity in order to induce the seller (S) to hand over an item that he is offering for sale in return for a cheque, which subsequently turns out to be worthless, R having in the meantime sold the item on to an innocent third party purchaser (D). The problem arrives in court when S sues D for the return of 'his' item and the question thus to be decided is whether S or D is the owner.[22] Now it is clear that such a contract is *voidable* for misrepresentation, but this is often of little help to S because a voidable contract will nevertheless pass title from S to R and, provided that the contract has not been unilaterally rescinded by S, R then has a title he can pass on to D.[23] However if the contract between S and R is *void* at common law because S's offer was aimed only and exclusively at the celebrity, title in the item cannot pass to R and S will thus succeed in his claim against D in the tort of conversion. The question, therefore, in these cases is whether the seller intended to contract with the celebrity or the person actually standing before them.[24]

In some legal systems this problem cannot arise because a possessor of a chattel vis-à-vis an innocent third party buyer is deemed to be owner (see eg CC art 2279). However English law has never adopted this rule in its entirety and, moreover, has held on occasions that contracts can be void for mistake of identity.[25] In 1972 the Court of Appeal appeared to come down, definitively, on the side of D[26] – for if anyone is in a position to prevent this kind of fraud it is S rather than D – but the definitiveness of this approach has recently been reversed by the House of Lords in yet another case involving a car.[27] As one dissenting Law Lord observed, '[g]enerations of law students have struggled with this problem' and they 'may be forgiven for thinking that it is contrived by their tutors to test their mettle'.[28] The Law Lord went on to observe that German law favours protection of the innocent third party buyer and that English law, having adopted a different approach, has now put itself in a position that 'would make the contemplated harmonisation of the general principles of European contract law very difficult to achieve'.[29]

---

[22] *Shogun Finance Ltd v Hudson* [2004] 1 AC 919, at para 56.
[23] Sale of Goods Act 1979, s 23.
[24] *Shogun Finance Ltd v Hudson* [2004] 1 AC 919.
[25] *Ingram v Little* [1961] 1 QB 31.
[26] *Lewis v Averay* [1972] 1 QB 198.
[27] *Shogun Finance Ltd v Hudson* [2004] 1 AC 919.
[28] Lord Millett in *Shogun Finance Ltd v Hudson* [2004] 1 AC 919, at para 56.
[29] *Shogun Finance Ltd v Hudson* [2004] 1 AC 919, at para 86.

A similar property problem can arise out of an error in respect to the nature of the transaction itself (*error in negotio*). Again these errors usually arise out of fraud when one party misrepresents to the other the nature of the contract or the document to be signed. The object of the misrepresentation is for the representor to get possession or title to property which is then transferred for money to an innocent third party. The point to note here is that the equitable remedy of rescission is not really helpful since it makes the contract only *voidable*; what the claimant wants is an order or declaration that the contract is *void* in order to prevent the third party obtaining a property right. In this situation the common law does not approach the problem as one of formation but one where the victim raises a defence of *non est factum* (this is not my deed). This plea was originally designed to apply to forgery cases where the victim had not signed at all, but it was extended to cover certain cases where the victim had signed.

However, for this defence to succeed and the victim to escape from the contract without property loss, the facts must be exceptional because there is a presumption that a contractor will read any contractual document presented to him or her. The plea will be effective (and the contract declared void), if, first, the representee signed without any negligence on his or her part and, secondly, if the contract is radically different from the one the signer believed it to be.[30] The object of this rule is to effect a compromise as between victim and innocent third party. However if the third party is less than innocent, it may find itself unable to enforce, for example, any contract it has as a result of the fraud with the victim.[31]

FRAUD AND DURESS

The French *Code civil* talks not just of error but also of fraud and duress as obstacles to consent (art 1109). Where they exist they create difficulties at the level of formation. In English law fraud and duress do not function at the level of formation even if they are seen as impacting on consent; a contract can certainly exist at common law despite the presence of these two factors. However they both have the capacity to make a contract voidable. As we have seen, there is no general rule that fraud vitiates consent. What fraud does is to give the victim a right to rescind the contract in equity (and perhaps at common law) and (or) to sue for damages in the tort of deceit. Many fraud cases involve a fraudulent statement by one party to the other

---

[30] *Saunders v Anglia Building Society* [1971] AC 1004.
[31] *Avon Finance Co Ltd v Bridger* [1985] 2 All ER 281.

and this means that most of the fraud cases end up under the heading of fraudulent misrepresentation.

Duress, like fraud, gives rise to a right to rescind the contract, but, as with fraud, it seems that the rules relating to duress are not strictly internal to the law of contract. No doubt it could be argued that certain kinds of menaces are so intense that they impact directly upon the very existence of consent, thus making the contract void rather than voidable. But this is not generally the approach of English law. Most fraud and duress cases were the concern of equity and the modern law probably reflects principles developed in Chancery.[32] Thus duress to the person or to goods will generally give rise to a right on the part of the victim to rescind provided that the duress has been a (and not necessarily the) cause for entering the contract.[33] Lesser forms of duress are more problematic.

One lesser form of duress that has given rise to a body of case law is where the threat is economic. Equity has been prepared to aid a victim of this form of behaviour in an indirect way,[34] but as a direct basis for obtaining rescission the development is relatively recent and belongs more to the law of restitution (unjust enrichment) than to contract. English law now accepts that the equitable remedy of rescission will be available for certain kinds of economic duress.[35]

The starting point is probably clear enough: a contractor who threatens to do a legally wrongful act (a crime, tort or breach of contract) will prima facie be guilty of economic duress rendering any contract resulting from the exercise of the threat voidable. This rescission rule is also to be found in the PECL (art 4.108(a)), but the provision in UNIDROIT is in many ways more interesting. 'A party may avoid the contract', states article 3.9, 'when he has been led to conclude the contract by the other party's unjustified threat which, having regard to the circumstances, is so imminent and serious as to leave the first party no reasonable alternative.' This provision is more restrictive than the one in the PECL in that it specifically incorporates the 'no reasonable alternative' test. As a result it may be closer to English law. Yet what both the PECL and UNIDROIT accept is that certain threats, even if not unlawful, may be sufficient to amount to economic duress ('lawful act duress'). There is some authority that this may be true of English law as well,[36] but a decision of the Court of

---

[32] Ibbetson (1999), at 235.
[33] *Barton v Armstrong* [1975] 2 All ER 465.
[34] *D & C Builders Ltd v Rees* [1966] 2 QB 617.
[35] *Pau On v Lau Yiu Long* [1980] AC 614.
[36] *Dimskal Shipping Co v ITWF (The Evia Luck)* [1992] 2 AC 152.

Appeal suggests otherwise.[37] This is an area of law that depends very much on the facts and the context within which the alleged economic duress is exercised.

Equity has made a further fundamental contribution to this area of 'lesser forms of duress' in recognising an equitable form called undue influence.[38] This form of duress grew out of the idea that certain relations of themselves gave rise to a situation where one party could exercise domination over the other.[39] In the 19th century undue influence remained largely confined to particular categories of relations such as parent and child, doctor and patient and the like, but in the latter half of the following century it saw an expansion into a fully developed principle applicable to commercial and consumer transactions.

Thus in *Lloyds Bank v Bundy*[40] the Court of Appeal set aside a contract between a bank and a farmer in which the farmer had charged his farm in support of his son's business debts. The court was of the view that the bank had abused its long-term relationship in failing to urge the elderly farmer to seek independent advice before signing the forms. In *Barclay's Bank v O'Brien*[41] the House of Lords went further and confirmed that a bank may be under an equitable duty to warn a client with whom it is negotiating a mortgage contract to seek independent advice even in cases where it is not the bank, but a third party, exercising the undue influence. If the bank has constructive knowledge of the undue influence, and fails to warn the client to seek independent advice, it will find that its contract might be subject to rescission. The case law is now complex, but if the undue influence is clear and obvious the bank will be under a high duty specifically to warn the client of his or her potential liabilities.[42] Where the influence is obvious and direct – for example the employer who induces a humble employee to mortgage his property for his boss's own interests – equity will use its remedy of rescission simply on the basis of conscience.[43]

The principal remedy for duress is rescission in equity. However economic duress could be said indirectly to have facilitated the victim's debt claim in *D & C Builders v Rees*[44] in that the court refused to allow the perpetrator to take advantage of promissory estoppel. And in *Williams v*

---

[37] *CTN Cash & Carry Ltd v Gallaher Ltd* [1994] 4 All ER 714.
[38] See *Royal Bank of Scotland v Etridge (No 2)* [2002] 2 AC 773, at paras 6–7.
[39] Ibbetson (1999), at 209.
[40] [1975] QB 326.
[41] [1994] 1 AC 180.
[42] *Royal Bank of Scotland v Etridge (No 2)* [2002] 2 AC 773.
[43] *Credit Lyonnais Bank Nederland v Burch* [1997] 1 All ER 144.
[44] [1966] 2 QB 617.

Roffey Brothers,[45] had the carpenter threatened not to continue with his existing contract, he would not have been able to claim the extra money. One who obtains a profit through duress might be liable to account to any victim through an action of account of profits. The interesting question is whether a victim can sue in damages. To be able to do this, the victim would have to prove damage and a cause of action in contract or tort. It is not easy to see how duress could amount to a breach of the actual contract that it induces, but causing damage through unlawful threats may give rise to a claim in the tort of intimidation. However the 'use of economic duress to induce another person to part with property or money is not a tort per se'.[46] But it will give rise to a claim in restitution (debt) for the return of any money paid, together with, of course, the rescission of any contract.

CAPACITY

In French contract law capacity is an essential condition for the formation of a contract (CC art 1108). Accordingly a minor cannot in principle contract (CC art 1124). In English law capacity is not an essential condition except perhaps in one or two situations. Thus a contract tainted by incapacity – usually one where one party is a minor (below the age of 18) or perhaps a contract with a mental incompetent – is prima facie valid and thus not void. It is only voidable or unenforceable and rescission or enforceability will depend upon the nature of the transaction and upon whether or not enforceability is unconscionable.[47] The exception is a public or a private corporation that has no power to contract; here the contract will be void on the basis that the corporation was acting *ultra vires*. In the case of commercial companies, thanks to statutory intervention, *ultra vires* contracts are no longer of great practical concern, but the same could not be said for public authorities,[48] although statute has now intervened in respect of the victims of *ultra vires* contracts with local authorities.[49]

One of the most serious problems that arises out of contracts made with a minor is in respect of money or property transferred to a minor under an unenforceable or voidable contract. Can the minor keep either the money or the property without having to pay? A minor or other human incompetent

---

[45] [1991] 1 QB 1.
[46] Lord Diplock in *Universe Tankships v International Transport Workers' Federation* [1983] 1 AC 366, at 385.
[47] *Hart v O'Connor* [1985] AC 1000 (PC).
[48] *Hazell v Hammersmith and Fulham LBC* [1992] 2 AC 1.
[49] See Turpin and Tompkins (2007), at 711.

must pay for necessary goods supplied to them[50] and now a court has been given power to order the return of 'property' acquired by a minor 'if it is just and equitable to do so'.[51] The Act does not define 'property' and so it is not clear from the text itself whether it covers money conveyed to a minor.

ILLEGALITY

Illegality is even more complex than capacity because, unlike French law which focuses on illegal cause (CC arts 1131, 1133) and object (art 1128), there is no single starting point and it is not even clear whether an illegal contract is void or unenforceable. Moreover the topic also embraces certain contracts that are not illegal in any moral sense but are void or unenforceable for reasons of public policy. The line between illegal and public policy contracts is not always easy to discern.

The first difficulty is to pin down exactly what is meant by illegality since it encompasses, at one extreme, serious criminal behaviour (*mala in se*) and, at the other extreme, breach of a technical statutory provision (*mala prohibita*). Historically no distinction, it seems, was made, but one key concept did emerge, that of public policy, and this proved useful because of its flexibility.[52] Flexibility is needed in this area because contracts can be tainted by illegality in a number of ways. There are contracts which in their very substance are illegal because the transaction itself is criminal (a contract to sell drugs or to have someone killed); there are other contracts which are illegal because of general social policy and (or) morality (for example prostitution). There is a further class of contracts which are not illegal per se but become illegal because of motive and performance (a contract to hire a carriage for prostitution).[53] In this latter situation the question then arises as to whether both parties were aware of the illegal motive or whether one party was innocent.

The primary practical question comes down to one of enforceability. Here two principles are said to govern. The first is the rule *ex turpi causa non oritur actio* (no action arises out of an illegal cause) which gives expression to the idea of unenforceability. Where both parties collude in the illegality it may well be that neither party will be allowed to sue if there is a breach of the contract.[54] Equally a contractor guilty of illegal behaviour

---

[50] Sale of Goods Act 1979, s 3. Mental Capacity Act 2005, s 7.
[51] Minors' Contracts Act 1987, s 3.
[52] Ibbetson (1999), at 212–3.
[53] *Pearce v Brooks* (1866) LR 1 Ex 213.
[54] *Ashmore, Benson, Pease & Co Ltd v A V Dawson Ltd* [1973] 1 WLR 828.

will not be allowed to sue on any contract connected with this behaviour if it would result in an unjustified enrichment.[55] Yet the rule is not rigidly applied and so much will depend upon the circumstances of the case and the relative guilt of each party.

The second principle used by the courts looks to the position of the parties: *in pari delicto potior est conditio defendentis (possidentis)* (where both parties are equally in the wrong, the position of the defendant (or possessor) is stronger). This rule evidently overlaps with the *ex turpi causa* maxim but it is wider in that it would prima facie seem to prohibit any action – even one that is not contractual – from coming to the aid of a party who has transferred money or property pursuant to an illegal contract.[56] One point to note is that both parties must be *in pari delicto* (equally guilty). Yet, more generally, it can be said that the rule is not rigidly applied and if a claimant is able to found his claim on a cause of action independent of the tainted contract – for example if he can sue in tort, quasi-contract or even on a collateral contract – he may succeed. Thus the owner of some machinery delivered under an illegal hire-purchase contract was able to sue for damages in the tort of conversion when the other party converted the property.[57]

There has been a further development in recent years with respect to the *in pari delicto* rule. In *Tinsley v Milligan*[58] a majority of the House of Lords decided that a woman who had transferred her share in a jointly purchased house to her partner, in order that the two of them could facilitate a social security fraud, could reclaim her equitable interest in the property despite the illegality. Several points emerge from the decision. First, that a person can at law enforce property rights against the possessor provided that one does not have to rely upon the illegal contract. Secondly, the court will no longer distinguish between common law and equitable property rights thus allowing the claimant to avoid (perhaps) the maxim that he who comes to equity must come with clean hands (one point that encouraged Lord Goff to dissent). Thirdly, that the courts are taking a measured approach towards restitution and illegal contracts; much will depend upon the facts including the nature and seriousness of the illegality, knowledge of the parties and so on. Two focal points perhaps emerge from this more flexible and discretionary approach: the courts will weigh deterrence (public interest) on the one hand against proportionality (private interests and unjusti-

---

[55] *Geismar v Sun Alliance Insurance* [1978] QB 383.
[56] See eg *Parkinson v College of Ambulance Ltd* [1925] 2 KB 1.
[57] *Bowmakers Ltd v Barnet Instruments Ltd* [1945] KB 65.
[58] [1994] 1 AC 340.

fied enrichment) on the other. If the judges had refused to aid the claimant in *Tinsley* the private interest and enrichment of one of the fraudsters would have been much enhanced thus affirming that, for her, crime pays. In other words, if the court had allowed the party effectively to escape from the contract it would have resulted in an unjustified benefit for the fraudster. The majority decision meant only that the status quo was restored.

In addition to contracts that are unenforceable because of illegality, common law and statute also treat certain other contracts as being 'void' for reasons of public policy. These contracts are not illegal as such since they often lack the moral dimension associated with illegality (although there is overlap). They are simply unenforceable for social or economic reasons. Thus gambling contracts were once 'null and void',[59] although insurance and investment transactions were always outside of this provision; and contracts in restraint of trade and certain anti-competitive agreements are void for economic policy reasons. Certain other contracts also fall into this public policy voidness class. Whether 'void' really means void or whether such contracts are just unenforceable is a debateable issue,[60] for parties to a gambling contract were not liable to make restitution[61] and restraint of trade provisions can be severed from unobjectionable parts of a contract. Yet, whatever the situation, restraint of trade and competition agreements are now specialist areas of commercial law and European economic law and the statute book itself is littered with sections declaring void or unenforceable either various types of agreements or particular provisions inserted into what are otherwise valid contracts.

CANCELLED CONTRACTS

A contract may also be in effect 'void' or 'voidable' if it is of a type in which one of the parties – normally a consumer – has a statutory right to cancel. Such a right is a real means of escape and, indeed, brings the whole idea of a binding contract concluded through offer and acceptance into question. Thus, with respect to a distance selling contract, a consumer has a right to cancel within seven working days of the receipt of the goods or services. If the consumer does cancel, 'the contract shall be treated as if it had not been made'.[62] In other words, the contract is void. This right of cancellation is

---

[59] But see now Gambling Act 2005, s 335.
[60] *Shell UK Ltd v Lostock Garages Ltd* [1976] 1 WLR 1187, at 1198 per Lord Denning MR.
[61] *Lipkin Gorman v Karpnale Ltd* [1991] 2 AC 548.
[62] Consumer Protection (Distance Selling) Regulations 2000, reg 10(2).

rather similar to the right of rescission accorded to a minor since they both could be said to depend upon the status of the contracting party. One might be tempted to say, therefore, that consumers are now a class of persons who should be considered from the angle of contractual capacity. Suppliers may well find that certain kinds of commercial contracts are not as binding as the traditional textbooks might lead them to believe.

NON-PERFORMANCE OF A CONTRACT

So far the primary, although not exclusive, means of escape from a contract has been via the equitable remedy of rescission or by claiming that the contract is inexistent or unenforceable. However the common law allows a contractor, both directly and indirectly, to escape from the contract in a number of situations where performance of the contract has failed or is defective. In particular a contractual party faced with a serious breach of a fundamental contractual promise (called a condition) has the remedy at common law of escaping from the contract and, if he has suffered damage, suing in damages. Put another way, one contractor is obliged to perform his promise only if the other contractor performs his basic promises.[63] This is a real escape hatch, so to speak, and a well-drafted commercial contract could be phrased in such a way as to allow a contractor to repudiate the whole contract even if, say, a payment is five minutes late.

A contractor may find himself freed from a contract as a result of an intervening event, arising through the fault of neither party, which destroys the commercial basis of the contract. Thus a contractor who undertook to pay a high rental sum for use of rooms to view the King's coronation was freed from the contractual debt when the coronation was cancelled.[64] Another means of escape is for a party to renegotiate the whole contract with the other party; if successful the first contract will be replaced by a second contract. Perhaps the most obvious way of 'escaping' from a contract is to perform one's promises. However all of these performance issues will be discussed in more depth in the next chapter since many such situations involve claims not just for freeing oneself from the obligation but, more importantly, for compensatory damages.

---

[63] *Bolton v Mahadeva* [1972] 1 WLR 1009.
[64] *Krell v Henry* [1903] 2 KB 740.

8. Unperformed contracts and appropriate remedies

English works on the law of contract do not on the whole have sections or chapters devoted to non-performance of contracts. Indeed to subdivide contract into just two parts – formation and non-performance – is very civilian. Moreover to try to approach English law from this general viewpoint has been described as 'somewhat alarming' because 'it is so general, too general for . . . intellectual comfort'.[1] Interestingly Tony Weir gives as one of the reasons for discomfort the distinction between promise and contract, pointing out that non-performance in English law tends to centre on the unperformed promise rather than the unperformed contract. Nevertheless in a general work on the law of obligations the idea of non-performance as a viewpoint can be helpful in the understanding of the structure of English contract law. It can also contribute to contract method since failure to perform is what usually gives rise to practical problems. Working back from these practical problems, one often has to examine and to interpret the contract itself.

INTERPRETATION AND LIABILITY

The contractual obligation having been formed, the next rational step is to examine its content. Where the contract has been reduced to writing this formal content will be evident from the written document. However because natural language can be ambiguous and because the parties cannot always foresee and provide for future events, certain clauses in the contract may well give rise to disputed interpretations. In substance, then, the content of the contract may be uncertain. Where a contract is silent about a particular event or factual circumstance a further interpretation problem arises. Can the court read into the contract certain obligations? However all this can be unrealistically abstract in as much as interpretation and content issues usually arise only when something has gone wrong

---

[1] Weir (1999).

and one of the parties is threatening to have recourse to a legal or self-help remedy. This is why content and interpretation should be seen as part of the more general topic of liability.

How, then, should contractual liability be approached? In civilian thinking a contract is more than the sum of its parts; it is an obligation – a *vinculum iuris* – binding two parties and having an existence, so to speak, of its own. English law, in contrast, enforces promises and thus a contract is simply a bundle of promises. As we shall see, these promises may vary in importance and status. Yet when things go wrong the reaction of contract lawyers is to locate the precise promise, or promises, that remain unfulfilled or broken.

Now this promise approach has the merit of focusing attention on very precise areas of the contract and in commercial contracts, which are normally reduced to writing, this means that the text becomes the object of attention. Contractual interpretation might easily, then, have developed rules analogous to interpretation of statutes. Yet this did not happen – or at least the rules of interpretation did not become fixed and assessable in quite the same way as for statutes – and one reason for this is that the structure and status of promises became so dominant that they focused attention on a number of terms of art. Remedies came to be dependent upon whether a promise (term) was a 'condition' or a 'warranty'. In addition, another dichotomy – that between express and implied terms – had the effect of fragmenting interpretation behind tests that looked to structure and content rather than linguistic analysis. And perhaps the same can be said of the distinction between 'terms' and 'representations'.[2] Interpretation and content have tended, therefore, to merge in English contract law.

In the civil law, however, interpretation of contracts is recognised as a specific aspect of contract knowledge. This is largely because the *Code civil* and other codes have a section specifically devoted to this issue (see PECL Chapter 5). Yet there is also a general tendency in the civilian world to treat interpretation of contracts within the topic of interpretation of texts in general and thus contracts are subjected to the same methods as statutory texts. In the common law world, in contrast, interpretation of contracts is not traditionally to be found as a free-standing topic in the textbooks (although there are exceptions). In addition, it is very rare for statutory interpretation methods to be cited as the means to be adopted with respect to contracts, although, again, there are exceptions.[3] In fact,

---

[2] See *Hopkins v Tanqueray* (1854) 15 CB 130; 139 ER 369.
[3] See eg Lord Denning MR in *Staffs Area Health Authority v South Staffs Waterworks Co* [1978] 1 WLR 1387.

while there are specific textual interpretation cases in the common law contract books, many problems are to be found in chapters on express terms, implied terms and exclusion clauses; and these problems often take as their starting point the issue of liability.

DIFFERENCES OF APPROACH

Common law and civil appear to take diametrically opposed approaches in respect of the interpretation of contracts. The PECL declare that a 'contract is to be interpreted according to the common intention of the parties even if this differs from the literal meaning of the words' (art 5.101(1)). And this provision in turn has doubtless been influenced by a provision in the French *Code civil* (art 1156). In the common law, in contrast, intention 'is determined by reference to expressed rather than actual intention'.[4] The policy behind this approach has been explained by Lord Bridge in *The Chikuma*:

> The ideal at which the courts should aim, in construing such clauses, is to produce a result, such that in any given situation both parties seeking legal advice as to their rights and obligations can expect the same clear and confident answer from their advisers and neither will be tempted to embark on long and expensive litigation in the belief that victory depends on winning the sympathy of the court.

As he admitted, this 'ideal may never be fully attainable, but we shall certainly never even approximate to it unless we strive to follow clear and consistent principles and steadfastly refuse to be blown off course by the supposed merits of individual cases'.[5] A similar view has been expressed by Lord Goff. An 'objective interpretation is of paramount importance in commercial affairs' since not only is it important that they can rely on courts and arbitrators but 'in the commercial world contracting parties have to look after their own interests'.[6]

These comments have of course to be understood in the context of the actual contracts in issue, namely charterparties. And these contracts are notorious not just because they often raise interpretation issues but also because they function within a 'hard nose' business world. It may well be that other contracts, even commercial ones, attract a more flexible

---

[4] Lord Steyn in *Genossenschaftsbank v Burnhope* [1995] 1 WLR 1580, at 1587.
[5] [1981] 1 WLR 314, at 322.
[6] *The General Capinpin* [1991] 1 Ll Rep 1, at 9.

approach. In *Mannai Investment Co v Eagle Star Life Assurance* Lord Hoffmann said that 'the restriction on the use of background has been quietly dropped'[7] and, in the same case, Lord Steyn was of the view that one looked for 'the intention of the parties' which often meant that 'the reasonable commercial person is hostile to technical interpretations and undue emphasis on niceties of language'.[8] Indeed Lord Hoffmann has subsequently gone on to reinforce what he calls the 'common sense' approach to interpretation and so, in short, a strictly literal approach to the interpretation of a contractual text has now seemingly been abandoned with respect to many commercial contracts.[9] The approach is probably much closer to the one to be found in the PECL (art 5.102), although much will depend on the facts and context and it is unlikely that English law would fully subscribe to the good faith provision.

One principle that English law does share – or at least partly share – with civil law is *contra proferentem* rule which states that where 'there is doubt about the meaning of a contract term not individually negotiated, an interpretation of the term against the party who supplied it is to be preferred' (PECL art 5.103). In English law this rule applies to any clause that attempts to take away or cut down the customer's common law rights[10] and thus it is usually encountered in the area of exclusion and limitation clauses. However it may equally have a role in the interpretation of insurance contracts.[11]

TERMS

The dichotomy between agreement and promise and the importance of promise with respect to the contents of an English contract has already been mentioned. Promise explains the English approach to the structure of a contract. A contract is not a *vinculum iuris* founded on a single obligation; it consists of a bundle of promises, called 'terms', of differing intensity and status. These different classes of terms have attracted their own labels and these labels in turn have determined the contents and structure. Two classification dichotomies are particularly important: the distinction

---

[7] [1997] AC 749, at 779.
[8] *Ibid*, at 771.
[9] *Investors Compensation Scheme Ltd v West Bromwich Building Society* [1998] 1 WLR 896; and see also *Sirius International Insurance Co v FAI General Insurance Ltd* [2004] 1 WLR 3251, at para 19.
[10] *Adams v Richard & Starling Ltd* [1969] 1 WLR 1645.
[11] *Houghton v Trafalgar Insurance Co Ltd* [1954] 1 QB 247.

between 'conditions' and 'warranties' and the distinction between express and implied terms.

Before examining these dichotomies, something must again be said about the starting point of an English contract. It is in structure nothing more than the sum of its parts, that is to say a bundle of promises. Nevertheless the courts have recognised that a contract usually has some fundamental, or basic, promise upon which the whole contract rests. Thus, in a contract for the sale of a car, the fundamental promise made by the seller is that he will pass ownership in the vehicle to the buyer and if he fails to do this (passing only possession) there will be a 'total failure of consideration' allowing the buyer to reclaim the whole of the price of the vehicle even if he has had use of the car for six months.[12] This kind of thinking has given rise to the idea that there are certain 'fundamental' terms in every contract. In principle there is nothing wrong with this idea, but in the context of English law the notion of a fundamental term proved unfortunate because the expression was used to mean different things. In particular the fundamental term was seized upon as a weapon in the war against exclusion clauses and this, in the end, resulted in its demise as a term of art. One is left, all the same, with the notion of a 'total failure of consideration' and by ricochet with the idea that some promises are fundamental to the whole contract.

CONDITIONS AND WARRANITES

The idea of a fundamental term proved difficult for another reason, namely that it seemed to share much the same status as a 'condition.' In civilian legal systems', observed Lord Steyn, 'a condition is sharply distinguished from the actual terms of a contract' in as much as it 'is reserved for an external fact upon which the existence of the contract depends'. In English law, in contrast 'a condition frequently means an actual term of the agreement' and thus it is 'necessary to distinguish between promissory and contingent conditions'.[13]

A contingent condition is one where the contract is dependent upon the happening of an event (PECL art 16.101). Thus Mrs Carlill was entitled to claim her reward of £100 only on the happening of a condition, that is that she caught flu (cf PECL art 16.103(1)).[14] But, as Lord Reid pointed out in

---

[12] *Rowland v Divall* [1923] 2 KB 500.
[13] *Total Gas v Arco British* [1998] 2 Lloyd's Rep 209, at 220.
[14] *Carlill v Carbolic Smoke Ball Co* [1893] 1 QB 256.

Schuler AG v Wickman Machine Tools, in 'the ordinary use of the English language "condition" has many meanings, some of which have nothing to do with agreements'. Thus 'it may mean a pre-condition: something which must happen or be done before the agreement can take effect' or 'it may mean some state of affairs which must continue to exist if the agreement is to remain in force'.[15] Lord Reid added a third meaning: it 'is a term the breach of which by one party gives to the other an option either to terminate the contract or to let the contract proceed and, if he so desires, sue for damages for the breach'.[16] According to this third meaning, a condition is a promise that is fundamental to the contract and this is why, if broken, the other party has the right to refuse to go on with the contract. One contractor's performance is conditionally dependant on the other party's performance, performance here signifying the 'fundamental' substance of the contract itself reflected in the idea of a fundamental promise or term.

However if the term broken is only a 'warranty' the other party will not have a right to terminate; he will have a right only to damages.[17] Like 'condition', the word 'warranty' has several different meanings and this, equally, can cause confusion. For example the expression 'warranty' is sometimes used to describe a pre-contractual statement that is more than a mere 'representation'. It is a term of the contract itself or, if not part of the main contract, a promise capable of being a contractual promise collateral to the main contract.[18] Again, in insurance contracts, the expression 'warranty' has a meaning of its own.[19]

The main purpose of the dichotomy between conditions and warranties is to distinguish between what a civil lawyer would call fundamental and non-fundamental failures to perform. Only if the other party's non-performance is fundamental may a contractor terminate the contract (PECL art 9.301(1)). In focusing on the term, English law is achieving the same objective; yet, in placing the emphasis on the status of the promise, it has created a structure whose logic could on occasions lead to difficulty. What if the harm arising from a breach of a promise labelled a condition turned out only to be slight? According to the logic of the dichotomy if the promise broken is a 'condition' the victim can terminate the contract irrespective of the extent or seriousness of the harm. The logic can seemingly apply in reverse: if a contracting party suffers very serious damage, yet the

---

[15] [1974] AC 235, at 250–1. And see PECL art 16.103(2).
[16] *Ibid*, at 251.
[17] Sale of Goods Act 1979, s 11(3).
[18] *Dick Bentley Productions Ltd v Harold Smith (Motors) Ltd* [1965] 1 WLR 623.
[19] See eg Marine Insurance Act 1906, ss 33–41.

term broken is only a minor one, it could be argued that he has no right to repudiate. Despite this logic, in such a situation, if the damage is serious, the victim of the breach has the right to bring the contract to an end.[20] In other words it is difficult not to judge the situation in the light of the damage actually suffered by the innocent party. In the PECL, where the focus is on the non-performance, the position is more flexible in that the effects of the non-performance are taken into account in assessing whether or not the non-performance is fundamental. The non-performance must substantially deprive the other party 'of what it was entitled to expect under the contract' (art 8.103(b)).

The logical difficulty created by the English approach was appreciated by the Court of Appeal in the 1962 case of *Hong Kong Fir Shipping v Kawasaki Kisen Kaisha*.[21] In this case the court attempted to introduce into English law an approach not dissimilar to the PECL: before a contractor could be allowed to terminate the contract for breach of a term it should be asked if the innocent party had been substantially deprived of the whole benefit of the contract. The conditions and warranties dichotomy might work well enough in the area of sale of goods but this was not necessarily true of undertakings in general in the common law (Diplock LJ). The effect of the *Hong Kong* case proved ambiguous. Was it abandoning the condition and warranties dichotomy as a model generally applicable in contract or was it introducing a third class of term or promise that fell mid-way between these two? Many commentators took the latter view and thus was created the 'innominate' term. Such a term has been accepted by the case law, but it was re-asserted in 1981 that freedom of contract and contractual certainty dictated that parties ought to be allowed to continue to use 'condition' as a term of art (that is to say, if broken, the remedy of termination will be available). And so if the parties clearly label a term as a condition the court should give effect to their intentions.[22] Indeed, this point is possibly recognised by the PECL (art 8.103(a)).

IMPLIED TERMS

The idea of promise equally explains one of the most important conceptual devices of English contract law, the implied term. To paraphrase Lord Wright, the expression is used in different senses; sometimes it denotes a

---

[20] *Aerial Advertising Co v Batchelor's Peas Ltd* [1938] 2 All ER 788.
[21] [1962] 2 QB 26.
[22] *Bunge Corpn v Tradax Export* [1981] 1 WLR 711.

term which is not dependent on the actual intention of the parties but on a rule of law, such as the terms, warranties or conditions which, if not expressly excluded, the law imports, as for instance under the Sale of Goods Act 1979 and the Marine Insurance Act 1906. Sometimes the law, in certain circumstances, holds that a contract is dissolved if there is a vital change of conditions (as we have seen with mistake). Sometimes what it is sought to be implied in a contract is based on an intention imputed to the parties from their actual circumstances.[23]

Implied terms are central to the whole question of contractual liability in the common law and although they are said to be based on the presumed intention of the parties, questions of risk and status may have their role as well. This is particularly so in cases where a party seeks to imply a term on the actual facts of a case. Here the test is one of giving 'efficacy to the transaction' which, in commercial contracts, is shortened to the business efficacy test.[24] The court will imply a term on its facts if the contract would otherwise fail. However a number of requirements or reference points will guide the court and some of these are helpfully set out in article 5.2 of UNIDROIT. They are (a) the nature and purpose of the contract; (b) the practices established between the parties and usages; (c) good faith and fair dealing; and (d) reasonableness. All of these reference points, except perhaps good faith,[25] are to be found in English law and so, for example, the term to be implied must be reasonable. Lord Denning once tried to raise reasonableness to the test itself of when to imply a term, but this was subsequently rejected by the House of Lords.[26]

Terms can also be implied by law. Here what the court or the legislator does is to stipulate that in certain classes of contract particular promises will be implied as rules of law. For example, before 1982, case law laid down that in commercial or consumer contracts to supply a service a term would be implied to the effect that the provider of the service would use skill and care; after 1982 this term is now implied by statute.[27] Equally an employer and employee both owe mutual duties of care, not just in tort, but as implied terms of the contract.[28] In contracts for the supply of goods, there is an implied term that the goods will be of satisfactory quality and

---

[23] *Luxor (Eastbourne) Ltd v Cooper* [1941] AC 108, at 137.
[24] *The Moorcock* (1889) 14 PD 64.
[25] *Reid v Rush & Tompkins Plc* [1990] 1 WLR 212.
[26] *Liverpool City Council v Irwin* [1977] AC 239.
[27] Supply of Goods and Services Act 1982, s 13; and see now *Platform Funding Ltd v Bank of Scotland* [2009] 2 WLR 1016 (CA).
[28] *Lister v Romford Ice & Cold Storage Co Ltd* [1957] AC 555.

reasonably fit for their purpose.[29] This distinction between contracts for the supply of a service and those for the supply of goods raises an important question about the link between liability and content of the implied term duty or obligation. In French law this is to be found in the famous distinction between *obligation de résultat* and *obligation de moyens*, a distinction that has been specifically adopted by UNIDROIT (art 5.4). Does a contractor promise or agree to achieve a specific result or just to use his best efforts? This question is clearly of importance in English law as well, but it has got hidden behind a distinction between a contract to supply goods and a contract to supply a service, as we saw in an earlier chapter.

UNFAIR TERMS

Express terms, unlike implied terms, tend to give rise to textual interpretation problems as one might expect. Yet there is one area that has proved particularly difficult. Indeed it is an area where express terms, interpretation and liability intersect with contract theory and ideology. This is the area of exclusion, limitation, indemnity and penal clauses. The area was once very difficult because the fundamental principle of freedom of contract clashed with the problem of abuse of economic power. In all of the EU countries it is generally true to say that, today, the consumer is largely protected and standard form contract terms even in commercial contracts might be avoided if very unreasonable.[30] However contract law tries to avoid declaring that parties should be under a duty to make reasonable contracts;[31] the emphasis, instead, is on open dealing and, in civil law thinking, on good faith.[32] The distinction between commercial and consumer contracts is thus vital.[33] In consumer contracts unfair terms are void (Unfair Terms in Consumer Contracts Regulations 1999), while in commercial standard form contracts clauses are subject to a reasonableness test (Unfair Contract Terms Act 1977, s 3). Clauses that attempt to exclude personal injury liability for negligence are void in business

---

[29] Sale of Goods Act 1979, s 14.
[30] UNIDROIT art 7.1.6; PECL art 4.110; Unfair Contract Terms Act 1977, s 3.
[31] Unfair Terms in Consumer Contracts Regulations 1999, reg 6(2). And see PECL art 4.110(2).
[32] Unfair Terms in Consumer Contracts Regulations 1999, reg 5(1). And see PECL art 4.110 but cf art 8:109.
[33] Unfair Contract Terms Act 1977, s 12; Unfair Terms in Consumer Contracts Regulations 1999, reg 3.

situations and must be reasonable in relation to other forms of damage (1977 Act, s 2).

Penal clauses have raised their own special problems. These are clauses whereby a contractor agrees to pay a fixed sum of money on failure to perform his contractual obligations and they can be unfair in that the sum stipulated could far exceed any damage suffered by the victim of the non-performance. Indeed, English law takes the view that if the sum stipulated is a fair estimation of the damage likely to be suffered the term will not be a penalty clause. It will be a liquidated damages clause and fully enforceable virtually as a debt.[34] However if it exceeds any likely estimation – that is to say if it was intended to operate *in terrorem* – it will become penal and, thanks to equity, will not be enforceable.[35]

PERFORMANCE AND NON-PERFORMANCE OF THE CONTRACT

Many cases concerning terms of the contract arise because one of the parties has either failed to perform his contractual promise or promises or has rendered defective performance. Interpretation of terms is necessary in order to discover what remedies are available to the innocent party. Of course it must not be forgotten that the great majority of contracts are formed and performed without giving rise to problems. And even in those statistically rare cases when things do go wrong, the victim may decide that the defective performance is not worth pursuing in or outside the courts. Other problems are solved mutually between the parties. Yet when a party to a contract does feel aggrieved the first question that needs to be asked is whether or not there has been performance. This may well involve looking back at the promises, but equally, as the *Hong Kong Fir Shipping*[36] case illustrates, it will require examination of the quality of the performance itself.

Non-performance is not an expression that is often used in English contract law and this is why it is necessary to look at the civil law and transnational contract codes in order to understand its significance. Non-performance of a contract 'is failure by a party to perform any of its obligations under the contract, including defective performance or late

---

[34] Ibbetson (1999), at 150–1.
[35] *Jobson v Johnson* [1989] 1 WLR 1026.
[36] *Hong Kong Fir Shipping Co Ltd v Kawasaki Kisen Kaisha Ltd* [1962] 2 QB 26.

performance' (UNIDROIT art 7.1.1). Two general questions arise from this definition. What amounts to performance (or alternatively non- or defective performance)? And what can the victim (aggrieved party) do when faced with such a non-performance? Now, civil law systems start off from this idea of non-performance and thus it is possible to approach these two questions from the top-down so to speak (PECL art 8:101). However common lawyers do not. They have tackled non-performance from the bottom up through a number of specific categories forming part of a general topic called discharge of contract. There is an equal logic or symmetry to this approach in that discharge or dissolution of contract is the mirror image of formation. Nevertheless when it comes to reconciling the two approaches – that is to say if one looks at the consequences of non-performance in English law – it is necessary to bring together a range of disparate areas.[37]

The question of what amounts to performance is vital both for the alleged non-performing party and for the aggrieved party. The alleged non-performer will no doubt be seeking performance from the other party (for example payment) while the aggrieved party will want to know what he can do about the non-performance. With regard to the question of what amounts to performance, the PECL state that 'a party must tender performance of at least average quality' (art 6:108) and UNIDROIT says it must be 'reasonable' (art 5.6). Common lawyers certainly talk from time to time about performance, but the emphasis on promise has resulted in many performance problems being dealt with under the heading of 'breach' of promise and the remedies available to the aggrieved party. Thus, prima facie, a failure to perform, including defective performance, amounts to a breach of contract. The question then becomes one of liability and remedies in turn relating back to the type of promise (term) breached. Was the promise one to pay a sum of money, to transfer a thing (of perhaps a particular quality) or to render a service? Was it a fundamental term (condition) or a non-fundamental term (warranty)?

These questions are vital with regard to remedies, but performance questions can arise when one party renders defective performance and the other party, as a result, refuses to perform his promise (usually an obligation to pay). If the defective performance is so defective that it amounts to no performance at all, then the aggrieved party can refuse to pay.[38] If however it amounts to defective but substantial performance, then the

---

[37] See Weir (1999).
[38] *Vigers v Cook* [1919] 2 KB 475; *Bolton v Mahadeva* [1972] 1 WLR 1009.

aggrieved party cannot refuse payment; he is liable for the price less an amount to remedy the defects[39] or which represents the damage.[40]

According to the French model a non-performing contractor will be liable in damages to the other contracting party (CC art 1147). However the non-performing party will have a defence to any such damages claim if he can show that the non-performance is due either to a *force majeure* or to a *cas fortuit* (CC art 1148). This is the model that has been adopted by the PECL (arts 8:101, 8:108) and by UNIDROIT (arts. 7.1.7, 7.4.1); in these codes *force majeure* is defined as an impediment beyond the control of the non-performing party and one which could not have been foreseen at the time of the conclusion of the contract (UNIDROIT art 7.1.7(1); PECL art 8:108(1)).

English law, as we have seen, does not operate in this top-down way. Instead it deals with the problem of *force majeure* as an event that frustrates the contractual venture and discharges the whole contract. The effect is often the same in as much as the discharge of the contract will prevent the non-performing party from being liable in damages. Yet the concept of frustration was developed on the basis of the implied term (implied condition precedent) and as a result shared a conceptual similarity with mistake at common law.[41] This conceptual similarity disappeared in 1956 when the implied term theory for frustration was abandoned on the basis that it was self-contradictory: how could the parties theoretically foresee something that was theoretically unforeseeable?[42] But it may be that the relation has been re-established now that the Court of Appeal has seemingly abandoned the implied term theory for mistake at common law.[43] At all events, the court now has a power to set aside a contract for frustration.

ONEROUS PERFORMANCE

According to Lord Simon,

> [f]rustration of a contract takes place when there supervenes an event (without default of either party and for which the contract makes no sufficient provision) which so significantly changes the nature (not merely the expense or onerousness) of the outstanding contractual rights and/or obligations from what the

---

[39] *Hoenig v Isaacs* [1952] 2 All ER 176.
[40] *Ruxley Electronics Ltd v Forsyth* [1996] 1 AC 344.
[41] *The Great Peace* [2003] QB 679, at paras 61–75.
[42] *Davis Contractors Ltd v Fareham UDC* [1956] AC 696.
[43] *The Great Peace* [2003] QB 679.

parties could reasonably have contemplated at the time of its execution that it would be unjust to hold them to the literal sense of its stipulations in the new circumstances; in such case the law declares both parties to be discharged from further performance.[44]

As Lord Simon makes clear, an increase in expense or onerousness does not amount to a frustrating event and a similar conclusion has been reached in French private law. Contracts, like statutes, are binding (CC art 1134) and severe inflation does not amount to a *force majeure*.[45]

However in administrative law the theory of unforeseen change of circumstances (*la théorie de l'imprévision*) was adopted in the famous *Gaz de Bordeaux* case of 1916 on the basis that the public interest takes precedence over the binding nature of contract; it was not in the public interest that the lighting company should go bankrupt (CE 30.3.1916). Interestingly English law has reached a similar result as the *Gaz de Bordeaux* case in *Staffs Area Health Authority v South Staffs Waterworks Co*,[46] although for the majority of the Court of Appeal this result was simply a matter of interpretation of the contractual document. Lord Denning, however, went beyond the interpretative approach and based his decision both on frustration and on a *rebus sic stantibus* (things remain the same) implied clause giving rise to a right to have the contract re-negotiated. In fact Denning's approach, although rejected by the other judges, now finds expression in both the PECL (art 6.111) and UNIDROIT (arts 6.2.1–6.2.3).

NON-PERFORMANCE AND EXCLUSION CLAUSES

A non-performing party may also be protected from the effects of non-performance by an express clause in the contract. Such clauses, as we have already mentioned, can take many forms and in principle, even if they exclude liability, are effective. However in order for a clause to be effective at common law it must have been properly incorporated into the contract.[47] Its language must cover both the actual event or breach that has occurred and the actual party attempting to rely upon the clause.[48] In addition, in cases of ambiguity, the clause must be read *contra*

---

[44] *National Carriers Ltd v Panalpina (Northern) Ltd* [1981] AC 675, at 700.
[45] Deroussin (2007), at 489–90.
[46] [1978] 1 WLR 1387.
[47] *Thornton v Shoe Lane Parking Ltd* [1971] 2 QB 163.
[48] See eg *Hollier v Rambler Motors Ltd* [1972] 2 QB 71.

proferentem. It seems, also, that if there is a very serious breach of contract – the breach of a fundamental term (see above) or a fundamental breach – the clause will specifically have to cover the breach and the damage that has occurred. For there is a 'rule of construction' that an exclusion clause or similar provision should not be interpreted as covering a fundamental breach of contract.[49] Put another way, 'the agreement must retain the legal characteristics of a contract'.[50]

Many of the abuse problems associated with standard form contracts have been alleviated by statutory intervention aimed at protecting the consumer.[51] Thus in consumer sale of goods and hire purchase contracts the statutory implied terms as to title, fitness for purpose and quality cannot now be excluded,[52] and in many other consumer transactions an exclusion clause will be effective at best only if it is 'fair and reasonable'.[53] This fair and reasonable provision also applies to any clause attempting to exclude any liability or any remedy available for misrepresentation, and it is unlikely that businesses will be able to have recourse to any collateral contracts to evade liability for their defective products.[54] In interpreting 'fair and reasonable' under the Unfair Contract Terms Act 1977 the courts will no doubt look at the circumstances of each case.[55] Yet the Act is, primarily, a piece of legislation designed to protect the consumer and so the courts are likely now to distinguish between the commercial and the consumer factual situation.[56] In the latter situation an attempt to exclude negligence, especially by a professional institution in a powerful economic position, will no doubt be treated with scepticism, especially where the institution can spread the loss via insurance and the loss itself is not open-ended.[57]

In addition to the 1977 legislation, the legislature has again intervened in order to give expression to the EU Council Directive of 5 April 1993 on unfair terms in consumer contracts.[58] The Unfair Terms in Consumer Contracts Regulations 1999[59] differs from the 1977 Act in that it applies

---

[49] *Suisse Atlantique etc v Rotterdamsche etc* [1967] 1 AC 361.
[50] *Photo Production Ltd v Securicor* [1980] AC 827, at 850.
[51] *George Mitchell (Chesterfield) Ltd v Finney Lock Seeds Ltd* [1983] QB 284, at 296–9; [1983] 2 AC 803, at 812–13.
[52] Unfair Contract Terms Act 1977, s 6.
[53] Sections 2(2), 3 and 11.
[54] Sections 5 and 10.
[55] Section 11.
[56] *Thompson v T Lohan (Plant) Ltd* [1987] 1 WLR 649.
[57] *Smith v Eric Bush* [1990] 1 AC 831.
[58] 3/13/EEC: L 95/29.
[59] SI 1999, No 2083.

exclusively to consumer contracts.[60] It decrees simply that an 'unfair term' shall not be binding upon the consumer[61] in situations where such a term has not been individually negotiated in a contract between seller or supplier and a consumer.[62] Following the Directive, it prohibits clauses that, 'contrary to the requirement of good faith, causes a significant imbalance in the parties' rights and obligations arising under the contract, to the detriment of the consumer'.[63] Power is also given to the Director of Fair Trading, together with other public officers and the Consumers' Association, to seek an injunction to prevent a contractor continuing to use unfair exclusion clauses in contracts.[64] What is particularly striking about this new regulation is that it formally introduces into the English law of contractual obligations the notion of good faith, something traditionally said to be absent, as a matter of form if not substance, from the English contract (see Chapter 5).

However this notion of good faith must be treated with caution for two reasons. First, because the actual regulation links good faith with the further requirement that the term 'causes a significant imbalance in the parties rights and obligations arising under the contract, to the detriment of the consumer' (reg 5(1)). If the term does not cause a significant imbalance to the detriment of the consumer it seems that it will not be regarded as unfair.[65] Indeed, even if there is some evidence that the contract might in the abstract contravene good faith, the clause will still be valid if the court considers that there is no imbalance and detriment to the consumer and that there has been open and fair dealing. For, according to Lord Bingham, regulation 4 of the 1999 text is directed to the unfairness of the term and not to the use which a party may make of the term.[66] Accordingly if the term is in itself fair it cannot become unfair as a result of its actual function within a contract. Such an approach might not appeal to a civil lawyer and suggests that the whole idea of 'good faith' will be given a

---

[60] Defined in reg 3 as 'any natural person'. This definition can be contrasted with the definition of 'dealing as consumer' in the Unfair Contract Terms Act 1977, s 12. In this latter definition a consumer is not limited to a natural person and may include a small company: *R & B Customs Brokers Co Ltd v UDT Ltd* [1988] 1 WLR 321; cf *Stevenson v Rogers* [1999] QB 1028.
[61] Reg 8.
[62] Reg 5(1). See also PECL art 4:110.
[63] Reg 5(1).
[64] Reg 12; Schedule 1.
[65] *Director General of Fair Trading v First National Bank plc* [2002] 1 AC 481.
[66] *Director General of Fair Trading v First National Bank plc* [2002] 1 AC 481, at para 24.

restricted meaning.[67] Whatever the situation, there is a second reason for caution in that the Law Commission has proposed suppressing the expression 'good faith' in any new unfair terms legislation and replacing it with the 'requirement of reasonableness'. For, according to its Report, 'good faith is a concept which is unfamiliar to English and Scots lawyers in this area of the law.'[68] Reasonableness, of course, might well do much of the work of good faith, but it has to be asked whether in a commercial context it will necessarily advantage the non-performing consumer caught out by the small print in a 'reasonable' contract.

PERFORMANCE AND THIRD PARTIES

A contract might stipulate that a benefit or burden be placed on a third party or that the contract will be performed by someone other than the contracting party (which is always the case with corporations). Can the third party demand performance? Can a contracting party disown performance if the third party performs defectively? Originally a person who was not a party to the contract could not sue, but this has now largely been modified in most systems. In English law a stipulation in favour of an identified third party is now enforceable in certain circumstances thanks to legislation.[69] Where performance is carried out by a third party the contractor will remain responsible for non- or defective performance (PECL art 8.107), unless, perhaps, the third party acted outside the scope of his employment[70] or is clearly independent of the contractor and whose performance is not warranted (through an implied term) by the contractor.[71]

The great danger for this area of contract law is that it becomes infected with what might be called 'tort thinking'. In tort an employer is liable for the tortious acts of its employees only if the latter were acting in the course of their employment (see Chapter 13). Ought a similar rule to apply in contract? That is to say, should a contractor be able to escape liability for breach of contract where the damage is caused by his employee or independent contractor? It is tempting to say that a contractor ought not to be liable if the damage is caused by a third party ('it is not my fault but his'),

---

[67] Vigneron (2008).
[68] Law Com No 292, cm 6464, 2004, para 3.86.
[69] Contracts (Rights of Third Parties) Act 1999.
[70] *Photo Production Ltd v Securicor* [1980] AC 827; *Wong Mee Wan v Kwan Kin Travel Services Ltd* [1996] 1 WLR 38.
[71] *Wilson v Best Travel Ltd* [1993] 1 All ER 353.

but difficulties arise when that third party is the very person charged with carrying out the contract.

In *Photo Production Ltd v Securicor*,[72] where a contractor's factory was destroyed thanks to the act of the other contractor's employee (in a contract to provide a security service to the factory premises), the House of Lords ended up by delivering an ambiguous decision. The House certainly refused to allow the security company to argue that their employee was acting outside the scope of his employment when he started a fire at the claimant's factory. But the House did allow the security company to rely upon an exclusion clause limiting its liability for acts committed by its own employee. From an insurance position – and it must be remembered that in truth this was an action between the subrogated insurance companies of the two contractors – it seems reasonable enough that the judges should see the whole case in terms of risk. Which insurance undertook the risk of this kind of fire? The problem is that it in putting the emphasis on the fire and building insurance risk, the House of Lords has suggested that a corporate contractor might be able to escape from liability for non-performance simply by pointing to a causal link between 'another person' and the innocent contractor's damage.[73]

NON-PERFORMANCE AND TERMINATION

Non- or defective performance, unless excused by agreement or frustration, will prima facie amount to a breach of contract. Now, breach of a contractual promise cannot of itself result in termination of the contract, although Lord Denning MR once tried to argue that it could.[74] What is required are two conditions. First, that the breach is serious enough to justify termination and, secondly, that the victim actually elects to terminate. An innocent party can thus choose to keep the contract alive and, in certain (limited) circumstances, render performance and then sue for the contract price in debt.[75]

The central question is the seriousness of the breach. It must go to the root of the contract before a party is entitled to discharge the contract for breach.[76] However, we have seen that the traditional approach of English law was not to look at the breach itself but at the status of the term broken;

---

[72] [1980] AC 827.
[73] cf *Tesco Supermarkets Ltd v Nattrass* [1972] AC 153.
[74] *Harbutts Plasticine Ltd v Wayne Tank and Pump Co Ltd* [1970] 1 QB 447.
[75] *White & Carter (Councils) Ltd v McGregor* [1962] AC 413.
[76] *Decro-Wall v Practitioners in Marketing Ltd* [1971] 2 All ER 216.

only if the promise or term broken was a 'condition' did the innocent party have the right to terminate. All the same, if the effect of the breach is not serious it may well be that a court would treat the term broken as an innominate one, thus allowing them to switch the emphasis to the seriousness of the breach itself. Equally the breach of what might appear to be a minor term could be enough to allow the other party to terminate the contract if the damage flowing from the breach turns out to be very serious.[77] One might add that a victim who wishes to terminate a contract for serious breach does not actually have to wait for the breach itself to occur. If the other party declares that he is not going to perform – or if he acts in a way that will prevent performance (for example going on an extended holiday in a far off land a day or so before he is to perform) – the victim can treat this declaration or act as an anticipatory breach and make his election from that moment. He may decide to keep the contract alive or he may terminate and sue immediately for damages.[78]

NON-PERFORMANCE AND AGREEMENT

A contract can of course be discharged before performance by agreement between the parties. However this is yet another area where the promise basis of English contract law manifests itself with something of a vengeance. The agreement to vary a contract or to discharge it completely is valid at common law only if it amounts to what is in effect a new contract; in other words the contract is discharged as a result of new promises moving from each party. If the contract has not been performed (executed) by either party there is no problem since each promise will act as consideration for the other. But if one party has performed his obligations under the contract to be discharged or varied, the new contract will fail because there can be no benefit for the new agreement and thus no enforceable promise (see Chapter 6). A contractor who agrees to pay a premium to his co-contractor over the agreed contract price might be seen to be providing only a gratuitous promise, although when this was tested the Court of Appeal did find consideration.[79] Equally the creditor who agrees to accept a lower sum than the one stipulated in the original contract is, at common law, not bound by this promise.[80] Equity will no doubt step in with its

---

[77] *Aerial Advertising Co v Batchelor's Peas Ltd* [1938] 2 All ER 788.
[78] *White & Carter (Councils) Ltd v McGregor* [1962] AC 413.
[79] *Williams v Roffey Bros & Nicholls (Contractors) Ltd* [1991] 1 QB 1.
[80] *D & C Builders Ltd v Rees* [1966] 2 QB 617.

remedy of estoppel, provided that the promisee comes with 'clean hands'; and a party who agrees not to enforce some term or other in the contract will be bound by such a variation under the doctrine of waiver.[81]

The rules on variation and discharge by agreement confirm that an English contract amounts to nothing more than its promissory parts. There is no obligation that transcends these promises. If there were, then the problem of variation and discharge would not need to be based on consideration. The contractual obligation having been formed, consideration, it could be said, ought no longer relevant since the sheer obligatory force of the contract now in existence could act as the means for variation or discharge. In other words any subsequent contractual promises would gain their contractual obligatory force from the existing contractual relation. The doctrine of waiver might appear to go some way in accepting this analysis, but *Williams v Roffey Brothers*[82] shows that this is wishful thinking. Every contractual promise, at common law, must be the product of a bargain.

---

[81] *Hartley v Hymans* [1920] 3 KB 475; *Rickards Ltd (Charles) v Oppenheim* [1950] 1 KB 616.
[82] [1991] 1 QB 1.

9. Tortious obligations: general provisions

When one moves from contractual to non-contractual obligations the idea of an abstract *vinculum iuris* which exists independently of the law of actions becomes more difficult to envisage. The distinction between the formation of an obligation and the performance of it has a practical dimension in a contractual obligation; parties may wish to know independently of any liability if they are under an obligation to do or to convey in some specific manner. With respect to non-contractual obligations it is often the causing of harm or the acquiring of a dubious enrichment that first gives rise to a legal question. And this question is as much concerned with the availability of any remedy as with any idea of a pre-existing obligation. In other words the remedy question in practice often precedes, or at least becomes combined with, the obligation question. Nevertheless, as we saw in an earlier chapter, the civil lawyers attempted to base liability for damage on the notion of fault (CC art 1382); the individual was under a general obligation to take care.

CIVILIAN APPROACH

Such a general principle can, as we have seen, be traced back to the Roman action for wrongful damage based on a statute called the *lex aquilia*. This action dealt with harm caused through fault (*culpa*) and thus became the foundation for a liability for individual acts motivated by intention or negligence. And in such actions even the slightest negligence was enough to found liability (D.9.2.44pr). However the Romans also recognised that the public interest required that control itself of property could on occasions give rise to an action on behalf of someone injured by the *res*. For example an occupier of a building adjacent to a public highway could find himself liable for damage caused to a passer-by from anything thrown or poured from the building. Such an action, according to the jurist Ulpian, was beneficial in that it was in the public interest that people should be able to move about without fear or danger (D.9.3.1.1). This, and other claims *quasi ex delicto*, provided the material from which the later civilians induced a general principle of liability without fault. And thus alongside the articles dealing with *culpa* liability for individual acts, the French *Code civil* lays down in article 1384 a principle that now stands in contrast to article 1382. Article 1384 states that: 'One is liable not only for damage caused by one's own act, but also for that caused by the acts of persons for which one must answer or for things under one's control (*sous sa garde*)'.

Despite these broad general statements of liability, it is still held that – in principle – everyone has to bear the risk of his own damage. In order to transfer one's loss, so to speak, a reason for the transfer has to be found and it is in the provision of such reasons that the law of obligations finds its role. Yet in fulfilling its role the law of obligations ends up by making significant inroads into the principle that the loss lies where it falls. As a result the law of obligations has to perform a balancing act between freedom to perform acts which carry a (statistical) risk of injury and the compensation of those victims who make up the statistics. In Roman law the balancing act was achieved by focusing on activities themselves and posing questions about the manner in which such activities were performed. Thus 'to do a certain act at a certain time and place was *culpa*, but at another time or place it was not'.[1] In modern civil law the inroads into the 'loss lies where it falls' principle are made by the legislator via a set of statutes which impose liability for damage caused by one person to another, of which the paradigm examples are articles 1382 and 1384 of the *Code civil*. Moreover, as the Advocate-General in a more recent French case observed, the 'law of insurance radiates today through the whole of social life'[2] and there is no doubt that today tort law and insurance are inseparable.[3]

However these French articles are very abstract in that they do not require particular *interests* to be invaded before a non-contractual damages claim can succeed. Accordingly they can be contrasted with the German approach where there is no obligation to pay damages unless there is the violation both of the standard or duty and of a specifically protected interest. Thus paragraph 823(1) of the BGB states that a 'person who intentionally or negligently injures the life, body, health, freedom, property, or other right of another contrary to law is obligated to compensate him for any damage thereby arising'. Merely to cause *damage* through *culpa* is not then enough; the claimant must also show that the defendant's act has invaded a protected *interest* or 'other *right*'.

---

[1] Lawson (1955), at 38.
[2] Cass.civ.19.2.1997; JCP 28.5.97.22848.
[3] Lewis (2005).

The law of non-contractual obligations is, then, highly individualistic in its approach to liability. It tends to start out from individuals (wilful or careless acts) and work towards more social ideas through the use of, for example, contract, vicarious liability (liability for people) and liability without fault (liability for things), although the New Dutch Civil Code has gone further and recognises a form of 'group' liability. According to article 166(1) of Book 6 '[i]f a member of a group of persons unlawfully causes damage and if the risk of causing this damage should have prevented these persons from their collective conduct, they are solidarily liable if the conduct can be imputed to them'.[4] Usually legal systems deal with this kind of problem through joint liability, although it is worth recalling that in Roman law where a group of persons stole something that was too heavy for any individual to carry the whole group was deemed guilty of theft and each was liable in delict to the owner (D.47.2.21.9). In strictly individualistic terms, as the Roman jurist recognised, this was *contra rationem* because it could be logically argued (*subtili ratione dici*) that no one should be liable since no individual could carry the thing (D.9.2.51.2). However one might say that in such a situation public policy took precedence over logic, for it would be more absurd (*longe absurdius*) if no one were to be liable.

ENGLISH APPROACH

Claiming a remedy was and is never enough to establish liability. A claimant, in both Roman and English law, had, and has, also to establish a cause of action upon which the remedy can be based since, as the Romans observed, actions and obligations are intimately bound together; 'obligations are the mother of actions' said the later Roman lawyers (cf D.3.3.42.2; D.44.7.53pr). Accordingly, in order to succeed in a damages claim in English law, a claimant must establish a cause of action in contract, tort or under statute. Equally to obtain an injunction in equity a claimant must in principle show the invasion, or threatened invasion, of some substantive legal or equitable right which is normally linked to a cause of action. Moreover, unlike contract, where non-performance (or defective performance) amounting to a breach is a cause of action in itself, there is no such cause of action as a 'breach of tortious duty'.[5] A claimant must always establish a specific cause of action such as negligence, nui-

---

[4] Translation: Haanappel and Mackaay (1990).
[5] *Bradford Corporation v Pickles* [1895] AC 587.

sance or defamation[6] and new liabilities are established often at the cost of deforming established heads of claim.[7]

In fact it might seem ironic that tort (trespass), having once been the father of contract (*assumpsit*), should find itself in the 20th century being the offspring of contract (in the sense of being a damages claim that could not be classified as contractual). Yet such historical developments help explain why a strict comparison between English and continental private law will always be difficult. The categories of contract and tort (delict), so well established in the civil law, are in truth a relatively modern phenomenon in English law. And this can mask the fact that in its formative days the common law tended to think, not in terms of a body of rules based on general principles, but in terms of separate compartments of factual situations, each compartment being founded on a particular writ.[8] This 'forms of action' approach gave rise to a system of liability attached to categories of fact situation and types of injury. Even today non-contractual damages cases can still be determined as much, for example, by the place where an accident happened[9] – or as much by the species of animal which causes damage[10] – as by any general principle of fault or risk. Of course the development of a general liability based on promise meant that a large section of the law of obligations was transferred from a law of debt and damages to a category of 'contract', but the apparent architectural perfection of this contract category did not of itself mean that the non-contractual debt and damages actions would also find themselves in categories unified by a common denominator.[11] Indeed English law has still not fully accepted that non-contractual debt claims are founded directly upon a general source principle of unjust enrichment (cf Chapter 16); and with regard to the non-contractual damages actions there is still a debate as to whether they belong to the category of torts or tort.

---

[6] See eg Denning LJ in *Southport Corporation v Esso Petroleum Co Ltd* [1954] 2 QB 182. And see *Kingdom of Spain v Christie, Mason & Woods Ltd* [1986] 1 WLR 1120.

[7] See eg *Khorasandjian v Bush* [1993] QB 727; but cf *Hunter v Canary Wharf Ltd* [1997] AC 655.

[8] 'The substantive law of torts in the Middle Ages was inherently messy, though perhaps no more messy than its twentieth-century counterpart': Ibbetson (1999), at 57.

[9] See eg *Jacobs v LCC* [1950] AC 361.

[10] Animals Act 1971.

[11] 'The medieval law, like that of the twentieth century, provided a mould within which issues could be raised but in itself provided few answers to the substantive questions that might have been asked': Ibbetson (1999), at 57.

DEFINITIONAL CONSIDERATIONS

The term 'tort' is an Anglo-Norman word that simply means 'wrong' and thus tort can be seen as the law of wrongs. In the common law, the law of tort, like the law of contract, is historically founded on the forms of action the most important of which was trespass which in the 18th century came to be seen as being concerned with damage *directly* caused. *Indirect* harm was covered by a development from trespass called the 'action on the case' (the boundary between trespass and case had earlier been much more fluid) and these actions hardened into form of action precedents such as nuisance, trover, deceit and so on. When the procedural forms of action were abolished in 1852 the category of 'tort' was used to house those claims for compensatory damages that could not be accommodated under contract. However the names of the old forms of action were retained and they acted as the basis for a cause of action in tort. Thus trespass, nuisance, conversion (trover), detinue and the like became specific 'torts'.

In 1932 the law of tort took an important step towards a general principle of liability when the House of Lords in *Donoghue v Stevenson*[12] established the tort of negligence based upon the idea of a general duty of care owed by one person to his 'neighbour'. Nevertheless the older causes of action did not disappear. Accordingly, as we have mentioned, there is no general theory of liability in tort; in order to succeed in a tort claim a claimant must establish the constituents of a specific tort. Nevertheless if one is going to talk in terms of a law of obligations it would seem logically to follow that tort is about non-contractual rights and duties. Yet the difficulty in trying to analyse English tort law in terms of a pre-existing obligation is that the analysis works, if at all, only at a very high level of abstraction. One can talk of an obligation not to harm others. In terms of actual vocabulary English law tends to use 'duty' and thus one can talk of 'duty of care' and 'breach of statutory duty'. But the language of duty does not easily work for torts like trespass[13] and, in addition, it often attaches to the nature of the harm and (or) the status of the defendant. Perhaps one could try to analyse tort liability in terms of 'rights', but in most personal injury cases (which statistically make up the bulk of tort claims) the emphasis is on claimants having to prove fault before they become entitled to any damages. Rights tend to suggest strict liability and so is not a very appropriate general term. The idea of the formation of a pre-existing abstract *vinculum iuris* – duties or rights – can, then, be

---

[12] [1932] AC 562.
[13] *Stubbings v Webb* [1993] AC 498, at 508.

unrealistic. Instead one must often think, at best, in terms of a mixture of duties (for example negligence), rights (for example defamation), interests and causes of action arising out of factual situations. Only with regard to certain activities like driving or manufacturing can one envisage a pre-existing undertaking or obligation. Might one talk here of a kind of 'contract' with those others undertaking the same activity?[14]

Accordingly the most realistic way to define tort is from an historical perspective. Tort claims are those causes of action (formerly forms of action) that cannot be classified under contract or, now, restitution. Such an historical approach partly informs those writers who are sceptical of normative definitions. For example Tony Weir writes in the preface to his introductory work on the subject that tort law 'is what is in the tort books, and the only thing holding it together is the binding'. He adds that the courts in tort cases 'function as a complaints department – though the claimant, unlike the customer, is not always right'. These 'complaints are of such different kinds that very different reactions may be appropriate, and though there are horses for courses, the tort course sports quite a lot of horses, and they are of very different breeds and speeds'. One cannot, according to Weir, produce a definitional theory or even discuss the purpose of tort without first becoming 'familiar with what that ragbag actually contains: otherwise we shall be like adolescents spending all night discussing the meaning of life before, perhaps instead of, experiencing it'.[15]

There is of course much truth in these observations. Nevertheless this has not stopped many authors in the common law world from producing definitions and these definitions can broadly be classed into two groups characterised in turn by two questions. What *is* tort? And what does tort *do*? The first group of definitions can be labelled *formalist* and they in turn fall into two sub-categories. There are formalist definitions based on inference from a pre-established model of rights, remedies, legal categories, legal rules or whatever; and there are formalist definitions based upon an axiological (science of morals) model. An example of the first kind of formalist approach is the definition fashioned by Winfield. He said that tortious 'liability arises from the breach of a duty primarily fixed by the law: such duty is towards persons generally and its breach is redressible by an action for unliquidated damages.'[16] Winfield goes on to explain how the terms 'fixed by the law', 'towards persons generally' and 'unliquidated

---

[14] cf *Clarke* v *Dunraven* [1897] AC 59.
[15] Weir (2006), at ix (Preface).
[16] Winfield (1931), at 32.

damages' mark off tort from other areas of the law such as contract, property and crime. Tort, in other words, is inferred from a classification model of legal rules.

A definition of tort based on principles of justice or upon the moral behaviour of individuals can be regarded as *axiological* in its approach and any resulting definition can be labelled as formalist. Perhaps one recent example of an axiological approach is to be found in Peter Cane's definition. He says that 'the law of tort can be viewed as a system of ethical rules and principles of personal responsibility for conduct'. Cane contrasts this approach 'to the traditional one of seeing tort law as made up of a number of discrete "torts", that is, legal formulae which can be used to obtain remedies from courts or as bargaining counters in out-of-court negotiations.'[17]

PURPOSE AND POLICY OF TORT

Another, and more common, approach is to fashion a definition in terms of the ends that tort is intended to achieve. This group of definitions can be called *functionalist*. What is the function of the law of tort? For example, John Fleming began his introductory work to tort by noting that the:

> toll on life, limb, and property exacted by today's industrial operations, methods of transport, and many another activity benignly associated with the 'modern way of life' has reached proportions so staggering that the economic cost of accidents represents a constant and mounting drain on the community's human and material resources.

He thus went on to assert that the 'task of the law of torts is to play an important regulatory role in the adjustment of these losses and the eventual allocation of their cost'.[18] Other writers have talked in a similar vein. Tort is about spreading the cost of accidents. In fact, as we shall see, although personal injury litigation statistically makes up the bulk of tort law, loss-spreading is not the only aim of this area of law.

Yet defining tort from the position of its purpose and function is by no means easy. The subject's fragmentary basis in a wide range of old forms (now causes) of action is at the heart of the problem since this fragmentation is equally reflected in its functions. One should note, also, that the absence of any formal distinction between administrative liability and civil

---

[17] Cane (1997), at 1.
[18] Fleming (1985), at 1.

liability means that tort ends up playing an important administrative and constitutional law role.[19] This constitutional role has become more acute, and in some ways more complex, with the incorporation of the European Convention for the Protection of Human Rights and Fundamental Freedoms into English law.[20] Moreover the further absence of any strict divisions, at the level of remedies at any rate, between property and obligations, and between personal and patrimonial rights, results in yet further roles for tort: it ends up as the category providing remedies for the 'vindication' of property rights[21] and of personal rights such as harassment, if not privacy.[22] This said, it must be remembered that statistically the great majority of tort claims are for personal injury arising out of accidents on the road or in the factory. Personal injury thus dominates the purpose and policy dimension.

ACTIONS FOR DAMAGES

One broad way of defining tort in terms of its purpose and policies is through the remedies associated with this category. By far the most important of these is damages; only the equitable remedy of injunction has any other real claim and this remedy is more or less limited to certain specific torts. Viewed from the position of damages one can talk of the law of tort as being concerned with compensation. However several qualifications must be made here.

First, an action for damages is an important remedy in contract and so tortious liability must be distinguished from contractual liability. To an extent this can be done by reference to aims – contract tends on the whole to protect economic interests as opposed to personal injury interests – but the overlap between the two areas is considerable.[23] Secondly, to talk in terms of compensation is to view tort from the position of the claimant; tort can, and must, equally be viewed from the position of the defendant. And one might add that the subject can also be viewed from the perspective of society: can society afford to compensate all accident victims? Thirdly, *damages* and *damage* are not the same; not all damage will attract compensation (damages) and thus a second descriptive concept, that of an *interest*, needs to be brought into the model. Tort can, accordingly, be seen

---

[19] See eg *Keegan v Chief Constable of Merseyside Police* [2003] 1 WLR 2187.
[20] Human Rights Act 1998.
[21] Torts (Interference with Goods) Act 1977.
[22] *Wainwright v Home Office* [2004] 2 AC 406.
[23] *Henderson v Merrett Syndicates Ltd* [1995] 2 AC 145.

as a matter of protected and unprotected interests, with perhaps varying degrees of protection between these two poles (see PETL art 2:102). However attempting to define tort in terms of protected interests will again prove extremely difficult not just because of overlap with other subjects (contract, public law, property etc) but also because some interests are protected at different levels in the law of tort. One cannot say that 'mental distress' is not a recognised interest, yet it is not always well protected (cf PETL art 2:102(5)).[24]

Fourthly, an award of damages in tort is not the only means of securing help and compensation for harm. Private insurance, social security, criminal injuries compensation, family support, charity and of course the National Health Service (NHS) are other support systems. Tort needs to be considered in relation to these other systems and not just because this contextual perspective is an accepted part of any tort course. These other systems are also of importance because they can influence, directly or indirectly, the actual reasoning and decisions of the judges.[25] Fifthly, damages as a remedy has a variety of aims and functions not all of which are compensatory. These differing functions are directly reflected back into the causes of action that give rise to the remedy and thus compensation has to be distinguished, for example, from restitution and from deterrence.

Finally, damages as a common law monetary remedy needs to be distinguished from other monetary claims such as an action for debt, an action for account or a claim for damages in equity. Indeed, some claims for 'damages' are in substance really 'debt'[26] or account actions and as a result they belong in substantive categories different from tort.

AIMS OF THE LAW OF TORT

In a famous article published half a century ago professor Glanville Williams identified a number of differing aims of the law of tort.[27] Moreover these aims have more recently been given a measure of judicial approval in a speech by Lord Steyn in *Smith New Court Securities v Vickers Ltd* where he reminds one of Glanville Williams' conclusion that '[w]here possible the law seems to like to ride two or three horses at once; but occasionally a situation occurs where one must be selected'.[28]

---

[24] Giliker (2000).
[25] See eg *Mitchell v Glasgow City Council* [2009] 2 WLR 481 (HL(Sc)).
[26] See eg *The Stonedale (No 1)* [1956] AC 1.
[27] Williams (1951); Williams and Hepple (1984), at 27–30.
[28] [1997] AC 254, at 280 quoting Williams (1951), at 172.

The first of these aims is the protection of an *expectation interest*.[29] Now this is normally an aim of the law of contract, but it needs to be added to the law of tort since it has been judicially recognised on occasions that tort fills the gaps of the law of contract and while an expectation interest is not normally the subject of a duty of care there are exceptions.[30] Moreover one might refer to the more general question of whether a breach of contract is itself a 'tort'. Secondly, there is compensation for harm. This is regarded as tort's most important aim and is sometimes described as the protection of a person's reliance interest. However, it might be better described as the protection of a restoration interest since in personal injury and physical damage (and indeed in many economic loss) actions the claimant is demanding to be put back into the position before the tort occurred. Thirdly, there is the rectification of unjust enrichments. This aim is less central to tort than it once was now that the law of restitution has become an independent category in English law (Chapter 16). Nevertheless conversion, trespass and exemplary damages can have an important restitutionary function and these claims remain formally within the category of tort.

Another important aim is punishment and *deterrence*. In Roman law these were central aspects of liability *ex delicto*, but this punishment objective was in later Europe taken over by criminal law. A similar development can be traced in the common law. Nevertheless the punishment and deterrence aim still has a place in tort law since it directly motivates exemplary damages, which are non-compensatory damages awarded to punish the defendant,[31] and has been used to justify more stringent damages in the tort of deceit than in negligence.[32] In other words, by making such a person pay, the law is attempting to deter certain kinds of behaviour that it considers particularly wrongful. One might add here that while this deterrence aim would appear to be totally undermined by the existence of insurance, the idea of punishment and deterrence might still be reflected indirectly via the contract of insurance. Lost no-claims bonuses and higher premiums could be seen as adjustment mechanisms that attempt to continue the deterrence aim.

A further aim of the law of tort is the protection of *rights*. At one level all legal categories could be said to be about rights. But the term 'right' has many meanings and in this tort context means rights in the strong

---

[29] As set out in Williams and Hepple (1984).
[30] See eg *White v Jones* [1995] 2 AC 207.
[31] On which see *Kuddus v Chief Constable of Leicestershire* [2002] 2 AC 122.
[32] *Smith New Court Securities Ltd v Scrimgeour Vickers Ltd* [1997] AC 254, at 279.

sense of the word (infringement rather than behaviour gives rise to an action). Thus causes of action such as conversion and trespass to goods protect property rights, while malicious prosecution and false imprisonment (trespass to the person) protect constitutional rights. Trespass to land and private nuisance protect rights in land, while some other rights are protected by statutory torts.[33] The incorporation of the European Convention of Human Rights into English law is clearly of major importance in respect of right protection. The Human Rights Act 1998 itself gives rise to a statutory action for damages against a public authority that infringes a human right, although it would seem that such a claim is not to be regarded as an action in tort.[34]

Finally, although this is not to suggest that the list of aims is closed, Williams and Hepple mention status as an indirect aim and cite how the tort of defamation might be used indirectly to declare a claimant's marital *status*.[35] One might add to this example the protection offered to a private purchaser of a motor vehicle which turns out not to have been owned by the seller but is the subject of a hire purchase agreement with a finance company. This is a tort problem in as much as, at common law, the purchaser might well be liable in conversion. However statute offers protection to private purchasers of such motor vehicles and the question of who is a 'trade and finance' buyer, who will not get protection, is, according to the Court of Appeal, one of status.[36] Yet perhaps this status aim is now too limited. Given that status forms part of the law of persons, it might be now possible, especially since the Protection from Harassment Act 1997 and the Human Rights Act 1998, to think in terms of personality rights. That is to say, tort will protect certain rights which are not patrimonial (that is having an economic worth) but attach directly to the person as a human. Such a category would include defamation, which protects the reputation interest, and certain other torts protecting, or coming close to protecting, privacy.[37]

In addition to the doctrinal work on the purpose, policy and aims of the law of tort, there is a huge body of literature, especially North American, devoted to the theory and philosophy behind tort liability. Indeed, there is enough to fill a whole course on the subject. Some theories are based directly on particular notions of justice; thus an emphasis on individual *corrective justice* usually focuses on the balance between individuals in

---

[33] See eg Protection from Harassment Act 1997.
[34] *R (Greenfield) v Secretary of State for the Home Department* [2005] 1 WLR 673, at para 19.
[35] See Williams and Hepple (1984), at 29–30.
[36] *Stevenson v Beverley Bentinck Ltd* [1976] 1 WLR 483.
[37] *Douglas v Hello! Ltd (No 3)* [2008] 1 AC 1.

society and the moral imperative behind the obligation to pay damages. Theories of *distributive justice* often emphasise the statistical cost (human and economic) of certain activities and the unrealistic nature of moral imperatives in a legal structure where most defendants are insured and accidents statistics are predictable. These theories motivate the debate between fault and no-fault liability. In the USA the law and economics school has been particularly active in the area of tort law, but old ideas about individual responsibility and freedom to act are by no means dead.

Given the discursive nature of common law judgments these policy, aims and philosophy questions remain important to the understanding of the case law itself. Different judgments can reveal differing theoretical perspectives. However the judges themselves do tend to agree on one thing, that English tort law has committed itself to no single theory.[38] Nevertheless the effect of such judicial statements is not of course to render aims, policy and philosophy irrelevant; for, as the Privy Council has put it, '[o]il and vinegar may not mix in solution but they combine to make an acceptable salad dressing'.[39] What the judicial scepticism indicates is a point made by Stephen Waddams in his analysis of common law reasoning and categorisation. Discussing the difficulty of trying accurately to 'map' English law, he points out that a 'related problem is the absence of uniformity in the reasoning and conclusions of judges, both within particular jurisdictions and from one jurisdiction to another.' Professor Waddams uses *White v Jones*[40] as an example. He notes that 'the three majority judges and the two dissenting judges all took different approaches' and that a 'differently constituted panel of English judges could very well have reached the opposite conclusion, as has indeed occurred on this question in other common law jurisdictions'.[41] It needs hardly to be stated that, if this is an accurate picture of English methodology (which arguably it is, as we shall see), then each judgment is likely to reflect a particular philosophical and policy bias. It is the very nature of the judicial system that prevents the adoption of a single theory.

TORT AND METHODOLOGY

These observations by Professor Waddams are fundamental to an understanding of the law of tort in general: for anyone who wishes to

---

[38] *Broome v Cassell & Co Ltd* [1972] AC 1027, at 1114.
[39] *Gleaner Co Ltd (The) v Abrahams* [2004] 1 AC 628, at para 54.
[40] [1995] 2 AC 207.
[41] Waddams (2003), at 13.

comprehend this (or in truth any) area of the common law must have an appreciation of much more than just the cases (precedents) and legislative texts that form the rule-basis of this subject area. Tort, in particular, requires a sophisticated appreciation of the common law method which in turn requires a sound grasp of both the history and the thought processes of common lawyers. An understanding of the law of tort requires, in short, a thorough understanding of its methodology.

It is of course trite knowledge that the English common law is uncodified and that the two main sources of law are case law and statute. It would, however, be dangerous if cases are approached as if they act as the source of 'unwritten' rules and principles which can be abstracted from their factual foundations. Statutes, also, are in style often rather different from the continental codes. Moreover these sources of law can be properly understood only in the context of the methods of reasoning which are brought to bear on them and these methods are in many ways more open-ended than those formally used by for example French lawyers.[42] In addition, there is a political and social mentality behind this reasoning that in some important ways is rather different from the political and social mentality to be found in other European countries which, at first sight, might appear to have similar principles in the area of non-contractual obligations.

The law of tort is one area of English law (and there are not so many these days) whose foundation is largely in precedent. The main concepts have been formed by the common lawyers over the centuries and even where the legislature has intervened to reform or alter the law, it often uses, without definition, these concepts. The precedents can be analysed in terms of rules, but such an approach is largely misleading for several reasons.

For a start, what binds is not actually a rule but the *ratio decidendi* of a precedent and this is a notion that by definition includes the 'material facts' of the precedent itself. This means that an important part of any judgment in a tort case will be devoted not just to the facts of the case in hand but equally to the facts of any relevant precedents. The problem here is that the relationship between facts and law is extremely complex. As Stephen Waddams explains, the facts 'may be stated at countless levels of particularity, and legal issues and legal rules may be formulated at countless levels of generality.' Thus no 'map or scheme could possibly classify all imaginable facts, for there is no limit whatever to the number of facts

---

[42] However it is important not to over-exaggerate the differences: see Lasser (1995).

that may be postulated of a sequence of human events.'[43] Moreover facts do not exist independently of their perception. A small ship sinks leaving no survivors: could it be said, as a question of fact, that all aboard the vessel died *simultaneously* or must one conclude that their deaths occurred at different times? How one processes this factual situation can of itself determine how a case will be decided.[44]

Yet the traditional ideal is that legal solutions in any litigation problem flow from a pre-defined set of rules and categories through the application of a syllogism. Lord Simon explained the method. 'A judicial decision', he says, 'will often be reached by a process of reasoning which can be reduced into a sort of complex syllogism, with the major premise consisting of a pre-existing rule of law (either statutory or judge-made) and with the minor premise consisting of the material facts of the case under immediate consideration.' And the 'conclusion is the decision of the case, which may or may not establish new law – in the vast majority of cases it will be merely the application of existing law to the facts judicially ascertained.' Lord Simon took as an example the case of *National Telephone Co v Baker*.[45] He said the major premise was the rule in *Rylands v Fletcher* [46] and the minor premise was that the defendant brought and stored electricity on his land for his own purpose; it escaped from the land; and in so doing it injured the plaintiff's property. The conclusion was that the defendant was liable in damages to the plaintiff (or would have been but for statutory protection).[47] The importance of this syllogistic approach is that the liability is seemingly not the result of the personal prejudices of the judges, but a matter of mechanical logic. It flows automatically from the rule in *Rylands v Fletcher*.

On closer inspection, however, Lord Simon's description of the reasoning process turns out to be more ambiguous. 'Analysis shows', he said, 'that the conclusion establishes a rule of law, which may be stated as "for the purpose of the rule in *Rylands v Fletcher* electricity is *analogous* to water" or "electricity is within the rule in *Rylands v Fletcher*"'. And that 'conclusion is now available as the major premise in the next case, in which some substance may be in question which in this context is not perhaps clearly analogous to water but is clearly analogous to electricity.'[48]

The point has already been made that the *ratio decidendi* of a precedent

---

[43] Waddams (2003), at 14.
[44] See *Re Rowland* [1963] Ch 1.
[45] [1893] 2 Ch 186.
[46] (1866) LR 1 Ex 265 (Ex); (1868) LR 3 HL 330 (HL).
[47] *Lupton v FA & AB Ltd* [1972] AC 634, at 658–9.
[48] [1972] AC 634, at 659 emphasis added.

includes its material facts and this means that when a new set of litigation facts arrives before a court, the barristers and judges need to compare two sets of facts in order to see if the new facts are governed by the *ratio* of the precedent. Lord Simon indicates that this is not actually a matter of logic but of *analogy*. This reasoning by analogy is of particular importance when it comes to extending the tort of negligence (duty of care) to new factual situations; the approach is not one of applying an abstract principle like CC art 1382 to a set of facts. The new situation needs to be analogous to the facts of an existing duty of care case.[49] Thus one reason why the claimant's action for damages was dismissed in *Goodwill v British Pregnancy Advisory Service*[50] was because the facts of her case were not analogous to those of the precedent established by *White v Jones*.[51] Reasoning by analogy does not, of course, of itself undermine the idea that legal reasoning in tort is a matter of applying rules. One is simply using analogy as a means of *applying* a legal rule. Nevertheless it does offer a certain latitude to judges (see the discussion of *Esso Petroleum v Southport Corporation* in Chapter 4).

POLICY AND FUNCTIONALISM

The complexity of reasoning in tort does not end with analogy. In *Home Office v Dorset Yacht Co*[52] Lord Diplock gave his own description of the reasoning methods used in negligence (duty of care) cases. At a formal level it was a matter of the induction out of all the duty of care precedents of a proposition about situations in which the courts have recognised a duty of care to exist. This induction stage was followed by a second, deductive, stage whereby the facts of the case before the court were examined in the light of the induced proposition. If the facts display all the characteristics to be found in the induced proposition, 'the conclusion follows that a duty of care does arise in the case for decision.' However Lord Diplock did not stop there. He went on to admit that there was an element of choice in reaching the conclusion since the facts of the case before the court will by definition *not* contain all the characteristics to be found in the induced proposition (and that is why the case has gone to court). This choice, said Lord Diplock, 'is exercised by making a *policy* decision'.[53] This notion of

---

[49] *Caparo Industries plc v Dickman* [1990] 2 AC 605, at 635.
[50] [1996] 1 WLR 1397.
[51] [1995] 2 AC 207.
[52] [1970] AC 1004.
[53] [1970] AC 1004, at 1059 (emphasis added).

policy has become a major reasoning focal point in the contemporary law of tort.[54]

Yet what does it mean? In terms of methodology, policy reasoning can be contrasted with syllogistic or logical reasoning in that solutions are not determined by way of *inference* from a model of rules. It is not like saying if A=B and B=C therefore A *must* equal C. Instead it represents a different kind of method called *functional* reasoning. A solution is fashioned in terms of the intended social *purpose* of the rule in question. In other words, one asks: what is the function of this rule?

A good example of this approach is to be found in the important tort precedent of *Spartan Steel & Alloys v Martin & Co*[55] where an action for damages was brought in negligence by the owner of an alloys factory against contractors working in the street outside the claimants' premises. The contractors had carelessly cut through an electricity cable and this deprived the owners of the factory of electricity for 15 hours or more with the result that the valuable metal in their furnaces hardened and caused damage. In addition to claiming compensation for the physical damage to the furnaces and the metal, the factory owners also demanded damages for the economic loss caused by their inability to use the furnaces during the power cut. Now there is, or at least was, a well-established rule that no duty of care in negligence exists in respect of pure economic loss. If one focused simply on the claim for lost profit, it would appear as a matter of logical inference that the factory owners were not entitled to damages for this head of damage. Yet not only was the rule ambiguous in this situation – cases do exist that have permitted a claimant who has suffered some physical damage to recover for any economic loss 'parasitic' to it – but some lawyers were beginning to question whether the rule itself was justified. Edmund Davies LJ, who dissented in *Spartan*, thought that the fine line between economic loss associated with physical damage and pure financial loss had nothing to do with legal principle.

Lord Denning MR, as one of the majority, took a different view. He certainly discussed the precedents but asserted that at 'bottom . . . the question of recovering economic loss is one of policy'.[56] He later explained that the cutting off of the supply of electricity is 'a hazard which we all run'; that in general 'most people are content to take the risk on themselves'; that 'they do not go running round to their solicitor'; and

---

[54] See eg *Hill v Chief Constable of West Yorkshire* [1989] AC 53.
[55] [1973] 1 QB 27.
[56] [1973] 1 QB 27, at 36.

that this 'is a healthy attitude which the law should encourage'.[57] The policy, in other words, is to spread the loss arising from hazards. Physical damage caused through the fault of another can be transferred onto the shoulders of the person at fault; but the *function* of the economic loss rule in negligence is to limit the amount that the defendant has to bear. These economic losses are spread more widely and between perpetrators and victims.

INTERESTS AND RIGHTS

One might note here how this economic loss rule can be translated into yet another concept that often has an important *functional* role to play in tort reasoning. This is the notion of an *interest* (see PETL art 2:102). The tort of negligence will protect some interests like personal injury and physical damage to property, but will on occasions exclude the pure economic interest.[58] In this context the notion of an interest is basically descriptive; it cannot in itself provide the *normative* force that will determine whether or not the interest is one that can attract compensation. This force has to come from a concept that does have normative force such as a 'right' or a 'duty' (determined in turn by the existence of a cause of action such as trespass or negligence). Consequently the law expresses the economic loss rule in terms of the defendants 'duty' (no duty of care) or the claimant's 'right' (no right to economic loss).

Nevertheless there are occasions in tort when 'interest' can be used in a normative way. In *Burris v Azadani*[59] the Court of Appeal had to decide if a woman being harassed by a particular man was entitled to the injunction that had been granted at first instance to prevent him from coming within 250 yards of her address. The man claimed that the injunction went too far and prevented him from exercising his lawful 'right' to use the public highway that passed by her house. However Sir Thomas Bingham MR analysed the situation in terms of two *interests* that needed to be reconciled. The defendant's liberty must be respected but, equally, 'the plaintiff has an interest which the court must be astute to protect'. Normally the court would grant an injunction only to restrain an actual tort such as trespass or interference with goods. However 'the court may properly judge that in the plaintiff's *interest* – and also, but indirectly, the defendant's – a

---

[57] [1973] 1 QB 27, at 38.
[58] See eg Consumer Protection Act 1987, s 5(1).
[59] [1995] 1 WLR 1372.

wider measure of restraint is called for'.[60] The Court of Appeal accordingly upheld the injunction on the functional basis of an interest.

AXIOLOGY AND ARGUMENTATION

In addition to logical, analogical and functional (policy) reasoning, the judges will often in tort cases employ moral (axiological) reasons. In *Smith New Court Securities Ltd v Scrimgeour Vickers*[61] the House of Lords had to decide whether a more generous measure of damages could be awarded in the tort of deceit than would have been the case if the claim had been one in say negligence. Lord Steyn stated that 'as between the fraudster and the innocent party, moral considerations militate in favour of requiring the fraudster to bear the risk of misfortunes directly caused by his fraud.' Moreover he made 'no apology for referring to moral considerations' since the 'law and morality are inextricably interwoven.' Indeed, to 'a large extent the law is simply formulated and declared morality'.[62] A couple of years later Lord Steyn made very similar comments in *McFarland v Tayside Health Board*.[63] Here he accepted that the role of the court is to apply the law; but the 'judges' sense of the moral answer to a question, or the justice of the case, has been one of the great shaping forces of the common law'.[64] Other judges have exhibited similar views. In *Fairchild v Glenhaven Funeral Services Ltd*[65] Lord Hoffmann stated that:

> as between the employer in breach of duty and the employee who has lost his life in consequence of a period of exposure to risk to which that employer has contributed, I think it would be both inconsistent with the policy of the law imposing the duty and morally wrong for your Lordships to impose causal requirements which exclude liability.[66]

Several other methodological points need to be stressed. The first is that it is not just the judges who are the sources of law; they make their decisions on the basis of arguments presented to them by the parties' barristers. Indeed, the judges rely on the barristers to research the law.[67] The presentation

---

[60] [1995] 1 WLR 1372, at 1380–1.
[61] [1997] AC 254.
[62] [1997] AC 254, at 280.
[63] [2000] 2 AC 59.
[64] [2000] 2 AC 59, at 82.
[65] [2003] 1 AC 32.
[66] [2003] 1 AC 32, at 75.
[67] *Copeland v Smith* [2000] 1 All ER 457.

of these arguments is itself dialectical (for and against) because of the nature of the legal process; thus nearly all English judgments consider in turn the arguments presented first by the claimant's counsel and then by the defendant's. The judge then decides between them, sometimes after a lengthy analysis of the precedents (and/or the statutory provisions) and sometimes after a detailed consideration of the factual context. This decision is often supported by a series of justifications that may, as we have seen, use reasoning internal to the law (for example the interpretation and application of a precedent or text) or external to strict positive law (for example arguments of policy or morality).

Recourse to metaphor is not unusual. For example in *Spartan Steel*[68] (discussed earlier) another form of reasoning employed by Lord Denning to reject the claim for 'parasitic' damages was to say that he did not like the very word 'parasite'. A 'parasite', he said, 'is one who is a useless hanger-on sucking the substance out of others' and the 'phrase "parasitic damages" conveys to my mind the idea of damages which ought not in justice to be awarded, but which somehow or other have been allowed to get through by hanging on to others.' And if 'such be the concept underlying the doctrine, then the sooner it is got rid of the better.' In contrast to this reasoning, one might note that in *White v Jones*[69] the decision of the majority allowing the claimant to succeed for what was in effect a pure economic loss claim was based on 'practical justice', a form of argumentation blending the *functional* with the *axiological*. A similar intermixing of the functional with the moral is often to be found in Lord Steyn's, and sometimes Lord Hoffmann's, judgments. Indeed Lord Hoffmann often brings in arguments from economics.[70]

STATUTORY INTERPRETATION

The foundational source of the law of torts is the common law (precedent). However, legislative intervention and the methods that attach to the interpretation of statutes cannot now be ignored in tort even if the intervention is relatively modest. In the remedial field of damages the intervention is such that the texts have an important role in personal injury claims.[71] And

---

[68] *Spartan Steel & Alloys Ltd v Martin & Co* [1973] 1 QB 27, at 35.
[69] [1995] 2 AC 207.
[70] See eg *Transco plc v Stockport MBC* [2004] 2 AC 1, at para 29; but cf Lord Hobhouse at paras 55–60.
[71] See eg Fatal Accidents Act 1976, Damages Act 1996, Social Security (Recovery of Benefits) Act 1997.

in the area of liability for defective premises (occupiers' liability) the foundation is almost entirely statutory as will be seen in a later chapter.

The methods applied to the interpretation and application of statutory texts are traditionally seen as being rather different from the application of precedents since the starting point is not analogy with pre-existing factual situations. The method is *hermeneutical* in the more traditional sense of working directly on the words of a text (signifier) to discover what Parliament 'intended' (signified). It is a matter of focusing on the text and *interpreting* the words in a way that will give expression to the author's intention. But this 'intention' is normally to be gauged only from the words of the text with the result that, in order to avoid circularity, other reasoning methods find themselves creeping into the justifications. These other methods are, as one might expect, those used in case law analysis and so, for example, one can apply a statutory text in a *literal* (what is the dictionary or legal definition of this word?) or a *functional* manner (what is the purpose of the statute?). The courts seem to oscillate between the two methods or indeed sometimes to combine them.[72]

Reasoning by *analogy* does not usually have a direct role in as much as one cannot normally use a statutory provision such as the Animals Act 1971, s 2(1) as the basis of creating by analogy a strict liability for, say, dangerous objects other than dangerous animals. But recourse to images by way of analogy is often used to test whether or not a word or phrase covers a particular fact ('an elephant is difficult to define but easy to recognise').[73] One might add, that traditional distinctions such as those between physical and mental injury and physical and pure economic damage can still influence the way texts are interpreted.[74]

In the past the approach was often quite literal, the judges stopping at the text itself and not considering the contextual situation.[75] It is not what the legislature aims at but what it hits that counts.[76] But some judges now approach statutory interpretation in a more flexible way. Thus where the statute is ambiguous the judges have partly abandoned their rule that they could not look at Parliamentary debates;[77] and where human rights are involved, the courts are under a statutory duty to interpret in such a way

---

[72] See eg *Birmingham CC v Oakley* [2001] 1 AC 617.
[73] Lawton LJ in *Young v Sun Alliance and London Insurance Ltd* [1977] 1 WLR 104, at 107.
[74] See eg *Morris v KLM Royal Dutch Airlines* [2002] 2 AC 628; *Merlin v British Nuclear Fuels plc* [1990] 2 QB 557.
[75] See eg *Haigh v Charles W Ireland* [1973] 3 All ER 1137.
[76] *St Aubyn v Att-Gen* [1952] AC 15, at 32.
[77] *Pepper v Hart* [1993] AC 593.

that, if at all possible, the Act in question is compatible with European Convention rights.[78] However artificial distinctions are still to be found especially in cases where for example the judges feel they are being forced to make policy decisions which would be better made by Parliament, especially if there are huge financial implications.[79]

The methodology associated with literal interpretation might also be termed a 'shallow' hermeneutical approach in that it takes as its point of focus only the text. This restricts of course the type of reasoning and research that can be applied, for the emphasis is on the dictionary and on technical legal concepts rather than the function of the rule. One searches out, for example, a definition of a 'road' and, logically applying it to the facts in issue, arrives at the conclusion that it does not include a 'car park'.[80] Had one looked at the function of the actual statute, and asked whether it had as its *policy* the exclusion of the claimant from receiving compensation, a wider definition of a 'road' might have resulted. One might add that this lack of partnership between judge and legislator has, in turn, resulted in textual characteristics that can only be described as detailed if not opaque.[81]

METHODOLOGY: CONCLUDING REMARKS

It is by no means easy to offer any general summary of the reasoning methods used in tort. One can say that judges by tradition focus on the case in hand and their primary aim, even in the House of Lords, is only to settle a dispute between two parties.[82] It is not the judges' job to rationalise the law. Yet this does not always mean they are backward-looking and irrational; what it does mean is that they take at best 'one step at a time' working from factual situation to factual situation often by way of analogy.[83] Thus English judges, on the whole, do not see the common law as a system of formal positive rules and concepts waiting to be applied in a logical manner. They tend to see problems in terms of their substantive social, moral and economic context, these contexts often being encapsulated in concepts such as 'practical' or even 'distributive justice'.[84]

---

[78] Human Rights Act 1998, s 3(1).
[79] See eg *Birmingham CC v Oakley* [2001] 1 AC 617; and see Samuel (2009).
[80] *Clarke v Kato* [1998] 1 WLR 1647.
[81] See eg *Mirvahedy v Henley* [2003] 2 AC 491.
[82] See Lord Macmillan in *Read v J Lyons & Co* [1947] AC 156, at 175.
[83] See Lord Simon in *Miliangos v George Frank (Textiles) Ltd* [1976] AC 443, at 481–2.
[84] See Lord Steyn in *McFarlane v Tayside Health Board* [2000] 2 AC 59, at 82.

This is not to suggest that they have abandoned 'applying the law'; but in the application judges are quite prepared to have recourse to open-ended reasoning tools such as 'policy', 'reasonableness' and 'justice'. Of course, different judges can take different approaches. Indeed, sometimes the same judge can adopt differing approaches in different cases. One might compare for example the judgment of Devlin J in *Esso v Southport*[85] with that of Denning LJ in the same case (see Chapter 4).[86] One adopted a reasoning approach to liability founded on general principle, the other started out from liability and duty attaching to particular tort categories. In other cases Lord Denning has seemingly abandoned the category approach in favour of broad-based principle.[87] Perhaps Stephen Waddams best sums up legal reasoning in private law cases. 'It is not so much that various *alternative* approaches are *permissible*', he says, 'as that various *complementary* approaches are *necessary* (to the understanding of a complex phenomenon)'.[88]

---

[85] [1953] 3 WLR 773.
[86] [1954] 2 QB 182.
[87] See eg *Letang v Cooper* [1965] 1 QB 232.
[88] Waddams (2003), at 232.

10. Liability and intentional harm

The frontiers between tort and other areas of the law of obligations suggest that tort obligations have a substantive existence of their own. Yet, as we have already seen with regard to contract, the notion of liability acts as a meeting point between the *vinculum iuris* (legal bond) and the *actio* (remedy). In the civilian world the distinction between obligation and liability is once again attracting attention even if in the common law the distinction is often masked by the emphasis on causes of action and on remedies. Accordingly liability, as a focal point in itself, has attracted its own theorising in that it raises a general question about accident liability and the factual sources of such accidents.

LIABILITY AND FAULT

In the civil law systems non-contractual compensation claims have traditionally been closely interrelated with fault (PETL art 1:101(2)(a)). Indeed, as we saw in the last chapter, it could generally be said that loss and damage accidentally caused would lie where it fell and could be transferred onto the shoulders of another only if that other was to blame for the harm. Roman law was particularly influential here given the central importance of *injuria* (wrongfulness) and *culpa* (blame) in both contractual (see D.13.6.5) and non-contractual damage claims (D.47.10.1pr). However this Roman foundation was given added support by the Christian notion of individual responsibility in the later civil law with the result that fault became an 'axiomatic truth'.[1]

With the rise of industry, technology and, later, widespread insurance this individualistic attitude to liability began to change and a second principle developed to challenge fault. This is the principle of risk (PETL art 1:101(2)(b)). The problem with fault is that, when viewed from the position of the victim, it is an arbitrary way of determining who should receive compensation, especially when statistics indicate that the accident rate is relatively constant from one year to the next. Moreover the statistics suggest

---

[1] Zimmermann (1996), at 1033–5.

that making wrongdoers pay was not a deterrence; indeed the existence of (often compulsory) insurance could, anyway, be said to negative such deterrence. Nevertheless, despite the growth of risk liability in France and in some other systems, the fault principle is proving harder to abandon than one might think. Its moral force seems irrepressible and it does have the economic advantage of limiting liability, thus providing scope for liberty of action for those engaged in activities that ultimately benefit the public.[2]

In English law the fault principle remains central to tort liability in a number of ways. First, despite the existence of several strict liability torts, the House of Lords went far in indicating that, in an action for personal injuries (by far the most important type of tort claim), fault normally had to be proved.[3] Secondly, the 'pull of the negligence principle – pay for the foreseeable harm you are at fault in causing – is immensely strong';[4] so strong, indeed, that it has tended to subvert other ideas. Thirdly, as we have seen, English law has committed itself to no single theory or aim when it comes to tort liability. 'It cannot lightly be taken for granted, even as a matter of theory, that the purpose of the law of tort is compensation' said Lord Wilberforce; as 'a matter of practice English law has not committed itself to any of these theories, it may have been wiser than it knew'.[5] English doctrine can sometimes be similarly sceptical, although some academics like to propound theories that can sometime seem far removed from judicial reality.

In fact, Lord Wilberforce's statement hides a continuing commitment to an 'individualistic philosophy' and to the requirement of fault.[6] At a formal level liability is dependent upon the existence or non-existence of a cause of action and in tort these causes of action are traditionally presented in list form seemingly bound together only by the alphabet. The result is that, at first sight, fault appears as a requirement of some but not all torts. However when tort is viewed from the perspective of damage, the picture changes in that personal injury damage and to some extent physical damage to property usually require fault before liability is established (strict liability cases becoming the exception).[7] Fault for this purpose

---

[2] See *Tomlinson v Congleton BC* [2004] 1 AC 46.
[3] *Read v J Lyons & Co* [1947] AC 156. But cf *In re Corby Group Litigation* [2009] 2 WLR 609 (CA).
[4] Weir (1998), at 137.
[5] *Broome v Cassell & Co Ltd* [1972] AC 1027, at 1114.
[6] Lord Hoffmann in *Reeves v Commissioner of Police for the Metropolis* [2000] 1 AC 360, at 368.
[7] See eg *Transco plc v Stockport MBC* [2004] 2 AC 1. But cf *In re Corby Group Litigation* [2009] 2 WLR 609 (CA).

does include illegal acts (breach of a statute) and in the area of industrial injuries this gave rise to the tort of breach of statutory duty which in turn resulted in a marked shift towards risk.[8] However such a regime was rejected in respect of traffic accidents.[9]

The position in France seems quite different in that the French *Cour de cassation*, during the 20th century, created a whole area of risk liability on the basis of CC art 1384. As the Advocate General in one of the principal decisions holding the family liable for a traffic accident caused by a young person stated: 'In civil liability law the notion of fault is becoming more and more restricted and the need to compensate victims for their harm is leading to the search for objective situations where a right to compensation will flow automatically.' And he continued, the 'liability for harm done by things under one's control, that of employers for their employees, the law of 5 July 1985 on traffic accident victims are examples of this'.[10] One should add that the French public law courts have been equally adventurous in developing no fault liability. This does not mean that liability for fault is redundant. This is very much not the case. What it means is that liability can now be presented under a number of broad general headings and these headings can perhaps be used to map out a general pattern of liability (and see also PETL art 1:101). These patterns of liability will be the focus of this chapter and the next.

LIABILITY FOR INDIVIDUAL ACTS: GENERAL ELEMENTS

The first head of liability is the one that normally attaches to fault and is expressed in its most concise and abstract form by CC art 1382. According to this article three conditions must be proved before liability is established: there must be (i) damage, (ii) fault and (iii) causation. Each condition has given rise to a mass of case law and doctrine in Western legal systems and it would be idle even to try to summarise this material or to try to draw out of it any normative propositions that can be succinctly stated. Several points ought nevertheless be made about each of these conditions of liability.

---

[8] *Groves v Wimborne* [1898] 2 QB 402.
[9] *Phillips v Britannia Hygienic Laundry Co* [1923] 2 KB 832.
[10] Cass.civ. 19.2.1997, JCP 1997 II.22848.

Damage

Physical damage to person or property is normally easy enough to identify. One can point to the broken limbs or to the wrecked car. However psychological damage can be much more difficult and has given rise to problems in various legal systems; pure economic loss is equally problematic in some systems (and see PETL art 2:102(4)). In fact the more intangible the damage – for example loss of a chance – the more likely it is that the case law in Western systems will be complex. In common law systems damage problems arising out of accidents are normally dealt with under what is called the 'duty of care' question. However negligence is not the only tort. In private nuisance, for example, an important distinction is made between tangible and intangible damage (in respect of the defence of locality); and, more generally, the relationship between damage and the remedy of damages has created a whole sub-section of case law precedents (since damage is defined in relation to 'a legally protected interest': PETL art 2:101).

A further problem that arises in the common law is the possibility of liability in situations where no damage is proved. Some torts such as trespass and defamation are said to be actionable *per se* and, with respect to the latter, large sums of money have been awarded in situations where the relationship between compensation and discernible damage can appear tenuous. In fact many unfortunate defendants have been forced to pay damages for failing to prove true in court things that subsequently turned out to be perfectly true. Trespass is a little different in that this tort has a range of aims and objectives. In situations where it is protecting constitutional rights (for example false imprisonment) the awarding of damages might be made to fulfil aims other than direct compensation. There are intangible aspects. In other trespass situations the award of damages might be made to fulfil restitutionary aims (cf Chapter 16). This restitutionary aim lies behind some of the exemplary damages cases, that is to say situations where damages are awarded not to compensate but to punish.

Fault

The second requirement for liability is normally fault (PETL art 4:101). In civil law systems fault is a broad category encompassing deliberate harm at one extreme and the slightest degree of negligence at the other (D.9.2.44pr). These two poles turn out, however, to be more complex than mere points either end of a spectrum. In the case of deliberate harm liability is based on what might be called a subjective state of mind; carelessly caused harm, in contrast, is different in that one cannot talk so easily of a particular state of mind. Thus in Roman law, as we have seen, the existence and non-existence of fault was determined objectively on the facts themselves. The result was that even a learner (mule) driver could be held liable for damage caused by his inexperience since, objectively, he should have known that he presented a danger to others (D.9.2.8.1). English law has arrived at a similar conclusion.[11] One effect of this approach is that fault comes to embrace not just behaviour as such but also risk which in turn can act as a means of moving liability beyond fault.

The idea of minimal fault as sufficient to trigger liability is usually to be found in most systems, although different degrees of fault can result in different measures of damages if not different forms of liability. But of course proof can be a problem.[12] Ideas of risk can again come into play here in that the law might deem some forms of damage arising from some forms of activity as raising a presumption of fault (PETL art 4:201); the onus will then be on the defendant to disprove fault if he wishes to escape liability. Equally, other activities might be treated more favourably by the courts, especially if they are perceived to have a high social and moral value (for example cricket).[13]

In the common law fault is not employed as a generic category since liability did not develop through abstract principle but through a system of individualised forms of action. The result is that different types of fault give rise to different torts. Fraudulent behaviour that causes damage will give rise to deceit, while negligent damage must be remedied through the tort of negligence. Deliberate physical harm to another will normally be a trespass and certain kinds of abuse of power by public officials may result in other specific torts.[14] Economic loss deliberately caused attracts yet other torts.[15] One point that must be made at the outset is this. In several famous late 19th century decisions the House of Lords confirmed that the intention and damage are not sufficient in themselves to generate liability in tort; there must be something more.[16] Nevertheless this categorisation of fault into specific kinds associated with specific torts has been breaking down to some extent with respect to negligent behaviour.

Yet the expansion of negligence as a general basis of liability in the common law world implies that there is a field of liability where fault does not have to be proved. In French law such strict liability is associated

---

[11] *Nettleship v Weston* [1971] 2 QB 691.
[12] As the victims of the Potters Bar rail crash discovered: letter *The Guardian*, 18 September 2003.
[13] See now Compensation Act 2006, s 1.
[14] See eg *Gibbs v Rea* [1998] AC 786.
[15] *OBG Ltd v Allan* [2008] 1 AC 1.
[16] See eg *Bradford Corporation v Pickles* [1895] AC 587.

with CC art 1384 which imposes liability upon a defendant in respect of persons and things under his control and which cause damage. The PETL base such liability on abnormally dangerous activities (art 5:101) and on liability for 'auxiliaries' (arts 1:101(2)(c), 6:102(1)). In English law, as one might expect, there is no equivalent general provision; there are, instead, a number of specific 'strict liability' torts such as trespass, public and private nuisance, breach of statutory duty, the rule in *Rylands v Fletcher* and defamation. There is also a more general rule that an employer will automatically be liable for a tort committed by an employee acting in the course of his employment (vicarious liability) (see Chapter 13). In some ways this category approach is valuable in that it operates quite close to the facts; yet it is also vulnerable to the reductionist principle of fault unless the strict liability categories are themselves underpinned by a powerful normative alternative.[17]

Causation

The third condition for liability is that there must be a causal link between the blameworthy act (or even non-blameworthy act in the case of liability without fault) and the damage (see Chapter 15). This is generally regarded as the most difficult, yet philosophically intriguing, part of obligations liability and the conundrums start in Roman law itself (cf D.9.2.11pr) to end up as competing theories in modern legal thinking (PETL arts 3:101–3:106). As a result the topic has two distinctive dimensions. There is the academic dimension dominated by theories of causation and there is the case law aspect where many judges profess a 'common sense' or 'practical' approach. Whether or not theory or common sense offers any kind of philosophical insight is a matter that can be decided only by examining the massive case law and doctrine. But what cannot be doubted is that in most systems intuition and social policy have a certain role in the recognition, or not, of a causal link (see Chapter 15).

INTENTIONAL HARM

Most English textbooks on the law of tort approach liability either from the position of particular categories of causes of action – trespass, negligence, nuisance, defamation and so on – or from the perspective of particular interests invaded (physical, economic, reputation and the like). Given the history of the forms of action and the absence of codification

---

[17] See eg *Transco plc v Stockport MBC* [2004] 2 AC 1.

such an approach is understandable. This cause of action approach to tort means, however, that it is not to look at tort strictly from the position of types of behaviour. Moreover the line between intention and negligence is sometimes difficult if not impossible to draw.[18] Nevertheless a types-of-behaviour perspective can be useful when it comes to an understanding of how liability functions in a European comparative context which, in turn, may provide new insights for analysing litigation problems.

It would be tempting to say that all intentionally caused damage ought to be actionable by the victim, but a moment's reflection will soon reveal that such a principle would be untenable. The deliberate causing of *physical* injury without legal justification is prima facie actionable and this includes psychological injury (nervous shock).[19] Indeed, to put someone in fear of violence can amount to trespass,[20] as might an indirect act which leads to personal injury.[21] Maliciously causing someone to be prosecuted can be a tort,[22] as can the malicious spreading of false statements about a person and (or) his business.[23] Maliciously abusing the legal process is equally actionable.[24] Creating a noise on one's property with the deliberate intention of annoying a neighbour will amount to a nuisance since no one has the right to create noise and deliberately causing it will by definition amount to an unreasonable use of land.[25] However intention alone can never constitute a tort since it is not the behaviour that generates liability in English law. Liability is always a matter of a cause of action and thus a claimant must prove the constituent elements of such a category.[26]

The deliberate causing of *economic loss* is more difficult, for if it were made generally actionable capitalism would no doubt grind to a halt. Deliberately caused economic loss will be actionable only in certain circumstances. Thus at common law (but not now under European law) one trader has the right to ruin a competitor by grossly under-pricing his goods or services;[27] only if the trader commits an 'unlawful act' might the loss be actionable. One difficulty with this area of 'economic torts' is to decide what amounts to unlawfulness for the purpose of an action. The courts

---

[18] See *Wainwright v Home Office* [2004] 2 AC 406, at para 37.
[19] *Wilkinson v Downton* [1897] 2 QB 57; cf *Wainwright v Home Office* [2004] 2 AC 406, at paras 36–47.
[20] *Read v Coker* (1853) 138 ER 1437.
[21] *Fagan v Metropolitan Police Commissioner* [1969] 1 QB 439.
[22] *Martin v Watson* [1996] AC 74.
[23] *Ratcliffe v Evans* [1892] 2 QB 524.
[24] *Keegan v Chief Constable of Merseyside Police* [2003] 1 WLR 2187.
[25] *Christie v Davey* [1893] 1 Ch 316.
[26] *Bradford Corporation v Pickles* [1895] AC 587.
[27] *Mogul SS Co v McGregor, Gow & Co* [1892] AC 25.

have attempted to define liability by requiring the existence of a number of conditional elements such as an intention directly to injure coupled with some kind of objective wrong (illegal threat, nuisance or whatever). But many cases are not free from ambiguity and circularity of reasoning.[28]

Another difficulty with these economic torts (a rather specialised area outside of this introductory survey) is to define their limits.[29] Not every intentional injury causing economic loss will be actionable otherwise all industrial action by ill-treated workers would be tortious (although much of it is) and all calls to boycott a product or service would equally be actionable. One notion developed by the courts is that of *legitimate interest* as related to the behaviour of the defendant. Thus if the defendant is acting to protect a well established interest this may give rise either to the non-existence of any economic tort or to a defence based on justification. For example a trade association can impose fines on its members and any threat of expulsion for non-payment will not amount to blackmail or an economic tort.[30] Even behaviour that is illegal might not be actionable in tort if it was not aimed at the claimant.[31] However if a defendant intentionally damages a claimant in circumstances where he has no interest of his own to protect, it may be that the damage will be actionable even if the behaviour itself does not actually fit into any civil or criminal wrong category.[32]

It is of course these latter cases that make this area so complex, particularly where the remedy sought is an interlocutory (emergency) injunction rather than damages. But if one was to try to formulate a rule-of-thumb principle it would be based on the idea that the direct intentional invasion of another's commercial interest might well be actionable if the means used are unlawful and there is an absence of any justification on the defendant's part. What amounts to 'direct', to 'unlawful' or to 'justification' is of course by no means clear and so if one is able to add a proprietary dimension – the defendant is interfering with the claimant's 'property *right*' – it sometimes gives further conceptual strength to the granting of a remedy.

INTENTIONAL TORTS

The nature of the damage is one important key, then, when it comes to harm intentionally caused. Yet despite movements towards some kind of

---

[28] But see now *OBG Ltd v Allan* [2008] 1 AC 1.
[29] *OBG Ltd v Allan* [2008] 1 AC 1.
[30] *Thorne v Motor Trade Association* [1937] AC 797.
[31] *Lonrho v Shell Petroleum Co Ltd (No 2)* [1982] AC 173.
[32] *Gulf Oil (GB) Ltd v Page* [1987] Ch 327.

general principle with respect both to physical and to economic loss, the only safe approach to liability is via specific existing torts.[33] Some of the principal torts dealing with intentionally (or maliciously) caused harm thus need to be examined in outline. As there is no common denominator, save a particular state of mind, the torts can only be approached alphabetically.[34]

Abuse of Civil (and Criminal) Process

Abuse of the criminal process can give rise, as we shall see, to the tort of malicious prosecution. Abuse of the civil process is also now to be a tort and one that seems to be an extension by analogy of malicious prosecution. Whereas malicious prosecution lies only in respect of criminal proceedings, the tort of abuse of process extends across the whole spectrum of civil proceedings. The foundational modern case is *Speed Seal Products v Paddington*[35] which in some ways is a rather weak authority being only a striking out action (whether a claimant has an arguable case). Nevertheless there have been subsequent first instance decisions that fall under this heading of abuse of process and the whole developmental logic of the law of tort would suggest that this is an established head of liability. One such (relatively) recent decision is *Gibbs v Rea*[36] which establishes that the malicious procurement of a search warrant is actionable if four conditions are fulfilled. These conditions, set out in a later case, are: '(1) a successful application for a search warrant, (2) lack of reasonable and probable cause to make the application, (3) malice and (4) resultant damage arising from the issue or execution of the warrant'.[37] What is interesting about this tort is that it seems to be a cause of action independent of malicious prosecution, abuse of public office and even perhaps abuse of civil process (although for convenience it is listed here under this more general heading), thus confirming that an alphabetical list of causes of action is still the approach when it comes to intentional damage.

Abuse of (Misfeasance in) Public Office

Another 'administrative' tort in some ways analogous to malicious prosecution and abuse of civil process is abuse of public office, more commonly known now as misfeasance in public office. This tort can be brought by

---

[33] Confirmed by *Wainwright v Home Office* [2004] 2 AC 406.
[34] B Rudden, Torticles (1991–2) 6/7 *Tulane Civil Law Forum* 105.
[35] [1985] 1 WLR 1327.
[36] [1998] AC 786.
[37] Kennedy LJ in *Keegan v Chief Constable of Merseyside Police* [2003] 1 WLR 2187, at para 13.

an individual against a public officer who has intentionally or recklessly damaged the claimant. The history and the requirements of the tort have been fully explored in recent years by the House of Lords in *Three Rivers DC v Bank of England* where Lord Steyn set out the conditions for liability.[38] These are that there must be an abusive exercise of power by a public officer aimed at the claimant, or a class of persons in which the claimant belongs, and the claimant him or herself must have a 'sufficient interest' in the action which will no doubt be fulfilled if serious economic loss (or other damage) is suffered. The abuse must also be the cause of the claimant's loss. As Lord Millet observed, the 'tort is an intentional tort which can be committed only by a public official' and from 'this two things follow.' The 'tort cannot be committed negligently or inadvertently' and, secondly, the 'core concept is abuse of power' which 'in turn involves other concepts, such as dishonesty, bad faith, and improper purpose.'[39] Another requirement is that damage must be proved.[40]

Breach of Statutory Duty

The tort of breach of statutory duty is not normally regarded as one of the intentional torts since its primary, although not exclusive, role is to act as one means for obtaining compensation for work injuries.[41] Nevertheless if the wilful behaviour of the defendant constitutes the breach of a statute it is possible that this cause of action might be relevant provided that the essential conditions for liability are fulfilled. The basis of the tort has been described by Lord Browne-Wilkinson: 'a private law cause of action will arise if it can be shown, as a matter of construction of the statute, that the statutory duty was imposed for the protection of a limited class of the public and that Parliament intended to confer on members of that class a private right of action for breach of the duty.'[42] An employer recklessly indifferent about the safety of his employees would no doubt be liable under this head.

Conspiracy

We have seen that a mere intention to cause damage is not in itself enough to give rise to liability in tort.[43] However if several people combine in order

---

[38] *Three Rivers DC v Bank of England (No 3)* [2003] 2 AC 1, at 191ff.
[39] *Ibid*, at 235.
[40] *Watkins v Home Office* [2006] 2 AC 395.
[41] *Groves v Wimborne* [1898] 2 QB 402.
[42] *X (Minors) v Bedfordshire County Council* [1995] 2 AC 633, at 731.
[43] *Mogul SS Co v McGregor, Gow & Co* [1892] AC 25.

deliberately to cause damage to another this may amount to the tort of civil conspiracy. Liability can be incurred even if the combination does not indulge in acts that are unlawful in themselves. This 'is the so-called "lawful means" conspiracy which is tortious notwithstanding that the means employed to cause the harm are themselves neither criminal nor tortious.' And the 'essential ingredient of this type of action is the combination of people all intent on causing harm to the victim, not on the type of means employed for doing so.'[44] However even if unlawful means are employed this does not always result in liability, for not 'every criminal act committed in order to injure can or should give rise to tortious liability to the person injured, even where the element of conspiracy is present.' Thus for example the 'pizza delivery business which obtains more custom, to the detriment of its competitors, because it instructs its drivers to ignore speed limits and jump red lights (. . .) should not be liable, even if the claim be put as a claim in conspiracy involving its drivers and directors.'[45] Conspiracy forms part of a group which has attracted the label 'economic torts'.

Conversion

Where one person aims his intention to injure not directly at the claimant but at the claimant's tangible property there is the possibility of the defendant being liable for wrongful interference with goods. This notion of wrongful interference is possibly not a tort in itself but a statutory creation which includes trespass, negligence and conversion.[46] Trespass to goods involves a direct interference with *possession* and thus a defendant will be liable if, for example, he deliberately rides off on the claimant's bicycle simply to annoy him. If the defendant were to sell the bicycle claiming it as his own the claimant would have an action in conversion, a tort remedying interference with *title*. Lord Nicholls has recently stated that conversion of goods 'can occur in so many different circumstances that framing a definition of universal application is well nigh impossible.' However he said that there are in general three basic features to the tort: that the defendant's conduct was inconsistent with the owner's rights or other person entitled to possession; that the conduct was deliberate and not accidental; and that 'the conduct was so extensive an encroachment on the rights of the owner as to exclude him from the use and possession

---

[44] Lord Scott in *Revenue and Customs Commissioners v Total Network SL* [2008] 2 WLR 711, at para 56.
[45] Lord Mance in *Revenue and Customs Commissioners v Total Network SL* [2008] 2 WLR 711, at para 119.
[46] Torts (Interference with Goods) Act 1977, s 1.

of the goods'. Lord Nicholls then added that these requirements are to be contrasted with lesser acts of interference such as trespass or negligence.[47] Conversion, then, can truly be an intentional tort, although it can also be committed even in situations where the defendant is innocent of any fault.[48]

Deceit

'For a plaintiff to succeed in the tort of deceit', said Hobhouse LJ, 'it is necessary for him to prove that (1) the representation was fraudulent, (2) it was material and (3) it induced the plaintiff to act (to his detriment).' And a 'representation is material when its tendency, or its natural and probable result, is to induce the representee to act on the faith of it in the kind of way in which he is proved to have in fact acted.' And, he added, the 'test is objective'.[49] This is an old tort and is the basis of most actions for damages where the loss arises from the defendant's fraud. Accordingly it can often have a role in situations involving contracts that have been entered into as a result of one party's fraudulent misrepresentation. The main difficulty facing claimants is that they must prove fraud. However, thanks to statute, any misrepresentation that induces a contract will now be actionable in tort without the claimant having to prove fraud, the defendant escaping liability only by proving the absence of fault.[50]

Defamation

Defamation is when one person publishes an untrue statement about another person that injures the reputation of the other and is a tort very easily incurred even in situations where the writer and (or) publisher had no intention of defaming the claimant. It is, therefore, a central tort against a person who deliberately sets out to damage another through the publication of statements. Although easily incurred – almost any statement critical of another will be defamatory provided it is published (defamation is strictly a three-party tort) – there are three important defences. These are justification (truth), fair comment and privilege. As a result of the Human Rights Act 1998, this last defence has been extended in recent

---

[47] *Kuwait Airways Corpn v Iraqi Airways Co (Nos 4 & 5)* [2002] 2 AC 883, at para 39.
[48] See eg *Willis & Son (RH) v British Car Auctions* [1978] 2 All ER 392.
[49] *Downs v Chappell* [1997] 1 WLR 426, at 433.
[50] Misrepresentation Act 1967, s 2(1).

years to cover the 'reasonable journalist' who reports in good faith a story in the public interest that turns out to be untrue.[51] Proof of damage is unnecessary in situations where the defamatory statement is in permanent (normally written) form (libel), but might be required where it is in spoken form (slander).

Harassment

One way of explaining the absence of proof of damage in libel cases is to say that it is a tort designed to protect a personality (law of persons) right, the assumed damage being a form of mental distress. But what if one deliberately causes mental distress in a way other than through publication? A number of established torts can be relevant; threats of violence might be a trespass and deliberate harassment of a neighbour can amount to a private nuisance. However, although there is no general tort of harassment (or privacy) at common law,[52] there is now a statutory one in which damages can be obtained for anxiety and any financial loss arising from the harassment.[53] In addition, it is possible, in equity, that a court might issue an injunction on the basis of preventing a person from being tempted to commit an existing tort such as trespass or public nuisance in situations where the problem is one of harassment and the claimant has a clear interest in need of protection.[54]

Human Rights

Even if there were no 1997 Act against harassment, it is possible that certain forms of conduct falling within it would also now amount to an invasion of a right protected by the European Convention of Human Rights and Fundamental Freedoms, now part of English law thanks to the Human Rights Act 1998. The 1998 Act impacts on tort in two main ways. First it has a vertical effect in declaring unlawful any act by a 'public authority' which is 'incompatible with a Convention right' (s 6) and granting the victim a remedy in damages against such an authority (s 8). Secondly, it has a horizontal effect in introducing into English law some new rights, for example privacy, which were not available at common law. It may be that if these rights are invaded by a

---

[51] *Reynolds v Times Newspapers Ltd* [2001] 2 AC 127.
[52] *Wainwright v Home Office* [2004] 2 AC 406.
[53] Protection from Harassment Act, 1997, s 3; *Majrowski v Guy's & St Thomas's NHS Trust* [2007] 1 AC 224.
[54] *Burris v Azadani* [1995] 1 WLR 1372.

private body or individual there will be no action for damages as such.[55] However Equity, whose jurisdiction is wider and encompasses all established legal rights, might well be prepared to grant one of its remedies to the victim of an invasion. It must be stressed, however, that, strictly speaking, an action for damages under the 1998 Act is not a claim in the law of tort.[56]

Inducing a Breach of Contract (Economic Torts)

Intentionally causing damage in the world of business is, as we have seen, a particularly difficult area for the law of tort since commercial competition is regarded as healthy and justified. This attitude was even extended to trade unions. If, in encouraging its members to go on strike, a union official committed no civil or criminal wrong, then such an official could not be liable in tort.[57] However it had been established earlier in the 19th century that if one person induced another to break his or her contract with a third party this third party would have an action in tort against the person who induced the breach.[58] In the later 20th century this tort was seemingly extended to include any interference (rather than actual breach) by one person with a contract between two others, but this extension has now been curbed.[59] In addition to this particular tort, the courts have developed others such as civil conspiracy (see above) that are both separate yet analogous.

Intimidation

Another analogous economic tort that is of importance with respect to intention to injure is the tort of intimidation. 'So long as the defendant only threatens to do what he has a legal right to do he is on safe ground', said Lord Reid. Provided that 'there is no conspiracy he would not be liable to anyone for doing the act, whatever his motive might be, and it would be absurd to make him liable for threatening to do it but not for doing it.' However Lord Reid then asserted 'that there is a chasm between doing what you have a legal right to do and doing what you have no legal right to do, and there seems to me to be the same chasm between

---

[55] *Wainwright v Home Office* [2004] 2 AC 406.
[56] *R (Greenfield) v Secretary of State for the Home Department* [2005] 1 WLR 673, at para 19.
[57] *Allen v Flood* [1898] AC 1.
[58] *Lumley v Gye* (1853) 2 E & B 216; 118 ER 749.
[59] *OBG Ltd v Allan* [2008] 1 AC 1.

threatening to do what you have a legal right to do and threatening to do what you have no legal right to do'.[60]

Malicious Falsehood

Malicious falsehood is a separate tort from defamation, although the two may overlap on occasions, in that it protects a person's business interest rather than reputation interest.[61] It is available where one person maliciously publishes a falsehood about another's trade or business. The claimant does not have to prove loss if the damage to the business was intentional and the publication is in a permanent form.[62] More recently the tort has been used in circumstances where one person has deliberately set out to blacken another's name and, even if the damages are modest (because the damage must be to a person's business interest rather than reputation), it can be useful to a claimant who wishes to clear his or her name.[63]

Malicious Prosecution

Malice is equally actionable where it has motivated a prosecution. In *Martin v Watson* Lord Keith quoting, *Clerk & Lindsell on Torts*, said that

> the plaintiff must show first that he was prosecuted by the defendant, that is to say, that the law was set in motion against him on a criminal charge; secondly, that the prosecution was determined in his favour; thirdly, that it was without reasonable and probable cause; fourthly, that it was malicious.

And the 'onus of proving every one of these is on the plaintiff.'[64] One might note here that malicious intention is not enough; the prosecution itself must be unreasonable. However although the tort is, in practice, one that is used mainly against the police and is thus an aspect of what a civil lawyer would call administrative liability, it can also be brought against private individuals if such an individual is the person who 'set the law in motion' (Lord Keith).

Negligence

It may seem very odd to include in a list of intentional torts the tort of negligence, for this is by definition a cause of action based on a state of

---

[60] *Rookes v Barnard* [1964] AC 1129, at 1168–9.
[61] *Joyce v Sengupta* [1993] 1 WLR 337.
[62] Defamation Act 1952, s 3.
[63] *Khodaparast v Shad* [2000] 1 WLR 618.
[64] [1996] AC 74, at 80.

mind that is different from wilfulness or malice. Yet the tort of negligence, which requires a breach of a duty of care that causes damage to the person to whom the duty is owed, might well be very relevant even if the damage has been caused intentionally since a defendant will not be able to escape from liability by arguing that he acted intentionally rather than negligently. Thus an employer who maliciously writes an untrue reference about an ex-employee can be liable in negligence in addition to any possible liability in defamation.[65] On a practical level, negligence might be useful where a claimant suspects that the defendant was acting intentionally, or fraudulently, but cannot prove it. One difficulty, however, is that where the damage is financial rather than physical, there is a presumption that no duty of care is owed, but there are important exceptions to this rule.

Passing Off

Because of the financial loss rule in negligence it is sometimes tempting to transcend this category of liability and state that economic loss in general is an interest that is imperfectly protected. Yet there are plenty of torts designed to protect interests beyond the physical. Where for example a defendant interferes with another's intangible property by passing off his goods as those of another there will be a tort. The action, which arose in the 19th century, has, according to Lord Diplock, five characteristics which must be present

> in order to create a valid cause of action for passing off: (1) misrepresentation, (2) made by a trader in the course of his trade, (3) to prospective customers of his or ultimate consumers of the goods and services supplied by him, (4) which is calculated to injure the business or goodwill of another trader (in the sense that this is a reasonably foreseeable consequence) and (5) which causes actual damage to a business or goodwill of the trader.[66]

From the defendant's position it is a kind of *deceit* practised on the public while from the claimant's position it is an invasion of a particular *commercial interest* bordering on a property right. It is, accordingly, a tort that can be put alongside malicious falsehood and the economic torts in as much as it is an action founded mainly on intentional wrongdoing which invades another's business or professional interests.

---

[65] *Spring v Guardian Assurance Plc* [1995] 2 AC 296.
[66] *Erven Warnink BV v J Townend & Sons* [1979] AC 731, at 742.

Private Nuisance

Land is another form of property that attracts the law of tort. Where one neighbour carries out an activity on his land with the sole purpose of intentionally annoying his neighbour this may amount to the tort of private nuisance if the behaviour is regarded as an unreasonable use of land. Private nuisance is available where a defendant has unreasonably 'used his own land or some other land in such a way as injuriously to affect the enjoyment of the plaintiffs' land'.[67] Intention to injure is important here because this of itself can turn a reasonable activity into an unreasonable one. Thus where one land owner set off shotguns on his land deliberately to cause injury to his neighbour's silver foxes this amounted to a nuisance.[68] As for the activity itself, there must normally be some element of continuity and thus a single, isolated escape of a dangerous thing will not be a nuisance although it may give rise to an action in negligence or under the rule in *Rylands v Fletcher*[69] (which is treated as a cause of action separate from nuisance).

Public Nuisance

Public nuisance, although it may on some occasions arise out of the same facts as private nuisance, is conceptually a quite distinct tort from private nuisance. It arises out of the crime of public nuisance and generates a claim in tort for any person who suffers special damage, a term which includes pure economic loss. Public nuisance is difficult to define – it 'covers a multitude of sins, great and small'[70] – but can be summed up as 'any nuisance . . . which materially affects the reasonable comfort and convenience of life of a class of Her Majesty's subjects'.[71] Any person who intentionally intends to cause annoyance or harm through behaviour that injuriously affects a section of the public at large (for example a demonstration on the highway) risks being sued for damages in public nuisance from any individual who suffers damage over and above the rest of the community. One might also note that indulging in criminal or unsocial activity, such as running a brothel, could well result in an

---

[67] Denning LJ in *Esso Petroleum Ltd v Southport Corporation* [1954] 2 QB 182, at 196.
[68] *Hollywood Silver Fox Farm v Emmett* [1936] 2 KB 468.
[69] (1866) LR 1 Ex 265 (Ex); (1868) LR 3 HL 330 (HL).
[70] Denning LJ in *Esso Petroleum Ltd v Southport Corporation* [1954] 2 QB 182, at 196.
[71] *Att-Gen v PYA Quarries Ltd* [1957] 2 QB 169, at 184.

action for an injunction based on public nuisance brought by an irate neighbour.[72]

Trespass

Nuisance is concerned with indirect damage, but if the damage is caused directly then the tort of trespass may be relevant. This comes in several forms depending upon the type of invasion. Direct violence to the person is assault and battery, while the unlawful restraint of a person is false imprisonment. Invasion of a person's possession of land or a chattel amounts to trespass to land or to goods. The main requirement is that the defendant directly invades the defendant's person or property without lawful authority. In theory the mere intentional touching of another is a battery and thus if D pushes C into a swimming pool and C is badly injured as a result D will be liable in trespass. But merely bumping into someone in a school playground, supermarket or busy street, even if it causes injury, might be different because there is an implied consent to this type of behaviour ('we live in a crowded world').[73] In false imprisonment, the defendant must be directly responsible for the imprisonment[74] and there must be no means of escape;[75] but technically speaking the claimant does not necessarily have to be aware of the imprisonment.[76] Consent is a defence to trespass and this can be implied in for example cases of necessity[77] or where various persons indulge in sport or even in horseplay.[78]

INTENTIONAL TORTS AND METHODOLOGY

The torts outlined above are not necessarily the only ones that can come into play in situations where one person has intentionally caused damage to another.[79] It is not, in other words, a definitive list. However it does set out the main torts that might be relevant in situations where one person intentionally causes harm to another and the principal point to emerge from this list is the importance of categorising factual situations around

---

[72] *Thompson-Schwab v Costaki* [1956] 1 WLR 335.
[73] *Wilson v Pringle* [1987] QB 237.
[74] *Harnett v Bond* [1925] AC 669.
[75] *Bird v Jones* (1845) 115 ER 668.
[76] *Murray v Ministry of Defence* [1988] 1 WLR 692.
[77] *F (In re)* [1990] 2 AC 1.
[78] *Blake v Galloway* [2004] 1 WLR 2844.
[79] See Rudden (1991–2).

a number of descriptive focal points. These focal points are the nature of the claimant's *harm*, itself often translatable into 'interest' (cf PETL art 2:101), and the *means used* by the defendant (cf PETL art 1:101).

Where the harm is physical the emphasis tends to shift immediately to the means used, the intensity of the defendant's behaviour and the causal relationship between the two. That is to say, the analysis is relatively straight-forward in terms of established legal concepts and institutions. Where acute problems can arise is with respect to invasions of non-physical interests. Here a distinction needs to be made between principles of law and underlying constitutional values. It may well be that English law is guided by underlying principles such as freedom of the Press, privacy and so on but, as Lord Hoffmann has recently asserted, there is a great difference between identifying say privacy 'as a value which underlies the existence of a rule of law' and 'privacy as a principle of law in itself'.[80] The same is true of freedom of speech. This is a value recognised by the common law,[81] yet 'no one has suggested that freedom of speech is in itself a legal principle which is capable of sufficient definition to enable one to deduce specific rules to be applied in concrete cases'. For that 'is not the way the common law works'.[82]

---

[80] *Wainwright v Home Office* [2004] 2 AC 406, at para 31.
[81] *Derbyshire CC v Times Newspapers* [1993] AC 534.
[82] *Wainwright v Home Office* [2004] 2 AC 406, at para 31.

11. Liability for unintentional harm

If there is one general statement that can be made about liability for intentional harm it is that it is not governed by any general principle. There is no tort of intentionally causing harm. In contrast, the obligation to make reparation for harm caused by negligent (careless) behaviour is rather different. Negligence today is not only an independent cause of action but a unifying idea whose influence is dominating the law of torts. It is such a large and complex subject that, in university courses, its study leaves little time for much else in the law of torts. This no doubt is another reason for its distorting effect on the category of 'tort'. Yet, that said, within the tort of negligence there is a struggle to control its generality. Conceptual devices, in particular the requirement of a duty of care, have assumed a kind of 'cause of action' category approach to liability.

TORT OF NEGLIGENCE

In English law negligence became an independent cause of action in tort in 1932. Yet even before this date *negligentia* had a very important role in that it 'was one of the range of terms commonly used since the fourteenth century to designate the basis of liability in trespass on the case' and from 'the second half of the eighteenth century "negligence" came more generally to play an increasingly central part in the analysis of tortious liability.'[1] This role is still increasing with the result that many independent torts such as trespass, nuisance and breach of statutory duty are being gradually subsumed under its influence; and one reason for this subsuming influence is the notion of 'reasonableness'.[2] This notion is used not just to define negligent behaviour itself, but to determine the existence of a duty of care and to act as a means of judging both factual and legal causation. Reasonable behaviour is a vehicle for breaking down the frontiers between different causes (forms) of action.

The classic definition of negligence was given by Alderson B in *Blyth v*

---

[1] Ibbetson (1999), at 164, 165.
[2] See eg *Transco plc v Stockport MBC* [2004] 2 AC 1, at para 96.

Proprietors of the Birmingham Waterworks.[3] Negligence, he said, 'is the omission to do something which a reasonable man, guided upon those considerations which ordinarily regulate the conduct of human affairs, would do, or doing something which a prudent and reasonable man would not do'. The point must be made at once that this is a definition of negligence and not the tort of negligence. The distinction is crucial because the mere causing of harm by a negligent act was, and is, never capable of giving rise to liability in itself; there has to be a pre-existing duty to take care and it is the breach of this duty – the negligent act or omission – which creates the liability.

Before 1932 the duty might arise as a result of contract[4] or as a result of certain clearly established extra-contractual situations such as products dangerous in themselves. Thus in order to establish liability a claimant had to show first that the defendant owed him a *specific duty* to take care (a question of law for the judge) and secondly that the defendant was in *breach* of this duty, that is to say that he was negligent (a question of fact for the jury). A third requirement was that the breach of duty *caused* (factually and legally) the claimant's damage. When juries started to disappear at the beginning of the 20th century there was no longer any need for a list of specific and fragmented duties of care.[5] Nevertheless the idea of negligence as a 'breach of duty' survived.

BREACH OF DUTY

This breach of duty question is a useful place to start since it is the central factual issue (see PETL art 4:102(1)). Was the defendant actually negligent? The absence of any duty of care or sufficient causal link can be as fatal to a victim's claim as the absence of any carelessness (breach of duty); however the duty and remoteness of damage questions are regarded as control devices. They limit as a pure question of law the scope of liability even in situations where actual carelessness can be proved. Of course, the distinction between fact and law becomes blurred at the level of conceptual analysis because concepts themselves – even so-called descriptive concepts – are rarely normatively neutral. Thus the application of the 'reasonable man' test, rather than sharply differentiating 'is' (descriptive) from 'ought' (normative), tends to merge the two by analysing a factual situation in

---

[3] (1856) 11 Exch 781, at 784; 156 ER 1047.
[4] See now Supply of Goods and Services Act 1982, s 13.
[5] Ibbetson, *op.cit*, at 188–9.

terms not just of how the defendant actually behaved but how he ought to have behaved. 'Is' becomes subsumed under 'ought' because deciding whether someone has been careless in any particular situation involves the court in measuring the actual behaviour of the defendant with some idealised behaviour (in turn determined with reference to a constructed individual such as the 'reasonable man').

For example it might not be careless (unreasonable) to fail to supply goggles to workers with normal sight in a vehicle repair shop. Yet it might be careless for the same employer not to supply a pair of goggles to a one-eyed worker since the loss of the good eye in an industrial accident would, for him, be catastrophic.[6] More controversially, perhaps, the learner driver's act of driving will be measured not against the reasonable learner driver, but against the reasonably competent and experienced driver.[7] The same objective test is applied to the Do-It-Yourself householder. If he or she does carpentry work around the house they must show a degree of care and skill of a reasonably competent carpenter, although this is not to be judged by reference to a professional carpenter doing work under a contract.[8] The reason why the law of tort takes this approach is because it has a mixture of aims (cf Chapter 9). On the one hand it wants to provide an arena in which entrepreneurs can act without fear of oppressive liabilities; on the other hand, the law of tort wants to remain partly true to its compensatory aim and to a commitment to risk. It does not want to see victims of road accidents go uncompensated on the basis of the vagaries of types of behaviour dictated by chance.

The reasonable man test is in theory, then, a test of fact and thus one which once belonged to the jury rather than judge. Juries may have disappeared,[9] but the distinction remains vital because decisions of juries never formed part of the precedent system; indeed juries never gave reasons for their verdicts. This means that breach of duty cases are not in themselves precedents. The point has been well put by Lord Somervell in a leading case on breach of duty. 'A judge naturally gives reasons for the conclusion formerly arrived at by a jury without reasons', he said; 'but if the reasons given by a judge for arriving at the conclusion previously reached by a jury are to be treated as "law" and citable, the precedent system will die from a surfeit of authorities'.[10] Care must be taken, therefore, when deciding the factual question of whether or not a person was

---

[6] *Paris v Stepney BC* [1951] AC 367.
[7] *Nettleship v Weston* [1971] 2 QB 691.
[8] *Wells v Cooper* [1958] 2 QB 265.
[9] *Ward v James* [1966] 1 QB 273.
[10] *Qualcast (Wolverhampton) Ltd v Haynes* [1959] AC 743, at 758.

negligent. This is a question of *fact* and not law and therefore precedent is, or ought to be, irrelevant.

The test for breach of duty is not, accordingly, one that can be found in the law reports. It all depends upon the circumstances. Nevertheless there are cases which act as guidelines and sometimes these guidelines can produce propositions that can be expressed as principles (see for example PETL art 4:102(1)). The leading case here is *Bolton v Stone*[11] which was an action for damages by a bystander in the street against a cricket club for an injury sustained by the bystander when she was struck on the head by a cricket ball hit out of the ground by a batsman. Cricket balls had been hit out of the ground before and so if one were to apply the foreseeability test it could be said that the accident was foreseeable. Did this mean that the cricket club did not behave reasonably in failing to provide a system of fencing that would ensure that cricket balls never reached the street? The House of Lords held that the cricket club had not been negligent and their judgments establish very clearly two propositions. First, that the test of breach of duty is not foreseeability; it is *reasonable behaviour* and this is not the same thing.

Secondly, that some risk is acceptable. The reasonable man does not have to guard against every conceivable risk particularly with respect to activities that are socially acceptable.[12] Indeed in cases of emergency the degree of acceptable risk may be higher.[13] Thus employers are not bound to sack an employee rather than expose her to some risk of dermatitis;[14] nor are they expected to shut down their factory when the floors become slippery as a result of a severe storm.[15] They are expected to act reasonably in the circumstances and in judging this behaviour the cost of precautions as measured against the gravity of the risk can be taken into account. Foreseeability can of course re-enter by the back door; and so those that dig up the streets must foresee that blind as well as normally sighted people will use the pavement and thus must erect suitable barriers.[16]

Two further general points need to be made. First, that professional defendants (for example doctors) are not judged by the ordinary reasonable man test but by the ordinary reasonably professional person

---

[11] [1951] AC 850.
[12] Compensation Act 2006, s 1.
[13] *Watt v Hertfordshire CC* [1954] 1 WLR 835.
[14] *Withers v Perry Chain* [1961] 1 WLR 1314; but cf *Coxall v Goodyear GB Ltd* [2003] 1 WLR 536.
[15] *Latimer v AEC Ltd* [1953] AC 643.
[16] *Hayley v London Electricity Board* [1965] AC 778.

(for example the reasonable doctor) professing those skills.[17] In medical negligence cases the courts have traditionally judged the behaviour in the light of prevailing medical opinion without ever subjecting the opinion to legal review.[18] Yet this attitude might now be changing.[19] The difficulty of course is that judges are not doctors, architects or engineers and thus have to rely on the expert evidence. In addition, they worry about defensive medicine.

Secondly, that although it is normally the claimant who must prove negligence there are some situations where 'the thing speaks for itself' (*res ipsa loquitur*) putting an onus on the defendant to at least provide some explanation other than carelessness for the accident (cf PETL art 4:201)). If the defendant can provide an explanation, that will put the onus back on the plaintiff.[20] Yet some cases seem to go further and virtually presume negligence, effectively reversing the burden of proof.[21]

DUTY OF CARE

It has already been stated that it is not the negligent act itself that generates liability in tort. It is the breach of a pre-existing duty of care owed by the careless actor to the person or class of persons damaged by the act. And thus, perhaps in contrast to French law, one can in theory talk of the formation of a non-contractual pre-existing obligation in respect of careless behaviour.

The starting point for the modern UK tort of negligence is *Donoghue v Stevenson*.[22] Despite being a Scottish case, it is equally an English precedent because the House of Lords stated that they were declaring the law of England as well that of Scotland. Mrs Donoghue brought an action for damages against the manufacturer of a bottle of ginger beer which, so she alleged, had caused her personal injury damage as a result of containing a decomposed snail. She had drunk the beer in a café after it had been bought for her by a friend. The manufacturer sought to have her claim struck out on a preliminary point of law: even if he had been careless in

---

[17] *Bolam v Friern Hospital Management Committee* [1957] 1 WLR 582.
[18] *Sidaway v Bethlem Royal Hospital* [1985] 1 AC 871.
[19] *Bolitho v City and Hackney Health Authority* [1998] AC 232.
[20] *Roe v Minister of Health* [1954] 2 QB 66.
[21] *Henderson v HE Jenkins & Sons* [1970] AC 282; *Ward v Tesco Stores Ltd* [1976] 1 WLR 810.
[22] [1932] AC 562.

allowing the snail to get into the beer he owed no duty of care to Mrs Donoghue. A majority in the House of Lords held that a duty did exist.

Why is the case so important? The answer is to be found in a number of factors. The first factor is the actual facts themselves. The immediate facts were (and to some extent still are) important in that they extended the structural symmetry of consumer protection. Before the decision, consumers injured by defective products could sue only if they had actually purchased the product;[23] the advantage of such a contract claim, however, is that a consumer does not have to prove fault.[24] *Donoghue* establishes that a consumer, even one who did not buy the product, injured by a defective product can sue the manufacturer. The seeming disadvantage is that the consumer must prove fault, but this is less of a burden than it might seem thanks to a later case establishing that the defect itself is prima facie evidence of negligence.[25] Legislation has further improved the position of third party consumers in that they *may* (it is not entirely clear) now be able to sue in contract.[26] A separate statute, anyway, allows consumers suffering personal injury and property damage to sue for damages without having to assert negligence.[27]

The second factor is the 'neighbour principle'. Normally a case is rarely an authority beyond its own material facts and thus it was argued in *Grant v Australian Knitting Mills*,[28] which involved defective underpants, that underpants were materially different from a bottle of ginger beer. Not surprisingly the argument was rejected (but was it such a daft argument for a lawyer to make?) and this was not just because both pants and ginger beer are 'products'. Lord Atkin in *Donoghue* famously said:

> The rule that you are to love your neighbour becomes in law, you must not injure your neighbour; and the lawyer's question, who is my neighbour? receives a restricted reply. You must take reasonable care to avoid acts or omissions which you can reasonably foresee would be likely to injure your neighbour. Who, then, in law is my neighbour? The answer seems to be – persons who are so closely and directly affected by my act that I ought reasonably to have them in contemplation as being so affected when I am directing my mind to the acts or omissions which are called in question.[29]

This is what lifts negligence liability out of its imprisonment within specific

---

[23] Sale of Goods Act 1893 (now 1979), s 14.
[24] *Frost v Aylesbury Dairy Co Ltd* [1905] 1 KB 608.
[25] *Grant v Australian Knitting Mills Ltd* [1936] AC 85.
[26] Contracts (Rights of Third Parties) Act 1999.
[27] Consumer Protection Act 1987, Part I.
[28] [1936] AC 85.
[29] [1932] AC 562, at 580.

factual categories and establishes the tort as a general cause of action prima facie applicable, seemingly, to any set of facts where damage is caused, by a careless act, to anyone within the 'neighbour' range of 'proximity'.

A key limiting factor, then, is the notion of 'proximity', a term used and developed by Lord Atkin himself in *Donoghue*. Yet, and this is a third factor, if 'duty' is based on 'proximity', what is the actual difference between these two notions? First, the former is *normative*, that is to say a concept that expresses a pure *ought* situation. To say that someone is under a 'duty' to do something is a moral and legal way of expressing what he ought to do. Proximity, in contrast, is purely *descriptive*; to say that one person is proximate to another is simply to describe a factual (an 'is') situation and implies in itself no 'ought' dimension.[30] Secondly, the two terms are not synonymous even when viewed from the standpoint of liability, for there can be situations of proximity but no duty.[31] Where 'proximity' and 'duty' are valuable is when the former can be used within a factual situation to organise the facts in such a way that the imposition (or non-imposition) of a duty becomes almost a natural consequence; it is, in other words, a valuable reasoning tool since it functions within the facts. Duty, in contrast, functions only in a world of normative rules.

However the neighbour principle was not to be as abstract as it might first have appeared and so a fourth factor is the scope of the duty of care. One material fact was the damage suffered by Mrs Donoghue: the decomposed snail made her physically ill and it was for this damage that Stevenson might potentially have been liable. However this was not the only harm suffered by Mrs Donoghue; she had also 'lost' the value of a bottle of ginger beer. Later cases, citing earlier ones, identified the 'interest' forming the object of manufacturer's duty as the threat to health, not the threat to the pocket.[32] Put another way, the physical injury suffered by Mrs Donoghue and her economic loss are two quite different types of 'damage'.[33] And thus the 1932 case is important in establishing (if retrospectively) the financial loss rule in the tort of negligence.

A fifth factor concerns a procedural aspect to the case. It is often said that it was never proved whether or not there was a snail in the ginger beer bottle[34] and this is because the case never went to trial. The appeal that reached the House of Lords was a 'striking out' action; that is to say the defendant asked the court on a preliminary question of law to strike

---

[30] cf *Caparo Industries plc v Dickman* [1990] 2 AC 605, at 633.
[31] See eg *Marc Rich & Co v Bishop Rock Marine Co Ltd* [1996] 1 AC 211.
[32] See now Consumer Protection Act 1987, s 5(2).
[33] *Birse Construction Ltd v Haiste Ltd* [1996] 2 All ER 1.
[34] *Freeman v Home Office (No 2)* [1984] QB 524, at 555–6.

out the case as disclosing no cause of action. Even if, argued the defendant, all the facts, including negligence, were proved by the claimant, these facts would still not make him liable since they disclosed no duty of care. What the House of Lords had to decide, then, was whether they did disclose a duty of care and, in order to decide this question, it was assumed that there was a snail in the bottle. Having lost the preliminary question of law action, Stevenson settled the case. Many subsequent duty of care cases are striking out claims; thus to say for example that the Home Office were found liable in negligence in *Home Office v Dorset Yacht Co*[35] is not exactly true. These striking out claims have proved problematic from a human rights position since they can appear arbitrarily to deny the claimant a remedy if not a fair trial.[36]

From a comparative law position, *Donoghue* can be linked to CC art 1382 and PETL art 4:101 in the way it lays down a general principle based on negligence. Indeed when put beside intentional physical damage to the person it is now possible to talk in terms of a general *culpa* liability.[37] However, given the limitation on liability imposed by the duty of care control device, the case is really closer to the German Civil Code paragraph 823 which requires, in addition to fault, cause and damage, the invasion of a specific interest ('life, body, health, freedom, ownership or any other right'). Duty of care, therefore, is in practice more than an abstract rule in that it is the means by which the tort of negligence protects only certain interests (cf PETL art 2:102).

EXTENSION OF DUTY OF CARE

The next major development in the tort of negligence was the decision in *Hedley Byrne & Co v Heller & Partners Ltd*.[38] The case itself involved a favourable credit reference letter gratuitously given by a bank in respect of a company that subsequently proved unable to pay its debts. The recipient of the reference, who had extended credit to the company on the strength of the letter, lost heavily when the company went into liquidation and they brought an action in negligence for their loss against the bank. Although the claimant lost its action because of a disclaimer in the credit reference letter, the House of Lords indicated that a duty of care could in principle

---

[35] [1970] AC 1004.
[36] See *Barrett v Enfield LBC* [2001] 2 AC 550; *Z v UK* [2001] 2 FLR 612.
[37] *Letang v Cooper* [1965] 1 QB 232.
[38] [1964] AC 465.

exist between the bank and the claimant. This decision thus extended liability to damage done by careless words (misrepresentation) and although it looks at first sight a major extension of *Donoghue v Stevenson*, it is probably more accurate to see the case as a development in the area of the tort of deceit,[39] perhaps with the idea of filling gaps in the law of contract rather than in extending *Donoghue* as such.[40] Those suffering loss as a result of a misstatement need no longer prove fraud provided they can establish a *special relationship*. In the words of Lord Steyn, 'the rule was established that irrespective of contract, if someone possessed of a special skill undertakes to apply that skill for the assistance of another person who relies upon such skill, a duty of care will arise'.[41]

What makes the case particularly special is that it appears to be a major exception to the established idea that *Donoghue v Stevenson* was concerned with physical rather than economic interests. However the key to the case is a *voluntary assumption* of responsibility by the defendant together with *reliance* by the claimant.[42] Yet it may be that 'reliance' will be interpreted quite generously when the duty problem is closely associated, directly or indirectly, with a contractual relationship and thus liability can attach to a reference from an ex-employer and to a breach of contract by a solicitor where only a third party (and not the contracting party) suffers loss as a result of the breach.[43] What is particularly important about *Hedley Byrne* is its central place in the law of obligations in as much as it both straddles the divide between contract and tort and acts as one starting point for recovering pure economic loss through the tort of negligence (see Chapter 14).

METHODOLOGICAL APPROACH TO DUTY

Negligence, then, is not just about behaviour but also about interests (types of damage) and these interests need to be examined in a little more depth since they form some of the key areas of difficulty within the tort of negligence. Two areas have proved to be particularly problematic: liability for pure economic loss and liability for causing what used to be called 'nervous shock' (psychiatric damage). An added complication is the fact

---

[39] *Peek v Derry* (1887) 37 Ch D 541 (CA); cf (1889) 14 App Cas 337 (HL).
[40] cf Supply of Goods and Services Act 1982, s 13
[41] *Hall (Arthur JS) & Co v Simons (a Firm)* [2002] 1 AC 615, at 676.
[42] See eg *Lennon v Commissioner of Police of the Metropolis* [2004] 1 WLR 2594.
[43] *Spring v Guardian Assurance Plc* [1995] 2 AC 296; *White v Jones* [1995] 2 AC 207.

that many defendants in these damage cases are public bodies, often local authorities or the police. These defendants create complications for two reasons. First, because they are often not the direct cause of the damage in issue; they are bodies that have allegedly failed to do their job properly and thus who have failed to prevent the claimant's damage (for example it was not the prison staff who damaged the yacht in *Dorset Yacht*).[44] This failure to act (mere omission) has, for duty of care purposes, been treated differently from positive acts.[45] Secondly, being public rather than private bodies, they have raised what might be called special policy problems. This, in turn, has propelled the courts into creating what might be called an extra requirement of negligence (besides duty, breach, causation and remoteness): is it fair and reasonable to impose a duty of care?[46]

Behind these duty and interest questions lay a problem of reasoning method. Is the *ratio decidendi* in *Donoghue* to be treated and applied as an abstract principle (the 'neighbour principle') like some continental code provision? Or is it a matter of moving more cautiously (incrementally) through reasoning by analogy, that is to say from factual situation to factual situation? In *Anns v Merton LBC*[47] Lord Wilberforce said that it was no longer necessary to bring the facts of any new case within those of previous situations in which a duty of care had been held to exist. One applied only the proximity test and then asked whether there were any considerations which ought to negative liability. However this two-stage principle approach has now been comprehensively rejected; 'the most that can be attempted', said another Law Lord, 'is a broad categorisation of the decided cases according to the type of situation in which liability has been established in the past in order to found an argument by analogy'.[48]

The facts of duty of care cases thus remain a fundamental part of the law itself; and what the lawyer must do is to compare the facts of any new problem with those in the precedents.[49] Of course whether or not one situation is analogous to another is itself a matter of some choice, as we have seen (Chapter 4). And thus behind this form of reasoning are often to be found other forms of argument. Reference may be found to policy, certainty, reasonableness, 'practical justice', fairness and so on.

---

[44] *Home Office v Dorset Yacht Co* [1970] AC 1004.
[45] See most recently *Mitchell v Glasgow City Council* [2009] 1 AC 874 (HL(Sc)).
[46] *Caparo Industries plc v Dickman* [1990] 2 AC 605.
[47] [1978] AC 728.
[48] Lord Oliver in *Caparo Industries plc v Dickman* [1990] 2 AC 605, at 635.
[49] See eg *Goodwill v British Pregnancy Advisory Service* [1996] 1 WLR 1397.

ECONOMIC LOSS

We have already seen that in *Donoghue v Stevenson* the claimant suffered not just 'damage' but also 'loss' (the ginger beer). This distinction became a fundamental one in the case law following the landmark decision of 1932. A defendant who had caused harm through a careless act owed a duty of care only to those who had suffered physical injury as a result of the act; those suffering pure economic loss had no claim. This rule applied even to claimants who had suffered some physical injury (two-party situations); if the court could make a clear distinction between *damnum emergens* (consequential loss) and *lucrum cessans* (failure to make a gain) the latter could be excluded as a head of damages.[50]

However care must be taken here. Economic loss could and can always be recovered in the tort of negligence as part of the loss *consequential* to the physical harm. Thus in *Spartan*, damages were recoverable in respect of the loss of profits on the ruined 'melt' because this was an economic 'interest' that attached to damaged tangible property.[51] It was only the 'pure' economic loss that attached to no item of damaged property – the loss of an expectation – that could not be recovered. Equally economic interests attaching to the claimant as a person can be recovered if the claimant has suffered personal injuries and this economic loss will include loss of earnings past, present and future; indeed damages are sub-divided into non-pecuniary and pecuniary. The so-called economic loss rule – which it must be noted applies for the main part only to the tort of negligence plus, on occasions, to breach of statutory duty[52] – has been justified in a number of ways. Lord Denning has said it is a matter of policy[53] while Tony Weir argued that people and tangible things are more important interests than money.[54] The PETL gives some support to the Weir approach (art 2:102).

Whatever the justification, the rule is breaking down, and at one point nearly disappeared.[55] What one can now say, then, is this. The causing of physical damage has universally to be justified whereas the infliction of pure economic loss does not.[56] Yet even although the logic of the rule

---

[50] See eg *Spartan Steel & Alloys Ltd v Martin & Co* [1973] 1 QB 27.
[51] *Spartan Steel & Alloys Ltd v Martin & Co* [1973] 1 QB 27.
[52] *Merlin v British Nuclear Fuels plc* [1990] 2 QB 557.
[53] See his judgment in *Spartan Steel & Alloys Ltd v Martin & Co* [1973] 1 QB 27.
[54] Weir (2004), at 6.
[55] *Junior Books Ltd v Veitchi Co Ltd* [1983] AC 520.
[56] *Customs and Excise Commissioners v Barclays Bank plc* [2006] 3 WLR 1 (HL).

suggests that where a defendant does carelessly cause physical damage to property there must, almost by definition, be a duty of care, it may be that a duty will be denied if policy and (or) fairness demand such a denial, say because of the insurance position or because the physical loss is analogous to economic loss.[57] One can still talk of an economic loss rule in negligence,[58] but one is forced back, these days, to the circumstances of each case. The rule is subject to exceptions, if only, sometimes, because the distinction between the physical and economic is not always an easy one.[59]

The first important major exception to the economic loss rule was, as we have seen, the decision in *Hedley Byrne*.[60] After this decision it was clear that a duty of care could be owed in respect of pure economic loss arising out of a misstatement. However the claimant had to show a *special relationship* based upon an *assumption of responsibility* by the defendant and *reliance* by the claimant. Thus the case, and its duty of care, could be placed in a category of its own: it was more an extension of the tort of deceit (where pure economic loss can always be recovered) within a relationship 'close to contract'. And even within this special category, it has not always been easy for a claimant to recover.[61] Nevertheless *Hedley Byrne* was to have far reaching consequences in the realm of professional liability in that breaches of contract that caused loss to third (non contractual) parties might result in liability in tort to the third party.[62]

Moreover, as with *Donoghue v Stevenson*, the effect of *Hedley Byrne* is to redefine tortious liability in general in as much as both cases cut across the old categories of liability approach. Thus factual situations thought to be confined to a particular cause of action (for example defamation) have now been redefined in terms of duty of care.[63] This has attracted criticism.[64] However it has to be remembered that when seen from an *interests* viewpoint the position turns out to be complex; a reference letter that contains a serious misstatement will invade not just the reputa-

---

[57] *Marc Rich & Co v Bishop Rock Marine Co Ltd* [1996] 1 AC 211.
[58] *Customs and Excise Commissioners v Barclays Bank plc* [2006] 3 WLR 1 (HL).
[59] *Murphy v Brentwood DC* [1991] 1 AC 398.
[60] [1964] AC 465.
[61] See eg *Mutual Life & Citizens Assurance Co Ltd v Evatt* [1971] AC 793; *Caparo Industries plc v Dickman* [1990] 2 AC 605.
[62] See in particular *Smith v Eric Bush* [1990] 1 AC 831; *White v Jones* [1995] 2 AC 207.
[63] *Spring v Guardian Assurance Plc* [1995] 2 AC 296.
[64] Birks (1996), at 5–6.

tion interest of the subject of the reference (defamation) but also his or her economic interest (duty of care). The point to be made about both *Donoghue* and *Hedley Byrne* is that they are continually, if only slowly, redefining the notion of tortious liability.[65] This redefinition means that even the scope of notions like 'misstatement' and 'reliance' are open to reinterpretation with the result that the 'misstatement' (does it include silence or inaction?) and even 'reliance' itself are continually being reassessed where, say, 'practical justice', 'fairness' or 'policy' require it.[66] The close relationship with contract does, however, raise another issue inherent in *Hedley Byrne* itself: a defendant always has the right expressly to exclude any duty of care, although this may fall foul of exclusion clause legislation.[67]

The development of duty of care to cover misstatement in situations close to contract creates a zone where the boundary between contract and tort becomes unclear. In French law the rule of *non cumul* once excluded any tort liability where the facts were governed by contract, but such a rule has been specifically rejected in English law.[68] Nevertheless the existence of a contract can impact upon the existence or non-existence of a duty of care. The courts may well refuse to allow a third party to avoid a contractual risk structure even if the party is outside the contract.[69] But much will depend upon the facts and this is why Lord Woolf made it clear in *Spring v Guardian Assurance* that cases are confined to their own factual classes. Or, as one other Law Lord has put it:

> Part of the function of appeal courts is to try to assist judges and practitioners by boiling down a mass of case law and distilling some shorter statement of the applicable law. The temptation to try to identify some compact underlying rule which can then be applied to solve all future cases is obvious. Mr Brindle submitted that in this area the House had identified such a rule in the need to find that the defendant had voluntarily assumed responsibility. But the unhappy experience with the rule so elegantly formulated by Lord Wilberforce in *Anns v Merton London Borough Council* [1978] AC 728, 751–2, suggests that appellate judges should follow the philosopher's advice to 'Seek simplicity, and distrust it'.[70]

---

[65] Weir (1998).
[66] See *White v Jones* [1995] 2 AC 207.
[67] *Smith v Eric Bush* [1990] 1 AC 831.
[68] *Henderson v Merrett Syndicates Ltd* [1995] 2 AC 145.
[69] *Norwich CC v Harvey* [1989] 1 WLR 828.
[70] Lord Rodger in *Customs and Excise Commissioners v Barclays Bank plc* [2007] 1 AC 181, at para 51.

PSYCHOLOGICAL DAMAGE (NERVOUS SHOCK)

Psychological damage, or nervous shock as it was once called, and 'mere omission' cases (discussed later in this chapter), together with on occasions those involving pure economic loss, often share a common structure. They involve three-party situations. This is often because serious accidents impact not just upon the victim but upon the victim's family as well. This impact is usually financial, but may be physical in the form of mental distress or worse.[71] To what extent should such family members be able independently to sue the tortfeasor? In particular, to what extent should they be able to sue for mental (nervous) shock? Alternatively the victim of an accident may find that the cause of his misfortune can be attributed not just to a primary defendant but also to a secondary defendant, such a secondary defendant having usually carelessly failed to prevent the first defendant from acting the way he did. Often these secondary defendants are public bodies like local authorities, who for example might negligently have failed to check, when it was being built, the foundations of the claimant's house,[72] or the police who might carelessly have failed to catch a dangerous criminal.[73] The family and public bodies thus form two central focal points in this area of duty of care.

Nervous shock is the old name given to psychiatric damage suffered by a victim and it gives rise to several types of problem in law. The first is one of definition; the law distinguishes between different types of actionable mental harm ranging from mental distress to severe psychiatric harm via pain and suffering and bereavement.[74] These different mental 'interests' are protected differently in the law of obligations. Thus mental distress *may* be recoverable in contract,[75] but not directly in the tort of negligence (except under the damages heading of pain and suffering in personal injury cases); only psychiatric illness ('nervous shock') can be recovered in negligence.[76]

The second problem is structural. Where the psychiatric illness is suffered by the primary victim (two-party situations) the problem is not really one of duty, because the defendant is already under a duty not to cause personal injury, but one of legal causation, that is to say remoteness of damage.[77] In this situation the question of psychiatric illness can be seen as

---

[71] See eg *Best v Samuel Fox & Co Ltd* [1952] AC 716.
[72] *Murphy v Brentwood DC* [1990] 3 WLR 414.
[73] *Hill v Chief Constable of West Yorkshire* [1989] AC 53.
[74] See *Heil v Rankin* [2001] QB 272 and Fatal Accidents Act 1976, s 1A.
[75] *Jarvis v Swan's Tours* [1973] QB 233.
[76] *Alcock v Chief Constable of South Yorkshire* [1992] 1 AC 310.
[77] *Page v Smith* [1996] 1 AC 155.

part of the general problem of defining personal injury damage, although it may even attach to property damage.[78] But sometimes it is not easy to determine whether the psychiatric illness victim is primary or secondary. Where, however, the claimant is a secondary victim (three-party situations) the problem becomes one of duty of care.

The starting point is that a third party (C) who witnesses an accident in which a victim (V) is injured or killed by the careless act of the defendant (D) will not have an action in negligence for psychiatric illness.[79] C is said to be too remote and owed no duty of care (the unforeseeable claimant). There were, however, exceptions to this rule based upon a relationship between V and C. The most important of these relationships was, and remains, a family one, now described as 'a close tie of love and affection'.[80] Thus if V is badly injured by D's negligent act and the accident is witnessed by C, his mother (or probably any family member), then D will be liable to C for C's psychiatric illness. And this will be true even if C does not witness the actual accident but sees the victim in a bad state in the hospital shortly (but how long?) after the accident.[81] Two other relationships were once (but probably no longer) of importance. If V and C were co-employees and C witnessed an accident at the workplace attributable to the employer's negligence there was some authority that this might allow C to sue for psychiatric illness.[82] Equally if C was a rescuer who intervened to help after an accident caused by D's negligence it seemed that C would have an action against D for psychiatric damage.[83] The symmetry once seemed fairly clear: a psychiatric illness claimant would no longer be 'unforeseeable' if there existed some relationship between the victim and claimant that brought him or her into the range of proximity and thus duty.

The structure and symmetry of the law regarding psychiatric illness was quite radically modified in two important cases arising out of the dreadful Hillsborough stadium tragedy in which the police were negligent in opening gates to a pressing crowd outside a football ground resulting in many deaths by suffocation. In the first case relatives and friends of those killed who witnessed, either directly or indirectly on television or radio, the events claimed damages for psychiatric illness; their claims were

---

[78] *Attia v British Gas Plc* [1988] QB 304.
[79] *Bourhill v Young* [1943] AC 92.
[80] Law Comm Report No 249, Draft Negligence (Psychiatric Illness) Bill, cl 1(3)(b).
[81] *McLoughlin v O'Brian* [1983] 1 AC 410.
[82] *Dooley v Cammell Laird & Co Ltd* [1951] 1 Ll Rep 271.
[83] *Chadwick v British Railways Board* [1967] 1 WLR 912.

dismissed on the ground that they were outside the scope of proximity.[84] Either there was not a sufficient close tie of love and affection or, if there was, the claimants were too far removed from the accident. Basically secondary claimants (three-party situations) must (i) have a close tie of love and affection with victims; (ii) be close to the incident; and (iii) witness the accident *directly* (sight and sound), although there might be some *very limited* exceptions.

In the second case police officers who had been present at the stadium brought claims for psychiatric injury on the basis that they were both rescuers and employees of the police force. The Court of Appeal allowed their claims, but in the House of Lords this was reversed by a majority.[85] One reason for this reversal was based upon public perception: it would not be fair to allow police officers to recover (especially as it was the police who had been negligent) but not the relatives of those killed and injured.[86] In giving effect to this public perception, however, the House of Lords has now discarded the employment and rescuer relationships as capable, in themselves, of giving rise to a foreseeable claimant in nervous shock cases. This is not to say that fellow employees or rescuers will never be able to claim for psychological damage; but they will have to show more than the mere relationship to bring themselves within the duty range. They will, for example, have to show that the tortious act threatened their personal safety.

One of the structural aspects of psychiatric illness problems that has come into focus thanks to these Hillsborough cases is the dichotomy between two-party and three-party situations. This dichotomy arose out of the nature of the damage itself; because mental injury has been treated differently from actual physical injury, claimants were treated as being outside the immediate accident event (and in one sense they often are of course). Nevertheless if psychiatric injury were to be treated as physical injury, all claimants would be primary victims and all could bring actions for their damage in the normal way against the tortfeasor. The law does not take this view except when the shock claimant was present at the scene of the accident and either suffered some physical injury or was immediately threatened.[87] Rescuers are on the whole secondary victims and thus must prove the three conditions laid down in *Alcock* before they can recover.[88] However, if their lives were immediately threatened by say

---

[84] *Alcock v Chief Constable of South Yorkshire* [1992] 1 AC 310.
[85] *Frost v Chief Constable of South Yorkshire Police* [1999] 2 AC 455.
[86] See Lord Steyn in *Frost* at 495.
[87] See *Page v Smith* [1996] 1 AC 155.
[88] *Alcock v Chief Constable of South Yorkshire* [1992] 1 AC 310.

falling masonry or whatever, they will be treated as primary victims.[89] In the second Hillsborough case (*Frost*) the police were not so threatened and thus had to prove the *Alcock* conditions, which they could not do.[90] These *Alcock* conditions mean, however, that factual analysis in nervous shock cases is now complex and the law 'a patchwork quilt of distinctions which are difficult to justify'.[91] Note again, with regard to this complexity, that bereavement has its own rule.[92]

OMISSIONS

Another complex area of duty of care is where a defendant's negligence consists, not in a positive act which causes damage, but in a failure to act. Here the direct cause is either an event of nature (for example a flood or landslide) or the act of a person other than the defendant (for example a thief, or a builder whose incompetence is not noticed by a local authority inspector). In principle there is no liability for such a mere omission on the basis of an absence of duty; one will be liable only if the negligence has made things worse.[93] This can be translated in turn into the principle that there is no duty to be a Good Samaritan.[94] As with psychiatric illness, there are however exceptions, usually based on some pre-existing relationship between claimant (C) and the person failing to act (D). For example if D owed a clear and defined pre-existing duty to C, then there might be liability;[95] equally once D has intervened he may be liable if he makes matters worse.[96] On the whole such defendants are usually public bodies and much may depend upon the nature of the statutory duty that D has failed to perform. Sometimes a range of factors may point one way or the other: the nature of the damage, the status of the defendant, the insurance position, the contractual relations and so on.[97]

---

[89] *Chadwick v British Railways Board* [1967] 1 WLR 912 as reinterpreted.
[90] *Frost v Chief Constable of South Yorkshire Police* [1999] 2 AC 455.
[91] Lord Stein in *Frost* at 500.
[92] Fatal Accidents Act 1976, s 1A.
[93] *East Suffolk Rivers Catchment Board v Kent* [1941] AC 74; *Mitchell v Glasgow City Council* [2009] 1 AC 874 (HL(Sc)).
[94] *Stovin v Wise* [1996] AC 923.
[95] *Reeves v Commissioner of Police for the Metropolis* [2000] 1 AC 360; and see the discussions in *Mitchell v Glasgow City Council* [2009] 1 AC 874 (HL(Sc)).
[96] *Barrett v Ministry of Defence* [1995] 1 WLR 1217.
[97] See now *Mitchell v Glasgow City Council* [2009] 2 WLR 481 (HL(Sc)).

PUBLIC BODIES

The fact that many defendants in mere omission cases have been local authorities is not surprising since their job is often to supervise. Now, in French law, a fundamental distinction is made between civil liability (*la responsabilité civile*) and administrative liability (*la responsabilité administrative*). Claims for compensation for damage caused by a public body or public agent usually have to be pursued in a quite different set of courts than claims against private persons or bodies. In the common law world no such formal distinction exists. In principle the law of tort applies equally to all persons, public and private; in substance, however, the position turns out to be more complicated.

The starting point for the liability of public bodies is simple enough: local authorities and central government bodies can be sued for damages where they wrongfully cause damage. Thus for example local authorities have been held liable in trespass, negligence, nuisance and so on. Indeed, occasionally one finds one government body suing another in tort[98] and while this might seem odd it is certainly less odd for a public agency to sue a private corporation if the latter has caused the former damage.[99] Central government can also be sued in tort where they damage citizens or where their employees have committed torts in the course of their employment.[100] And damages claims in negligence against NHS hospitals (or Area Health Authorities) have become a specialist area of tort law.

However the courts recognise that subjecting public bodies to tort liability can raise difficult questions of policy in that an action for damages might not always be an appropriate vehicle for investigating the efficiency of the police force or a local government social services department.[101] In negligence actions this issue is dealt with as a duty of care problem. Thus if the courts think an action for damages is inappropriate they deny the existence of a duty between public body defendant and claimant. This denial in turn can be based on a number of more formal notions. For example, the absence of a duty might be justified on the mere omissions rule or upon the fact that the damage is pure economic loss. More generally the judges often now refer to the idea that it is not 'fair, just and reasonable' to impose such a duty.[102] And behind all these formal notions

---

[98] *Ministry of Housing and Local Government v Sharp* [1970] 2 QB 223.
[99] See eg *Customs and Excise Commissioners v Barclays Bank Plc* [2006] 3 WLR 1.
[100] See eg *Home Office v Dorset Yacht Co* [1970] AC 1004.
[101] *Van Colle v Chief Constable of the Hertfordshire Police* [2009] 1 AC 225.
[102] See eg *Elguzouli-Daf v Commissioner of Police of the Metropolis* [1995] QB 335; *Customs and Excise Commissioners v Barclays Bank plc* [2006] 3 WLR 1.

lie policy considerations: 'In a wide range of cases', said Lord Browne-Wilkinson, 'public policy has led to the decision that the imposition of liability would not be fair and reasonable in the circumstances, eg some activities of financial regulators, building inspectors, ship surveyors, social workers dealing with sex abuse cases.' And he continued, in 'all these cases and many others the view has been taken that the proper performance of the defendant's primary functions for the benefit of society as a whole will be inhibited if they are required to look over their shoulder to avoid liability in negligence'. For in 'English law the decision as to whether it is fair, just and reasonable to impose a liability in negligence on a particular class of would-be defendants depends on weighing in the balance the total detriment to the public interest in all cases from holding such class liable in negligence as against the total loss to all would-be plaintiffs if they are not to have a cause of action in respect of the loss they have individually suffered.'[103] This kind of policy argument has also been used to deny the existence of a duty of care in situations where the police have negligently failed to give adequate protection to a victim threatened by another.[104]

These words of Lord Browne-Wilkinson might seem convincing enough, but one can reflect upon whether they have any foundation in social reality.[105] Certainly the judgments themselves are often completely devoid of any sociological evidence and this exposes a serious problem with legal reasoning in the common law. Admirable as it may be that the judges are prepared to go beyond mere rule application, functional reasoning does actually require something more than mere armchair philosophy. There may well be very pertinent reasons why the liability of local authorities ought not to be open-ended (for example it might seriously threaten the viability of public liability insurance); but the judgments sometimes read like tabloid newspaper editorials. This is, perhaps, an area where comparative law could make a useful contribution.[106]

A particular problem encountered with respect to local authorities is that they are statutory creations whose duties and powers are determined by the legislator. They discharge statutory functions operating within a statutory framework. The view of the courts is that because the will of the legislator is paramount when it comes to such functions, a 'common law duty must not be inconsistent with the performance by the authority of

---

[103] *Barrett v Enfield LBC* [2001] 2 AC 550, at 559.
[104] *Van Colle v Chief Constable of the Hertfordshire Police* [2009] 1 AC 225; and see *Mitchell v Glasgow City Council* [2009] 1 AC 874 (HL(Sc)).
[105] See eg *Van Colle v Chief Constable of the Hertfordshire Police* [2009] 1 AC 225.
[106] Markesinis, Auby, Coester-Waltjen and Deakin (1999).

its statutory duties and powers in the manner intended by Parliament, or contrary in any other way to the presumed legislative intention'.[107]

What has made matters difficult is the question of discretion often conferred upon public authorities and what the courts have attempted to do is to distinguish between a policy decision (for example not to build a new sports centre) and an operational decision (for example making a careless decision about the safety of a building). 'The greater the element of policy involved', said Lord Slynn, 'the wider the area of discretion accorded, the more likely it is that the matter is not justiciable so that no action in negligence can be brought'.[108] The result is that a

> claim of negligence in the taking of a decision to exercise a statutory discretion is likely to be barred, unless it is wholly unreasonable so as not to be a real exercise of the discretion, or if it involves the making of a policy decision involving the balancing of different public interests; acts done pursuant to the lawful exercise of the discretion can, however, in my view be subject to a duty of care, even if some element of discretion is involved.[109]

Subsequent to this statement, Lord Slynn and his colleagues have held that educational psychologists and teachers, working for a local authority, might owe duties of care to pupils in their care and that the local authority would be vicariously liable for breach of such a duty.[110]

HUMAN RIGHTS

A whole new dimension has been added to the question of liability of public bodies with the incorporation of the Convention for the Protection of Human Rights and Fundamental Freedoms by the Human Rights Act 1998. The effects of the incorporation of the Convention go much further than establishing a statutory remedy against public bodies. Many of the leading negligence cases (including *Donoghue v Stevenson* itself) are what are called striking out actions. This is where the defendant, as a preliminary question of law, asks the court to put an end to the whole case because of the absence of a duty of care and thus a cause of action in negligence. If the court agrees the claimant is in effect left with no right to proceed. One such case was *Osman v Ferguson* where a claim for damages against the police

---

[107] Lord Nicholls in *Stovin v Wise* [1996] AC 923, at 935.
[108] *Barrett v Enfield LBC* [2001] 2 AC 550, at 571.
[109] Lord Slynn in *Barrett, ibid*, at 572.
[110] *Phelps v Hillingdon LBC* [2001] 2 AC 619; and see *D v East Berkshire Community NHS Trust* [2005] 2 AC 373.

was struck out on policy grounds; however the European Court of Human Rights ruled that this striking out fell foul of the right to a fair trial as set out in Art 6(1) of the Human Rights Convention.[111] Although academics and judges were critical of this Strasbourg ruling, the House of Lords have appeared to retreat from the position they had formerly adopted in cases like *X (Minors) v Bedfordshire County Council*.[112] There is now more of a reluctance to strike out cases on a preliminary motion.[113] This development is important because it means that the courts have had to be more generous in holding that a public body is under a duty of care and thus the 1998 Act has had an important impact on substantive questions within the tort of negligence.

In fact, since these decisions, the *X (Minors)* case (which involved child abuse) has been heard by the Strasbourg court which has changed its position from the one adopted in *Osman*. The court admitted that it was wrong to regard the striking out procedure as a breach of Article 6 since the striking out cases clearly went into substantive detail with respect to the policy issues behind the duty of care question. However the Strasbourg court went on to say that it was nonetheless the case that the interpretation of domestic law by the House of Lords resulted in the applicants' case being struck out. Yet the experiences of the claimants, according to the evidence, were 'horrific'; this meant that, in preventing the applicants from suing, there was a gap in the UK domestic law and 'one that gives rise to an issue under the Convention, but in the Court's view it is an issue under Article 13, not Article 6 § 1'.[114] There was also, the court held, a violation of Article 3.[115]

COMPARATIVE REFLECTIONS

Before leaving the topic of liability of public bodies mention should be made of one of the disadvantages of failing to develop a thesis of administrative liability. In French law the *Conseil d'État*, the highest

---

[111] *Osman v Ferguson* [1993] 4 All ER 344; *Osman v United Kingdom* [1999] 1 FLR 193. But see now *Van Colle v Chief Constable of the Hertfordshire Police* [2009] 1 AC 225.
[112] [1995] 2 AC 633.
[113] cf *Van Colle v Chief Constable of the Hertfordshire Police* [2009] 1 AC 225.
[114] *Z v UK* [2001] 2 FLR 612, at para 102.
[115] See generally Lord Bingham in *D v East Berkshire NHS Trust* [2005] 2 AC 373, at paras 22–5.

administrative court, with the help of academic doctrine, has developed a whole field of liability without fault. The court has been able to do this through the application of constitutional ideas in the area of what an English lawyer would see as tort liability. One such idea is the principle of equality (*égalité*). This principle has been used, alongside that of risk, to justify the imposition of strict liability in a number of situations where, in English law, given the same facts, negligence would have to be proved.

Take for example the situation that arose in one English case. In order to recapture a dangerous criminal who had barricaded himself into the claimant's gun shop, the police fired CS gas into the building with the result that the shop caught fire and was destroyed. The owner of the shop (or perhaps his insurance company) brought an action against the police in tort and the judge made it clear that in order for the action to succeed negligence would have to be proved. Any strict liability claim would fail because of the defence of necessity. In fact the claimant was able to show negligence and so damages were awarded.[116] But what if there had been no carelessness? The logic seems to be that the owner of the destroyed building would be left to carry the loss himself (although in truth the loss may fall on the building insurer). French administrative lawyers would regard such a result as both unjust and unconstitutional since the community has benefited while a single individual has been left with the burden. Consequently, in French law, damages might well have been awarded to the shop owner, without proof of fault, on the basis of the principle that equality demands the sharing of burdens suffered in the pursuit of the public interest.

This strict liability (no fault) principle flows naturally from public lawyers who are continually having to balance the community interest against the interests of individuals. Private lawyers, at least in the UK, find such thinking more difficult. Indeed the idea of community benefit has been used to arrive at the opposite conclusion from the French one; negligence must be proved before a public body supplying a community benefit like gas, water or electricity can be liable to a citizen injured by for example a gas explosion. 'Gas, water and also electricity services are well-nigh a necessity of modern life,' said Sellers LJ in 1964, 'or at least are generally demanded as a requirement for the common good'. He concluded from this premise that it 'would seem odd that facilities so much sought after by the community and approved by their legislators should be actionable at common law because they have been brought to places where they are

---

[116] *Rigby v Chief Constable of Northamptonshire* [1985] 1 WLR 1242.

required and have escaped without negligence by an unforeseen sequence of mishaps.'[117]

In addition to this equality principle, administrative lawyers in France take the view that public authority activities involving risk should equally give rise to no fault liability. However, in English law, the fact that the injured claimant is a civil servant (or public service employee) injured in the exercise of his or her duties in a situation involving danger is irrelevant. If such a person is injured during the course of his or her duties fault or the unlawful breach of a statute must be shown.[118] Indeed, those involved in dangerous public service jobs are deemed to have gone some way in accepting the risks involved.[119] Equality appears, at least traditionally, to be neither a constitutional nor a private law principle. Risk also appears to be a principle with only a limited direct influence on liability theory; indirectly, of course, it can find expression through maxims such as *res ipsa loquitur*.

Has the position been modified by the Human Rights Act 1998? In a recent nuisance case involving noise from military jet aircraft Buckley J observed that the 'problem with putting the public interest into the scales when deciding whether a nuisance exists, is simply that if the answer is no, not because the claimant is being over sensitive, but because his private rights must be subjugated to the public interest, it might well be unjust that he should suffer the damage for the benefit of all'.[120] And he continued:

> If it is to be held that there is no nuisance, there can be no remedy at common law. As this case illustrates, the greater the public interest, the greater may be the interference. If public interest is considered at the remedy stage and since the court has a discretion, the nuisance may continue but the public, in one way or another, pays for its own benefit . . . Allowing a human rights claim but denying a remedy in nuisance would, of course, be another solution, but it would be one that reflected adversely on the flexibility of the common law . . .

One might hope that the 1998 Act would equally impact on another administrative liability case. In *Elguzouli-Daf v Commissioner of Police for the Metropolis*[121] two claimants brought an action against the Crown Prosecution Service (CPS) claiming that they had been held in prison on remand as a result of the negligence of the defendants. The Court of Appeal dismissed their claims on the basis of an absence of a duty of care,

---

[117] *Dunne v NW Gas Board* [1964] 2 QB 806, at 832.
[118] *Read v J Lyons & Co* [1947] AC 156.
[119] *Watt v Hertfordshire CC* [1954] 1 WLR 835.
[120] *Dennis v MOD* [2003] EWHC 793, at para 46.
[121] [1995] QB 335.

Steyn LJ asserting that 'that the interests of the whole community are better served by not imposing a duty of care on the CPS' because 'such a duty of care would tend to have an inhibiting effect on the discharge by the CPS of its central function of prosecuting crime.' Imposing a duty, he continued, 'would in some cases lead to a defensive approach by prosecutors to their multifarious duties.' Steyn LJ offered no evidence whatsoever to support the claim that the 'CPS would have to spend valuable time and use scarce resources in order to prevent law suits in negligence against the CPS'.[122] And even if it did involve some extra work, it is by no means clear that the interests of the community are served in depriving individuals of recourse against the administration in situations where they have suffered horrifying invasions of their family life, privacy and (or) other human rights as a result of the careless exercise of state power. And thus Steyn LJ's judgement stands as a warning. If judges are happy to replace a formalist approach with a functionalist one, rationalism still demands that the functions envisaged be supported by empirical evidence. If not the reasoning becomes invalid at the level either of authority (precedent) or of empiricism. One form of empirical research would be to examine how these kinds of abuse of power through negligence problems are treated in other jurisdictions. However, with respect to the police, the Steyn LJ form of reasoning has been confirmed by the House of Lords (again without recourse to any empirical evidence or research).[123]

UNLAWFUL ACTS

Another complication is the existence of two sets of remedies in respect of public bodies: there are the 'private law' claims for damages and the 'public law' actions for judicial review. As Lord Browne-Wilkinson observed in *X (Minors) v Bedfordshire County Council*, actions to recover damages founded on a private law cause of action have to be distinguished from judicial review actions in public law to enforce the performance of statutory duties. For the breach of a public law right does not of itself give rise to a claim for damages; such a damages claim can only be founded on a cause of action in (normally) contract or tort.[124] The Law Lord then went on to classify the private law damages claims into four kinds: actions for breach of statutory duty; actions based solely on the careless

---

[122] [1995] QB 335, at 349.
[123] *Van Colle v Chief Constable of the Hertfordshire Police* [2009] 1 AC 225.
[124] [1995] 2 AC 633, at 730–1.

performance of a statutory duty in the absence of any other common law right of action; actions based on a common law duty of care arising either from the imposition of the statutory duty or from the performance of it; and actions based on misfeasance in public office. With regard to this last tort, the claimant would have to prove that the public agent wilfully acted unlawfully. Besides negligence (and nuisance), then, the torts of breach of statutory duty and misfeasance in public office have a role to play in the liability of public bodies or officials.

The tort of breach of statutory duty, as described by Lord Browne-Wilkinson, 'will arise if it can be shown, as a matter of construction of the statute, that the statutory duty was imposed for the protection of a limited class of the public and that Parliament intended to confer on members of that class a private right of action for breach of the duty.' In determining whether a statute does give rise to a private action, there is no general rule of reference; instead there are a number of indicators. Thus:

> If the statute provides no other remedy for its breach and the Parliamentary intention to protect a limited class is shown, that indicates that there may be a private right of action since otherwise there is no method of securing the protection the statute was intended to confer. If the statute does provide some other means of enforcing the duty that will normally indicate that the statutory right was intended to be enforceable by those means and not by private right of action: *Cutler v Wandsworth Stadium Ltd* [1949] AC 398; *Lonrho Ltd v Shell Petroleum Co Ltd (No 2)* [1982] AC 173. However, the mere existence of some other statutory remedy is not necessarily decisive. It is still possible to show that on the true construction of the statute the protected class was intended by Parliament to have a private remedy. Thus the specific duties imposed on employers in relation to factory premises are enforceable by an action for damages, notwithstanding the imposition by the statutes of criminal penalties for any breach: see *Groves v Wimborne (Lord)* [1898] 2 QB 402.[125]

The reason why this tort is of relevance to public authority liability is that many such authorities are created by statute and their powers to act are defined by statute. The tort can, accordingly, be relevant if a public body or one of its employees act in breach of a statute. In fact, as Lord Browne-Wilkinson indicates, the tort is of particular importance in one of the great sources of tort claims, namely accidents at work, and so it may well be a means by which an employee of a public or a private employer can gain compensation for injuries sustained in the course of employment. In one sense, of course, it is a liability arising out of an individual act and therefore deserves to be classified alongside negligence. However in reality many cases involve defective industrial plant, machinery, buildings

---

[125] [1995] 2 AC 633, at 731.

or other things and so it is equally a tort that can be categorised under a 'liability for things' heading. The point to be emphasised in this chapter is that behaving *unlawfully*, as opposed to carelessly, gives rise to a separate cause of action, although of course the two different kinds of behaviour can overlap. And, as a result, the approach of the court, when assessing liability, will be different. The focus will not be on the *behaviour* of the defendant but on the wording of the statutory text. Do the facts fall within the words of the Act? If they do, then there will prima facie be liability, even if the defendant was not negligent; if they do not, then there cannot be liability under this particular tort.

12. Liability for things

Article 1384 of the *Code civil* declares that one is 'liable not only for the damage which one has caused by one's own act, but also for that which is caused by the act of persons for whom he is responsible, or by things which he has in his keeping.' The French private law courts have, during the 20th century, used this article as the basis for the construction of a major area of no fault civil liability. English law has no such general principle. Nevertheless it does have pockets of no fault liability some of which can be analysed in terms of a liability attaching to things that cause damage. Indeed even aspects of fault liability can be seen in terms of damage done by things under the control of another. In addition English law also recognises a principle of vicarious liability whereby an employer is automatically liable for a tort committed by his employee acting in the course of his employment (see Chapter 13).

LIABILITY FOR MOVEABLE THINGS

CC art 1384 imposes a liability for damage done by a thing under the control (*sous sa garde*) of another. For well over a century this statement was thought to be simply a general introduction to arts 1385 and 1386 and thus restricted to damage resulting from dilapidated buildings and from animals. However during the 20th century the *Cour de cassation* used this principle to develop a liability for things in general and one particular landmark was the application of this strict liability article to motor vehicles in the famous *Jand'heur* decision in 1930.[1] Such a general liability is to be found in few other systems (cf PETL art 5:102)), although many do now have special traffic accident regimes (including France since 1985). Instead the tendency is to create specific areas of liability, one of the most important being the EU-inspired liability for defective products.

In English law liability without fault attaches to dangerous animals and, in certain circumstances, to non-dangerous ones as well. In addition

---

[1] Ch réun 13.2.1930; DP 1930.1.57, note Ripert; Terré, Simler and Lequette (2002), at 722–3.

there are one or two other strict liabilities. The tort of private nuisance can make a landowner liable for damage arising from the unreasonable use of his land and 'unreasonable' in this context is not confined to fault. Public nuisance can be used in respect of dangerous structures that injure members of the public and it can equally extend to vehicles parked on the highway.[2] A landowner or occupier may also be liable under the rule in *Rylands v Fletcher* for the escape of a dangerous thing brought onto the land, although it seems that this rule has to some extent been subverted by the torts of negligence and nuisance.[3] Factory machinery and other things that are dangerous may well entail an employer in liability through the tort of breach of statutory duty or negligence (see Chapter 11) and there are a number of statutory strict liability regimes.[4] Contract also has a central role to play in respect of a liability for things. Thus the victim of defective goods may well have a contractual claim and, even if he does not, all EU systems now have, or should have, delictual liability regimes in place.

DANGEROUS PRODUCTS

Products liability is central to the tort of negligence in as much as the foundational case of *Donoghue v Stevenson*[5] was of course a products case. Damage arising from a defective product also transcends tort in that a purchaser of goods that are not reasonably fit for their purpose and (or) not of satisfactory quality can sue the seller for damages without having to prove fault.[6] Similar provisions apply where goods are hired. In addition to these existing claims there is now a statutory regime (Consumer Protection Act 1987), itself the result of a European Directive in respect of dangerous products.[7] The key provision states that 'where any damage is caused wholly or partly by a defect in a product' the producer 'shall be liable for the damage'.[8] The Act goes on to state that 'there is a defect in a product . . . if the safety of the product is not such as persons generally are entitled to expect' (s 3). The statutory regime follows the common law negligence position with respect to the type of damage remedied. The regime does not apply to pure economic loss and thus the defective product must

---

[2] *Benjamin v Storr* (1874) LR 9 CP 400.
[3] See *Transco plc v Stockport MBC* [2004] 2 AC 1.
[4] See *Transco plc v Stockport MBC* [2004] 2 AC 1, paras 42, 45, 108.
[5] [1932] AC 562.
[6] Sale of Goods Act 1979, s 14.
[7] Council Directive of 25 July 1985 No 85/374/EEC.
[8] Consumer Protection Act 1987, s 2.

cause either personal injury or physical damage to property (s 5(1)) other than to itself (s 5(2)).

The main question here is likely to focus upon what consumers are 'entitled to expect'. This is not as simple as it may seem for several reasons. First, because some products are themselves controversial; one thinks here not just of tobacco and alcohol but complex and or potentially dangerous mechanical products such as microwave ovens, lawnmowers, mobile telephones and the like. If such products come without adequate warnings are they defective? Or what if a consumer fails to warn his or her hairdresser of an undue sensitivity with respect to a particular product that can be dangerous for some people?[9] Secondly some products such as chicken, pork and possibly eggs have at some time or other been food items that have properly to be cooked for them to become safe to eat. What if a customer fails to cook pork properly?[10] Thirdly, much will depend upon whether the court puts the emphasis on the product itself – does the public expect it to be 100 per cent perfect? – or whether account is also taken of the producer's manufacturing processes: did the manufacturer have in place a system of safety that meets public expectations? With respect to infected blood it has been held that one looks at the product rather than the system;[11] and this approach is valuable for the claimant since strict liability becomes less 'strict' so to speak the moment one begins to take account of the defendant's 'act' (of producing).

Indeed, here one must mention another ambiguous point in the legislation. To what extent does the Act take consumer protection beyond the existing position at common law, that is to say beyond the protection offered by the tort of negligence and the law of contract? One point of contention is section 4(1)(e) whose wording can be compared with the words in the Directive. The Directive states that the 'producer shall not be liable . . . if he proves: . . . that the state of scientific and technical knowledge at the time when he put the product into circulation was not such as to enable the existence of the defect to be discovered' (art 7(e)). The Act, however, says 'that the state of scientific and technical knowledge at the relevant time was not such that a producer of products of the same description as the product in question might be expected to have discovered the defect if it had existed in his products while they were under his control'. The European Commission took the view that section 4(1)(e) was not compatible with article 7(e), but the European Court of Justice held that the two

---

[9] See *Ingham v Emes* [1955] 2 QB 366.
[10] *Heil v Hedges* [1951] 1 TLR 512.
[11] *A v National Blood Authority* [2001] 3 All ER 289.

were not necessarily incompatible.[12] The European Court stated that it is not just a matter of the wording in the text but how national courts actually interpret the legislation and on this point the Court noted section 1(1) of the 1987 Act which states that the Act 'shall have effect for the purpose of making such provision as is necessary in order to comply with the product liability Directive and shall be construed accordingly'. In other words the European Court is looking less at the words in section 4(1)(e) and more at the interpretative leeway given to the judges to read the text in conformity with the Directive.

DEFECTIVE EQUIPMENT

One of the great sources of personal injury is the workplace and many accidents are caused by dangerous things such as machinery, plant, tools and other equipment. As a result the workplace is covered by detailed safety legislation the breach of which, if it leads to injury, will be actionable via the tort of breach of statutory duty and (or) the tort of negligence. Breach of statutory duty is very much a liability for things in that emphasis is put on the thing rather than the behaviour of the defendant; if a piece of dangerous machinery must be fenced and, in breach of statute it is not, the employer will be strictly liable.[13] The problem for claimants is when an employee is injured by a thing that does not fall within any statutory definition. If the court is not prepared to give a wide definition to the statutory term,[14] then a claimant will have to rely on the tort of negligence, always assuming that this tort has been pleaded.[15]

Where an employee is injured by equipment dangerous as a result of a manufacturing defect the employer who supplied the equipment will be liable, at common law, only if he himself is in breach of a duty of care towards the employee.[16] This in effect meant that the employer would often not be liable since he would on the whole be unaware of any latent manufacturing defect in a piece of equipment. This position came in for criticism and Parliament stepped in with the Employers' Liability (Defective Equipment) Act 1969 which deems the employer liable where

---

[12] *European Commission v UK* [1997] CMLR 923.
[13] *John Summers & Sons Ltd v Frost* [1955] AC 740; *Millard v Serck Tubes Ltd* [1969] 1 WLR 211.
[14] See eg *Haigh v Charles W Ireland* [1973] 3 All ER 1137; but cf *Coltman v Bibby Tankers Ltd* [1988] AC 276.
[15] *Morris v National Coal Board* [1963] 1 WLR 1382.
[16] *Davie v New Merton Board Mills Ltd* [1959] AC 604.

'the defect is attributable wholly or partly to the fault of a third party (whether identified or not)'. What is interesting from a liability for things point of view is that 'fault' 'means negligence, breach of statutory duty *or other act or omission which gives rise to liability in tort*' (emphasis added). Logically therefore it would seem that the employer will now be deemed liable for any liability that would attach to the manufacturer of the defective equipment under the Consumer Protection Act 1967.

ANIMALS

Liability for damage done by animals is also the subject of a statutory regime and, with respect to a dangerous animal, there is a strict liability which attaches, via the animal, to the keeper.[17] Much more difficult is the strict liability that can attach to non-dangerous animals. There will be liability only if the damage was of the type that the animal was 'likely to cause' or, if caused, 'was likely to be severe' and 'the likelihood of the damage or of its being severe was due to characteristics of the animal which are not normally found in animals of the same species or are not normally so found except at particular times or in particular circumstances'. Moreover these characteristics had to be known to the keeper (Animals Act 1971, s 2(2)). Not surprisingly, this section has been described by the judiciary, on several occasions, as 'opaque' and it is, for example, by no means clear that if a cat eats a neighbour's canary the keeper of the cat will be strictly liable.

In a major House of Lords decision on section 2(2) a bare majority held that the keeper of a horse that escaped from a field, without any negligence on the part of its owners, and caused a serious car accident was to be strictly liable and this suggests that the judiciary are prepared to give a generous interpretation to the difficult section.[18] The position is not entirely clear, of course, given the two dissenting opinions and in consequence much will depend on the facts of each case. But, as things stand, the majority have established a genuine liability for things regime on the basis of an ambiguous legislative section. In addition the case is valuable for the background depth it gives both to the Animals Act 1971 in general and to section 2 in particular. However one should add that the 1971 Act goes on to deal with further types of damage done by other types of animal; and thus strict liability attaches to dogs which injure livestock

---

[17] Animals Act 1971, s 2(1).
[18] *Mirvahedy v Henley* [2003] 2 AC 491.

(s 3) and for livestock which stray on to the land of another and cause property damage (s 4). The Act, in other words, is, as a French Professor once observed, more an exercise in animal character studies than legal principle, a view that seems to be confirmed by the Court of Appeal who once devoted pages to the study of a dog's character.[19]

MOTOR VEHICLES

It may seem odd that animals (especially horses) are subjected to a statutory regime at a time when their importance in terms of transport has been completely eclipsed by motor vehicles. One might, instead, have expected a 'Motor Vehicles Act' perhaps along the lines of the French Law of 1985 which aimed to ameliorate the legal position of victims injured on the roads.[20] For, alongside accidents at work, traffic accidents are the other great source of personal injury litigation. Yet English law has, on the whole, refused to establish a no fault liability of things regime for motor vehicles with the result that civil liability for accidental harm is entirely dependent on the tort of negligence. Indeed, even the tort of breach of statutory duty – applicable to things in the workplace – was excluded from things on the road.[21] Thus a victim must prove fault before damages can be obtained.[22]

However two points do need to be noted. First, there is a kind of liability for things that can apply to motor vehicles when a car owned by one person is driven by another and when a taxi, owned by one person, is directed to customers by another firm (see Chapter 14). Secondly, there is one case which suggests that those who put commercial vehicles on the road which cause damage through a defect in for example the brakes might be put into a position where they virtually have to disprove fault.[23] But such a principle, if in fact there is such a principle, probably does not in general extend to private vehicles. Despite these two exceptional situations, the civil liability position is controversial when compared with France. Victims of traffic accidents in France do not, on the whole, have to prove fault and, in addition, they can use the criminal proceedings to obtain civil compensation. It is, arguably, much less of a lottery in an area

---

[19] *Curtis v Betts* [1990] 1 WLR 459.
[20] See Terré, Simler and Lequette (2002), at 884–94.
[21] *Phillips v Britannia Hygienic Laundry Co* [1923] 2 KB 832.
[22] *Mansfield v Weetabix Ltd* [1998] 1 WLR 1263.
[23] *Henderson v HE Jenkins & Sons* [1970] AC 282.

of personal injury where statistics are able fairly accurately to predict how many will be killed or injured on the roads in any one year.

AIRCRAFT

A statutory strict liability regime does apply, however, to 'material loss or damage' that 'is caused to any person or property on land or water' by things falling from an aircraft.[24] The 'cost' to the individual is that the same statute limits the right to bring an action for nuisance in respect of annoyance caused by aircraft and prohibits any action in trespass.[25] Nevertheless the courts seem to take the view that an action in nuisance is not completely excluded and in one recent decision it was held that the Ministry of Defence could be liable in private nuisance for the considerable noise caused to an occupier of land over which military jets flew. Such over-flights are no doubt in the public interest, said the judge; but 'it might well be unjust that he [the claimant] should suffer the damage for the benefit of all'.[26]

The judge also thought that the over-flights constituted an invasion of the claimant's human right under the Human Rights Act 1998. However it has recently been held by the Grand Chamber of the European Court of Human Rights that night flights at Heathrow would not amount to an invasion of article 8 provided that the government had seriously weighed the interests of the individual against the general economic interest of the country. The Court concluded that it:

> does not find that, in substance, the authorities overstepped their margin of appreciation by failing to strike a fair balance between the right of the individuals affected by those regulations to respect for their private life and home, and the conflicting interests of others and of the community as a whole, nor does it find that there have been fundamental procedural flaws in the preparation of the 1993 regulations on limitations for night flights.[27]

LAND AND BUILDINGS: HARM ON THE PREMISES

Where damage has been caused by things on land the position becomes complex because the sources of such liability are complex. Statute plays a

---

[24] Civil Aviation Act 1982, s 76(2).
[25] Civil Aviation Act 1982, s 76(1) and s 77.
[26] *Dennis v MOD* [2003] EWHC 793.
[27] *Hatton v UK* (2003) 37 EHRR 611, at para 129. See also *Marcic v Thames Water Utilities Ltd* [2004] 2 AC 42, at para 41.

fundamental role, yet not only are several different statutes to be considered, but the common law continues to have a background role as well.[28] It might be useful, therefore, to approach this area from the viewpoint of the formal source of liability, that is to say the various relevant statutes. However one fundamental starting point must always be kept in mind, the actual premises (land, buildings and natural objects on the land) themselves.

Where damage was caused by things on land the position at common law was, before 1957, particularly complex because of the differing kinds of status of all those connected with the land. Occupiers might well have to be differentiated from landlords and those coming on to land might enter under a contract (for example football spectators) or because they were invited (guests) or because they were given an implied licence to enter (for example travelling salesman). The common law once had different levels of duty attaching to these different classes of people. The aim of the Occupiers' Liability Act 1957 was to simplify the position and it did this by reducing all the duties owed by an 'occupier' to a 'visitor' to a 'common duty of care' (s 2(1)).

The duty itself is one of taking such care as in all the circumstances of the case is reasonable to see that the visitor will be reasonably safe in using the premises (s 2(2)). This is, therefore, negligence liability, but a particular liability because it attaches to the state of the premises and extends to omissions (failure to make safe). Thus if the visitor is injured by a dangerous product on the premises the source of any liability might be outside of the Act (but what about a collapsing stack of chairs?). The Act specifically mentions certain relevant circumstances: an occupier must be prepared for children to be less careful than adults (s 2(3)(a)), but he can expect that those who enter 'in the exercise of a calling' will guard against any risks attaching to this calling (s 2(3)(b)). Thus an occupier who calls in a specialist to deal with a defective installation can reasonably expect the specialist to appreciate and guard against the dangers arising from the defect.[29]

The statutory 'common duty' exists, however, only between an 'occupier' and a 'visitor' which gives rise to two questions. Who is an 'occupier'? And who is a 'visitor'? The occupier is a person who has *sufficient degree of control* over the premises[30] – and thus there might be two occupiers of the same premises (landlord and tenant) – while a visitor covers the old invitee (guest) and licensee (permitted to enter).

---

[28] See *Gwilliam v West Hertfordshire Hospital NHS Trust* [2003] QB 443, at paras 35–44.
[29] *Roles v Nathan* [1963] 1 WLR 1117.
[30] *Wheat v E Lacon & Co Ltd* [1966] AC 552.

What the term 'visitor' in the 1957 Act did not cover was the uninvited person who enters land as a 'trespasser'.[31] Thus, in principle, it would seem that no duty of care was owed to trespassers, save a duty not intentionally to injury them.[32] The position was modified at common law mainly in respect of the problems caused by children: trespassers were owed a duty of common humanity, a much more limited duty than the ordinary duty of care.[33]

Today uninvited persons are covered by the Occupiers' Liability Act 1984. An occupier owes a duty to 'persons other than his visitors in respect of any risk of their suffering injury on the premises by reason of any danger due to the state of the premises or to things done or omitted to be done on them' (ss 1(1)(a); 1(3)). However the occupier must be *aware* both of the *danger*, or has reasonable grounds to believe that it exists, and of the *uninvited person* being 'in the vicinity of the danger' (s 1(3), emphasis added). Moreover the risk must be one that it is *reasonable* in all the circumstances for the occupier to offer to the other some protection (s 1(3) (c), emphasis added). As to the duty itself, it is only 'to take such care as is reasonable in all the circumstances . . . to see that he does not suffer *injury* on the premises by reason of the danger concerned' (s 1(4), emphasis added), the definition of 'injury' being confined to personal injury (s 1(9)). The duty is thus a very limited one (and one should note the interest protected) and much will depend upon the age of the trespasser and whether the danger was an obvious one or not. Indeed it may well be that it is only on rare occasions that an occupier will be liable to adult trespassers injured by obvious dangers, even at night.[34] Children might be treated with more sympathy, especially if the occupier is a large enterprise and (or) there is an allurement on the land.[35] But again it may be that an occupier is entitled to assume that parents will not normally allow their little children to go out unaccompanied[36] and that when judging whether something on the land is dangerous or not the occupier is entitled to judge it in relation to adults.[37] The occupier owes no duty to those with a statutory 'right to roam' in respect of natural features of the landscape (s 1(6A)).

---

[31] See Law Comm Report No 75, Cmnd 6429, 1976.
[32] *Edwards v Railway Executive* [1952] AC 737; *Revill v Newbery* [1996] QB 567.
[33] *Herrington v British Railways Board* [1972] AC 877.
[34] *Ratcliff v McConnell* [1999] 1 WLR 670; *Tomlinson v Congleton BC* [2004] 1 AC 46.
[35] *Jolley v Sutton LBC* [2000] 1 WLR 1082.
[36] *Phipps v Rochester Corporation* [1955] 1 QB 450.
[37] *Keown v Coventry Healthcare NHS trust* [2006] 1 WLR 953.

In *Tomlinson v Congleton BC*,[38] a major case to reach the House of Lords on the 1984 Act, a teenager entered land owned by a local authority and dived into a lake on the property suffering severe injury when his head struck the bottom. The defendant local authority was aware that people were attracted by the lake, but prominent notices declared that swimming was prohibited. The defendants were equally aware that these notices were often ignored and they intended, when finances permitted, to plant vegetation around the lake that would physically prevent people from entering the water. However at the time of the accident the planting plan had not been executed. A majority of the Court of Appeal gave judgment for the teenager, but this was reversed by the House of Lords. There were a number of reasons put forward as to why the occupier should not be liable, but perhaps the general policy basis was expressed by Lord Hoffmann:

> I think it will be extremely rare for an occupier of land to be under a duty to prevent people from taking risks which are inherent in the activities they freely choose to undertake upon the land. If people want to climb mountains, go hang-gliding or swim or dive in ponds or lakes, that is their affair. Of course the landowner may for his own reasons wish to prohibit such activities. He may think that they are a danger or inconvenience to himself or others. Or he may take a paternalist view and prefer people not to undertake risky activities on his land. He is entitled to impose such conditions, as the Council did by prohibiting swimming. But the law does not require him to do so.[39]

One problem with this observation of Lord Hoffmann is that it appears to be propounding a policy that actually conflicts with the careful wording, and thus possibly the intention, behind the 1984 Act. The Law Lord seems to be envisaging that the risk is almost entirely on the trespasser, yet the language of the Act does not fully confirm this view. Where there is a danger attaching to land and premises there is some obligation that in turn attaches to the occupier. Nevertheless *Tomlinson* does seem to have sent an important message: ordinary things on land such as trees, lakes and fire escapes will not easily attract liability.[40]

The two occupiers' liability statutes are concerned with the duties owed by occupiers. But it is also necessary to consider the position of landlords where the latter are not occupiers and this is where the Defective Premises Act 1972 is relevant. It puts a landlord under a duty of care 'to *all persons* who might reasonably be expected to be affected by the *defects* . . . to see that they are *reasonably safe* from personal injury or from damage to their

---

[38] [2004] 1 AC 46.
[39] [2004] 1 AC 46, at para 45.
[40] See *Keown v Coventry Healthcare NHS trust* [2006] 1 WLR 953.

property caused by a relevant defect' (s 4(1), emphasis added; and one should note again the interests protected). However this duty exists only in respect of let premises where the landlord is under an obligation to the tenant for the maintenance or repair of the premises. This of course means that where a third party (C) is injured as a result of defective premises, any claim against the landlord (D) might well depend, not on the legal relationship between C and D, but upon the exact nature of a tenancy contract between D and tenant, reducing liability to a matter of chance.[41] No doubt the tenant might well be liable if the landlord is not, but if the person was off the premises when injured by the defect (for example by a collapsing wall) the 1957 and 1984 Act will not apply (see s 1(7) of the 1984 Act). The question then is whether there is liability of occupier and (or) landlord at common law for public[42] or private nuisance.[43]

If one returns to the Occupiers' Liability Act 1957, it specifically allows an occupier to 'extend, restrict, modify or exclude his duty' (s 2(1)). Thus before 1977 all occupiers could potentially exclude liability by erecting a notice containing an exclusion provision; provided the notice was clear the occupier would not be liable.[44] However the Unfair Contract Terms Act 1977 now renders void any attempt to exclude liability for personal injury (s 2(1)) arising out of a 'business liability' (s 1(3)(a)); in the case of damage to property the exclusion will have to pass the reasonableness test (s 2(2)). The non-business occupier can therefore continue to exclude liability through a general notice (s 1(3)(b)). One anomaly is that a visitor may be, in theory, in a worse position than a trespasser, although it is unlikely that the judges will be over-impressed with such logic.[45] One might note also that a notice, if ignored, might turn a visitor into a trespasser, although much will depend here on the actual facts.[46] However it is difficult to imagine that a notice would be held to be binding against a young child.[47]

LAND AND BUILDINGS: HARM OFF THE PREMISES

Occupiers' liability, as expressed in legislation, is primarily (although not exclusively) concerned with the liability of an occupier to those on

---

[41] *McCauley v Bristol CC* [1991] 1 All ER 749.
[42] *Mint v Good* [1951] 1 KB 517.
[43] *Brew Brothers Ltd v Snax (Ross) Ltd* [1970] 1 QB 612.
[44] *White v Blackmore* [1972] 1 QB 651.
[45] See *Tomlinson v Congleton BC* [2004] 1 AC 46.
[46] *Tomlinson v Congleton BC* [2004] 1 AC 46.
[47] But see *Keown v Coventry Healthcare NHS Trust* [2006] 1 WLR 953.

the land under his control. However dangerous premises can equally injure or damage people off the premises. A collapsing wall might fall onto a passer-by or an activity carried out by the occupier might seriously annoy, if not physically damage, a neighbour. An activity attached or associated with a particular piece of land can, of course, physically spread itself beyond the premises and spill onto the public highway. And this can cause problems for neighbours if not the community in general.

Several specific torts are of importance when it comes to the liability of an occupier and (or) owner of premises to those off the land. The most important are trespass, private nuisance, public nuisance and the rule in *Rylands v Fletcher*. One must not, of course, forget negligence since one foundational case involved injury to a person on the highway (public road) as a result of an activity (cricket) carried on by an occupier.[48] This case also raised the difficult issue of the relationship between the torts of nuisance and negligence. In many ways it is a sterile exercise to try to compare the so-called strict liability torts like nuisance with negligence at the formal level; it is more often a question of the nature of the damage suffered and the activity producing this damage, not forgetting, either, the remedy and interests (public or private) in issue.[49] The actual requirements of many of these torts have been set out by Denning LJ in *Esso Petroleum Ltd v Southport Corporation*.[50]

In addition to these torts one must not forget public law. There is now a range of statutes empowering public authorities such as a local authority or the police to act in situations where a person or commercial enterprise is carrying out an anti-social activity. For example the Environmental Protection Act 1990 gives to local authorities the power to serve abatement notices where a statutory nuisance exists (ss 79-80) and the Anti-Social Behaviour Act 2003 empowers a local authority to make a closure order where noise amounts to a public nuisance (s 40). It must be remembered, also, that a severe interference with family life might well amount to an invasion of a human right. Some of these statutory protections are not as effective as one might at first think. The European Court of Human Rights has expressed the view that the rights of individuals are to be balanced against the economic interests of the community as a whole[51] and the Environmental Protection Act

---

[48] *Bolton v Stone* [1951] AC 850.
[49] See generally *Transco plc v Stockport MBC* [2004] 2 AC 1.
[50] [1954] 2 QB 182.
[51] *Hatton v UK* (2003) 37 EHRR 611.

1990 allows a firm that is prima facie committing a statutory nuisance the defence of 'best practicable means' in countering the nuisance (s 80(7)).[52]

Trespass

An occupier of land can be liable for trespass to a neighbour if he directly invades the land of the latter. Thus if he builds a garage on his land that by several inches transgresses onto the land of his neighbour there will liability; however the victim probably does not have the right to destroy that part of the garage that transgresses the boundary, even if in principle a victim can abate a nuisance (self-help remedy).[53] He can seek damages and (or) an injunction. The same trespass principle applies to a crane jib that transgresses the air space of a landowner;[54] but merely to photograph a person's house without actually entering the premises or airspace will not be a trespass,[55] although it might amount to a contravention of Article 8 of the European Convention of Human Rights. The damage must normally be direct if it is to constitute trespass,[56] but a person who deliberately sets a pack of dogs in pursuit of say a stag or a fox, knowing that there is a real risk that the dogs will enter on another's land without permission of the landowner, will be liable in trespass.[57] One could also talk here of a liability for animals.

Private nuisance

Trespass is about direct invasions of a person's land while nuisance is about indirect invasions. However these indirect invasions must result from an activity carried out by a landowner that amounts to an *unreasonable use of land*. The essence of the tort of private nuisance is not so much the behaviour of one person vis-à-vis the damage suffered by another person. The essence is the activity, or state of affairs, associated with one piece of land and its effect on a neighbouring property with the result that the damage arising from nuisance is damage to *land*.[58] Accordingly the claimant must

---

[52] cf *Hounslow LBC v Thames Water Utilities Ltd* [2004] QB 212, at para 52.
[53] *Burton v Winters* [1993] 1 WLR 1077.
[54] *Anchor Brewhouse Developments Ltd v Berkley House (Docklands Developments) Ltd* (1987) 38 BLR 82.
[55] *Bernstein v Skyviews & General Ltd* [1978] QB 497.
[56] *Esso Petroleum Ltd v Southport Corporation* [1954] 2 QB 182, at 195.
[57] *League Against Cruel Sports v Scott* [1986] 1 QB 240.
[58] *Hunter v Canary Wharf Ltd* [1997] AC 655.

have an *interest* in the land affected.[59] The use of the word 'unreasonable' means that the behaviour of the defendant *might* be relevant on occasions; encroaching tree roots or direct physical damage often requires an 'unreasonableness' that is close to the Lord Atkin neighbour formula.[60] Moreover if an occupier deliberately indulges in an activity with the sole purpose of irritating his neighbour he will be liable.[61] Equally a failure to remedy a dangerous state of affairs – a mere omission in the eyes of the tort of negligence but not in the tort of private nuisance – could result in liability.[62]

Nevertheless the type of damage is important. If the damage is *intangible* (noise, smell and the like) the nature of the locality and the activity will play a vital role in determining liability. If it is *tangible* – physical damage to persons or property – then locality will be irrelevant.[63] Often this distinction is reflected in the type of the remedy in issue: intangible damage is usually the subject of an injunction claim and here the public interest might be balanced against the private.[64] The remedy of damages in contrast usually focuses on where the loss should fall which in turn tends to emphasise interference, activity and causation.[65] An important defence to nuisance is its authorisation by statute; indeed the tort may be inapplicable where a statutory scheme is in place.[66] However the mere granting of planning permission is not a licence to commit a nuisance.[67]

Public nuisance

Private nuisance involves a claim by one land user against another and is concerned with private interests; public nuisance – whose origins are conceptually different – usually involves a claim for interference with a person's use and enjoyment of a public highway (including waterways) and thus must involve an invasion of the public interest.[68] The interference must amount to the crime of public nuisance and to sue in tort the claimant must suffer *special damage* over and above other members of the

---

[59] *Hunter v Canary Wharf Ltd* [1997] AC 655.
[60] *Delaware Mansions Ltd v Westminster CC* [2002] 1 AC 321, at 1017–18; *Transco plc v Stockport MBC* [2004] 2 AC 1, at para 96.
[61] *Hollywood Silver Fox Farm v Emmett* [1936] 2 KB 468.
[62] *Goldman v Hargrave* [1967] 1 AC 645; *Delaware Mansions Ltd v Westminster CC* [2002] 1 AC 321.
[63] *Halsey v Esso Petroleum & Co Ltd* [1961] 1 WLR 683.
[64] *Miller v Jackson* [1977] QB 966.
[65] *Holbeck Hall Hotel Ltd v Scarborough CC* [2000] QB 836.
[66] *Marcic v Thames Water Utilities Ltd* [2004] 2 AC 42.
[67] *Wheeler v JJ Saunders Ltd* [1996] Ch 19.
[68] *Att-Gen v PYA Quarries Ltd* [1957] 2 QB 169.

public.[69] Here, however, it is important to note that pure financial loss will suffice. Consequently an action in public nuisance could succeed where the tort of negligence would fail.[70]

What the court does, according to Edmund Davies LJ in a case involving personal injury on the road, in an action for public nuisance is not to look at the conduct of the defendant and ask whether he was negligent. What it does is to look at the actual state of affairs as it exists in or adjoining the highway, without regard to the merits or demerits of the defendant's act; and if the state of affairs is such as to be a danger to persons using the highway it will amount to a public nuisance. Once it is held to be a danger, the person who created it is liable unless he can show sufficient justification or excuse.[71] This tort can thus be used to gain damages for injury, damage or loss suffered by public highway users as a result of dangerous buildings and structures which adjoin the highway (that is to say a public road, path or waterway).[72] Even an activity that is prima facie a private nuisance – that is to say where private interests are affected – can become a public nuisance if the effects are wide enough to affect the community as a whole, for in such a situation the public interest comes into play. And in such cases the Attorney-General (and now the local authority thanks to legislation) can seek an injunction to restrain the nuisance.[73]

Rylands v Fletcher

Private nuisance liability involves a continuing state of affairs. Accordingly a single isolated escape – for example an explosion or the escape of water or electricity – does not normally give rise to a claim based on the unreasonable use of land. There may be liability in public nuisance and, of course, it may be possible to argue that the storage of hazardous material is a continuing activity that amounts to the unreasonable use of land. However if an isolated escape does cause damage off the premises and it involves a dangerous thing there may be liability under the rule of *Rylands v Fletcher*.[74] In this case the owner of land was held liable for the

---

[69] *In re Corby Group Litigation* [2009] QB 335.
[70] *Tate & Lyle v GLC* [1983] 2 AC 509.
[71] *Dymond v Pearce* [1972] 1 QB 496, at 506–507.
[72] See *Tarry v Ashton* (1876) 1 QBD 314; *Wringe v Cohen* [1940] 1 KB 229; *Mint v Good* [1951] 1 KB 517; Defective Premises Act 1972, s 4.
[73] See Lord Bingham in *R v Rimmington* [2006] 1 AC 459, para 7; Local Government Act 1972, s 222. See also *Att-Gen v PYA Quarries Ltd* [1957] 2 QB 169; *In re Corby Group Litigation* [2009] QB 335.
[74] (1866) LR 1 Ex 265 (Ex); (1868) LR 3 HL 330 (HL).

escape of water from a reservoir that had been defectively constructed by an independent contractor. This case is not just a precedent but has traditionally been considered as the basis of an independent cause of action in tort. 'We think', said Blackburn J in his Court of Exchequer Chamber judgment, 'that the true rule of law is, that the person who for his own purposes brings on his lands and collects and keeps there anything likely to do mischief if it escapes, must keep it in at his peril, and, if he does not do so, is *prima facie* answerable for all the damage which is the natural consequence of its escape'.[75] In the House of Lords, Lord Cairns added the requirement of 'non natural use' (replacing 'not naturally there').[76] Whether the judges and Law Lords thought they were laying down new law is open to question.[77] But the case became separated from nuisance and in the United States it has become the basis for 'extra hazardous liability'. Its subsequent history in England, however, was to take a very different course.

LIABILITY FOR DANGEROUS THINGS

If one was looking for one single authority that appears closest, in spirit at least, to the idea of a liability for a thing under the control of another (cf CC art 1384) it is this decision of *Rylands v Fletcher*. However in the United Kingdom later cases severely restricted its scope by focusing on one or more of what are three basic requirements. These are that the thing must be dangerous (thus bringing in an element of foreseeability);[78] that the dangerous thing must escape from the defendant's land (and so no liability under the rule to someone injured on the premises);[79] and that the accumulation on the land must be a 'non-natural use'. This last requirement has now been subsumed to some extent under the foreseeability principle which means that the focal point is now the 'dangerousness' of the thing brought onto land.[80] The escape rule is a serious restriction in that a person injured *on the premises* will not it seems have a claim under the rule and will have to prove a breach of a common duty of care. Moreover if the escape of the thing results from the act of

---

[75] (1866) LR 1 Ex 265, at 279.
[76] (1868) LR 3 HL 330, at 340.
[77] See *Transco plc v Stockport MBC* [2004] 2 AC 1.
[78] *Cambridge Water Co v Eastern Counties Leather Plc* [1994] 2 AC 264.
[79] *Read v J Lyons & Co* [1947] AC 156.
[80] *Cambridge Water Co v Eastern Counties Leather Plc* [1994] 2 AC 264.

a stranger[81] or an 'act of God'[82] the landowner may have a defence; and it is unlikely that the rule now applies to personal injury.[83] In Australia the rule has been absorbed into the tort of negligence,[84] but in a quite recent decision the House of Lords has decided to maintain *Rylands* as an independent cause of action, though very confined in its scope. As Lord Hoffmann concluded: 'It is hard to escape the conclusion that the intellectual effort devoted to the rule by judges and writers over many years has brought forth a mouse'.[85]

Dangerous animals and fire might seem to be covered by *Rylands v Fletcher*. However liability for damage done by animals is, as we have seen, now governed by a separate statutory regime. With respect to damage caused by fire, there is a statutory defence 'against any person in whose house, chamber, stable, barn or other building, or in whose estate any fire shall *accidentally* begin'.[86] The word 'accidentally' has been construed narrowly with the result that spreading fire can give rise to liability under a number of heads: *Rylands v Fletcher*;[87] private nuisance;[88] and of course negligence. If the fire has been caused by a trespasser the occupier from whose land the fire spreads may be able to escape liability in negligence provided he has not allured the trespasser onto the property.[89] But the property owner upon whose property a fire accidentally starts will probably not be allowed to avail himself of the mere omission rule if he fails to tackle the fire or to call the fire brigade.[90] Fire also brings into play fire insurance and contractual structures in complex commercial situations and this may lead to the following question often posed implicitly, if not explicitly, by the judges. Upon which insurance policy should the fire risk fall? Certainly damage done to property by water can now attract this kind of insurance analysis[91] and the same is no doubt true for damage by fire.[92]

---

[81] *Perry v Kendricks Transport Ltd* [1956] 1 WLR 85.
[82] *Nichols v Marsland* (1876) 2 Ex.D 1.
[83] *Read v J Lyons & Co* [1947] AC 156; *Transco plc v Stockport MBC* [2004] 2 AC 1. cf *In re Corby Group Litigation* [2009] 2 WLR 609 (CA).
[84] See *Transco plc v Stockport MBC* [2004] 2 AC 1, at para 40.
[85] [2004] 2 AC 1, at para 39.
[86] Fires Prevention (Metropolis) Act 1774, s 86 [emphasis added].
[87] *Mason v Levy Auto Parts* [1967] 2 QB 530.
[88] *Goldman v Hargrave* [1967] 1 AC 645.
[89] *Smith v Littlewoods Organisation Ltd* [1987] AC 241.
[90] *Goldman v Hargrave* [1967] 1 AC 645.
[91] *Transco plc v Stockport MBC* [2004] 2 AC 1, at paras 46 and 60.
[92] *Photo Production Ltd v Securicor* [1980] AC 827.

OCCUPIER'S LIABILITY: METHODOLOGICAL CONSIDERATIONS

Before leaving the topic of occupiers' liability something should perhaps be said about the methods involved in handling problems arising in this area. The supposed strength of the 1957 Act was that it was designed to simplify the situation with respect to liability and duty. Instead of differing duties at different levels, the Act imposed a common duty of care. Yet it should be obvious that the plethora of duties that attach to an occupier have not in general been simplified. If a wall collapses harming three different persons – one on the land on which the wall was constructed, another on the public highway and one living next door whose property is damaged – the situation will be complex. The owner of the wall will find that he owes three quite different duties. To the person on the highway the duty is strict, or almost strict;[93] to the person next door, the duty might be quite strict;[94] while to the person on the land the duty will be one where the injured person has to prove fault.[95] Such a difference of duties will also be found where, for example, a shed full of fireworks explodes and causes all kinds of damage to property both on and off the premises. To those off the premises the duty will probably be strict whereas to the owners of property parked on the premises the duty will be the common duty of care. Indeed, if a trespasser has left property on the premises, there will be no duty owed by the occupier.

All these differing duties result, of course, from different kinds of causes of action. To those off the premises the duties will be determined by the torts of public nuisance, private nuisance and *Rylands v Fletcher*; to those on the premises the duties will be defined by statute and much will depend upon whether the claimant is a 'visitor' or a 'trespasser'. Yet even where the duty is fixed by statute complexity can still resurface. If the occupier brings onto to his land an independent contractor to provide entertainment for his visitors, the occupier may remain under some residual duties, perhaps to check the contractor's insurance if the activity is a risky one.[96] Over and above the statutory regime, it may well be that the occupier continues to owe a duty at common law in respect of the kind of safety system that is in operation; and thus in one case a woman injured in a supermarket when she slipped on a pot of spilt yoghurt was able to recover damages

---

[93] *Mint v Good* [1951] 1 KB 517.
[94] *Wringe v Cohen* [1940] 1 KB 229.
[95] Occupiers' Liability Act 1957, s 2.
[96] *Gwilliam v West Hertfordshire Hospital NHS Trust* [2003] QB 443.

when she indicated that the supermarket might have a faulty system for handling such spillages.[97]

When faced, therefore, with a set of facts involving land and (or) buildings it remains important to identify exactly where the accident took place, the nature of the damage and how it occurred. Was the claimant injured on or off the premises? If the latter, then the Occupiers' Liability Act 1957 or 1984 will not be applicable; one will need to look at one of the strict liability torts and the common law tort of negligence. What was the nature of the damage? If it was intangible (smell, noise), locality might be relevant. If it was economic or damage to property, the status of the claimant could be vital. If a trespasser, the occupier will owe him a duty only in respect of personal injury.

How did the damage occur? If it was of a continuing nature, then the tort of nuisance might be relevant; if a single event, like an explosion or escape, then *Rylands v Fletcher* would be the cause of action (although this cause of action probably will not apply to personal injury). Was the damage caused by an activity started and operated by the defendant or did it arise from a situation of which he was not the immediate cause? If a neighbour suffers damage as a result of a commercial activity it may well be that the occupier will be liable in nuisance even if he is not at fault; the mere causing of damage by the activity could well deem it an unreasonable use of land vis-à-vis the person who individually suffers as a result of the defendant's activity.[98] However if the damage is caused by some process of nature, or some activity reasonable in itself, then the occupier will probably be liable only if he *adopted* the nuisance, that is if he was aware, or ought to have been aware, of the danger.[99] In this latter situation nuisance and negligence to some extent merge via the notion of *unreasonable*. If the activity causes annoyance to more than just one or two neighbours, it may be that the local authority will be able to seek an injunction since the interests of the community are in play; in other words public nuisance might provoke a community remedy whereas private nuisance is actionable only by the person affected.[100] If the activity is governed by a statutory scheme there may be no scope for a liability at common law.[101] However if injury occurs as a result of a breach of some safety statute, perhaps the tort of breach of statutory duty might be relevant.

---

[97] *Ward v Tesco Stores Ltd* [1976] 1 WLR 810.
[98] *Bamford v Turnley* (1862) 3 B & S 62; 122 ER 27; *Dennis v MOD* [2003] EWHC 793.
[99] *Delaware Mansions Ltd v Westminster CC* [2002] 1 AC 321.
[100] *Att-Gen v PYA Quarries Ltd* [1957] 2 QB 169.
[101] *Marcic v Thames Water Utilities Ltd* [2004] 2 AC 42.

The intervention of statute in 1957 has, admittedly, probably not exacerbated the duty complexity which attaches to an occupier. Yet it has not really simplified the overall picture either. Nor, perhaps, could or should, statute do this. The situation is complex because the activities carried out on land are complex and give rise to a range of different types of problem. The advantage of the forms of action approach – trespass, public nuisance, private nuisance, *Rylands v Fletcher* and negligence – is that it forces legal problem-solvers to operate at the level of fact and to distinguish between different types of damage, causes, actors and activities. Or, put another way, it offers a range of possibilities when it comes to categorising the facts in order to apply the law. The difficulty is, of course, that the forms of action are not watertight; concepts from one can infect others and this immediately gives rise to a conceptual problem of boundaries. What is the difference between nuisance and negligence? Why does Baron Bramwell in *Bamford v Turnley*[102] seem to be applying a criterion that is different from, say, the one used by Lord Hoffmann in *Transco v Stockport MBC*?[103] One reason, perhaps, is that a commercial brick factory is not quite the same as a statutory concern charged with supplying water and sewerage facilities (although privatisation has 'muddied the waters' to use an apt metaphor). Judges do not always openly say such things, but the concepts they apply can reflect differences in social fact and in historical outlook.

Perhaps, however, the biggest challenge in the area of occupiers' liability is to fashion a methodology suitable for dealing with the new environmental concerns, no doubt more challenging than those that had to be faced in former times. How does the public interest, or the interest of future generations, get recognised, for example, in a private nuisance action? In addition to all of this, one must not forget the Human Rights Act 1998 which might impose even further duties on an occupier. One thing is certain, merely applying a 'common duty of care' across the whole spectrum of liability for things would be far too simplistic and possibly rather dangerous for local, national and international environmental interests.

---

[102] (1862) 3 B & S 62; 122 ER 27.
[103] [2004] 2 AC 1.

13. Liability for people

The idea of a liability for things is balanced, symmetrically speaking, in CC art 1384 by the further idea of a liability for people. We have seen that English law does give *some* expression to the idea of a liability based on the control of a thing. Does it also give expression to the idea of a liability arising out of the control of a person? As with liability for things, the answer is not entirely negative by any means, but the conceptual structure of English tort law can make comparison with French law complex.

Accordingly there is no general principle in English law similar to the liability for persons in CC art 1384. Instead there are a number of specific situations where one person will be liable for a tortious act committed by another person. These specific situations fall broadly into three categories: (i) the liability of an employer for torts committed by an employee (vicarious liability); (ii) certain direct liabilities arising out of torts committed by persons who might or might not be employees; and (iii) the specific liability of an owner of a car for the careless driving of another using the car when the owner has an interest in the journey. In addition to these categories there are a number of further specific situations where the act of one person may result in liability for another person. All these categories are not scientific creations, particularly the second; they are simply designed to orientate the researcher towards the main groups of cases where one person can be held liable for the tortious act of another. One complicating factor, of course, is the notion of legal personality since such an 'abstract' person (or *personne morale* as the French say, developing an idea first found in medieval Roman law scholarship) can act only through human persons. Where an employee or other contractor causes damage to a third person the latter is immediately confronted with two possible defendants, the corporation and the individual actor.[1]

VICARIOUS LIABILITY

The starting point of liability for another's tort is the well-established principle of vicarious liability whereby an employer ('master') is liable for

---

[1] See *In re Supply of Ready Mixed Concrete (No 2)* [1995] 1 AC 456, at 465.

torts committed by an employee ('servant'). The liability is based on three sub-rules: (i) there must be a tort (ii) committed by a servant (iii) acting within the course of his employment. All of these rules have given rise to case law.

Tort

The claimant injured by an employee must establish a tort, that is to say he must establish that the employee's act that has caused the damage amounted to trespass, negligence, conversion, defamation or whatever. If there is no tort there is no employer's liability.[2] The claimant might be able to derive some help from the maxim *res ipsa loquitur*; and so if someone goes into a hospital operating theatre for a minor operation on his hand and comes out minus his arm there will be a prima facie assumption that this is due to a tort committed by the hospital.[3] But such an aid does not amount to a reversal of the burden of proof;[4] all that the defendant need show to put the burden of proving negligence back onto the claimant is that the accident could have happened without fault.[5] Most of the torts committed by employees are unintentional ones – normally negligent behaviour or breach of a statute – but an employer can also be liable for wilful behaviour. Thus an employer has been held liable for harassment by one employee towards a co-employee.[6]

Servant (Employee)

The individual who has committed a tort must be a 'servant', that is to say an employee and not an independent contractor.[7] Thus a business enterprise will be liable for the careless driving of a driver on the payroll but not for a taxi driver who drives some of the managers to the station. There are some ambiguous situations however. Some firms hire out not just vehicles but also drivers: thus if the driver carelessly injures a third person it may not always be clear whether it is the owner or hirer of the vehicle who is to be vicariously liable.[8] Recently, however, the Court of Appeal has

---

[2] *Staveley Iron & Chemical Co v Jones* [1956] AC 627.
[3] *Cassidy v Ministry of Health* [1951] 2 KB 343.
[4] *The Kite* [1933] P 154.
[5] *Roe v Minister of Health* [1954] 2 QB 66.
[6] *Majrowski v Guy's and St Thomas' NHS Trust* [2007] 1 AC 224.
[7] *Rowe v Herman* [1997] 1 WLR 1390.
[8] *Mersey Docks & Harbour Board v Coggins & Griffiths (Liverpool) Ltd & McFarlane* [1947] AC 1.

held that both companies may be vicariously liable since there is nothing in the precedents that definitively restricts the concept to one employer.[9] Another difficulty is that some contracts of employment specifically state that employees are not 'servants' but independent contractors; here the courts may or may not be influenced by form.[10]

In fact the line between employee and independent contractor can be very difficult to discern on occasions. In *Hall v Lorimer*[11] the first instance judge said that the process was not a 'mechanical exercise of running through items on a check list to see whether they are present in, or absent from, a given situation.' The 'exercise is to paint a picture from the accumulation of detail' and then to evaluate 'the overall effect of the detail', which is not necessarily the same as the sum total of the individual details.[12] In *Market Investigations Ltd v Ministry of Social Security*[13] Cooke J broadly adopted this approach but by asking two questions. The first was 'whether the extent and degree of the control exercised by the company, if no other factors were taken into account, be consistent with her being employed under a contract of service'. And the second question was, 'whether when the contract is looked at as a whole, its nature and provisions are consistent or inconsistent with its being a contract of service'.[14] The question that he had to decide was whether a woman interviewer employed from time to time to carry out interviews was acting as an employee (contract of service) or as an independent contractor in business on her own account (contract of services). After weighing up a number of considerations – including the degree of *control* exercised by the employer over her work plus the fact that there was nothing in the contracts that was actually *inconsistent* with it being a contract of service – Cooke J decided that she was an employee.

Course of Employment

The third requirement is perhaps the most difficult since there is a large grey area between acting for one's employer and acting for oneself (a 'frolic of one's own'). For example, the company van driver who carelessly injures another road user while delivering his employer's goods

---

[9] *Viasystems (Tynside) Ltd v Thermal Transfer (Northern) Ltd* [2006] QB 510.
[10] *Ready Mixed Concrete v Minister of Pensions* [1968] 2 QB 497; cf *Ferguson v John Dawson & Partners (Contractors) Ltd* [1976] 1 WLR 1213.
[11] [1992] 1 WLR 939 (QBD); [1994] 1 All ER 250 (CA).
[12] [1992] 1 WLR 939, at 944.
[13] [1969] 2 QB 173.
[14] [1969] 2 QB 173, at 185.

will involve the employer in liability. However if the driver was using the company van to take his family out to a picnic one Sunday the employer will probably not be liable. The test used to be summed up by this question: was the actor doing something he was employed to do? Thus in one case a bus company was held not liable for an assault by a bus conductor on a passenger since assaulting passengers was not what he was employed to do.[15] But in another case the House of Lords insisted that an employer of a security guard would have been liable (but for an exclusion clause) for his criminal act in deliberately burning down the premises of a client whose factory he had been sent to guard.[16]

One leading case involved the theft of a valuable mink stole by an employee of a firm of cleaners. The firm was held liable to the owner of the stole because he was employed to 'handle' it and thus his theft was an extension of doing what he was employed to do.[17] If the stole had been stolen by a secretary or night porter presumably there would have been no liability. In fact the case is complicated because there was a direct bailment duty between owner and cleaners and this makes it more of a property than an obligations case. Nevertheless it acted as the basis for the most recent major decision in this area: the law ought not to protect property owners better than human victims. Thus the employers of a warden who abused children in his care were held to be vicariously liable since he abused his position of trust.[18] The test now is the 'connection' between employment duty and tortious act and thus a nightclub has been held liable for a doorman who took violent revenge on a member of the public leaving him severely handicapped.[19]

THEORY OF VICARIOUS LIABILITY

Just why an employer is, in English law at least, automatically liable for torts committed by employees is not that easy to determine. Of course at first sight one can fashion a number of seemingly convincing theories based, for example, on the idea of those who profit from another's work should take the risk or on the thesis that the employer is in the best position to insure.[20] On closer examination many of these theories do not stand up to scrutiny. Thus the insurance argument breaks down because liability is

---

[15] *Keppel Bus Co v Sa'ad bin Ahmad* [1974] 2 All ER 700.
[16] *Photo Production Ltd v Securicor* [1980] AC 827.
[17] *Morris v C W Martin & Sons Ltd* [1966] 1 QB 716.
[18] *Lister v Hesley Hall Ltd* [2002] 1 AC 215.
[19] *Mattis v Pollock* [2003] 1 WLR 2158.
[20] *Morris v Ford Motor Co Ltd* [1973] 1 QB 792.

joint; the victim has the choice of suing either the servant or the employer and even if the employer is sued the insurance company, subrogated to the rights of the employer, is entitled in law to recoup the money from the employee who committed the tort.[21] Indeed, the insurance company could also do this as a matter of contribution.[22]

Possibly vicarious liability was once an extension of the principle of agency: *qui facit per alium facit per se* (he who acts through another acts for himself). But recently Lord Millett has stated that it 'is best understood as a loss-distribution device' whose 'theoretical underpinning of the doctrine is unclear.' He went on to suggest that the employer 'is liable only if the risk is one which experience shows is inherent in the nature of the business'.[23] Again Lord Millett's thesis is open to attack on the ground that it is the person at fault who is, in theory, ultimately liable to pay. Yet if he is reflecting what most judges believe then one further valuable reform that they might undertake is to remove the right of the employer (or in effect its insurance company) to reclaim from the employee an indemnity. In practice insurance companies do not do this and so any reform by the judiciary would have the added advantage of mirroring social practice.

Another justification that has been advanced recently in support of vicarious liability is its functional role. According to Lord Nicholls the rationale can be found 'in a combination of policy factors.' And he continued:

> They are summarised in Professor Fleming's *Law of Torts*, 9th ed (1998), pp 409–10. Stated shortly, these factors are that all forms of economic activity carry a risk of harm to others, and fairness requires that those responsible for such activities should be liable to persons suffering loss from wrongs committed in the conduct of the enterprise. This is 'fair', because it means injured persons can look for recompense to a source better placed financially than individual wrongdoing employees. It means also that the financial loss arising from the wrongs can be spread more widely, by liability insurance and higher prices. In addition, and importantly, imposing strict liability on employers encourages them to maintain standards of 'good practice' by their employees. For these reasons employers are to be held liable for wrongs committed by their employees in the course of their employment.[24]

These justifications for vicarious liability are not open to attack in themselves but they do beg a number of questions about the law of tort itself. If strict liability is to be justified on the ground of 'fairness' why is it so restricted? Why are these 'good practices' restricted just to employers?

---

[21] *Lister v Romford Ice & Cold Storage Co Ltd* [1957] AC 555.
[22] Civil Liability (Contribution) Act 1978.
[23] *Lister v Hesley Hall Ltd* [2002] 1 AC 215, at para 65.
[24] *Majrowski v Guy's and St Thomas' NHS Trust* [2007] 1 AC 224, at para 9.

Ought not car drivers or those who indulge in risky activities to be under such a strict duty? Would not drivers and manufacturers be encouraged to maintain higher standards? It is all very well justifying vicarious liability on the basis of fairness, but if this is to be a policy issue why is it not extended into other areas of liability? Is it 'fair' that the claimant in *Read v Lyons*[25] went away empty handed because she could not prove the operator of a munitions factory negligent and because she was inside the premises rather than outside them? French administrative law judges, and probably private law judges as well, would certainly have taken a different view.[26] Is it fair that two men should spend time in prison as a result of the incompetence of a public body and then be denied any compensation by the courts?[27] The problem with attempting to theorise about vicarious liability is that it soon becomes evident that the English law of tort has committed itself neither to a consistent theory nor to a consistent policy. And this makes theories of vicarious liability look unconvincing.

NON-DELEGABLE DUTY

Vicarious liability cannot apply where an *independent contractor* commits a tort since he is not a 'servant'.[28] Yet there appear to be cases that contradict this logic; there are decisions where an employer of an independent contractor is seemingly held liable for the tort committed by the contractor. For example in *Rylands v Fletcher*,[29] as we have seen (Chapter 12), the owner of land who hired a firm of independent contractors to build a reservoir on the property was held liable for the negligent work carried out by the contractor. However the liability of the employer in these exceptional cases is not vicarious; it is based on the breach of a direct *non-delegable* duty between victim and employer. In addition to any statutory duties, such a duty can arise from the keeping of a dangerous thing, an extra-hazardous act,[30] a bailment relationship,[31] a public nuisance[32] and of course a contractual relationship between victim and employer.[33]

---

[25] [1947] AC 156.
[26] Jolowicz [1985] CLJ 370.
[27] *Elguzouli-Daf v Commissioner of Police of the Metropolis* [1995] QB 335.
[28] *Salsbury v Woodland* [1970] 1 QB 324.
[29] (1866) LR 1 Ex 265 (Ex); (1868) LR 3 HL 330 (HL).
[30] *Honeywill & Stein v Larkin Brothers* [1934] 1 KB 191.
[31] *Riverstone Meat Co v Lancashire Shipping Co* [1961] AC 807.
[32] *Tarry v Ashton* (1876) 1 QBD 314.
[33] *Photo Production Ltd v Securicor* [1980] AC 827; *Wong Mee Wan v Kwan Kin Travel Services Ltd* [1996] 1 WLR 38.

This last relationship is of particular importance because it so clearly indicates how the law of obligations can become distorted by the relationship between legal personality and liability. When a company contracts to do something it can perform the contract *only* through its employees – as Lord Templeman quoted earlier in this chapter observed – and thus vicarious liability is irrelevant.[34] If an employee fails to perform his employer's contractual promise the employer cannot claim that the employee's act (or failure) is not *their* act; it is they, the employer, who have promised and thus it is they who will be in breach of contract. In other words the contractual performance and duty cannot be delegated, in the sense of freeing the employer of his contractual responsibility, to an employee.

Land can also give rise to a non-delegable duty attaching to the owner or occupier. In one recent case it was held that a local authority could be liable (it was a striking out claim) for a nuisance caused by a group of travellers who had occupied land belonging to the council. As one judge pointed out, this was not a matter of vicarious liability, but a matter of whether the council had *adopted* the nuisance in as much as it was connected with their land.[35] If there were no local authority land to which the nuisance could attach the result would be different.[36] The key question for the employer, contractor or landowner is whether he can use the person who actually commits the tort to isolate himself from liability. Thus the householder who hires a reputable firm of contractors to build, say, a garage will probably not be liable if the contractors commit a public nuisance.[37] But the employer cannot always isolate himself from a general duty to provide safe premises simply by hiring a firm of independent contractors.[38]

Thus another form of non-delegable duty is where the employer himself owes a direct duty of care to the victim. Take the case of *Home Office v Dorset Yacht Co*[39] where the claimant's yacht was damaged by borstal boys out on a supervised camping trip. There is no doubt that this actual case was a vicarious liability decision in that the House of Lords had to decide if the prison warders themselves owed a duty of care to the yacht owner to supervise the borstal boys; if they did, and were in breach of it, the Home Office would be vicariously liable for the prison officers' tort. Yet the facts raise further issues. Could the Home Office itself, as a legal person, owe

---

[34] *In re Supply of Ready Mixed Concrete (No 2)* [1995] 1 AC 456, at 465.
[35] *Lippiatt v South Gloucestershire Council* [2000] 1 QB 51.
[36] *Hussain v Lancaster CC* [2000] 1 QB 1.
[37] *Rowe v Herman* [1997] 1 WLR 1390.
[38] *Gwilliam v West Hertfordshire Hospital NHS Trust* [2003] QB 443.
[39] [1970] AC 1004.

a direct duty of care in respect of supervising inmates to the population living close to a prison? This question is not the same as the vicarious liability one in that the court would have to examine the security *system* that operated in prisons. If the system itself was found wanting, then the Home Office might be in breach of a direct duty of care if a prisoner had escaped, due to the faulty system, and had harmed a nearby resident.[40] Another interesting question, of course, is whether the Home Office might be vicariously liable for torts committed by prisoners. One could immediately respond by saying that prisoners are not servants. But what if they were out doing prison work in return for payment by the Home Office?

This systems point is well brought out by *McDermid v Nash Dredging and Reclamation Co*.[41] This case involved an accident on a tug which arose out of the negligence of the captain who was not actually an employee of the defendants. The House of Lords nevertheless held the defendants liable, not on the ground of vicarious liability, but on the basis that an unsafe system of work was being operated on the tug. The defendants were liable, in other words, for the breach of a *direct* duty of care owed to the claimant. Again, more recently, the House of Lords has stated that in these kinds of cases it is important to identify the correct basis of liability.[42]

The principle of vicarious liability in English law does not extend to families as it does in French law.[43] A young child wanders into the road and causes an accident in which a motorist is injured: in French law the parents are strictly liable whereas in English law the parents would be responsible only if it were proved that they were careless in supervising the child. This idea of want of supervision was once the rule in France, but in 1997 the *Cour de cassation* ruled that 'only *force majeure* or the fault of the victim could free [the parent] from the strict liability arising from the damage caused by the act of his son, a minor, living with him'. Thus 'the *Cour d'appel* did not have to look into the existence of a failure of supervision by the father'.[44] Two points can usefully be made with respect to this liability for children question. The first is that the whole subject indicates the relevance of theory in vicarious liability. If the courts accepted that the liability of the master for his servant is founded on the idea of control and authority, it would be very difficult not to extend the idea to parents or

---

[40] cf *Ward v Tesco Stores Ltd* [1976] 1 WLR 810.
[41] [1987] AC 906.
[42] *Phelps v Hillingdon LBC* [2001] 2 AC 619.
[43] CC art 1384 line 4.
[44] Cass.civ.19.2.1997; JCP 28.5.97.22848 note Viney.

other supervisors of children.⁴⁵ The fact that parents and teachers are not automatically liable for torts committed by their children indicates that vicarious liability cannot easily be rationalised along these lines.

The second point to be made about the liability of a parent for a child is that there are exceptions. A child who acts as an 'employee' of the parent – for example a child doing a paper round for his parents' newsagent business or two sons employed by an MP on public money – might involve the parent in liability under the ordinary principles of vicarious liability if the child commits a tort in the course of his employment. Parents can also be liable for torts if they are in breach of a direct duty of care to supervise or if their children were committing a nuisance said to have been adopted by the parents. Thus in one case a local authority was held in breach of its duty of care when a child ran into the road from one of its nursery schools and caused a serious accident.⁴⁶ Yet another possible liability, as we shall see, is when a child has a car accident while using his or her parents' car.

OWNERS OF MOTOR VEHICLES

One apparent extension of the principle of vicarious liability beyond the employment relationship is where an owner of a car is held liable for the negligent driving of the car by another person. The liability is based on a form of 'agency' (*qui facit per alium facit per se*) and thus the owner must have a real interest in the journey; that is to say that the driver must be undertaking a specific task for the owner.⁴⁷ If there is no interest – the owner is just lending the car as a favour – then there will be no liability under this principle. However in *Morgans*,⁴⁸ where the husband was using a car owned by his wife and, when he got too drunk handed over the keys to a friend so that he could drive, it was held that the husband was *vicariously liable* for the friend's negligent driving.⁴⁹ Most insurance policies will, however, extend to drivers named by the owner, so in practice this form of vicarious liability is less important than it may seem.

Non-delegable duty can also play a role. In one case, where a taxi customer was injured as a result of the defective condition of the taxi, the customer was able to obtain damages, not from the owner of the taxi, but from the mini-cab firm who had supplied a radio to the taxi used to

---

⁴⁵ cf Animals Act 1971.
⁴⁶ *Carmarthenshire CC v Lewis* [1955] AC 549.
⁴⁷ *Morgans v Launchbury* [1973] AC 127.
⁴⁸ *Morgans v Launchbury* [1973] AC 127.
⁴⁹ See *Nottingham v Aldridge* [1971] 2 QB 739.

direct the owner towards customers.⁵⁰ The mini-cab firm was in breach of a direct non-delegable duty that the taxi was reasonably fit for its purpose. This decision has attracted criticism, but it can be justified on the basis that taxi customers direct their 'offers' towards the mini-cab firm seemingly to be 'accepted' or rejected by the firm. It is not necessarily unreasonable (unfair?) that such a relationship, even if not actually contractual, should contain a guarantee of safety.

PUBLISHERS

Another form of 'non-delegable duty' can be found in the world of publishing. The publisher of a defamatory article written by another will, prima facie, be just as liable in the tort of defamation as the person who wrote the libellous piece, although the publisher does now have a statutory defence if it did not know of the defamatory nature and had acted reasonably.⁵¹ This form of liability is not one based on any extension of an agency or vicarious liability principle; it is just that the tort attaches both to the writer and to the publisher of the defamatory piece. Nevertheless it is a kind of liability for the act of another in as much as the publisher can be said to be responsible for words written by their authors.

---

⁵⁰ *Rogers v Night Riders (a firm)* [1983] RTR 324.
⁵¹ Defamation Act 1996, s 1.

14. Liability for words

The previous chapter ended with an overview of the liability of publishers for words written by another, but such a liability could equally have been put under the heading of liability for words. This heading is useful for a number of reasons. First it aligns itself with the two previous liabilities, namely liability for things and liability for people. It suggests a kind of extension of liability for physical things to a liability for abstract 'things'. Secondly it transcends the categories of contract and tort in as much as a liability for words can often involve the two types of obligation; and even where the liability is, in the end, allocated to one or other category often the facts are close to the borderline between contract and tort. Thirdly many of the cases involving liability for misleading statements (including omissions) involve professional defendants such as accountants, lawyers and sometimes even doctors. Liability for words can thus encompass professional liability.

Statements are capable of being categorised in a number of ways. They can be interpreted as promises which, if supported by consideration, might well give rise to liability in contract or they might simply be regarded as lies, threats or insults. Equally they may be seen as something upon which the recipient of the statement might act. Where a statement causes loss or damage to another the question arises as to whether such a statement can act as the basis of a damages claim. However the forms of action continue to play an important role in the determination of this question in that a number of quite different causes of action have come to govern the outcome of the liability question.

DECEIT AND NEGLIGENCE

Until the middle of the last century a damages action was, in the absence of a contractual or a fiduciary relationship, generally available only in cases of fraudulent misstatement (the tort of deceit) or defamation (the torts of libel and slander). However the problem with deceit was, and remains (except with regard to misrepresentations inducing contracts),[1]

---

[1] On which see Misrepresentation Act 1967, s 2(1).

that fraud, by no means easy to prove, was essential.[2] But if a claimant does manage to overcome the hurdle of proof and to succeed in deceit, there is a good chance that liability, in terms of damages recoverable, will be wider than if the action had been one of negligence. Liability for fraudulent misrepresentation is, in other words, more severe than for negligent misrepresentation.[3]

Before 1964 if one could not establish that a misrepresentation was either fraudulent or contractual, then there was no basis for an action for damages at common law.[4] However in 1964 all of this changed with the recognition in *Hedley Byrne & Co Ltd v Heller & Partners Ltd*[5] that the tort of negligence might be available for misstatement in situations where there had been a 'special relationship' between the parties at the time the statement was made (see Chapter 11). This special relationship is certainly less intense than a fiduciary relationship, but it nevertheless seems to be a development from this equitable bond in that the reasoning moves outwards from a fiduciary duty to one of fiduciary care.[6] In order for an action to be available under the *Hedley Byrne* principle the reliance connection must be close or equivalent to a contractual relationship.[7] No doubt the House of Lords were coming close to re-establishing the old 19th century idea of equitable 'fraud' (or negligent 'deceit')[8] and, of course, statute was to confirm this development with respect to misrepresentations made to induce contracts.[9] But from a law of obligations position, one very important effect of this new duty of care was that it effectively turned certain negligent breaches of contract into torts with implications for third parties in business and commercial transactions.[10] Thus if A contracts with B to produce a valuation report on a house to be purchased by C and the report turns out to be carelessly inaccurate causing loss to C, then C may have an action against B in tort.[11]

It has to be stressed however that liability in these negligent survey three-party cases is not automatic. Much might depend on the established

---

[2] *Derry v Peek* (1889) 14 App Cas 337.
[3] *Smith New Court Securities Ltd v Scrimgeour Vickers Ltd* [1997] AC 254.
[4] Equity might grant an action where a defendant was in breach of a fiduciary obligation: *Nocton v Lord Ashburton* [1914] AC 932.
[5] [1964] AC 465.
[6] cf *Nocton v Lord Ashburton* [1914] AC 932, 947.
[7] *Hedley Byrne & Co Ltd v Heller & Parnters Ltd* [1964] AC 465, 486, 528–9; *Smith v Bush* [1990] 1 AC 831.
[8] *Peek v Derry* (1887) 37 Ch D 541.
[9] Misrepresentation Act 1967, s 2(1).
[10] *Henderson v Merrett Syndicates Ltd* [1995] 2 AC 145.
[11] *Smith v Bush* [1990] 1 AC 831.

structure of obligations as reflected in contractual risk allocation and the insurance position. Thus while liability might be imposed on a surveyor in the interests of consumer protection the same might not be true, even if the pattern of relationships is analogous, in the purely commercial arena.[12] Liability for statements is thus an area that benefits from being viewed within a category that transcends the strict dichotomy between contract and tort.[13] The courts may well be prepared to use the tort of negligence to 'fill a gap' in the law of contract but will only do so by considering all the relevant obligations.[14] One might add that the position has been made more complex by changes within the law of contract itself. The reform of the privity rule *might* mean that contractual liability will be imposed in certain situations where, before the reform, only a tort claim would have been possible.[15]

DEFAMATION

The tort of defamation is said to protect the reputation interest and any award of damages is designed to compensate him, her or it for this particular damage.[16] The tort is quite unlike negligence in that it is based on the claimant's right rather than the defendant's wrong. Accordingly fault on behalf of the speaker (slander) or writer (libel) is largely irrelevant; all that need be shown is that words capable of being defamatory – in effect critical of the claimant[17] – were spoken or published to a third party, however obscure the three party situation.[18] Not surprisingly there is a considerable body of case law devoted both to the meaning of words – was the actual statement capable of bearing the meaning alleged by the claimant?[19] – and to what can amount to publication.[20] The position

---

[12] *Marc Rich & Co v Bishop Rock Marine Co Ltd* [1996] 1 AC 211.
[13] *Henderson v Merrett Syndicates Ltd* [1995] 2 AC 145.
[14] *White v Jones* [1995] 2 AC 207; *British Telecom Plc v James Thomson & Sons Ltd* [1999] 1 WLR 9.
[15] Contracts (Rights of Third Parties) Act 1999.
[16] *John v MGN Ltd* [1997] QB 586, at 607–08.
[17] See eg *Cornwell v Myskow* [1987] 2 All ER 504; *Berkoff v Burchill* [1996] 4 All ER 1008.
[18] *Morgan v Odhams Press* [1971] 1 WLR 1239 HL.
[19] See eg *Lewis v Daily Telegraph* [1964] AC 234.
[20] See eg *Morgan v Odhams Press Ltd* [1971] 1 WLR 1239. The effect of this rule means that a person living in a foreign country and who has no connection with the UK can nevertheless sue in London for damages a publication which is principally published outside the UK. This has led to an accusation that London, as the libel capital of the world, is a global threat to Press freedom.

is made more complex by the fact that innuendo is a form of defamation.[21]

Given the strictness of liability, the defences in defamation play a central constitutional role. To escape liability the publisher must successfully plead truth, fair comment or privilege, but this is not so easy as these defences are not as wide as they might first appear.[22] Until quite recently the law seemed more interested in protecting the private rather than the public interest. Thus to criticise public figures, to file complaints about public officials (and it would seem doctors)[23] or even to attempt to debate in the Press issues such as blood sports[24] could be an expensive exercise given that the damages awarded by juries originally had little relation with those awarded by judges for serious personal injury.[25] Admittedly this damages problem has been alleviated to some extent now that the Court of Appeal has power to intervene in the quantum question.[26] Yet part of the problem here was that there was no constitutional principle upholding freedom of speech,[27] and so one often found the private law of defamation acting as a forum for what are in truth issues of public law.[28] All this is in the process of some change as a result of the Human Rights Act 1998 which guarantees in article 10 freedom of expression.

The first change was with regard to the use of defamation by public bodies and public officials. The House of Lords held that it 'is of the highest public importance that a democratically elected governmental body, or indeed any governmental body, should be open to uninhibited public criticism'. And the 'threat of a civil action for defamation must inevitably have an inhibiting effect on freedom of speech'.[29] Individual politicians and civil servants will, no doubt, continue to be able to sue in their private capacity backed, perhaps, by public funds, but this privilege is certainly likely to be curtailed if it is used to stifle public interest criticism.

---

[21] *Tolley v Fry* [1931] AC 333.
[22] See generally *Reynolds v Times Newspapers Ltd* [2001] 2 AC 127; *Jameel (Mohammed) v Wall Street Journal* [2007] 1 AC 359.
[23] *The Observer*, 2 July 2000, at 11.
[24] *The Guardian*, 15 January 1990, at 2. And see eg *Blackshaw v Lord* [1984] 1 QB 1.
[25] *Blackshaw v Lord* [1984] QB 1; *Sutcliffe v Pressdram Ltd* [1991] 1 QB 153.
[26] Courts and Legal Services Act 1990, s 8. See *Rantzen v Mirror Group Newspapers Ltd* [1994] QB 670; *John v MGN Ltd* [1996] 2 All ER 35.
[27] cf *Hector v A G of Antigua & Barbuda* [1990] 2 AC 312 PC.
[28] See eg John Pilger, Letter, *The Guardian* 9 July 1991; but see now *Derbyshire CC v Times Newspapers* [1993] AC 534.
[29] Lord Keith in *Derbyshire CC v Times Newspapers* [1993] AC 534, at 547.

The second development concerns the defence of qualified privilege. This defence is based on the notion that certain statements, even if defamatory, will be privileged if the recipient of the statement has a clear interest in receiving it. Thus the managing director of a company has an interest in hearing an allegation about a fellow director.[30] This privilege will protect the maker of the statement unless the claimant can prove malice.[31] However from the constitutional viewpoint the question arises as to whether qualified privilege might be available to protect a journalist who reports in good faith, but without being able to prove all the facts and allegations in a court of law. The traditional answer to this question is that the defence was far too narrow to cover this kind of problem and statutory defences were far too restrictive to offer any real relief.[32] But this has now changed thanks to the Human Rights Act 1998 and the defence has been extended to cover media reporting.[33] A publisher will now be able to plead qualified privilege even if some of the allegations prove to be untrue provided that the writer fulfils the test of the 'reasonable journalist'.[34] A publisher who thinks that he will not be able to rely on qualified privilege can now make an 'offer of amends' which, if unreasonably refused by the claimant, could act as a defence to any action in defamation.[35]

BEYOND DEFAMATION

However there are some factual situations that can be analysed from another 'interest' point of view. Take the case of an employer who writes an inaccurate and damning reference of an employee and as a result the employee finds it extremely difficult to secure another job. There is certainly an invasion of the employee's reputation interest, yet, equally, there is also an invasion of his economic interest in not being able to secure another job. The reference has caused him quantifiable loss. Now if the employee were to sue the employer in defamation he would be met by the defence of qualified privilege; and in order to defeat this defence he would

---

[30] *Watt v Longsdon* [1930] 1 KB 130.
[31] Thus those who complain, say, about doctors ought to have their complaints covered by such privilege; however this does not appear to prevent some doctors threatening those who complain with defamation proceedings: *The Observer*, 2 July 2000, at 11.
[32] See Defamation Act 1952, ss 5–6; *Blackshaw v Lord* [1984] QB 1.
[33] *Reynolds v Times Newspapers Ltd* [2001] 2 AC 127.
[34] *Jameel (Mohammed) v Wall Street Journal* [2007] 1 AC 359.
[35] Defamation Act 1996, ss 2–4.

have to prove malice. If he could not prove malice, ought the facts to give rise to a claim in the tort of negligence for careless misrepresentation causing economic loss? In *Spring v Guardian Assurance plc*[36] the House of Lords responded positively to this question: the tort of defamation provides a wholly inadequate remedy for an employee who is caused damage by an inaccurate and negligent reference. Consequently the employee should be able to sue in negligence.

This decision has attracted criticism on the ground that two torts intersect with respect to a single set of facts.[37] This is to be criticised, according to the late Professor Birks, because defamation, which is an infringement of the reputation interest, intersects with negligence, which is a wrong based on a species of fault. This results in a situation where a careless invasion of the reputation interest could give rise to two wrongs, namely defamation and negligence, when a rational system ought to see only one wrong. Whatever the intellectual merits of this criticism,[38] the intersection of the two torts was inevitable once English law extended the tort of negligence to misstatements causing economic loss. Liability that attaches to statements can either attach to the statement itself, as in defamation, or to the behaviour of the defendant, as in negligence, and the only way to avoid intersection is by a specific rule excluding the tort of negligence. Such exclusion is by no means self-evident even as a matter of rationality since *Hedley Byrne* itself concerned a reference which caused economic loss. One might claim, perhaps, that there are too many concepts (reputation interest, fault, economic interest, duty of care etc,) chasing too few factual patterns, but others might argue that this is exactly what makes legal reasoning so effective. What the House of Lords did in *Spring* was just to shift the point of emphasis both from the statement to the behaviour and from the reputation interest to the economic interest. Of course, in doing this they changed, in a subtle way, the facts themselves: for the notion of an interest is a concept that functions at one and the same time in the world of law and the world of social fact.

A not dissimilar exercise was carried out in another case involving the intersection of the reputation and the economic interests. Two employees who worked for the BCCI bank found themselves out of work when the bank collapsed amid allegations of the most serious fraud and incompetence. The two employees sued the bank claiming that they had lost more than their jobs: they also suffered an invasion of their reputation interest

---

[36] [1995] 2 AC 296.
[37] Birks (1996), at 5–6.
[38] cf Samuel (2000).

through the stigma which attached to them having worked for a dishonest and corrupt employer.[39] This invasion of their reputation interest translated into an economic interest in that they were put at a serious disadvantage in finding new jobs. The House of Lords held that the facts disclosed a good cause of action. However the defendants had put forward two basic arguments against liability. First they said that if an action were to be allowed for breach of an implied contractual obligation of mutual trust and confidence, this would side-step the tort of defamation. The real interest in play, so it was argued, was reputation. This argument was rejected on the ground that the possible availability of defamation on the same facts was not a reason in itself for excluding damages from being recoverable for breach of contract. The two claims were not mutually exclusive. Secondly they argued that the claimants were trying to recover damages for an intangible interest that was not recognised as a head of damages in the law of contract.[40] This was rejected on the ground that a claimant was entitled to recover damages for actual financial losses incurred as a result of a breach of contract even if this economic loss attached to an injury to reputation. The separation of the reputation and the economic interest is not always possible. Or, put another way, facts can be construed in such a way so as to construct the interest in play.

To argue, as Professor Birks has done, that a tort which has as its object a single interest like reputation should not intersect with a tort based on a wrong is to assume that legal taxonomy is like taxonomy in the natural sciences. This is not the case since a set of facts like those disclosed in *Spring v Guardian Assurance* or in the BCCI case are not an object unchanging in nature and disclosing fixed properties. They are facts constructed out of quasi-normative concepts such as 'interest' and 'fault' whose properties are as dependent upon the taxonomy – the rules in play – as upon the object of the taxonomy, that is to say social reality. In brief, the judges go some way in constructing their own social reality and this is inherent in the nature of law and legal reasoning.[41]

INTELLECTUAL PROPERTY RIGHTS

The torts of passing off and trade libel are further forms of liability attaching to statements. These torts are primarily designed to protect intellectual

---

[39] *Mahmud v BCCI* [1998] AC 20.
[40] See *Addis v Gramophone Co Ltd* [1909] AC 488.
[41] Samuel (2000). And see generally Waddams (2003).

property rights and business interests, but the emphasis is rather different depending upon whether the complaint is 'misappropriation' of the claimant's words[42] or damage incurred as a result of the statement.[43] A defendant does no wrong by entering a market created by another (an area of course dealt with by national and EU law on fair trading and competition). However he must not attempt to deceive the public or maliciously to injure the claimant's products or business reputation. Thus a person may be prohibited by injunction from marketing goods in a container the distinctive shape of which has become a form of (intellectual) property in itself.[44] If the defendant wrongfully uses the claimant's property (including confidential information) in order to make a profit for himself by, say, publishing a book he might well find that he has to disgorge such a profit through the remedy of account on the basis of unjust enrichment. Indeed it may be that confidential information, protected in equity as a property right, is now the basis of a new tort of misuse of confidential information. In *Douglas v Hello! Ltd (No 3)*[45] the House of Lords held that a magazine that had been given exclusive rights to publish the wedding photographs of two film stars was entitled to claim damages at common law against another magazine that had published photographs of the wedding in circumstances where they knew they had no right to publish.

PRIVACY

The *Douglas* case is not just a precedent in respect of the misuse of confidential information. It is also an important case for the protection of the right of privacy. Such a right has never existed at common law,[46] but it is given specific recognition by article 8 of the European Convention for the Protection of Human Rights and Fundamental Freedoms, now of course incorporated into English law. Consequently the common law is probably obliged to provide remedies to ensure that privacy is a properly protected interest. One constitutional issue that arises here is that the European Convention equally protects freedom of speech (article 10) and thus if the Press wishes to publish words that may infringe a person's right of privacy the courts will have to think carefully about how to develop the law in such a way as to give expression, at one and the same time, to both empirical interests.

---

[42] *Cadbury Schweppes v Pub Squash Co* [1981] 1 All ER 213, 223.
[43] Defamation Act 1952, s 3.
[44] *Reckitt & Colman Properties Ltd v Borden Inc* [1990] 1 WLR 491 HL.
[45] [2008] 1 AC 1.
[46] *Wainwright v Home Office* [2004] 2 AC 406.

There are three technical means by which they can develop liability law. The first is to adapt existing causes of action – in particular torts such as trespass, defamation and breach of confidence (confidential information) – to cover those factual situations involving privacy. The second is to use the equitable remedy of injunction (and perhaps account) which will be available, even in the absence of a tort of privacy, to protect any established right. Over time this equitable protection might well harden, if not into a specific tort, then into some kind of right analogous to a property right. The third is to exclude certain rights like privacy from the law of tort as such and to allow claimants only to seek a remedy under the Human Rights Act 1998. The difficulty with this last approach is that a claim under the Act will lie only against a public authority.

Whatever approach is adopted – and it seems from the *Douglas* case that breach of confidence is one principal cause of action now dealing with the privacy interest (at least where it involves confidential information) – the main problem that the courts will have to face is, as we have mentioned, balancing the private interest (privacy) with the public interest of Press freedom. As with the defence of qualified privilege, one can see the courts having recourse to notions such as the 'reasonable journalist'. Is there a public interest issue in revealing by words or pictures certain personal details with respect to individuals? What about public figures: should they be able to stop the Press publishing details about their private lives? And who, for these purposes, amounts to a public figure?

One further difficulty is that a confusion of interests can easily occur in situations where a claimant appeals to rights such as privacy. In the *Wainwright* case the claimant was humiliated by prison officers during a strip search and privacy was one of the grounds of her claim. Her action was unsuccessful in the UK courts on the basis that humiliation is different from an invasion of privacy. 'If a shop assistant or a bouncer or barman at a club is publicly offensive to a customer, the customer may well be humiliated and distressed', said Lord Scott; but 'that is no[t] sufficient reason why the law of tort should be fashioned and developed with a view to providing compensation in money to the victim.'.[47] What this observation overlooks is the difference of context between the private and the public. It may well be that privacy was not the correct interest in play here; the issue in *Wainwright* was more one of dignity, a separately protected law of persons right in some civil law systems (see for example CC art 16). Yet should *public* officials be free to humiliate, to denigrate the dignity of, a citizen in the absence of direct statutory authority? Insults and humiliation

---

[47] *Ibid*, at para 62.

in the private sphere are one thing, but when carried out by agents of the state some might say that this is another matter.[48]

Here, of course, is a problem that attaches to privacy. It is not an interest that is tightly defined; it is sometimes a genuinely personal, as opposed to economic, interest but it can equally be turned into an economic asset as the *Douglas* case illustrates. Where public figures are concerned there is the further issue of trying to disentangle the genuinely personal from the politically embarrassing piece of information. Is the public entitled to know what the viewing habits are of the spouse of a leading politician? What if the politician advocates strong moral views about what the public should or should not watch? One can accordingly understand the reluctance of the courts to develop a distinct tort of privacy. 'At least within the realm of tort law,' said Lord Rodger, 'questions about the availability of a remedy are best answered by looking at the substance of the supposed wrong rather than by reference to a somewhat imprecise label which lawyers might attach to it in another connection.' The problem is that privacy (plus perhaps dignity) is not a wrong, but a constitutional right[49] and often a commercial right as well. And there seems on occasions to be a reluctance on the part of the judges to see constitutional rights as being worthy of special treatment in the law of obligations.[50] Instead the issue appears to come down to a conflict between the commercial interests of the Press and those of well-known film stars and models. In other words if privacy can be reduced to a question of private property the courts seem happier.[51] The interests of prisoners and their relatives (for example Mrs Wainwright) attract, in contrast, little sympathy from UK tort, property or even public law.

PROFESSIONAL LIABILITY

Privacy is about liability attaching to statements that are true. If they are untrue then it is a matter for the tort of defamation (reputation interest) or negligence (economic interest). In fact liability for misstatement is, as we have seen, an area that now straddles both contract and tort in that the 'implied duty to take care' now extends beyond the contract itself.[52] Accordingly the professional valuer, the accountant and the solicitor may

---

[48] *Wainwright v United Kingdom* (2006) (12350/04) (2007) 44 EHRR 40.
[49] *Watkins v Home Office* [2006] 2 AC 395, at para 62.
[50] See eg *Watkins v Home Office* [2006] 2 AC 395, as well as *Wainwright v Home Office* [2004] 2 AC 406.
[51] See eg Lord Brown in *Douglas v Hello! Ltd (No 3)* [2008] 1 AC 1, at para 325.
[52] cf Supply of Goods and Services Act 1982, s 13.

find themselves owing duties not just to the person who commissioned them for a report, but to other proximate persons who might foreseeably rely upon the report.[53]

No doubt the duty test will remain very strict indeed in the economic loss cases.[54] Accordingly in one of the most important negligence cases to be decided by the House of Lords in the last 20 years or so it was held that a firm of accountants acting as auditors of one company owed no duty of care to another company considering a potential takeover.[55] Indeed even in physical damage cases the courts will be reluctant to impose liability in situations where it would unfairly affect the balance of contractual and insurance relations between commercial parties.[56] Moreover the nature of the relationship between claimant and negligent advisor will, as we have seen, be of the utmost importance when it comes to the question of a duty of care.[57] Nevertheless, in both contractual and non-contractual situations negligence has an important role to play in compensation claims against doctors, lawyers, architects and the like.

The liability is in form no different from any other liability under the fault principle. However in substance there are two special characteristics. First, where a professional skill is concerned, the test for a breach of duty is not governed by the reasonable man test as such; it is governed by the standard of the reasonable person exercising that professional skill.[58] The test is the standard of the ordinary skilled man exercising and professing to have that professional skill. Accountants, architects, lawyers or doctors need not possess the highest expert skill; all they must exercise is 'the ordinary skill of an ordinary competent man exercising that particular art'.[59] Thus when a medical operation goes wrong, although it may raise a presumption of fault under the *res ipsa loquitur* maxim, liability is by no means automatic because the risk of medical accident is, in the absence of carelessness, very much on the patient.[60] The law might impose a duty of care on doctors as a question of law, but the standard of care, a question of fact, is always a matter of sound medical judgment.[61] Of course risk also

---

[53] *Morgan Crucible Co Plc v Hill Samuel & Co Ltd* [1991] Ch 295.
[54] *Customs and Excise Commissioners v Barclays Bank plc* [2006] 3 WLR 1.
[55] *Caparo Industries plc v Dickman* [1990] 2 AC 605.
[56] *Marc Rich & Co v Bishop Rock Marine Co Ltd* [1996] 1 AC 211.
[57] See eg *Goodwill v British Pregnancy Advisory Service* [1996] 1 WLR 1397.
[58] *Bolam v Friern Hospital Management Committee* [1957] 1 WLR 582.
[59] *Bolam v Friern Hospital Management Committee* [1957] 1 WLR 582, at 586 per McNair J (to the jury).
[60] *Roe v Minister of Health* [1954] 2 QB 66.
[61] *Sidaway v Bethlem Royal Hospital* [1985] AC 871, 881; cf *Bolitho v City and Hackney HA* [1998] AC 232.

implies informed consent and so the medical profession must take care to furnish any necessary information, provided such information is in the 'best interests' of the patient.[62] Yet the courts are not over ready to hold doctors and surgeons liable when things go wrong in the surgery or on the operating table.

This reluctance also results from a second characteristic of professional liability, the role of policy and the public interest.[63] No doubt all duty, breach and causation decisions contain an important policy element, but in certain areas this policy factor, sometimes under the guise of the public interest, can play a more direct role. Thus incompetent barristers were once immune from being sued for the way they conducted a case in court. This rule has now been reversed on the basis that both the tort of negligence and the functioning of the legal profession have changed.[64] However immunity still attaches to the detective who fails to catch the murderer.[65] This is not to say that public bodies cannot be sued – indeed they are a regular source of litigation. The point to be made is that institutions like the National Health Service and the constabulary are public law institutions and actions in the law of tort can raise issues of an administrative law nature (see Chapter 11).[66]

Since the decision of *Hedley Byrne v Heller & Partners*[67] there is a temptation to treat all cases of professional liability as falling into the category of tort. For it is often the case that the act complained of is misleading or incompetent professional advice and thus the problem appears at first sight to be one of professional misstatement. Such an analysis is not wrong; indeed the tort analysis may be of relevance if there is a limitation problem.[68] But it can easily overlook the fact that the relationship between professional and client is governed by a contract. Thus any breach of duty will be a breach of an implied term of the contract and this implied term now has as its source a specific statutory provision.[69] If the professional is negligent he or she (or it) will thus be liable, not under the *Hedley Byrne*

---

[62] *Sidaway v Bethlem Royal Hospital* [1985] AC 871.

[63] See eg *Marc Rich & Co v Bishop Rock Marine Co Ltd* [1996] 1 AC 211, 240–1; *Arthur JS Hall & Co v Simons* [2002] 1 AC 615; *Phelps v Hillingdon LBC* [2001] 2 AC 619.

[64] *Arthur JS Hall & Co v Simons* [2002] 1 AC 615.

[65] *Hill v Chief Constable of West Yorkshire* [1989] AC 53; *Van Colle v Chief Constable of the Hertfordshire Police* [2009] 1 AC 225.

[66] But cf *Kent v Griffiths* [2001] QB 36.

[67] [1964] AC 465.

[68] In contract time runs from the breach of contract whereas in tort it runs from the incurring of the damage: see Limitation Act 1980.

[69] Supply of Goods and Services Act 1982, s 13.

duty of care, but under the statutory contractual duty. Of course if the advice is given without charge, then the tort analysis will become of relevance; yet most dealings between professional and client are pursuant to a contract. One might note, also, that an important advantage in suing on the contract is that the award of damages may well be greater than in tort. The victim of a breach of contract is entitled to be put into the position they would have been in had the contract been performed. Moreover, by definition, a contractual duty claim does not run into the 'fairness' and 'policy' issue that underpins the duty of care and financial loss question in the tort of negligence.

The implied term duty will not be applicable in medical negligence cases unless the patient was in a private hospital pursuant to a contract. Liability under the National Health Scheme is always a tort liability.[70] Where contract might have a role, however, is in situations where a person goes to a private clinic for a vasectomy and the relevance of the contract is that it might affect the level of the duty. Is such a clinic under a contractual duty to render a client permanently sterile or is it only under a duty to use skill and care? In *Thake v Maurice*[71] one Court of Appeal judge thought that a clinic could be under a strict duty to achieve the desired result, but the majority disagreed. The point is, nevertheless, an important one in professional liability cases, as Lord Denning once pointed out,[72] and was taken up by one of the majority judges in *Thake*.[73] Outside of medical cases it may well be that if a client hires a professional firm to achieve a certain level of skill, then the achievement of that standard will be a term of the contract. For example it may be that a firm of contractors will not only be under a contractual duty, but also under an obligation to conform to certain specific building regulations.[74] Moreover the imposing of a strict liability on a contractor may in turn impact upon whether loss should be shared between client and professional if the former was in some way guilty of contributory negligence. The court may well be unwilling to allow apportionment where the defendant is under a strict liability duty.[75]

The medical cases can be seen not just as private law problems but equally as matters that a French lawyer would see as falling under

---

[70] *Roe v Minister of Health* [1954] 2 QB 66.
[71] [1986] QB 644.
[72] See his judgment in *Greaves & Co v Baynham Meikle & Partners* [1975] 1 WLR 1095.
[73] See Nourse LJ [1986] QB 644, at 687–8.
[74] *Barclays Bank Plc v Fairclough Building Ltd* [1995] QB 214; and see now *Platform Funding Ltd v Bank of Scotland* [2009] 2 WLR 1016.
[75] *Barclays Bank Plc v Fairclough Building Ltd* [1995] QB 214.

administrative law. Similar category questions are associated with tort claims against local authorities or other governmental bodies.[76] The 'public law' tort problems can raise special policy questions that are not found in purely private law professional liability cases and this can give them an extra dimension of complexity (see Chapter 11). The complexity is increased if the damage is of a special kind – in particular nervous shock or pure economic loss – or was incurred more by an omission rather than a positive act.[77] Public law liability, economic loss, nervous shock and the like thus deserve special treatment as we saw in earlier chapters.

---

[76] *D v East Berkshire NHS Trust* [2005] 2 AC 373; cf *Kent v Griffiths* [2001] QB 36.
[77] See *Stovin v Wise* [1996] AC 923; *Gorringe v Calderdale MBC* [2004] 1 WLR 1057.

15. Escaping liability

Devoting a chapter to escaping from liability might at first sight appear somewhat cynical. In addition it is probably not a fully comprehensive term vis-à-vis everything that will be covered in this chapter. Nevertheless this perspective has a number of strengths, the most important of which is to shift the emphasis off claimants, and off things, and onto the defendant. What means are open to a defendant, faced with a possible liability, to mount a full or partial defence against damages, or some other remedy, demanded by the claimant?

If one was to look for one single notion that would more or less cover most of the possible defences it might be 'causation'. Now it has to be said at once that this is not readily obvious from most contract and tort textbooks or even from the cases themselves. But that is because 'causation' is something of a term of art in itself and, as a specific legal notion, is relatively narrow in scope. Yet if one takes a wide view of causation it can be seen to cover many areas that do not appear in the causation chapter to be found in many of the textbooks. For example, self-induced frustration or consent is not normally dealt with as a matter of causation even although each functions as a means for cutting the connection between cause (or intervention) and effect. This chapter will, accordingly, interpret causation in its widest sense and as a result it will include many of the main defences available to a defendant in a law of obligations action.

CAUSATION: INTRODUCTION

In the tort of negligence, in addition to establishing that a defendant was under a duty of care to the claimant and that he was in breach of this duty, a claimant must prove that the breach of duty (the negligence) *caused* the damage incurred. In fact this requirement is to be found across the whole spectrum of the law of obligations and thus a defendant will escape liability for a breach of contract, a breach of a statutory duty and a breach of a strict liability duty if he can prove that he was not the cause of the claimant's damage. Indeed causation problems can even arise in the tort of conversion.[1] In the common law tradition, probably because of the jury, this causal requirement usually sub-divides into two questions. Was the defendant's wrongful act the *factual* cause of the claimant's damage? And was it the *legal* cause? However, as we have mentioned, causation as a topic stretches beyond these two sub-questions. It is a requirement in all torts (and of course in contractual liability) and it finds expression in other tort notions such as the defences of contributory negligence and mitigation of damage.

Causation, when viewed generally in the law of obligations, is not a unitary subject since it tends to be split up into different rules and concepts. It can be found as part of the definition of some torts (actionability) or as a defence in others (measure of damages). It is of course a substantive requirement in all torts where damage has to be specifically proved (factual causation) in that if the defendant is able to show that the damage has no causal connection with the tort or breach of contract he will escape liability for this particular damage. Thus in one case the employers of a lorry driver escaped liability in public nuisance for a dangerously parked lorry, into which a motor cycle crashed, because the accident was actually caused by the motorcyclist looking at girls on the pavement.[2]

A defendant can still escape liability, even if a factual cause can be shown, if he establishes that the damage is too remote (legal causation). Here the court is not actually saying that the defendant was not the cause of the damage; it is allowing the defendant to escape liability in whole or in part because the connection between breach and damage is too weak. The damage is *too remote* from the breach of duty. This rule is to be found in systems other than the common law and so for example the *Code civil* contains an article in its section on contract which lays down that a defendant 'is held liable only for damages which were *foreseen* or which *could have been foreseen* at the time of the contract, when it is not by his *wilfulness* that the obligation is not executed' (art 1150, emphasis added). What remoteness adds to causation is, supposedly, a subjective element and this is as true for English law as it is for French. However, whereas causation in fact is a question of fact (in the sense that it was once a question for the jury), remoteness is a question of law; it is for the judge to decide upon the subjective element according to the appropriate legal test.

Causation can also function at the level of the remedy of damages. A defendant who is partly responsible for his own damage may find his

---

[1] *Kuwait Airways Corpn v Iraqi Airways Co (Nos 4 & 5)* [2002] 2 AC 883.
[2] *Dymond v Pearce* [1972] 1 QB 496.

damages reduced by a percentage that reflects his share of the blame.[3] Equally, a defendant who fails to take reasonable steps to mitigate his damage may have to face a reduction in his damages deemed to be caused by his own unreasonableness. Here, of course, one is not taking a strictly objective approach to causation since one has moved from connection between breach and damage to the subjective notion of blame. Thus much could depend upon the behaviour of the defendant. One tort writer (Tony Weir) fashioned the adage that 'bad people pay more' and this moral maxim has now seemingly been openly adopted by the House of Lords.[4]

Given these different levels of causation – actionability, fact, law and damages – it will be useful to approach causation across the whole spectrum of tort and contract law, especially as the different levels have their own conceptual expressions and requirements. Indeed, even when focusing only on the tort of negligence, causation is to be found in areas other than just the 'causation and remoteness' question. As has been mentioned, it often has a role in the duty question (actionability) and is an issue in many defences to negligence.[5] However before looking at these different levels something must be said about the various theories of causation.

THEORIES OF CAUSATION

The literature on causation is massive but its existence has done nothing to make the subject any easier or clearer in the law of obligations. Indeed, according to Honoré, the 'theories tend to induce a feeling of frustration, because they either have little empirical content and so fail to point the way, or are clear-cut but apply to only a segment of the circle of problems which present themselves'.[6]

The idea of competing theories starts with the Roman jurists one of whom famously repeated a problem posed by an earlier jurist. Several persons were playing with a ball near a place where a barber had set up his chair. One of the players hit the ball rather hard and it knocked against the hand of a barber, who was in the process of shaving a slave, with the result that the barber cut the throat of his client. Who is causally to blame? The jurist poses the problem as if the choice is between ballplayer and barber, one jurist, we are told, suggesting that the liability is with the barber for

---

[3] Law Reform (Contributory Negligence) Act 1945.
[4] *Smith New Court Securities Ltd v Scrimgeour Vickers Ltd* [1997] AC 254.
[5] See eg *Tomlinson v Congleton BC* [2004] 1 AC 46.
[6] Honoré (1969), at para 1.

setting up his chair in a place where people were accustomed to play ball. The jurist who posed the problem however adds a third possibility: anyone who allows himself to be shaved under such circumstances only has himself to blame (D.9.2.11pr). In this practical problem a number of theory points seem to lie under the surface; there are ideas about directness of cause, about foreseeability, about blame, about contributory negligence, about last opportunity and so on. What is interesting, of course, is that the Roman jurists did not appear to have had (or want) a definitive answer to the actual problem.

Little has changed today. One problem is that causation itself has never been properly defined and thus can mean a range of different things depending upon whether the term, at one extreme, is purely objective or, at another extreme, embraces notions of fault, harm, policy and imputability. Common law judges like to avoid these theory questions by claiming that the law adopts a 'common sense' approach. But, as Lord Hobhouse has pointed out, 'causation as discussed in the authorities has been complicated both by conflicting statements about whether causation is a question of fact or of law or, even, "common sense" and by the use of metaphor and Latin terminology, eg, *causa sine qua non*, *causa causans*, *novus actus* and *volenti*, which in themselves provide little enlightenment and are not consistently used.'[7] These Latin terms and metaphors seem at first sight scientifically impressive, but as Honoré has pointed out, they are largely empty of content. They do not directly relate to facts. 'But in any case', says Honoré, 'the problems to be answered are so various that they cannot be solved by a single formula which remains at all meaningful'.[8]

Instead, then, of examining all the various theories it might be better to state those that have received some practical application. Broadly there are two approaches. One can examine causation in terms of applicable principles – a kind of axiomatic approach – or one can look at how it operates at a lower level of abstraction, this second approach being more casuistic in its attitude. To some extent this difference of approach is reflected in the two European traditions of law. In the civil law an attempt has been made in the recent *Principles of European Tort Law* (PETL), drawn up by the European Tort Law Group, to state the relevant principles of causation. In English law, on the other hand, the problem of causation, as we have mentioned, has tended to be distributed among a range of different concepts many of which function at different levels of operation. This does not mean that causation as an issue in itself is never of importance in the

---

[7] *Reeves v Commissioner of Police for the Metropolis* [2000] 1 AC 360, at 391.
[8] Honoré (1969), at para 105.

common law; there are plenty of cases where a court has had to decide whether or not there is sufficient causal connection at the factual level to establish liability. The point to be made is that these factual causation cases only form part of a much bigger picture.

There are, nevertheless, some common points that can be identified in both the civil and the common law traditions. The first is the distinction between cause-in-fact and cause-in-law. The distinction is to be found in the PETL in that article 3:201 states that even if causation can be established at the level of fact, the damage may not be attributed to the actor if for example it was unforeseeable or that the interest invaded was not one well protected in private law. This distinction between fact and law was clearly adopted by the common law in 1961.[9]

A second common principle is the definition of factual causation. Both the common law and the civil law tend to start from an axiom called the 'but for' test or *conditio sine qua non* (PETL art 3:101) but then often retreat from it because it offers only limited help. Indeed what is of particular interest about this test is that it is clearly inadequate. Take the following example once put by Lord Hoffmann:

> A mountaineer about to undertake a difficult climb is concerned about the fitness of his knee. He goes to a doctor who negligently makes a superficial examination and pronounces the knee fit. The climber goes on the expedition, which he would not have undertaken if the doctor had told him the true state of his knee. He suffers an injury which is an entirely foreseeable consequence of mountaineering but has nothing to do with his knee.[10]

Lord Hoffmann went on to assert that to make the doctor liable would offend 'common sense because it makes the doctor responsible for consequences which, though in general terms foreseeable, do not appear to have a sufficient causal connection with the subject matter of the duty.' And he added that there 'seems no reason of policy which requires that the negligence of the doctor should require the transfer to him of all the foreseeable risks of the expedition.'[11] Yet if one applies the 'but for' test then 'but for' the doctor's negligence the mountaineer would not be injured. The doctor's omission to state the true condition of the knee was thus, according to article 3:101, a cause of the damage. In fact the test is useful in assessing the potency of the causal link, but it does not come anywhere near defining causation at the level of fact.

---

[9] *The Wagon Mound (No 1)* [1961] AC 388.
[10] *Banque Bruxelles Lambert SA v Eagle Star Insurance Co Ltd* [1997] AC 191, at 213.
[11] *Ibid*, at 214.

A third shared principle is the idea that risk of damage should be given some force within the causation question. Thus article 3:103(1) of the PETL states that in the 'case of multiple activities, where each of them alone would have been sufficient to cause the damage, but it remains uncertain which one in fact caused it, each activity is regarded as a cause to the extent corresponding to the likelihood that it may have caused the victim's damage.' The House of Lords has now gone some way in incorporating this idea into English law,[12] although a subsequent case has confirmed that the damage is not the actual physical damage suffered by the claimant but the risk of suffering the damage.[13] In other words the damage is a loss of a chance not to suffer the damage.

A fourth shared principle is with respect to overlapping damage. C has a car which is wrongfully damaged by D1; before the damage is repaired C's car is wrongfully hit by D2's car which, had C's car not already been damaged, would have suffered the same damage. C fails to get any satisfaction from D1 and the question thus arises as to whether he can sue D2. According to both the PETL (article 3:104(1)) and English precedent it would seem that C has no right of action with respect to the second defendant.[14] This situation is sometimes summed up by the maxim that a tortfeasor must take his victim as he finds him. In the above situation of overlapping damage the principle can work in favour of the tortfeasor; but this is not always the case since the principle applies equally where the victim has an extra-sensitivity that results in his suffering greater damage than would be the case with an ordinary person.

A fifth principle that may be shared by both the civil law (as expressed in the PETL) is with respect to multiple events which have all contributed to the claimant's damage. According to article 3:105 of the PETL in 'the case of multiple activities, when it is certain that none of them has caused the entire damage or any determinable part thereof, those that are likely to have minimally contributed to the damage are presumed to have caused equal shares thereof.' This article could suggest that the law is permitted to take what might be called a 'nominalist' approach to causation. For example in one English case an employee had been attacked by two youths while working in a branch of a fast food chain and as a result had to undergo an eye operation which went wrong resulting in a loss of sight in that eye. This loss of an eye was not the only damage; the employee also endured pain and suffering, loss of future earnings and then severe psy-

---

[12] *Fairchild v Glenhaven Funeral Services Ltd* [2003] 1 AC 32.
[13] *Barker v Corus UK Ltd* [2006] 2 AC 572.
[14] *Performance Cars Ltd v Abraham* [1962] 1 QB 33.

chological harm. Both the employer and the hospital were found to have been negligent but the causal responsibility was split between the various actors.[15] In one sense this might seem fair and reasonable, but normally in this situation one actor is held liable for all the damage, the latter reclaiming contribution from other actors who might also have been liable for the 'same damage'.[16] If one adopts a nominalist analysis in respect of both the damage and the actors – that is to say if one splits up the damage into different and independent kinds each attributable to different wrongdoers – the contribution approach seemingly fails.

It is not of course being suggested that the PETL represent English law. What they do is to give expression to some theory ideas that are to be found not just in the case law of various continental legal systems but, to some extent, in the English case law and judgments as well. Thus these principles can act as a reference point for understanding the way causation and remoteness function in English contract and tort law in that they suggest various categories under which causal problems might be classed. In the end, however, the problem of causation cannot be understood through a set of axiomatic principles; what matters are the factual situations themselves and the reasoning processes adopted in each case by the judge or judges. Accordingly theories of causation will be of little or no help in understanding English law, especially as causal problems permeate every level of operation. And this is the reason why it might be more useful to examine causation at its various levels of operation.

LEVEL 1: ACTIONABILITY

The first level where causation can function is 'actionability'. This is to say it can function as a requirement for getting certain tort actions off the ground; if the required causal relationship between harm and act is not present then the tort itself will not be present. Thus trespass will not normally lie where damage results from the indirect act of the defendant; accordingly, in false imprisonment, the defendant must have *directly* imprisoned the claimant and not be just part of a causal chain of events.[17] This trespass requirement emerges out of the old distinction between the writ of trespass and the action on the case; and so in the past causation could play a role in determining whether a claimant had

---

[15] *Rahman v Arearose* [2001] QB 351.
[16] Civil Liability (Contribution) Act 1978.
[17] *Harnett v Bond* [1925] AC 669.

brought the right form of action.[18] Historically, then, actionability was a question of procedure (and to an extent jurisdiction), yet the point can return today as one of substantive law. For example, in *Esso Petroleum v Southport Corporation* Denning LJ said that he was 'clearly of opinion that the Southport Corporation cannot here sue in trespass' because the 'discharge of oil was not done directly on to their foreshore, but outside in the estuary'; and it 'was carried by the tide on to their land, but that was only consequential, not direct'.[19] Similar requirements apply to malicious prosecution and in a tort such as inducing breach of contract the causal link between the 'inducing' and the 'breach' probably needs to be strong before there can be liability. Thus merely furnishing the means by which others can break a contract will not be enough.[20]

Causation issues can also emerge in duty of care cases. For example the cause of psychological harm is a vital ingredient in the establishing of a duty of care; if the victim has suffered the shock by indirect means – through seeing a disaster in which a loved one is involved on television or learning of it by word of mouth – the required causal connection will not be enough.[21] The mere omission rule can be viewed in similar terms. In *East Suffolk Rivers Catchment Board v Kent*[22] the defendants were held not to owe a duty of care because their carelessness had not actually caused the claimant's flooding damage. That was an act of nature. All that the defendants could be accused of was not making it better. Similarly *Tomlinson v Congleton BC*[23] can be viewed as a case in which the claimant was the cause of his own misfortune in diving into such shallow water. The local authority could perhaps have prevented the accident if they had put better fencing or whatever around the lake, but in the end the real cause of the disaster was to be located in the act of the claimant.

An action can fail to get off the ground if the defendant can show that the claimant consented to the damage (PETL art 7:101(1)(d)). Thus the surgeon is not liable in trespass for the invasion of the patient's body because the patient will have consented to the operation; equally the victim of a legitimate tackle in sport will be taken to have consented to the injury and this may even extend to horseplay.[24] Of course, just what

---

[18] *Scott v Shepherd* (1773) 96 ER 525.
[19] [1954] 2 QB 182, at 196.
[20] *CBS Songs Ltd v Amstrad Plc* [1988] AC 1013.
[21] cf *Page v Smith* [1996] 1 AC 155.
[22] [1941] AC 74. And see now *Mitchell v Glasgow City Council* [2009] 1 AC 874 (HL(Sc)).
[23] [2004] 1 AC 46.
[24] *Blake v Galloway* [2004] 1 WLR 2844.

amounts to consent can on occasions be difficult and one old case which suggests that submission can amount to *volenti* is probably no longer good law.[25] Equally the surgeon who fails to inform a patient of the full risks associated in any operation can undermine any consent. But such a situation may not result in a trespass claim, for the law takes the view that the patient consented to the invasion so to speak; it may give rise, instead, to liability in negligence if a risk materialises.

A particular difficulty arises in this area of medical law where the patient, perhaps through unconsciousness, is unable to give consent. Here the courts have applied the notion of the patient's 'best interests' adding also the presumption that the medical profession, and thus public policy, is under an obligation to save life. However where absence of consent is very clear, the doctors cannot act. Consent, in other words, has a causal aspect in respect of any invasion and damage. One distinction that is fundamental is that between knowledge and consent: mere knowledge of a risk will not act as defence.[26] The risk has to be 'willingly accepted'.[27] In contract, the defence of consent will normally operate as a contractual promise, often in the form of an exclusion or limitation clause or perhaps even via a notice; but these clauses are not automatically valid thanks to restrictive interpretation or consumer legislation (see Chapter 8).

Another defence that, in medical law, is often associated with consent is necessity. 'That there exists in the common law', said Lord Goff, 'a principle of necessity which may justify action which would otherwise be unlawful is not in doubt'.[28] The emergency treatment of patients without their consent can be justified as a matter of necessity if such treatment is reasonable and in the best interests of the patients; and such a defence will extend to for example a sterilisation operation on a mentally weak person provided it is reasonable and in her own best interest.[29] More difficult is the problem that arose in one case where the police, in order to recapture a dangerous criminal, ended up by destroying, through the use of CS gas, the shop in which the criminal had barricaded himself. If the police had not been negligent – for necessity is not a defence to negligence – the owner of the shop would not have succeeded in any of the strict liability torts because the police would have had the defence of necessity.[30] One can speculate if such a defence will today always be valid in such situations

---

[25] *Latter v Braddell* (1881) 50 LJQB 448.
[26] *Smith v Baker & Sons* [1891] AC 325.
[27] See eg Occupier's Liability Act 1957, s 2(5).
[28] *F (In Re)* [1990] 2 AC 1, at 74.
[29] See *F (In Re)* [1990] 2 AC 1.
[30] *Rigby v Chief Constable of Northamptonshire* [1985] 1 WLR 1242.

now that the Human Rights Act 1998 is in force, for it seems hard that an individual should have to suffer an invasion of his property and perhaps family life for the benefit of the community.[31] But much might depend upon the insurance position.

The PETL provide that a strict liability claim 'can be excluded or reduced if the injury was caused by an unforeseeable and irresistible (a) force of nature (*force majeure*), or (b) conduct of a third party' (art 7:102). This article represents English law as well since there is authority that both an 'Act of God'[32] and an act of a third party[33] are defences to action under the rule in *Rylands v Fletcher*. The stricter the liability, it might be argued, the stricter the causal link. But it may be that these defences will be interpreted more narrowly where the thing brought onto land creates a serious risk to surrounding neighbours.[34] In fact the problem will now probably be treated as one of foreseeability: was the intervening factor that triggered the escape of the dangerous thing foreseeable?

A defendant may also escape liability if it can be shown that the claimant was engaged in an illegal activity when he sustained the damage. The maxim here is the one that applies in contract: *ex turpi causa non oritur actio* (no action arises out of an illegal cause). In contract such a defence functions more at the level of the remedy rather than the right – the contract is unenforceable rather than void – but in tort one can say that it is a matter of actionablity. The courts will not enforce a right if such enforcement can be regarded 'as sufficiently anti-social and contrary to public policy'.[35]

LEVEL 2: CAUSE IN FACT

The second level that causation can operate is at the level of fact (and thus was originally a question for the jury). Did the defendant's tortious act cause the claimant's harm? In the *Barnet* case a night-watchman, who had been drinking some tea with co-employees, became very ill and went to a hospital for treatment; the duty doctor sent him home without proper examination and the man later died. The doctor was found to have been negligent in sending him home without examination, but the hospital was held not liable

---

[31] cf *Dennis v MOD* [2003] EWHC 793.
[32] *Nichols v Marsland* (1876) 2 Ex D 1.
[33] *Perry v Kendricks Transport Ltd* [1956] 1 WLR 85.
[34] *Cambridge Water Co v Eastern Counties Leather Plc* [1994] 2 AC 264.
[35] *Pitts v Hunt* [1991] 1 QB 24; *Gray v Thames Trains Ltd* [2009] 3 WLR 167 (HL).

because the cause of the illness was poisoning by arsenic. Even if the nightwatchman had been admitted for treatment he still would have died since, by the time he had arrived at the hospital, it was too late to save his life.[36] Similarly, in *McWilliams v Sir William Arrol & Co*,[37] Lord Devlin stated curtly that the 'courts below have held that the employers were in breach of their duty in failing to provide a safety belt, but that was not the cause of the deceased's death since he would not have worn it if it had been provided'. The general test said to apply in these factual causation cases is the 'but for' test (see PETL art 3.101), yet this text does not always work as we have seen. Causation problems often prove too complex for such a simple test. Thus the other causation tests set out in the PETL can become relevant. One must add, of course, that policy issues do seemingly play a role at this level of 'fact', as Lord Hoffmann (cited earlier) indicated.

A similar causal rule applies in the tort of breach of statutory duty. It must be the breach of the statutory regulation that actually causes the claimant's injury; and so even where an employer is in breach of a statute, there will be no liability if the employer can prove that the damage would have occurred despite the breach.[38] Accordingly in *Gorris v Scott*[39] the defendant shippers were able to avoid liability in breach of statutory duty for the loss of a cargo of sheep washed overboard in a storm by arguing that their breach of statute did not cause the loss. The object of the statute, which required ships carrying sheep to be divided into pens, was not to protect sheep from being washed overboard; it was to protect against the spread of disease.

LOSS OF A CHANCE

The facts of the *Barnett* and *McWilliams* cases appear, at first sight, as clear examples of the absence of cause and connection between careless act and damage suffered. Yet there is another way such facts can be envisaged, at least in cases where there is more uncertainty as to the effects or lack of them of the careless act. What if there had been some chance, however remote, of saving the out-patient's life had the doctor acted without negligence? If such a chance were to exist, then the doctor's negligence would have led to some loss even if the careless act cannot be deemed the actual

---

[36] *Barnett v Chelsea and Kensington Hospital Management Committee* [1969] 1 QB 428.
[37] [1962] 1 WLR 295, at 308.
[38] *Bailey v Ayr Engineering Co Ltd* [1958] 2 All ER 222.
[39] (1874) LR 9 Ex 125.

cause of the death. The out-patient would have lost the chance of having his life saved.

Loss of a chance has been recognised as a head of damage in the English law of obligations[40] and there is even a Court of Appeal decision in a medical negligence case in which a careless diagnosis and treatment of an accident victim was held to have caused the loss of a chance of avoiding a serious physical handicap (negligent act → loss of a chance). However this Court of Appeal decision was overturned by the House of Lords who insisted on seeing the damage, not as the loss of a chance, but as the actual disabled condition.[41] This latter structure (negligent act → physical condition) allowed the Law lords to deny a causal link between negligent treatment and final handicap; the physical handicap was the result of the *accident* not the medical negligence (original accident → physical condition).

The idea of a loss of a chance can be extended to embrace risk. An employer fails to provide washing facilities to employees working in a dirty and dusty brick kiln and one of the employees contracts dermatitis. The failure to supply the facilities amounts to a tort, but what if the employee cannot actually establish cause and connection between absence of facilities and the dermatitis (negligent omission → ? → physical condition)? Expert medical evidence says only that there is a chance (? in the diagram) that the washing facilities might have prevented the dermatitis. One way around this problem is to focus on the loss of this chance and hold the employers liable for in effect creating an enhanced risk of dermatitis (negligent omission → loss of a chance of avoiding dermatitis; or: negligent omission → risk of contracting dermatitis). And this is exactly what the House of Lords did in *McGhee v NCB*, Lord Wilberforce asserting that 'the employers should be liable for an injury, squarely within the risk which they created and that they, not the pursuer, should suffer the consequence of the impossibility, foreseeably inherent in the nature of his injury, of segregating the precise consequence of their default'.[42]

However in *Hotson v East Berks AHA*[43] the Law Lords distinguished, and seemingly marginalised, *McGhee* and although the decision was rehabilitated in *Fairchild v Glenhaven Funeral Services Ltd* (discussed below), the force of the *Hotson* case (together with *Wilsher v Essex AHA*)[44] has by

---

[40] *Chaplin v Hicks* [1911] 2 KB 786; *Allied Maples Group Ltd v Simmons & Simmons* [1995] 1 WLR 1602.
[41] *Hotson v East Berks Area Health Authority* [1987] AC 750.
[42] [1973] 1 WLR 1, at 7.
[43] [1987] AC 750.
[44] [1988] AC 1074.

no means disappeared. A majority of the House of Lords has recently reaffirmed the need for a claimant to prove beyond the balance of probabilities (50 per cent) that the negligence of the defendant has caused the adverse consequences suffered; if the statistical probability of the wrong causing the damage is less than 50 per cent the action will fail.[45] As Baroness Hale observed, almost 'any claim for loss of an outcome, could be reformulated as a claim for loss of a chance of that outcome'[46] and the 'complexities of attempting to introduce liability for the loss of a chance of a more favourable outcome in personal injury claims have driven me, not without regret, to conclude that it should not be done.'[47] In short it is not enough for a claimant to show that the defendant's negligent act *might possibly* (less than 50 per cent chance) have caused the claimant's loss of a chance for a more favourable medical outcome; it must be shown that it *probably* (more than 50 per cent chance) did cause it.

In *Fairchild* the causation problem seemed at first to be rather different from a loss of a chance one since the causation difficulty arose, not from the inexistence of causal relation between fault and disease, but from uncertainty about where to locate the relation in respect of the negligent actor.[48] The claimant was negligently exposed to asbestos dust by two employers but, on contracting mesothelioma, he was not able to establish which workplace exposure had actually triggered the disease; accordingly the Court of Appeal dismissed his claim against the employers on the ground of failing to prove causation. They rejected in effect the rule expressed in article 3:103 of the PETL (in the 'case of multiple activities, where each of them alone would have been sufficient to cause the damage, but it remains uncertain which one in fact caused it, each activity is regarded as a cause to the extent corresponding to the likelihood that it may have caused the victim's damage.') The House of Lords allowed an appeal, Lord Bingham stating 'that such injustice as may be involved in imposing liability on a duty-breaking employer in these circumstances is heavily outweighed by the injustice of denying redress to a victim'.[49]

What is clear of course from the judgements is that factual causation is not just a question of fact (a point discussed in some detail by Lord Hoffmann in the case). Policy and axiological considerations equally have their role. Interestingly in *Fairchild* the judges asked counsel to cast their net wider than common law precedents; they wanted to know how such

---

[45] *Gregg v Scott* [2005] 2 AC 176.
[46] [2005] 2 AC 176, at para 224.
[47] [2005] 2 AC 176, at para 226.
[48] *Fairchild v Glenhaven Funeral Services Ltd* [2003] 1 AC 32.
[49] [2003] 1 AC 32, at para 33.

problems were handled in the civil law and Lord Hope even spent time examining the Roman jurists. As Lord Bingham explained, this was not a question of finding out the law but discovering where justice lay. Yet in the end much comes down, not to some theory or other about causation, but to how one views, or perhaps one should say constructs, the facts. Two hunters carelessly fire their guns at the same time and wound someone out for a walk. One can either accept the mutually exclusive causal defence based on the argument 'it is not me, it is him'; or one can see the two hunters as a single 'actor' and hold both liable. Escaping liability, in other words, becomes something of an ontological (what exists) question; it depends on how one 'sees' the world (do forests exist or are there only trees?)

However *Fairchild* subsequently turned out to be a loss of a chance case. In *Barker v Corus UK*[50] the claimants had negligently been exposed to asbestos by a variety of employers many of whom had become insolvent. The question arose as to whether those employers who were still solvent were to be liable jointly and severally for all the damage suffered by the employees or for only a proportion of it (severally only). The House of Lords held that liability should be several only. Lord Scott said that he would 'hold that the extent of the liability of each defendant in a *Fairchild* type of case, where it cannot be shown which defendant's breach of duty caused the damage but where each defendant, in breach of duty, has exposed the claimant to a significant risk of the eventual damage, should be liability commensurate with the degree of risk for which that defendant was responsible.'[51] As Lord Rodger, who dissented, observed, this was a 'new analysis'[52] putting the risk of insolvency not on the other tortfeasors but on the victims; but Baroness Hale made it clear that although the harm might be indivisible the material contribution to the risk can be divided up among the different actors. The question, she said, was one of fairness.[53] What this reasoning appears to mask is the fact that the real defendants were not the employers at all but their insurance companies. Accordingly if one re-poses the question of fairness from the point of view of insurance, it is difficult to escape the conclusion that the issue is one of risk, as Lord Rodger noted. Who should bear the risk of this terrible disease: the victims or the insurance companies? The legislator seems to have arrived at a different conclusion than the majority in *Barker*.[54]

---

[50] [2006] 2 AC 572.
[51] [2006] 2 AC 572, at para 62.
[52] [2006] 2 AC 572, at para 85.
[53] [2006] 2 AC 572, at para 126.
[54] See Compensation Act 2006, s 3.

The *Fairchild* case was followed by a further decision of the House of Lords that could be said to modify the normal causation rule in the tort of negligence.[55] The claimant underwent surgery which resulted in significant nerve damage that left her partially paralysed. The trial judge held that the surgeon had not been negligent in the performance of the operation but had failed in his duty adequately to warn her of the risks which attached to such surgery. What made the case difficult was that the claimant did not argue that had she known the risks she would never at any time have consented to surgery and this resulted in the judge not being able to state as a fact that the claimant would never have had the operation. Could it be said, therefore, that the absence of the warning was the cause of her partial paralysis? Two of the Law Lords thought that that the causal test had not been satisfied; the claimant had 'not established that but for the failure to warn she would not have undergone surgery'[56] In other words, she had not proved that she 'would have taken the opportunity to avoid or reduce that risk'.[57] However the majority thought there was sufficient causal connection. Lord Steyn asserted that 'in the context of attributing legal responsibility, it is necessary to identify precisely the protected interests at stake'. And that the duty to warn not only 'tends to avoid the occurrence of the particular physical injury the risk of which a patient is not prepared to accept' but 'also ensures that respect is given to the autonomy and dignity of each patient'.[58] Accordingly 'policy and corrective justice pull powerfully in favour of vindicating the patient's right to know.'[59]

This last point made by Lord Steyn has to be appreciated in the context of the particular facts of the case. Failure to warn can of course be seen (and normally is seen) as a 'negligent act'. Yet it also goes beyond negligence and into the tort of trespass in that it is the patient's informed consent to surgery that prevents the surgical operation amounting to a trespass. Trespass of course is a tort that protects constitutional as well as health interests and thus it is not unreasonable to bring into play interests other than the ones protected by the tort of negligence. As Lord Hope pointed out, the 'function of the law is to protect the patient's right to choose'.[60] And 'if the application of logic is to provide the answer, the consequences ... are stark' in as much as there is duty, breach of duty and injury within the scope of the duty but 'the patient to whom the duty was owed is left

---

[55] *Chester v Afshar* [2005] 1 AC 134.
[56] [2005] 1 AC 134, at para 8 per Lord Bingham.
[57] [2005] 1 AC 134, at para 29 per Lord Lord Hoffmann.
[58] [2005] 1 AC 134, at para 18.
[59] [2005] 1 AC 134, at para 22.
[60] [2005] 1 AC 134, at para 56.

without a remedy.'[61] Causation in the tort of negligence is, accordingly, normally applied as between negligent act or omission and actual injury sustained (act/omission → partial paralysis). But an omission to warn brings into play a mediating 'law of persons' (dignity) interest which allows a weaker form of causation to function as between the omission and the ultimate injury on the basis that there was a clear invasion of the patient's *right* to choose (omission → absence of right to choose → physical injury). If this *right* were ignored it would, as Lord Hope observed, leave the *duty* 'useless in the cases where it may be needed the most'.[62] *Chester v Afshar* indicates once again how the law of tort often has to protect a range of quite different interests which in turn can reflect themselves in the relationship between a defendant's 'duty' and a claimant's 'right'.

All the same, much will depend upon the actual facts and the way the damage is envisaged (physical outcome or loss of a chance). If the defendant had argued that the claimant had simply not proved beyond the balance of probabilities (more than 50 per cent chance) that the failure to warn had caused her physical injury, the result might have been different as a later House of Lords decision indicates.[63] Indeed, in his dissenting judgment in *Afshar*, Lord Hoffmann denounced the whole decision as being 'about as logical as saying that if one had been told, on entering a casino, that the odds on the number 7 coming up at roulette were only 1 in 37, one would have gone away and come back next week or gone to a different casino'.[64] However one can ask whether an analogy between invasive surgery and casino gambling is a particularly sensitive one.

OVERLAPPING CAUSES AND OVERLAPPING DAMAGE

Another difficulty to be encountered in factual causation is where damage is aggravated, or indeed just incurred again, by a second independent cause (cf PETL art 3:104). C's car is involved in two separate accidents both the fault of the other party (D1 and D2 respectively) and each accident, if viewed independently, necessitates a re-spray of the vehicle; C sues D1 for the re-spray and although successful does not get satisfaction (D1 is bankrupt). It would seem that C cannot sue D2 for the re-spray since D2

---

[61] [2005] 1 AC 134, at para 73.
[62] [2005] 1 AC 134, at para 87.
[63] *Gregg v Scott* [2005] 2 AC 176.
[64] *Chester v Afshar* [2005] 1 AC 134, at para 31.

takes the car as he finds it, that is to say already damaged.[65] D damages C's ship and temporary repairs are effected to make her seaworthy, but the damage is such that the ship will need to return to the USA for more long-term repairs. While crossing the Atlantic she suffers further damage from a storm and again becomes unseaworthy. Both sets of repairs are carried out in the USA which means that the ship is in dry dock for a longer period than would have been the case if there had been no storm; the owners cannot recover their loss of profits from D for any part of the period while in dry dock.[66]

There were grounds for thinking that personal injury may have been treated differently. D damages C's leg and is sued by C for this damage; just before the trial C is shot in the damaged leg by robbers and this results in C having his leg amputated. D's argument that C has literally lost the cause of his damage (his leg) will, it seems, be unsuccessful; D must pay for the original damage.[67] Yet the position is not clear. In 1973 C suffered a back injury at work due to the negligence of D his employer; in 1976 C became totally disabled owing to an illness that was completely independent of the employment accident; D was liable for C's damage only up to 1976.[68] More recently the decision in *Performance Cars v Abraham*[69] has been directly applied to a personal injury action where the earlier precedent was described as 'still good law' and as 'a matter of logic and common sense, it is clearly correct'. The judgment went on to hold that since 'the claimant had already suffered that damage, the second defendant did not cause it' and thus this 'is not a case of concurrent torfeasors.'[70]

The situation seems to be, then, that if two hunters both carelessly fire off a shot and a passer-by is hit by a single bullet, both hunters will be liable to the victim, if it can be proved that the bullet came from one or other of the guns.[71] However if one hunter carelessly fires a shot which smashes the passer-by's right knee and, a few minutes later, a second hunter fires a shot that would have smashed the victim's right knee if it had not already been smashed, the second hunter will not be liable.[72] But if one hunter fires off

---

[65] *Performance Cars Ltd v Abraham* [1962] 1 QB 33; *Halsey v Milton Keynes General NHS Trust* [2004 1 WLR 3002.
[66] *Carslogie SS Co v Royal Norwegian Government* [1952] AC 292.
[67] *Baker v Willoughby* [1970] AC 467.
[68] *Jobling v Associated Dairies Ltd* [1982] AC 794; and see now *Gray v Thames Trains Ltd* [2009] 3 WLR 167 (HL).
[69] [1962] 1 QB 33.
[70] *Halsey v Milton Keynes General NHS Trust* [2004] 1 WLR 3002, at para 70.
[71] *Fairchild v Glenhaven Funeral Services Ltd* [2003] 1 AC 32.
[72] *Halsey v Milton Keynes General NHS Trust* [2004 1 WLR 3002.

a shot which hits the passer-by's right knee and a second hunter fires off a shot that hits the passer-by's left knee, each hunter will, apparently, be liable for one knee each.[73] The position will of course become complicated if the victim is hit in one knee by one hunter and the other knee by another hunter and, as a result of the cumulative effect of both injuries, suffers very severe psychological shock. One possibility is to treat the different injuries as a single form of personal injury damage and make one or other hunter liable for all this damage, the hunter held liable then being able to claim contribution from the other hunter through the Civil Liability (Contribution) Act 1978. It is, however, uncertain, thanks to the *Rahman* case,[74] how this last situation might be analysed.

Matters will become even more complicated if the hunters carelessly injure one knee each with their shots and, subsequently, the victim is run over in the street, losing both legs by amputation that would not have been necessary if the knees had not already been smashed by bullets. Will each hunter be liable for: (i) just one injured knee; (ii) the loss of one leg; (iii) the loss of both legs; (iv) the loss of a chance of not having to lose one leg; or (v) the loss of a chance of not having to lose two legs? This problem cannot be answered by recourse to a set of abstract and axiomatic rules or principles since the real source of any solution will depend upon how the reasoner views the facts. How is 'damage' to be understood? And how is this damage (if viewed holistically), or the different separate types of damage (if viewed in its parts), to be linked causally to each actor? The patterns or models applicable are various, if not endless.

NOVUS ACTUS INTERVENIENS

Some of these cases can be approached from the position of a supervening event that can then be characterised as a new intervening act (*novus actus interveniens*). In fact new intervening acts can be of different kinds. First, the intervening act can be that of a third party (including an 'Act of God'). D's ship negligently collides with a ship on which C is a sailor; the captain of C's ship decides to set out in a small boat, with a crew including C, to liaise with the captain of D's ship. While crossing between the two ships in a rough sea, the small boat capsizes and C is drowned; the act of the captain in deciding to set out in the small boat does not break the chain of causation (it is a 'natural consequence' of the accident) and D is liable to

---

[73] *Rahman v Arearose Ltd* [2001] QB 351.
[74] *Rahman v Arearose Ltd* [2001] QB 351.

C.[75] D, a decorator, working in C's house goes out for lunch leaving the front door unlocked; a thief slips in and steals C's goods. D is liable to C (but one might note the contractual relationship).[76]

Secondly, the intervener can be the claimant himself. D negligently injures V which causes such depression that V subsequently commits suicide; the chain of causation is not necessarily broken and D may be liable (to V's wife C or to V's estate) for the death.[77] This is particularly so if D is under an actual duty to guard against V's suicide and thus the police have been held liable, although subject to a reduction for contributory negligence, where they have failed to prevent V from killing himself.[78] However where D has carelessly injured C, the latter must conduct himself with care and must not take unreasonable risks which may result in him suffering further injury; if he does, then D will not be liable for the second injury.[79] But much depends on the nature of the risk and the situation of the claimant. Some judges try to answer the question by asking whose fault caused the accident,[80] but this tends to extend factual causation into the realm of duty which, of course, might be unavoidable on occasions.[81]

Thirdly, there is the intervention by a rescuer. Here the chain of causation is not broken in situations where a rescuer intervenes to save life and limb, for such an intervention is not deemed unreasonable.[82] However a rescuer who intervenes just to save property might not be treated so generously;[83] and psychological damage suffered by a rescuer causes particular difficulties (see Chapter 11).[84]

The general test to emerge from these situations is that of 'reasonableness'.[85] Yet it is important to stress that this test is to be understood in a causal sense and thus must not be confused with the reasonable test in breach of duty cases. For example, objectively, suicide might be unreasonable, but in the context of causation things are different; there are

---

[75] *Oropesa (The)* [1943] P 32.
[76] *Stansbie v Troman* [1948] 2 KB 48.
[77] *Pigney v Pointers Transport Services Ltd* [1957] 1 WLR 1121; *Corr v IBC Vehicles Ltd* [2008] AC 884; *Gray v Thames Trains Ltd* [2009] 3 WLR 167.
[78] *Reeves v Commissioner of Police for the Metropolis* [2000] 1 AC 360.
[79] *McKew v Holland & Hannen & Cubitts* [1969] 3 All ER 1621.
[80] See eg *Ginty v Belmont Building Supplies Ltd* [1959] 1 All ER 414.
[81] See eg *Corr v IBC Vehicles Ltd* [2008] 2 AC 884.
[82] *Haynes v Harwood & Son* [1935] 1 KB 146.
[83] *Cutler v United Dairies (London) Ltd* [1933] 2 KB 297.
[84] *Frost v Chief Constable of South Yorkshire Police* [1999] 2 AC 455.
[85] *McKew v Holland & Hannen & Cubitts* [1969] 3 All ER 1621.

situations where suicide will not break the chain of causation.[86] Yet care must be taken with regard to factual causation. In *Fairchild v Glenhaven Funeral Services Ltd* Lord Hoffmann was of the opinion that 'one is never simply liable, one is always liable for something – to make compensation for damage, the nature and extent of which is delimited by the law.' And he added that once 'it is appreciated that the rules laying down causal requirements are not autonomous expressions of some form of logic or judicial instinct but creatures of the law, part of the conditions of liability, it is possible to explain their content on the grounds of fairness and justice in exactly the same way as the other conditions of liability.'[87]

What the Law Lord seems to be saying here is that while it is perfectly proper to distinguish between all the different levels of causation (cause in fact, remoteness, duty), they are nevertheless only control devices and thus may all, either overall or in their individual parts, be infused with axiological considerations. And so escaping liability on grounds of factual causation must now, it seems, be considered within the whole context of the legal obligation itself.[88] Indeed this approach has been specifically reaffirmed by Lord Steyn.[89] The problem, of course, is what might appear 'fair' to one judge could well prove 'unfair' to another.[90] This is why it might be better to give expression to these 'legal conditions of liability' through a balancing act between, on the one hand, the various causal concepts (causal here being understood in its wider context) and, on the other hand, the nature of the behaviour (PETL art 1:101) and protected interests (PETL art 2:102). European law expresses these conditions of liability through abstract general principles and while such an approach is not necessarily that helpful when it comes to solving actual factual problems of causation, it must nevertheless be remembered that recourse to 'fairness' is equally not necessarily a helpful alternative. The strength of a code like the PETL lies in what it does not state but implicitly assumes, namely that all the various sections and articles are to be balanced against each other. The rules on causation (PETL chapter 3) are always to be read in conjunction with the rules on damage and interest (PETL chapter 2). This

---

[86] *Corr v IBC Vehicles Ltd* [2008] AC 884. But cf *Gray v Thames Trains Ltd* [2009] 3 WLR 167 (HL).

[87] [2003] 1 AC 32, at para 54.

[88] See now *Corr v IBC Vehicles Ltd* [2008] AC 884 and *Gray v Thames Trains Ltd* [2009] 3 WLR 167 (HL).

[89] *Chester v Afshar* [2005] 1 AC 134, at para 22.

[90] See eg the dissenting judgments in *Reeves v Commissioner of Police for the Metropolis* [2000] 1 AC 360 and in *Corr v IBC Vehicles Ltd* [2007] QB 46. See also *Gray v Thames Trains Ltd* [2009] 3 WLR 167.

is probably what Lord Hoffmann means when he talks of the 'conditions of liability'. Thus factual causation remains an important level of analysis, but the cases that have been examined on this level implicitly have, on the whole, equally taken account of the nature of the damage and the interests in play.

LEVEL 3: REMOTENESS OF DAMAGE

The third level at which causation operates is that of law in the full sense of the meaning. That is to say, in the days of juries, it was a question for the judge rather than the jury. The point to stress here is that one is not applying a factual-orientated concept like 'reasonable' because the problem is not one of making sense of fact as such. The question is one of limitation of liability; a defendant is not to be liable for every consequence flowing from the wrongful behaviour.[91] As a legal question, therefore, the concepts in play are much more normative in nature and try to reflect policy issues as much as causal (cf PETL art 3:201). There are of course plenty of cases that, not surprisingly (now the jury has gone), confuse factual and legal causation,[92] but the starting point for legal causation is the test to be applied and this test has varied. Being a legal issue this is a matter of precedent, yet, while it is true to say that the test formulated in the 19th century has been replaced by one laid down in 1961, the older test(s) cannot be completely ignored.

The test of liability for a particular head of damage formulated in the 19th century was founded upon the principle of directness. A defendant would be liable for all damage directly and naturally flowing from the negligent act. Thus a railway company was held liable for the destruction of the plaintiff's cottage by fire; the company had negligently caused a fire on its embankment and the fire spread across a field and then a road and finally arrived at the cottage. The company was liable because the link between fire destruction and negligent act was one of directness.[93] This test was subsequently confirmed in a leading Court of Appeal decision. An employee of a company that had chartered a ship carelessly allowed a plank to fall into the hold of the vessel; the falling plank caused a spark which ignited some petrol vapour in the hold leading to an explosion

---

[91] This is well brought out by Ward LJ's dissenting judgment in *Corr v IBC Vehicles Ltd* [2007] QB 46; cf [2008] AC 884.
[92] cf *Corr v IBC Vehicles Ltd* [2008] AC 884.
[93] *Smith v London & South Western Railway Co* (1870) LR 6 CP 14.

that completely destroyed the ship. The charterer was held liable for the destruction even although such extensive damage was an unforeseeable result of a falling plank.[94]

However this directness test, which had come under some doctrinal criticism, was, formally speaking, abandoned in 1961. Oil was carelessly discharged from a ship during its bunkering operations in Sydney harbour and it spread to the claimant's wharf some 200 yards away where another ship was being repaired. The claimant halted its welding operations until assured by scientific opinion that oil on water would not ignite; subsequently, when a spark from the claimant's welding fell onto a piece of floating rag, the oil did ignite and the claimant's wharf was destroyed in the ensuing fire. The Australian courts, applying the directness test, held the charterers of the ship liable to the claimants, but an appeal was allowed by the Privy Council on the ground that the damage was unforeseeable.[95] Foreseeability thus replaced the directness test.

The shift effected by the Privy Council is an interesting one from a methodological point of view. The directness test was one that put the emphasis on the relation between tortious act and damage; if unbroken in the 'directness' sense there would be liability irrespective of any subjective element on the part of the tortfeasor. The test was genuinely causal in its method. However the foreseeablity test introduced a whole new approach in that the facts were now to be reconstructed in terms of an *actor* whose subjective view of the world was to determine the limits of liability. In a sense this has introduced a more 'contractual' flavour into the analysis in as much as the link between tortious act and damage will depend partly upon what the constituted actor (the reasonable man) had in mind when any particular activity is undertaken. In other words the 'reasonable man', so central to the breach of duty question,[96] has moved to a new stage where duty, breach and causation become, at least in part, merged within the idea of foreseeability. This in turn will affect the other tests including that of breach of duty which, it may be recalled, was originally one of reasonable behaviour.[97]

In fact the two levels – breach of duty and remoteness – can become very easily confused. Thus in *Tomlinson v Congleton BC* Lord Hoffmann stated that the reason Miss Stone failed in her claim was that she was owed no duty of care by the cricket club.[98] This analysis must be wrong since all

---

[94] *Polemis (In Re)* [1921] 3 KB 560.
[95] *Wagon Mound (No 1) (The)* [1961] AC 388.
[96] *Bolton v Stone* [1951] AC 850.
[97] See eg *Corr v IBC Vehicles Ltd* [2008] AC 884.
[98] [2004] 1 AC 46, at para 44.

occupiers owe a duty of care (if not a higher duty) to highway users not to cause physical injury. The club was not liable because they were not *in breach* of the duty. Yet what seems to be creeping into the analysis is foreseeability; but even this is wrong, since the cricket ball accident, according to Lord Radcliffe, was quite foreseeable. An 'actor' approach to liability thus becomes all-consuming in a *functional* way. Is it the function of the tort of negligence (or any other tort) for this *actor* to remedy this particular *damage*? Here, of course, one is effecting a shift, via the 'subjective actor', off the idea that tort consists of rules or definable structures and onto the aims and objectives of tort. Decisions are to be justified by reference to social history, economic theory or whatever.[99]

The result is not as enlightening as one might think because there is a general reluctance to approach liability from the point of view of the cost of an activity. In *Re Polemis* if the employee, in carelessly dropping a plank, had killed an employee of the owners of the ship, would the charterers have been liable or could they have claimed that the victim had been 'unforeseeable'? This question cannot easily be answered by reference to economic theory in conjunction with the foreseeability of the reasonable man. Is the presence of a person any more or any less foreseeable than petrol vapour? Yet it can be answered by reference to PETL art 2:102(2): people are worth more than ships. In other words the foreseeability test is in the end a means of giving expression to protected interests without having to look at the *activity* in question. How many port workers are killed in any one year and should this cost be borne by the employers or by the victims? The moment one asks this activity question, the law of tort – with its vision of a world full of individual actors – begins to look unconvincing.

This more unconvincing aspect is intensified if one looks at the law of bailment in which a person who takes possession of another's chattel becomes strictly liable (in the tort of wrongful interference with goods) for the chattel if the chattel is stolen or destroyed. The burden is on the bailee to prove that there was no fault. Now if one applies this to a ship, the actual decision in *Re Polemis* becomes understandable; the charterers were like 'bailees' of the ship and it was their employee who sank it.[100] Yet the law of bailment does not apply to people which means that had the plank killed someone rather than just destroyed the ship the family of the dead person would have had to prove fault and foreseeability. The

---

[99] See eg Lord Hoffmann in *Transco plc v Stockport MBC* [2004] 2 AC 1.
[100] Weir (2004), at 307. As Weir points out, the hirers (charterers) of a ship, unlike the hirers of a self-drive car, are not technically bailees of the vessel.

PETL article 2:102 does not, in other words, properly reflect English tort law. For chattels are better protected than people in as much as negligence must be proved if people are injured in a train crash but not if goods of another are destroyed.[101]

Yet this emphasis on the actor might well be seen as the remoteness test that has always operated in contract, for the *Code civil* (and now the PECL and UNIDROIT) state that a contractor who fails to perform, or is in breach to use the common law language, is liable only for damage that was foreseeable at the time of entering the contract (CC art 1150). This rule was incorporated into English law in the 19th century decision of *Hadley v Baxendale*,[102] although the term employed was 'contemplation' rather than 'foreseeable'. Thus the actual remoteness rule in contract is that a contractor is liable only for damage that was in his contemplation. In a bailment contract what is contemplated, according to *Hadley*, unless the bailee is made aware of some greater risk, is the value of the thing bailed.

In terms of aims and objectives of contract this contemplation rule can however be more generous than the tort rule in that damages for failure to gain a profit are not automatically excluded under a financial loss rule. Thus if *Spartan Steel*[103] had been a contract case the claimant would probably have recovered damages under all of the heads claimed since it is not difficult to hold that a contractor acting under a contract with the claimant who negligently cuts through a cable will contemplate both stoppage and loss of profits.[104] One also has to add the more general damages rule in contract that the aim is to put the contractor in the position he would have been in had the contract been performed (expectation interest). Nevertheless the effect of *Hadley v Baxendale*, according to the French analysis that attaches to CC art 1150, is that it is an implied limitation clause. The aim is to shield a contractor from liability when, say, an object sold is put to an unsuitable and unforeseeable use by the buyer resulting in serious damage. In other words a contractor must be able to assess the risk of entering into the contract.[105] Thus a swimming pool contractor who constructs a pool that is not in accordance with the contract will not be

---

[101] *Readhead v Midland Railway Co* (1869) LR 4 QB 379.
[102] (1854) 9 Ex 341; 156 ER 145; and see now *Transfield Shipping Inc v Mercator Shipping Inc* [2009] 1 AC 61.
[103] *Spartan Steel & Alloys Ltd v Martin & Co* [1973] 1 QB 27. But now see *Transfield Shipping Inc v Mercator Shipping Inc* [2009] 1 AC 61 where liability in contractual damages is now based on the presumed intention of the parties.
[104] See eg *Parsons (Livestock) Ltd v Uttley Ingham & Co* [1978] QB 791.
[105] See now *Transfield Shipping Inc v Mercator Shipping Inc* [2009] 1 AC 61, para 12.

liable for the whole cost of a new pool if this is way outside the economic risk.[106] A surveyor will, in contrast, be liable for the mental distress caused by over-flying aircraft when this kind of harm was the central risk in the surveying contract of which he was in breach.[107]

Is the same true of tort? Is the foreseeability test one whereby the actor can assess the risk of entering into some course of conduct like driving or manufacturing ginger beer? It has been authoritatively stated that the contemplation (contract) and foreseeability (tort) tests are different, the latter being wider in terms of probability or likelihood.[108] This analysis was viewed with a sceptical eye by Lord Denning MR in *Parsons v Uttley Ingham*[109] who preferred to emphasise a more general law of obligations rule based on the distinction between physical damage and pure economic loss; but this distinction was not accepted by the other two judges in the case. The present law seems to be, then, that foreseeability is wider in scope and thus encompasses a greater degree of risk.

UNTYPICAL DAMAGE

Nevertheless foreseeability can be deceptive here in that this test can end up excluding certain types of harm for reasons that are not strictly relevant in terms of risk. This point is well illustrated by a particular difficulty that arose after the adoption of the foreseeability test. A farmer carelessly allowed his farm to become infested with rats with the result that a farm worker became infected with what was then considered to be a very rare disease contracted from rats' urine (Weil's Disease). The farmer was held not liable since this particular damage was unforeseeable; had the worker been infected through a rat's bite, he would have recovered.[110] What foreseeability (of the actor) has done here is to introduce a problem of genus and species: one must foresee not only damage (genus) but the particular species of harm. Breach of duty (reasonableness) becomes intertwined with remoteness.[111]

The courts had begun to grapple with this genus and species problem in

---

[106] *Ruxley Electronics Ltd v Forsyth* [1996] 1 AC 344 and see now *Transfield Shipping Inc v Mercator Shipping Inc* [2009] 1 AC 61.
[107] *Farley v Skinner* [2002] 2 AC 732.
[108] *Heron II (The)* [1969] 1 AC 350; *Transfield Shipping Inc v Mercator Shipping Inc* [2009] 1 AC 61, at paras 31–32.
[109] [1978] QB 791.
[110] *Tremain v Pike* [1969] 3 All ER 1303.
[111] See eg *Doughty v Turner Manufacturing Co Ltd* [1964] 1 QB 518.

a case where a small boy entered a shelter erected by the defendants over a manhole in the street and started to play with a paraffin warning lamp; the lamp fell down the manhole and exploded causing the boy serious burns. The defendants argued that while injury by fire was foreseeable, injury by explosion was not; but the House of Lords rejected this defence on the ground that the harm was of a recognised type.[112] The problem surfaced again more recently when two friends decided to repair an old boat which had been left on local authority land. The boat collapsed on one of the boys causing him very serious injury, yet his damages claim was rejected in the Court of Appeal on the ground that it was unforeseeable that the boys would jack up and prop up the boat. In other words the species of *accident* was unforeseeable. This decision was overturned in the House of Lords: the 'foreseeability is not as to the particulars but the genus', said Lord Hoffmann.[113] Such an approach is clearly right in that foreseeability of the species of damage becomes relevant only if one wishes to exclude particular *interests* (cf PETL art 2:102).

One area which seemingly remained untouched by the foreseeability test was the principle that a tortfeasor must take his victim as he finds him. A worker was burnt on the lip by some molten metal, an injury that might have been prevented had the employer not been negligent; however the burn turned cancerous owing to the plaintiff's special susceptibility to cancer and he died. The employer was held liable for the death.[114] Again, as with the genus and species issue, this kind of damage simply cannot be excluded by reference to the foreseeability test. If it is to be excluded it should be on the basis of a more structured and objective relationship between the category of damage suffered and the risk attaching to the actor. In other words the forseeability test is by no means as useful as it might seem.

LEVEL 4: CAUSATION AND REMEDIES

The fourth level at which causation operates is at the level of remedies, in particular the remedy of damages. With respect to a remedy like debt causation may well be used to deny liability completely; thus, for example, a defendant sued by a creditor for a sum owing in respect of an alleged service might argue that there was no causal link between the contractual

---

[112] *Hughes v Lord Advocate* [1963] AC 837.
[113] *Jolley v Sutton LBC* [2000] 1 WLR 1082, at 1091.
[114] *Smith v Leech Brain & Co* [1962] 2 QB 405. See also *Robinson v Post Office* [1974] 1 WLR 1176.

promise and the alleged service (for instance the estate agent who claims a fee when it is questionable if he has been instrumental in selling the defendant's house). But in this situation it could equally be said that the causal issue is operating at the level of substantive law. It is with regard to the remedy of damages that causation can have an important role.

At this level of damages causation tends to operate not to deny liability but to exclude certain heads of damage. D negligently cuts the power supply to C's factory and this caused three types of harm: (i) damage to valuable molten metal in the furnaces when they cooled; (ii) loss of profit on this ruined melt; (iii) loss of profits that the factory could have made during the period it was closed through lack of power. The Court of Appeal has held that C was entitled to damages under heads (i) and (ii) but not for head (iii) since this damage, being pure economic loss, was *inter alia* too remote.[115] In this example the exclusion of head (iii) was a question of legal causation; however factual causation can also be used at this level to limit the extent of liability in damages.[116] In addition to this general operation of causation and remoteness to limit liability, several specific defences now operate at this level of damages.

The first defence is contributory negligence. Before 1945 if the claimant (C) had causally contributed to his own damage this was regarded as a *novus actus interveniens* isolating the defendant (D) from liability; contributory negligence, in other words, was once a matter of factual causation. In 1945 the law changed. The courts now have a statutory power to apportion responsibility between C and D and thus if C is 40 per cent to blame for his damage his damages from D will be reduced by this amount.[117] Contributory negligence is mainly now a question of damages. Nevertheless the courts can still have recourse to factual causation so as to deny any liability where C himself is the cause of his own damage.[118] The 1945 Act does not, it seems, apply to contract unless the facts giving rise to the contractual claim also disclose a cause of action in tort.[119]

The second defence is mitigation (PECL art 9:505). This has been expressed as follows: 'a plaintiff suing for breach of contract or, for that matter, for tort cannot call upon a defendant to pay the full direct consequences unless he himself has acted reasonably to mitigate the loss.' The judge went on to comment that it 'is sometimes loosely described as a

---

[115] *Spartan Steel & Alloys Ltd v Martin & Co* [1973] 1 QB 27.
[116] *Liesbosch (The)* [1933] AC 449.
[117] Law Reform (Contributory Negligence) Act 1945.
[118] *McWilliams v Sir William Arrol* [1962] 1 WLR 295.
[119] *Barclays Bank Plc v Fairclough Building Ltd* [1995] QB 214.

plaintiff's duty to mitigate'.[120] But in a 1983 case Sir John Donaldson MR stated that a 'plaintiff is under no duty to mitigate his loss, despite the habitual use by the lawyers of the phrase'. The claimant 'is completely free to act as he judges to be in his best interests'. However 'a defendant is not liable for all loss suffered by the plaintiff in consequence of his so acting'; he 'is only liable for such part of the plaintiff's loss as is properly to be regarded as caused by the defendant's breach of duty'.[121] One should note, of course, that mitigation is irrelevant when the remedy is debt rather than damages.[122]

This assertion by Sir John Donaldson is helpful in as much as it clearly locates mitigation in the realm of causation and links it to the interests in play.[123] Moreover it makes clear that failure to mitigate is not a wrong in itself. Yet it remains an odd comment in that from the claimant's viewpoint mitigation is dependent upon how he acts and this can be explained in normative terms. For example, in one leading case, a claimant was not allowed the full cost of restoring his motor car written off by the defendant's negligence; he could only claim the cost of a similar car on the second-hand market.[124] Of course in having his car, something of a collector's item, restored he could be said to be acting in his own best interests; yet the judges in the case did not focus on this interest aspect. The test they applied was one focused on the claimant as an actor: did the claimant behave as a reasonable businessman? In other words defendants are entitled to expect to pay only for risks that are strictly commercial and mitigation gives expression to this expectation by saying that a claimant must not 'abuse' his position. This is, in other words, a question of 'duty', but, equally, it is a matter of causation.[125]

MEASURE OF DAMAGES

Causation might also be seen as operating, at least in a loose sense, behind all the detailed rules that now govern the measure of damages in contract and tort cases. Such damages rules require a textbook in itself because the courts and the legislator have had to produce very detailed provisions in

---

[120] Rougier J in *Thomas v Countryside Council for Wales* [1994] 4 All ER 853, at 860.
[121] *Solholt (The)* [1983] 1 Ll Rep 605, at 608.
[122] *White & Carter (Councils) Ltd v McGregor* [1962] AC 413.
[123] See also *The Borag* [1981] 1 WLR 274.
[124] *Darbishire v Warran* [1963] 1 WLR 1067.
[125] *The Borag* [1981] 1 WLR 274.

respect of personal injury claims, if not property damage cases. One is not talking here, of course, of escaping liability *per se*. The question is one of escaping from part of the liability, for substantial sums of money can still be at stake.

The general rule is simple enough: 'the measure of damages recoverable for the invasion of a legal right, whether by breach of contract or by the commission of a tort, is that damages are compensatory'.[126] Several difficulties immediately arise even at this general level. Are all damages compensatory? In fact some damages, known as exemplary damages, are not.[127] Does 'compensation' mean the same thing in contract and in tort? If one examines this question from the position of interests, there are differences.[128] In contract the aim of an award of damages is normally to compensate for an *expectation interest* (that is to put the claimant in the position he would have been in had the contract been performed: see PECL art 9.502). In tort the interest is one of restoration, that is to say to restore the claimant to the position he was in before the damage (see PETL art 10:101). Behaviour may play a role; the defendant found liable in fraud will quite possibly be liable for more extensive damage than if he had been held liable in negligence (PETL art 10:301(2)).[129] Even the nature of the interest invaded can have a dramatic effect on amounts payable. A claimant whose reputation interest has been invaded may receive as much, perhaps even more, than someone badly injured in a road accident.[130]

As one descends to lower levels of generality the problems become more detailed but no less difficult. There is the general problem of trying to compensate in money for debilitating personal injury. Clearly non-economic losses such as pain and suffering will by nature be difficult; yet trying to establish the future economic loss is no easier in a once-and-for-all lump sum damages award.[131] 'The aim', as Lord Hope has said, 'is to award such a sum of money as will amount to no more, and at the same time no less, than the net loss'.[132] However, as Lord Steyn in the same case noted, the system might work well enough in cases where the injuries are relatively minor. 'But', he continued, 'the lump sum system causes acute problems in

---

[126] Lord Diplock in *The Albazero* [1977] AC 774, at 841.
[127] *Kuddus v Chief Constable of Leicestershire* [2002] 2 AC 122.
[128] *Transfield Shipping Inc v Mercator Shipping Inc* [2009] 1 AC 61.
[129] *Smith New Court Securities Ltd v Scrimgeour Vickers Ltd* [1997] AC 254.
[130] See eg *John v MGN Ltd* [1997] QB 586.
[131] But see now Courts Act 2003, ss 100–01; Lewis (2009).
[132] *Wells v Wells* [1999] 1 AC 345, at 390.

cases of serious injuries with consequences enduring after the assessment of damages' and in 'such cases the judge must often resort to guesswork about the future'.[133] The courts try to go beyond guesswork by resorting to tariffs (how much an arm is worth) and discount rates (multiplicand); they aim to be 'fair' and to achieve 'consistency',[134] although whether they always achieve this depends upon one's view of these terms. One of course must add that the lump sum system may be on the way out with respect to very serious personal injury awards.[135]

Some of the more specific questions are these. What if the claimant is rendered permanently unconscious: should he or she still be compensated for loss of amenity? The answer is that substantial damages can be awarded.[136] Should money received from public donations or from private accident insurance be taken into account when assessing damages for personal injuries? If such money results only because the claimant is the victim of an accident for which the tortfeasor is liable there is a clear cause and connection between damage and private compensation. Yet why should the tortfeasor benefit from the public's generosity or from the claimant's own prudence? The PETL state that when 'determining the amount of damages benefits which the injured party gains through the damaging event are to be taken into account unless this cannot be reconciled with the purpose of the benefit' (art 10:103); and this possibly represents English law, although much will depend upon how one interprets 'purpose of the benefit'.[137] Accidents also impact on the victim's family. If the victim is killed as a result of a tort, the dependents will have their own claim against the tortfeasor independent of any claim by the victim's estate.[138] But what if the victim is not killed and a family member gives up his or her job to look after the victim: is this loss recoverable? And, if so, by whom? The law of damages may well have to grant 'rights' by ricochet and thus the House of Lords has held that a carer can receive compensation via damages awarded to the victim but it will be held on trust for the carer.[139] If a victim has his life shortened as a result of the tortious damage he can

---

[133] *Wells v Wells* [1999] 1 AC 345, at 384.
[134] *Heil v Rankin* [2001] QB 272.
[135] Courts Act 2003, ss 100–01.
[136] *West (H) & Son Ltd v Shephard* [1964] AC 326.
[137] *Parry v Cleaver* [1970] AC 1; *Hussain v New Taplow Paper Mills Ltd* [1988] AC 514.
[138] Fatal Accidents Act 1976.
[139] *Hunt v Severs* [1994] 2 AC 350.

still be awarded damages for these lost years on the basis of protecting the interests of his dependents.[140]

Damage to property may seem very much easier to assess than damage to a human, but it is not without its own problems. Even if one starts out from the idea that property has a market value (PETL art 10:203(1)), it is not always easy to assess such value. Is the owner of a wrongfully destroyed factory or house entitled to full rebuilding cost, or just the difference in land value before and after the destruction? Is the owner of a wrongfully destroyed herd of pigs entitled to the replacement value or their sale value? Where the owner has been deprived of the use of a thing, damages may be awarded for this loss of use (PETL art 10:203(2)) and this could well prove more than the value of the thing itself.[141] The case law is not entirely consistent and much will depend upon the facts of an individual case together with the choices made by a claimant when faced with a destroyed commercial asset.

Severe psychological damage is regarded as a form of personal injury if suffered directly and thus can be compensated by an award of damages.[142] If suffered indirectly, the issue becomes one of the existence or non-existence of a duty of care and so is a 'causation' problem that functions at the level either of actionability[143] or remoteness.[144] Mental distress arising from pain and suffering and loss of amenity is recoverable if attached to physical personal injury; it is one of the heads of personal injury damage. However, more generally, mental injury (mental distress) is generally not considered to be 'damage' and is, then, not a well-protected interest.[145] Yet there are exceptions. It is a protected interest in certain contract situations where mental wellbeing is the object of the contract itself. Thus a holiday that turns out to be miserable as a result of a breach of contract will attract damages for mental distress[146] as will a contract with a surveyor specifically asked to report on aircraft nuisance.[147] Bereavement is recognised by statute as an interest in need of protection;[148] and aggravated damages awarded in, for example, a defamation case might also be viewed as a form of compensation for mental distress. Equally damages awarded for the

---

[140] *Pickett v British Rail Engineering Ltd* [1980] AC 126.
[141] *Mediana (The)* [1900] AC 113; *Liesbosch (The)* [1933] AC 449.
[142] *Page v Smith* [1996] 1 AC 155.
[143] *Alcock v Chief Constable of South Yorkshire* [1992] 1 AC 310.
[144] *Attia v British Gas Plc* [1988] QB 304.
[145] *Rothwell v Chemical & Insulating Co Ltd* [2008] 1 AC 281.
[146] *Jackson v Horizon Holidays Ltd* [1975] 1 WLR 1468.
[147] *Farley v Skinner* [2002] 2 AC 732.
[148] Fatal Accidents Act 1976, s 1A.

invasion of constitutional rights – for example false imprisonment – can be seen as compensating a mental interest, although awards by juries are now, thanks to legislation, controlled by the judges. This control has been exercised very much in the favour of defendants.[149] The police have, therefore, not escaped from liability when they wrongfully assault or imprison; but the judges have made their lives easier, perhaps to the detriment of constitutional and administrative law. The English law of tort has too many masters and it is the faithful servant to none of them. But can it ever be otherwise?

---

[149] *Thompson v Commissioner of Police for the Metropolis* [1998] QB 498.

16. Beyond contract and tort: restitution

The aim of this chapter is to move beyond contractual and tortious obligations and to look, briefly, at liability arising in situations where there is neither promise nor wrong. The need for a category, or categories, of obligation in addition to contract and delict (tort) was recognised, as we saw in an earlier chapter, even in Roman times. Having divided the law of obligations into contract and delict, the 2nd century jurist Gaius observed that there were some situations which could not be accommodated within this twofold division (G.3.91). This jurist subsequently added a third category of 'various causes' (D.44.7.1pr). The 6th century Byzantine jurists went further and added to contract and delict the two further categories of quasi-contract and quasi-delict.

LIABILITY FOR GAIN

Delictual (tortious) liability is on the whole concerned with damage and loss incurred by a claimant. The object of the action is to secure compensation and this is achieved through a liability to pay damages. It is a question of corrective justice, although in certain situations policy considerations might require an appeal to distributive justice.[1] Quasi-contractual (unjust enrichment) liability is different; here the emphasis is not on the claimant's loss or damage (although these may well be relevant), but on the defendant's gain. When viewed through the eyes of a common lawyer, the relevant action is more likely to be debt rather than damages since one is often seeking the repayment of a specific amount of money, although of course other remedies might be relevant as well.[2] In terms of moral philosophy, the remedy often responds more to distributive rather than corrective justice and this is one reason why the legislator has intervened.[3]

---

[1] *McFarlane v Tayside Health Board* [2000] 2 AC 59, at 82.
[2] See generally Lord Atkin in *United Australia Ltd v Barclays Bank Ltd* [1941] AC 1.
[3] Proceeds of Crime Act 2002.

The general principle governing liability in respect of a gain, since Roman times, is this: no one should be unjustly enriched at the expense of another (D.50.17.206). This principle would appear to contain several essential elements. There must be (i) an enrichment (ii) which is unjust (or *sans cause* in French law) and (iii) gained at the expense of another.[4] As with delictual liability, two approaches can be discerned. First, liability can be approached through a number of specific remedies or causes of action each of which is governed by its own set of rules. This was the Roman approach where liability depended on the availability of particular types of *actio*; and it is more or less the Roman approach that is to be found in the *Code civil* (*quasi contrats*: arts 1371–81).[5]

The use of the word 'contract' in this context comes from the idea that this kind of liability arises out of a situation 'as if' there was a contract between the parties.[6] This 'as if' idea was however to be problematic for some later civilians. Either a meeting of the minds existed or such a meeting did not exist; and if there was no *consensus* there could be no contract. Accordingly a second approach is one where liability rests directly on the unjust enrichment principle itself.[7] In German law, for example, liability is based on such a general principle (BGB § 812), though the practical application of this code paragraph is not always easy.

English law has recently recognised these enrichment claims as falling under a liability that is neither contractual nor tortious.[8] Nevertheless contract, tort and unjust enrichment can overlap in situations where a defendant has for example profited from a breach of contract or a tort. If the claimant has suffered damage equivalent to the gain there is no problem since the remedy of damages will normally solve the problem (corrective justice). Difficulties occur when the claimant has suffered no damage. In this situation the English judges have turned to equity: a person who profits from a wrong but causes no damage to the victim of a breach of contract or a tort might be held liable in equity via its remedy of account of profits (distributive justice).[9] Some commentators regard this situation as an example of restitutionary damages, but this is an error since account is an equitable debt claim rather than a damages remedy.

The distinction between common law and equity, and between rights and remedies, might seem to make restitution a complex area of law

---

[4] *Cressman v Coys of Kensington (Sales) Ltd* [2004] 1 WLR 2775, at para 22.
[5] Terré, Simler and Lequette (2002), at 998–9.
[6] *Ibid*, at 973.
[7] *Ibid*, at 998ff.
[8] See eg *Kleinwort Benson Ltd v Glasgow CC* [1999] 1 AC 153.
[9] *Att-Gen v Blake* [2001] 1 AC 268.

and to an extent it is. But despite these complexities, the Scottish Law Commission has made a major contribution to the unjust enrichment approach to liability for gain in that it has produced a set of Draft Rules on Unjustified Enrichment based upon the general principle (see rule 1).[10] In the absence (as yet) of any other international or European (as opposed to national) code, these draft principles might act as a useful starting point for a general approach which shifts the emphasis off remedies and onto more substantive ideas.

ENRICHMENT

The Draft Rules deal first of all with enrichment which it defines as an 'economic benefit' (rule 2(1)). It goes on to state that a person is enriched 'if his net worth is increased or is prevented from being decreased' (rule 2(2)); and it illustrates this with four examples. These are acquiring money or other property; having value added to property; being freed in whole or in part from an obligation; or being saved from loss or expenditure. These examples can usefully be compared with similar provisions identified in the civil law, but it should not be thought that the notion of enrichment does not present serious problems in either system.

In one English case the purchaser of a motor car discovered six months after the purchase that he had no title to the vehicle and he thus had to surrender it to the real owner. The purchaser successfully sued the vendor in debt for return of the purchase price, which of course meant that he had had six months free use of the car.[11] Did this six months amount to an enrichment (cf Draft Rules rule 3(4))? In another case a householder was held to be justified in refusing to pay for a central heating system that would not work.[12] Did he nevertheless receive an enrichment in respect of the boiler, pipes, radiators and the like? Another problem mentioned in a French textbook is the child who receives private lessons from a teacher who is unable to recover payment because the parents have become bankrupt.[13] Has the child been enriched? A further problem is one that has been discussed with respect to the English law of frustration.[14] A claimant contractor renders services which improve the defendant's house; however, before the services are complete, the house is destroyed by lightning. Has

---

[10] Scottish Law Commission DP No 99.
[11] *Rowland v Divall* [1923] 2 KB 500.
[12] *Bolton v Mahadeva* [1972] 1 WLR 1009.
[13] Terré, Simler and Lequette (2002), at 1001.
[14] On which see Law Reform (Frustrated Contracts) Act 1943.

the defendant been enriched or has the enrichment disappeared with the house? This problem may become more acute where there is no contract to render services but the claimant interferes to protect the house while the owner is absent. Here it could be said that any claim ought to be measured with respect, not to the expenditure by the claimant, but to the enrichment of the defendant (D.3.5.6.3; cf D.3.5.10.1; D.3.5.22).

This problem of deciding what amounts to 'enrichment' is as complex as the problem of trying to determine what amounts to 'damage'. The danger with putting too much emphasis on the fact of enrichment is that policy considerations that attach say to the law of contract can become undermined if one then introduces a whole new set of rules that attach, independently, to gain. In *Bolton v Mahadeva*[15] the policy that a non-performer cannot claim the contract price is perfectly coherent with regard both to the law of contract itself and to the law of consumer protection. Suggesting that the victim of the non-performance has gained an unjustified enrichment simply undermines this dual policy factor, a point seemingly recognised in a recent House of Lords decision.[16]

Of course, there are situations where focusing on the gain rather than on the apparent policy of contract or tort law can be valuable. For example, allowing an insurance company to be subrogated to the rights of a tort party whose liability it has covered so that it can pursue any other potential defendant can result in a situation where the loss-spreading aim of tort is undermined by an apparent unjustified enrichment. Thus in one famous case, where a careless employee injured a co-employee, the employer, having been held vicariously liable to the co-employee, was allowed to recoup the damages paid out from the employee at fault.[17] Given that the real claimant was the employer's insurance company, the point can be made – and was made by several tort specialists – that the loss-spreading aim of tort law was undermined by an insurance company who had in truth been paid to carry this very risk.[18] An independent law of restitution, focusing on unjust enrichment, might well have concluded that the insurance company ought to be denied its remedy of subrogation on the basis that in such a situation other potential defendants of the tort victim have not suffered an *unjust* enrichment by not having to make contribution. The loss should fall uniquely on the insurance company since they had been paid to carry this very risk (damage arising out of

---

[15] [1972] 1 WLR 1009.
[16] *Wilson v First County Trust Ltd (No 2)* [2004] 1 AC 816.
[17] *Lister v Romford Ice & Cold Storage Co Ltd* [1957] AC 555.
[18] cf *Morris v Ford Motor Co Ltd* [1973] 1 QB 792.

accidents caused by employees of the insured). Enrichment, in brief, is a delicate term that often transgresses the frontier between corrective and distributive justice.

EXPENSE OF ANOTHER

The second requirement is the impoverishment of another. According to the Draft Rules there is enrichment at the expense of another 'if it is the direct result of' a payment, grant, transfer, incurring of liability, or rendering of services by another person to the enriched person (rule 3). This transfer may be in fulfilment of an obligation of the enriched person; in adding value to the enriched person's property; in acquiring some other economic benefit for the enriched person; or in any other case where there is an interference with the patrimonial rights of the other person otherwise than by operation of natural forces (rule 3(1)). Such an interference will include for example the unauthorised use of property belonging to another; but it will not include a mere breach of contract (rule 3(2)). Thus if D uses C's property while C is away, and unknown to C, it may well be that D will be liable to C for a commercial hire fee.[19]

One possible problem is illustrated by the case of the wine seller who sells as litres of wine, bottles that in fact contain only 98 centilitres. The seller after several years makes a huge profit out of this wrongful behaviour, but the loss to each individual consumer is so small as to amount to no loss at all. The benefit is at the expense of the consumers only as a class, but if the wine seller is to be relieved of the profit who should sue? One might note on this the recent English case of *Att-Gen v Blake* [20] where the equitable remedy of account of profits was used to deprive a person of a wrongful profit even although the claimant had suffered no damage. However the claimant here was the government and thus the extracted profit did not go into a private patrimony. Perhaps all unjust gains made from criminal conduct can now be retrieved by a government agency in criminal and (or) civil proceedings thanks to the Proceeds of Crime Act 2002. This statute has the potential to replace a large part of the private law of restitution for wrongs, thus making the non-statutory remedies of restitutionary damages, account and tracing largely irrelevant.

---

[19] *Strand Electric Co Ltd v Brisford Entertainments Ltd* [1952] 2 QB 246.
[20] [2001] 1 AC 268.

'UNJUST' (*SANS CAUSE*)

The final element of the principle is that the enrichment must be unjust. In civil law this is often rather differently described as being '*sans cause*',[21] but the Draft Rules indicate that the two terms are seemingly synonymous in that rule 4 states that an 'enrichment is unjustified unless it is justified under rules 5 or 6'. And rule 5 is headed 'Enrichment justified by legal cause'. In French law an enrichment will be *sans cause* 'when there is no legal mechanism, no legal title – statutory, agreement, judicial – which can justify the flow of value from the patrimony of the person impoverished to the person enriched'.[22] Rule 5 of the Draft Rules list these causes, which are much the same as those in French law, although there is added at the end of the list 'or (g) some other legal cause'. An enrichment is therefore 'justified' if the enriched person is entitled to it by virtue of a statutory provision, rule of law or court decree; or as a result of a contract, will, trust, gift or some other legal cause (rule 5(1)).

The rule makes explicit, also, that the mere acquisition of title does not in itself mean that the enrichment is justified (rule 5(4)). Rule 6 states that an enrichment can be justified by public policy. These include incidental benefits enjoyed by another when one person undertakes work and expenditure for himself (cf D.3.5.6.3),[23] together with various other examples of what in English law is often referred to as a voluntary payment. 'Voluntary' and 'policy' in this context have perhaps a moral dimension.[24] One interesting situation is where a debtor repays a debt and, having paid, discovers that the debt was in fact statute-barred; no recovery is possible here if the creditor had himself performed his obligation which created the debt (rule 6(c)). A civil lawyer might talk here of a 'natural obligation'. Another example in the English case law of a voluntary payment is *Regalian Properties Plc v London Docklands Development Corpn* where 'pending the conclusion of a binding contract any cost incurred by [a potential party] in preparation for the intended contract will be incurred at his own risk, in the sense that he will have no recompense for those costs if no contract results'.[25] Things might be different if one party expressly or impliedly requests the other to perform services or supply goods in anticipation of a contract that never actually materialises.[26]

---

[21] Terré, Simler and Lequette (2002), at 1002–4.
[22] *Ibid.*
[23] *Ibid*, at 1005–6.
[24] *Ibid*, at 1005.
[25] [1995] 1 WLR 212, at 231 per Rattee J.
[26] *British Steel Corporation v Cleveland Bridge & Engineering Co Ltd* [1984] 1 All ER 504.

Several difficult cases remain. What if a window cleaner mistakenly cleans the windows of the wrong house: must the householder who benefits pay? In English law the answer is traditionally, and sensibly, that payment is refused on the basis that liabilities cannot be forced upon people behind their backs. Nevertheless some have argued that the householder should pay on the basis of an analogy with a mistaken payment; if C by mistake gives D too much change D is under a clear obligation to return the overpayment. Why should services be different? One answer is that services are different and cannot be valued in the same way as money.[27] Another difficult problem is where a contractor only partly performs his contract. The part performance, even where it does not amount to substantial performance, may nevertheless confer a benefit on the aggrieved party. Should the latter be under an unjust enrichment obligation to repay? English law would appear once again to deny liability.[28]

REMEDIES AND UNJUST ENRICHMENT

This approach to unjust enrichment liability through the principle itself is, as far as the common law is concerned, rather misleading. The subject has been, and to an extent still is, very much remedy-driven which means that rules attach as much to damages, debt, account, subrogation, tracing and the like as to any substantive law of obligation relationship. In turn these remedies can cut across, say, the frontier between owing and owning, between contract and tort and between law and equity. Quasi-contract in English law has, for example, traditionally focused on the three non-contractual debt remedies of an action for money had and received, an action for money paid, and an action on a *quantum meruit*. And while these debt actions are clearly *in personam*, they can sometimes be based on an *in rem* (proprietary) substantive right because a debt, as a chose in action, is a form of property.[29] In addition equity offers its own independent *in rem* claim called 'tracing'; a claimant can reclaim money in another's bank account on the basis, not of an obligation, but of ownership.[30] The claimant simply asserts that the money in another's patrimony is his property.

---

[27] cf Terré, Simler and Lequette (2002), at 1006–7.
[28] *Bolton v Mahadeva* [1972] 1 WLR 1009.
[29] *Lipkin Gorman v Karpnale Ltd* [1991] 2 AC 548. And see Proceeds of Crime Act 2002, s 316(4)(c).
[30] See *Agip (Africa) Ltd v Jackson* [1990] Ch 265 (ChD); [1991] Ch 547 (CA). And see Proceeds of Crime Act 2002, ss 304–10.

Action of Money Had and Received

Returning to the three quasi-contractual claims, the first is an action for money had and received which in some ways resembles, indeed may even have taken its 19th century motivation, from the old Roman *condictio*. It is thus available for the return of money paid under a mistake of fact, under compulsion or under a transaction whose consideration has wholly failed. For example, where a bank mistakenly credits a customer's account the bank can, in principle, recover such an amount via an action for money had and received.[31] Equally if a person pays over money to another on the basis of a 'contract' that later turns out to be void the payer can recover the money using this common law action.[32] Furthermore the action for money had and received is available in situations where the defendant has received money from a third party of which account ought to be made to the claimant,[33] and where the defendant has profited at the claimant's expense through the commission of an unlawful act. In this latter situation the action for money had and received might be a useful alternative to a damages claim for breach of statutory duty. Thus where the defendant has made a profit from his crime, the common law claim will be available to recover the illegal profit,[34] although it is likely that the equitable remedy of account will now be more relevant.[35] An action for money had and received is, then, likely to be the main claim in situations where a claimant has transferred, directly or indirectly, to a defendant a sum of money which in all the circumstances it would be unjust for the defendant to keep.[36]

Action for Money Paid

The second form of quasi-contractual debt claim is available in cases where the defendant has received a benefit by reason of money paid by the claimant to a third party. This claim is useful in situations where the claimant has paid money on the defendant's behalf in circumstances of necessity and thus it can resemble the Roman action of *negotiorum gestio* which allowed the good neighbour who unofficiously intervened to protect

---

[31] *United Overseas Bank v Jiwani* [1977] 1 All ER 733.
[32] *Westdeutsche Landesbank Girozentrale v Islington LBC* [1996] AC 669.
[33] *Lipkin Gorman v Karpnale Ltd* [1991] 2 AC 548, at 572–3.
[34] *Reading v Att-Gen* [1951] AC 507.
[35] *Att-Gen v Guardian Newspapers (No 2)* [1990] AC 109; *Att-Gen v Blake* [2001] 1 AC 268.
[36] *Kleinwort Benson Ltd v Lincoln CC* [1999] 2 AC 349.

the property of another to recover his expenses.[37] However in contrast to *negotiorum gestio* the action for money paid is probably available only in situations where there is some pre-existing relationship between the parties such as agency or bailment. Thus the existence of a factual emergency will not *per se* be enough to give rise to quasi-contractual liability.[38] The action for money paid is also available in situations where the claimant has been compelled by law to pay money on behalf of another. Thus if O stores goods in P's bonded warehouse O will, prima facie, be liable to reimburse P for any duties that P might be forced to pay in respect of the goods.[39] Whether or not this liability will be incurred in situations where the compulsion is moral rather than legal is a more difficult question. In *Owen v Tate* Scarman LJ said that if 'without an antecedent request a person assumes an obligation or makes a payment for the benefit of another, the law will, as a general rule, refuse him a right of indemnity.' However if the person 'can show that in the particular circumstances of the case there was some necessity for the obligation to be assumed, then the law will grant him a right of reimbursement if in all the circumstances it is just and reasonable to do so'.[40]

Quantum Meruit

The third form of debt claim is available, together with its sister *quantum valebat*, to recover money for services or for property supplied to the defendant. However it must be remembered that it is an established principle of English law that the mere rendering of services or property to another is not enough, in itself, to give rise to restitutionary liability since 'liabilities are not to be forced upon people behind their backs'.[41] For example if P cleans D's windows without D's permission and with no pre-arranged course of dealing, P will not be able to claim any money. Accordingly in a *quantum meruit* or *valebat* action the claimant must normally show that the defendant expressly or impliedly requested, or at least he freely accepted, the services or goods in question.[42] If such services or goods were rendered pursuant to a contract incompletely performed then it is unlikely that the courts would allow a quasi-contractual claim unless there is evidence that the defendant had agreed to accept

---

[37] Zimmermann (1996), at 433–50.
[38] *The Winson* [1982] AC 939; *In Re F* [1990] 2 AC 1.
[39] *Brook's Wharf & Bull Wharf Ltd v Goodman Brothers* [1937] 1 KB 534.
[40] [1975] 2 All ER 129, at 135.
[41] *Falcke v Scottish Imperial Insurance Co* (1886) 34 Ch D 234, at 248.
[42] *Sumpter v Hedges* [1898] 1 QB 673.

incomplete performance. But where services have been rendered under a void contract the court will in principle allow a quasi-contractual action for their value[43] provided that the principle of restitution takes account of any policy considerations which underlie the rule that makes the contract void, illegal or unenforceable. The courts are not prepared indirectly to enforce certain contracts that statute has made illegal or void.[44] One exception to the general principle of services performed without prior request is maritime salvage. One who saves another's ship or cargo is entitled to reward from the owners of the ship or cargo. This is a true restitution claim in as much as the entitlement is measured in terms of the property saved and thus the salvor who fails to save the defendant's ship is entitled to nothing since the defendant has not been enriched by the salvor's (intervenor's) act.

Defences

Given that most of these non-contractual debt claims have their foundation, traditionally speaking, in the law of actions rather than in some rationalised structure of restitutionary rights, it has not been that easy to develop a coherent set of defences to such claims. Furthermore the vagueness of the whole area (of 'unjust' enrichment) has also meant that defences have tended to become swallowed up by the discretionary nature of the 'right' itself. However there have been developments. A claimant who, in full knowledge of a possible ground on which to contest liability, nevertheless pays a claimed debt in consequence of a deliberate decision not to contest the claim may be met with the defence of voluntary payment should he ever wish to claim restitution.[45] And a defendant who can show that he has changed his position as a result of the payment – for example by giving the money in question to a charity – now has a substantive defence provided he can show that he was neither a wrongdoer nor one who has paid in bad faith.[46] It must be stressed, however, that merely showing that the money received has been paid to some third party will not of itself amount to the defence of change of position.[47]

---

[43] *Craven-Ellis v Canons Ltd* [1936] 2 KB 403.
[44] *Orakpo v Manson Investments Ltd* [1978] AC 95.
[45] *R v Tower Hamlets LBC, Ex p. Chetnik Ltd* [1988] AC 858, at 880–1, 882–3.
[46] *Lipkin Gorman v Karpnale Ltd* [1991] 2 AC 548.
[47] *Lipkin Gorman v Karpnale Ltd* [1991] 2 AC 548, at 580.

EQUITABLE REMEDIES

In addition to the quasi-contractual debt claims, equity has available a number of remedies that can be used to prevent unjust enrichment. Indeed, it might be said that the idea of unjust enrichment is one of the great motivating principles of Chancery and so each time equity intervenes in the area of contractual obligations it could be said that it is preventing a means of justified enrichment being turned into, because of say undue influence or misrepresentation, a vehicle of unjustified enrichment. Such intervention can be positive or negative in operation. It is positive when equity grants a remedy such as rectification, rescission or injunction; it is negative when it refuses to grant, for example, specific performance or injunction. In other words equity can simply refuse to order the performance of a contract and this will have the effect of forcing the contractor demanding performance to sue for damages at common law.[48] If such a contractor cannot show damage, or is deemed to be the cause of his own loss, the common law court, again perhaps reflecting the principle of unjust enrichment, will award only nominal damages.[49]

What equity cannot normally do, although there are statutory exceptions, is to award damages since there does not appear to have any inherent jurisdiction to award this remedy.[50] Accordingly it cannot restore an enrichment through the protection of the restitutionary interest by means of a compensation claim as such. What it has is the remedy of account which can be used to extract unjustified profits or receipts of money. Indeed the remedy of account has been specifically described as an equitable debt claim and it is of use in situations where the parties are in a fiduciary relationship.[51] It may also be available as an alternative to an action for money had and received where one person has profited from a wrong at the expense of another or in exceptional situations where other normal remedies prove inadequate.[52]

The principle of unjust enrichment can cut across, then, such established boundaries as the one between common law and equity and property and obligations. Another boundary is the one between tort liability in damages and unjust enrichment liability in debt. Where a victim suffers damage

---

[48] See eg *Co-operative Insurance Society Ltd v Argyll Stores Ltd* [1998] AC 1.
[49] See eg *The Albazero* [1977] AC 774.
[50] *Jaggard v Sawyer* [1995] 1 WLR 269.
[51] *English v Dedham Vale Properties* [1978] 1 All ER 382.
[52] *Att-Gen v Blake* [2001] 1 AC 268.

as a result of a breach of contract or a tort by more than one defendant, the victim can sue any particular defendant for all his damage (unless the damage itself is causally apportioned between two or more defendants).[53] However the defendant condemned to pay has a statutory right to 'recover contribution from any other person liable in respect of the same damage'.[54] Thus in the terrible Selby train disaster, where a driver fell asleep at the wheel of his car and his vehicle ended up on a railway line in front of an oncoming train, the driver's insurance company was liable to all the victims. The insurance company attempted, unsuccessfully, to gain contribution from the highway authority on the basis, so it was argued, that the authority's inadequate road barriers contributed to the accident. Had they been held to be at fault and a part cause of the train crash, they may well have had to contribute to the final compensation bill. This contribution right is not, strictly speaking, an equitable remedy since its source is statute. Yet the principles are based on what is 'just and equitable' and so it is not unreasonable to see the claim for contribution as being one closer to account than quasi-contract.

Another area where equity, restitution and tort come together is subrogation which has been described as a remedy rather than a cause of action.[55] However it would be better to see it as an institutional structure rather than as a remedy defined and governed by rules. Subrogation is based on a formal relationship either between two persons or between a person and a thing and is a means by which one thing or one person is substituted for another thing or person without the actual form of the relationship changing. There are thus two forms: real subrogation is where one object is substituted for another object and personal subrogation is where one person 'stands in the shoes' of another person. Take for example the situation where D owes C a debt and this debt is secured on D's house. If S pays off C with his own money the law may on occasions allow S to become subrogated to C's position with the result that S 'stands in the shoes' of C and takes over the security attached to D's house. The form of the legal structure stays the same, but an individual part changes. Subrogation plays a central role in the English law of obligations since it is the means by which an insurance company is able to gain access to the courts. Thus in many tort cases the real claimant or defendant is not the named party but an insurance company subrogated to the rights of the insured named party.

---

[53] *Rahman v Arearose Ltd* [2001] QB 351.
[54] Civil Liability (Contribution) Act 1978, s 1.
[55] *Boscawen v Bajwa* [1996] 1 WLR 328.

TRACING

A more developed equitable 'quasi' monetary remedy central to restitution is the remedy of tracing. This, seemingly, is a remedy founded not on an obligation right as such (*ius in personam*) but on a right *in rem*; the claimant entitled to trace is held to be the owner of the money claimed from the defendant's patrimony. An equitable tracing action is thus an *actio in rem*. In truth the exact status of tracing is, today, not easy to discern. For it has been asserted recently that tracing 'is neither a claim nor a remedy but a process' which 'is not confined to the case where the plaintiff seeks a proprietary remedy; it is equally necessary where he seeks a personal remedy against the knowing recipient or knowing assistant'.[56] In addition to the equitable remedy of tracing, common law also recognises the notion of tracing. However, once again, it is by no means so clear whether this action is a claim *in rem* in the full Roman sense of the term.

A claim in equitable tracing is associated with the trust. Indeed it started out as a means of protection accorded by the Court of Chancery to the beneficiary of a trust and this helps explain its proprietary nature.[57] The remedy depends upon the continued existence of the trust property in the patrimony of the defendant, but the latter will have a complete defence if he can show that he is a *bona fide* purchaser for value without notice or that he has innocently changed his position.[58] One great advantage of tracing in equity over its counterpart in common law is that money can be traced into a mixed fund. However if the defendant has parted with the trust property he will not be liable to an action for account in equity unless it can be shown that he disposed of the money knowing of the existence of the trust. Moreover there must at some point have existed a fiduciary relationship which gives rise to the equitable jurisdiction to intervene.[59]

In the field of restitution, the law of equitable tracing was once particularly important in those situations where, because of the implied contract theory underpinning quasi-contractual claims, common law debt was unavailable. The key case was *Sinclair v Brougham*[60] in which depositors of money in a building society found that their contracts were void because the society had been acting *ultra vires*. When the depositors tried to recover their money in an action for money had and received they were met with the argument,

---

[56] *Boscawen v Bajwa* [1996] 1 WLR 328, at 334 per Millett LJ.
[57] Lawson (1980), at 147–60.
[58] *Boscawen v Bajwa* [1996] 1 WLR 328, 334.
[59] See generally *Agip (Africa) Ltd v Jackson* [1991] Ch 547, 566; *Boscawen v Bajwa* [1996] 1 WLR 328, 335.
[60] [1914] AC 398.

accepted by the House of Lords, that these claims were invalid since they were based on implied contracts which themselves must be equally void. In order to get around this logic the House of Lords allowed the depositors to trace their money in equity on the basis that the society held the money as trustees under a resulting trust. The actual solution was no doubt equitable enough, but, being claims based on equitable ownership, it meant that the depositors were in effect privileged creditors which put them in an advantageous position vis-à-vis the position they would have had had the contracts been valid. *Sinclair v Brougham* has now been overruled on the ground that the implied contract theory is no longer the basis for a quasi-contractual personal claim.[61] Accordingly, if the facts of *Sinclair* were to arise again, the depositors would be entitled to an action for money had and received. As several writers have pointed out, the problem with the equitable remedy of tracing, in the context of the law of restitution, is that it seems to cover many of the same factual situations as the common law action for money had and received.[62] Does the claimant who has paid over money in a situation where the contract turns out to be void have an *in rem* or just an *in personam* remedy? Whatever the final answer, the confusion at the level of remedies indicates, once again, the difficulty of isolating a law of obligations from a law of property.[63] At this level of remedies the distinction between *owing* and *owning* is functional rather than conceptual.

Tracing at common law is, in some ways, an even more difficult concept than tracing in equity because there is no actual *in rem* remedy at common law which itself gives expression to the property right. The actions are all *in personam* claims in damages, debt or, in the case of a chattel, one of the property torts.[64] This is mainly because English law has no concept of ownership in the civil law sense of the term of a direct relationship between person and thing (CC art 544). Remedies dealing with the protection of property are based largely on possession. Thus tracing goods is achieved through the tort of conversion, which is an action for damages based upon the interference with a right of property; however this 'right of property' is in the end determined through the better right to possession.[65] Now there is no doubt that such a property right is, at a substantive level, independent from the obligation relationship just as bailment is independent of contract.[66] But at the level of remedies the actions which give expression to the

---

[61] *Westdeutsche Landesbank Girozentrale v Islington LBC* [1996] AC 669.
[62] See eg Burrows (1995).
[63] cf Ibbetson (1999), at 290–3.
[64] See the Torts (Interference with Goods) Act 1977.
[65] See Weir (2004), at 483–7.
[66] *Bowmakers Ltd v Barnet Instruments Ltd* [1945] KB 65.

property right are all classed as torts with the result that there is confusion between the law of obligations and the law of actions. Equally the tracing of money is effected through an action for money had and received which, again, is a personal rather than a real remedy. Thus it has been said that while a claimant may have no proprietary *remedy* at common law, he may have a proprietary *claim*.[67]

PRESENT STATUS OF RESTITUTION

Given all the different quasi-contractual and equitable remedies which appear to be designed to prevent unjust enrichment, it is not difficult to claim that there exists in England the general principle of unjust enrichment. This claim becomes even stronger when one looks at the historical basis of the common law which for many centuries thought in terms of debt and trespass (damages) rather than in terms of a strict dichotomy between contract and tort. Debt, as Lord Atkin pointed out, 'was not necessarily based upon the existence of a contract'.[68] And even with the adoption of the civilian categories of contract and tort the need for an independent law of restitution founded on the principle of unjust enrichment did, as Lord Wright subsequently pointed out, not diminish.[69]

However the problem became one of looking for a conceptual basis upon which one could found a duty to repay a debt in situations where there was no actual wrong. Such a conceptual basis was found in the existing law of contract: 'for there was no action possible other than debt or assumpsit on the one side and action for damages for tort on the other'. And the 'action . . . for money had and received . . . was therefore supported by the imputation by the Court to the defendant of a promise to repay'.[70] This notion of an implied contract no doubt worked well enough in a range of cases, but it could create logical difficulties in certain situations. For example, as we have already seen, if an enriched defendant was, as a matter of law, incapable of making contracts through a lack of capacity, it logically followed that no contract could be implied and thus no quasi-contractual action allowable.[71] This implied contract theory

---

[67] *Jones & Sons v Jones* [1997] Ch 159, at 168.
[68] *United Australia Ltd v Barclays Bank Ltd* [1941] AC 1, at 26.
[69] *Fibrosa Spolka Akcyjna v Fairbairn Lawson Combe Barbour Ltd* [1943] AC 32, at 61.
[70] Lord Atkin in *United Australia Ltd v Barclays Bank Ltd* [1941] AC 1, at 27.
[71] *Sinclair v Brougham* [1914] AC 398.

has now been abandoned, but its replacement with a theory based upon a property right in the debt owed is just as much a fiction and may well cause problems for the future.[72] Consequently the idea of a general action based directly upon the Roman unjust enrichment principle has, for some, become attractive.

There is no doubt now that the principle exists as the basis for a category within the law of obligations quite independent of those of contract and tort.[73] Accordingly the principle seems to have been used as the basis for decision in a few cases and it even appears in a modern statute.[74] Yet it would be wrong to say that the principle exists in England as a *direct* source of obligations. What does exist are a number of *in personam* and *in rem* remedies which can be used, *inter alia*, to prevent unjust enrichment.[75] In other words, if there is a principle of unjust enrichment, it is a principle that operates only through the existing categories of substantive law. It operates through contract, tort, equity or bailment and through certain 'empirical' remedies belonging to the law of actions (action for money had and received, tracing, subrogation and the like). To go further than this would be to introduce a general enrichment action similar to the one found in German and Dutch law, and this would run counter to the traditional *mentalité* of English method and reasoning. Merely because enrichment is something of a mirror image of damage, it does not follow that the two are in a symmetrical relationship. Causing damage, for example, is not a goal of society even if it is a by-product, whereas personal and corporate enrichment is a specific goal. Those that cut corners and cause damage are not necessarily in the same class as those that cut corners to enrich themselves, particularly where the enrichment causes no specific loss to a specific legal person.[76]

What is valuable about unjust enrichment is that it provides a substantive idea to underpin non-contractual debt actions in much the same way as 'tort' provides a basis for non-contractual damages actions. Tort, however, is not a normative idea in itself; it is simply a general category or common denominator containing, or underpinning, a range of independent causes of action (trespass, negligence, nuisance, defamation and so on). Unjust enrichment should be viewed in a similar way. Consequently what is important from a normative position is the remedy or cause of action (or even 'process') that is relevant to the factual situation. This means, in turn,

---

[72] *Lipkin Gorman v Karpnale Ltd* [1991] 2 AC 548.
[73] *Kleinwort Benson Ltd v Glasgow CC* [1999] 1 AC 153, at 184–5.
[74] Torts (Interference with Goods) Act 1977, s. 7(4).
[75] *Lipkin Gorman v Karpnale Ltd* [1991] 2 AC 548, at 578.
[76] See eg, *Surrey CC v Bredero Homes Ltd* [1993] 1 WLR 1361

that, from a law of obligations position, it continues to be important to think both in abstract (unjust enrichment) and in concrete terms (remedy, cause of action). But this, of course, is typical of English law. As a Court of Appeal judge put it, now that 'the mists have cleared still further' one can recognise 'that these different forms [of action] spring from a single underlying principle, which is described as the right to recover on grounds of unjust enrichment; that is to say, the defendant has been unjustly enriched by the payment made to him and which the plaintiff seeks to recover'.[77]

---

[77] *Kleinwort Benson Ltd v Birmingham CC* [1997] QB 380, at 386. Note that recovery is now possible for mistakes of law: *Kleinwort Benson Ltd v Lincoln CC* [1999] 2 AC 349.

17. Transnational law of obligations?

The adoption by common lawyers of, first, the categories of contract, tort and (later) unjust enrichment, and then, secondly, of the civilian generic category of the law of obligations goes far in suggesting, if not actually implying, the possibility of European harmonisation of private law. This possibility was given added impetus not only by the European Parliament's calls in 1989 and 1994 for the elaboration of a European civil code,[1] but by the completion and publication of the *Principles of European Contract Law* (PECL) and the *Principles of European Tort Law* (PETL). In addition, there seems to be considerable doctrinal support, among civil lawyers if not among those trained in the common law tradition, for increasing harmonisation. For example, in 1994 a collaborative work *Towards a European Civil Code* (now in its third edition) was published in English by a Dutch academic press.[2] This collaborative work, while accepting that harmonisation of private law was not yet a realistic project, nevertheless viewed with 'enthusiasm' the possibility of a European code capable of acting as a framework and a 'source of inspiration' for convergence.[3]

However, in the face of some hostility, the idea of a civil code has now been replaced by a European Commission Action Plan which proposes a Common Frame of Reference (CFR) containing inter alia the fundamental principles of European Contract Law. Although it is unlikely that the PECL/CFR will, in the foreseeable future, replace the present English law of contract,[4] codes such as the PECL remain of importance for legal education purposes, in particular for those studying the comparative law of obligations. It is the purpose of this concluding chapter to reflect not just upon English law in the context of a European law of obligations, but more importantly upon the complex theoretical issues and debates that lie beneath any attempt at harmonisation of the law of obligations.

---

[1] Resolution of 26 May 1989 OJEC No C 158/401 of June 26 1989; EP 207 670/13 [1994] OJ C 205/518.
[2] Hartkamp *et al* (2004).
[3] Hondius (2004), at 16.
[4] Ashton (Baroness) (2006).

POSSIBILITY OF HARMONISATION

Similarity and difference is often a question of degree and it would thus be idle to suggest that between all the legal systems of Europe there is an absence of much that is common.[5] Contract in France and in England might well be based upon different starting points, but the idea of a *vinculum iuris* between two persons acting as a form of private legislation is a notion that, more or less, is probably shared by many French and English lawyers. Or, put another way, a law of enforceable agreements is something that the common law would be happy to accept even if promise and consideration turn out to be quite different ideas than *conventio* and *causa*. In addition, the principles of wrongfully caused harm and unjustly acquired benefits act, at varying degrees of abstraction (even within the civilian systems), as direct or indirect normative motivators of damages and debt claims throughout the European Union.

Of course, from an historical position it has to be said that at first sight there appears to be little in common between the civil and the common law. Yet according to Reinhard Zimmermann 'a common European legal culture, centred around a common legal science and informed by the same sources, did once exist'.[6] Up until the 17th century there was the tradition of the *ius commune* which gave Europe a common legal grammar and this common grammar informed not only all the systems of the civilian tradition, but also endowed English law with a certain European character.[7] Indeed Zimmermann castigates Baker's statement that 'English law flourished in noble isolation from Europe'[8] as a complete myth.[9] In reality, says Zimmermann, English legal thought was never cut off from the continental culture in that Roman law, canon law and the *lex mercatoria* all influenced aspects of English and Scottish legal literature. Moreover in the 18th and 19th centuries the links between civil and common law were particularly strong.[10] Accordingly, the possibility that Roman law could act as a means for achieving European legal unity is 'a programmatic topic'. Legal historians can contribute to harmonisation by 'fostering an awareness that a common legal tradition (which has indelibly been imprinted by Roman law) still informs our modern national legal systems'. A new *ius commune*, asserts the author, can be carved out of a common systematic,

---

[5] On this point see the comments by John Merryman: Legrand (1999), at 42.
[6] Zimmermann (2004), at 24. See also Zimmermann (1996a).
[7] Zimmermann (2006), at 69, 75ff.
[8] Baker (2002), at 29.
[9] Zimmermann (2006), at 75.
[10] On this point see also Stein (1988).

conceptual, dogmatic and ideological foundation which has been buried under the debris of legal particularisation over the past 200 years. And a renewed intellectual contact can be made between positive law, comparative law, doctrinal legal scholarship – 'a contact which has largely been disrupted by the modern codifications'.[11]

HARMONISATION THROUGH SCIENCE AND SYSTEM

Given the very different procedural structure of the common law before the 20th century – in particular the central role of the jury – and given the absence of law faculties in England teaching the common law before 1846, much of what Professor Zimmermann asserts is probably at best an exaggeration.[12] Yet behind his thesis and its insistence that a knowledge of Roman law remains vital to any harmonisation project,[13] there does emerge an important issue. This issue has been articulated by Alan Watson in his assertion about the central role of the *Institutes of Justinian* in the formation of the civil law tradition in modern Europe and beyond.[14]

Watson argues that the importance of Roman law lies in the way it has shaped modern civilian national laws in terms of their systematisation and legal attitudes.[15] What got transferred to Europe were not just concepts and rules but a whole legal structure which could then be discussed 'quite independently of any original setting . . . in a specific historical, political, social, and economic context.'[16] Indeed the structure itself became a fundamental foundation of legal knowledge with the result that it transcended Roman culture to form the basis of the *ius commune*, the *ius naturale* and the *scientia iuris*.[17] Watson thus emphasises the importance of Gaius whose institutional system (see Chapter 1) acted, from the 11th century onwards, as 'both the gateway to knowledge of the law, and also the organising instrument of the developing systems',[18] bequeathing 'the basic structure

---

[11] Zimmermann (2006), at 80.
[12] See in particular Baker (2003), at 48–52.
[13] Zimmermann (1996a), at 597.
[14] See eg Watson (1994).
[15] Watson (1981), at 15.
[16] *Ibid*, at 19.
[17] See generally Stein (1999). Note also Stein (1980), at 123.
[18] Watson (1994), at 10.

to Napoleon's *Code civil*,[19] and then to the subsequent European codes.[20] The important point to emerge from this argument goes to the heart of what might be called the epistemological (theory of knowledge) debate about 'legal transplants' and is this. That there exists a 'system' that transcends particular cultures and as a result can be regarded as 'natural' in as much as such a system is empty of social, economic and political content. 'In what sense', asks Watson, 'does Gaius' *Institutes* reflect the society of pagan Rome and with some modifications, Christian Byzantium?' Indeed, he says, if 'the *Institutes* had mirrored Byzantine conditions, it would have been influential in the west only with difficulty.'[21]

This idea that there exists a transnational *scientia iuris* (science of law), *ius commune* (common law) and (or) *lex mercatoria* (law merchant) lies at the heart of the harmonisation of private law debate in Europe.[22] Legal rules or legal norms can be invoked under the heading of legal science to support the assertion that since all legal systems can be reduced to a set of linguistic propositions, harmonisation or unification of law ought to be possible. It is just a matter of bringing these propositions into line.[23] The same kind of argument can be applied to legal categories and to the structure and organisation of legal systems. Accordingly Peter Birks, mirroring Watson's argument, has asserted that Gaius had provided *all* lawyers with a 'map' of the law or, better, with their 'software'.[24] Here of course Birks is simply echoing an older view 'that some concepts and principles found in Roman law are so fundamental as to be of universal application and to form in a very real sense part of the *nature of things*.'[25] But the point is, as we have said, central to the whole harmonisation debate. If the idea of a 'law of obligations' transcends legal cultures and exists as a 'scientific' or 'natural' structure, then it would seem that through adjustment and transplantation a common law of Europe (and beyond) is a real possibility.

Yet even if one is sceptical about a new *ius commune*, or about any meeting of minds between English and continental jurists, there remains another argument founded on the importance of Roman law. In its original form, it was a system which had as little in common with the modern codes as it supposedly has with the common law.[26] Consequently Roman

---

[19] *Ibid*, at 18.
[20] See generally Jolowicz (1957), at 61–81.
[21] Watson (1994), at 21.
[22] See eg Berger (2004), at 43.
[23] See eg Mincke (1992).
[24] Birks (2000), at xliv–xlv.
[25] Jones (1940), at 65, emphasis added.
[26] Villey (2006), at 468–70, 487.

law might have the potential to act as a mediating system between English law and continental law. Indeed for Franz Pringsheim classical Roman law actually has more in common with modern English law than it has with modern civil law.[27] According to Pringsheim classical Roman law and common law were connected by an 'inner relationship'. This inner relationship was based on the idea that both systems had a 'taste for the particular, for the characteristic, for reality and reasonableness apart from all abstract ideas';[28] and, in turn, these similar tastes were based upon a similarity of 'spirit'. This *Volksgeist* was not, according to Pringsheim, amenable to rational explanation since it was an aspect of 'the fundamental character of a nation' which 'will always remain a secret'. Indeed 'it is not at all desirable to attack' such national characteristics 'with rational considerations'.[29] Roman law and common law were, accordingly, bound together, not by a genealogical history, but by a spiritual bond that lay deep in the national characters of two peoples. It was a connection that transcended history.

Evidently such a thesis is open to ridicule. Nevertheless weak concepts like the *Volksgeist* can prove extremely fertile in facilitating a re-orientation in theoretical thinking and it has to be observed that Pringsheim was not alone in his view that Roman and common lawyers appear to exhibit similar mentalities. Michel Villey and Zweigert and Kötz also comment upon the similarity of methods between English and Roman lawyers.[30] More importantly, perhaps, when one examines the texts from the two legal systems there are some striking similarities. For example, the classical Roman jurist, like the traditional common lawyer, thought in terms of remedies rather than rights; that is to say both sets of jurists started out from the form of an action and worked from there towards a solution. *Ubi remedium ibi ius* (where there is a remedy there is a right). Furthermore Roman lawyers and common lawyers tend to reason at the level of facts rather than at the level of a structured set of interrelating and abstract principles. Now this is not to suggest that within these facts there are not conceptual models of institutions and institutional relationships in play. The point to be made is that legal development is largely a matter of pushing outwards from the facts: it is a matter of jurists hypothetically varying the facts and considering, on a 'what-if?' (*quid enim si*) basis, what the legal effect of such hypothetical variations would be.[31] It is a matter of *ex facto ius oritur* (law arises out of fact).

---

[27] Pringsheim (1935).
[28] *Ibid*, at 358.
[29] *Ibid*, at 365.
[30] Villey (2006), at 611–2; Zweigert and Kötz (1998), at 186–7.
[31] Weir (1992), at 1617; Salter (1992), at 172; Samuel (1994), at 191–6.

These similarities do not of course depend upon any common *Volksgeist* as such. They can be explained quite rationally by the history of science which shows that it is a common feature of scientific development that a science passes through four stages of development. According to Robert Blanché one should not think in terms of a binary division between the concrete and the abstract sciences; rather, one should see all sciences following the same development, although at different times, from an initial to a final stage. The initial stage is the descriptive and the final stage the axiomatic; in between these two stages there is an inductive and deductive stage respectively.[32] When this scheme is applied to legal science the inner relationship between classical Roman and common law becomes evident. Both systems functioned within the inductive stage of scientific development with the result that they appear at odds with the modern codified civilian systems. For in the 16th to 18th centuries civil law thinking passed from the inductive to the deductive stages to arrive, in the era of the codes, at an axiomatic stage.[33] This axiomatic stage is characterised by a model of rules functioning as a closed system – a pyramid – where all concepts are rigorously defined and completely divorced from the world of fact.[34]

The methodology associated with the deductive and axiomatic stages of legal science is quite different from that used in the descriptive and inductive stages. For a start, the axiomatic approach is one that sees legal knowledge as being completely divorced from the facts of society and social disputes. Legal rules are analogous to numbers and thus function according to their own conceptual symmetries and systematics.[35] The result, in terms of the methodology associated with such an approach, is that the application of the law aspires to be simply a matter of formal logic. 'The premiss of this method, rooted in the epistemology of formal idealism', said Franz Wieacker in his famous historical account of the history of private law, 'is that if a scientific rule is conceptually logical and fits into the system then it must be right'.[36] In other words epistemological validity is conferred not by *correspondence* with an external object but by internal *coherence*. The logical result was the civil code. Accordingly an abstract rule as found in a code provision forms the major premise and the set of litigation facts the minor premise; the conclusion – that is to say the solution to the legal problem – automatically follows from the juxtaposition of the two premises. In terms of 'spirit', one can talk of a *mos geometricus*

---

[32] Blanché (1983), at 65.
[33] Villey (2006), at 454–87.
[34] See generally Jouanjan (2005).
[35] Wieacker (1995), at 243–56, 292–9, 341–53.
[36] *Ibid*, at 343.

where 'the articles of the Code are no more than the number of theorems required to demonstrate the connection and to draw out the consequences: the pure jurist is a mathematician'.[37] In other words, an essential part of legal knowledge is to be found in the symmetrical architecture of the reasoning (deductive) model itself.

Of course the methodology to be found in the inductive stage of legal science is, in contrast, very different even if it does on occasions make use of the syllogism. One searches for the legal solution within the facts themselves rather than within some abstract conceptual model. Definition of various notions such as 'possession' or 'consent' might vary according to the circumstances in play.[38] Moreover there is no clear distinction between substantive and procedural ideas and so, for example, success or failure can depend upon whether electricity is analogous to water or an explosive shell is analogous to a dangerous animal.[39] The role of the court in an inductive system is simply to do justice between the parties, for there is no duty on the judges to rationalise the law since facts themselves have a tendency to baffle even the most intelligent human mind (D.22.6.2). In an inductive legal science the art of deciding (*ars judicandi*) is still to be distinguished from the abstract organisation of law (*scientia iuris*) since the practitioner, unlike the professor, is little interested in constructing universal theories of knowledge.[40] The practitioner is happy with a patchwork of concepts operating at a low level of abstraction.[41]

HARMONISATION THROUGH CASUISTIC METHODS

The difference of mentality seemingly so clearly evident in any comparison of an English law report with its French counterpart is, then, a difference not of spirit but of science and technique. In the civil law tradition *scientia iuris* and *ars judicandi* became merged in a *jurisprudentia rationalis*.[42] However in the common law there is little sympathy for the view that 'a judicial decision should be arrived at solely by an abstract juridical dialectic, without regard to those reasons of the heart for which the reason has

---

[37] Dubouchet (1991), at 127 quoting Liard (1894), at 397.
[38] See Legrand and Samuel (2005).
[39] *Lupton v FA & AB Ltd* [1972] AC 634, at 659; *Read v J Lyons & Co* [1947] AC 156.
[40] Samuel (1994), at 103–16.
[41] For an historical viewpoint see Ibbetson (1999), at 294–302.
[42] Dubouchet (1991), at 78.

at best but an indifferent understanding'.[43] Reasoning in the common law stretches beyond logic and formalism.

Now there is no doubt that when Pringsheim gave his lecture the gap between the inductive and axiomatic approaches was real enough in the minds of jurists, however much of a myth the language of mathematics was proving to be in the face of the reality of case law problem-solving. But it has to be asked if today this dichotomy between the inductive and the axiomatic is still valid. Do French and German judges still believe that the solutions to all legal problems are to be found in some abstract model constructed along the lines of mathematical logic? One answer is to assert that this axiomatic obsession no longer dominates the reasoning mentality in the civil law tradition and that the reality of judging is not so different from what goes on the common law world.[44] In truth monolithic images of 'civilian' and 'common law' judges are likely to be false; the picture, even within national systems, is more fragmented.[45]

Some argue that this movement beyond the axiomatic is evidenced, at the level of methodology, by the increasing movement away from logic towards argumentation. Civil law writers, on the whole, no longer think that legal method consists of formal logic and hard conceptual models. Instead the focus is on dialectical reasoning and the methods of rhetoric,[46] for it is now recognised that law cannot be limited just to exercises in thinking since it has to allow for the satisfaction of the concrete requirements of everyday social life.[47] There is an increasing acceptance that behind the formality of the structured syllogism an interpretative process is at work which cannot be explained just in terms of *scientia iuris*.[48] It is the lawyer and judge and not the abstract proposition who act as the true source of law when it comes to actual problem-solving.

Théodore Ivanier in France for example argues that the *ars judicandi* is not in truth a matter of propositional knowledge founded on a logical application of the code.[49] It is a matter of interpretation of the facts. The approach, he claims, is still interpretative (hermeneutic) in method in that one is teasing out 'hidden facts' (*les faits inconnus*) from known facts (*les*

---

[43] Lord Simon in *Att-Gen v Times Newspapers Ltd* [1974] AC 273, at 315.
[44] Bergel (2003), at 292–5.
[45] Bell (2006).
[46] See eg Perelman (1979).
[47] Bergel (2003), at 286–95.
[48] *Ibid*, at 291–5. See also Bengoetxea (1993).
[49] Ivainer (1988).

faits connus).[50] But the point he emphasises is that the *ars judicandi* – the art of judging – is to be found in the movement from structuring the facts to choosing and inventing the normative principle, a process which involves the use of fuzzy concepts (*les concepts flous*). These concepts – for example fault, damage, interests, good faith – act not only as the bridge between the facts and the text but also as the means by which the judges can inject into the act of interpretation their system, or systems, of values. 'If the starting point (fuzzy) is to be found in the legislative text', writes Ivanier, 'the evaluation of the context will be in the system of values chosen by the judge'. And so 'although the legal information is abstract and rigid, the legislative text never having its feet on the ground since it sets it sights only on categories, the distinctive feature of axiology is to operate *in concreto* in getting into the innermost recesses of life as it actually unfolds.'[51]

Instead of continuing to talk, then, of a clash between the inductive (common law) and the axiomatic (codes) it might be argued that it is more desirable for those legal scientists keen on harmonisation in Europe to think in terms of a new epistemological stage beyond that of the axiomatic. Indeed, one German academic talks of the need to abandon old models in the face of the complexity of EU law and economics.[52] This new stage would be forward-looking in that it would invite the European lawyer to think not in terms of a backward step to the inductive and descriptive. It would invite one to progress towards a dialectical creation arising out of the tensions between descriptive and inductive methodology on the one hand and deductive and axiomatic techniques on the other. The 'post-axiomatic' stage might be one where the dichotomy between science (law) and object of science (legal facts) is seen in terms of a single model: the 'geometry', in other words, becomes more concrete and the concrete more abstract. For 'the concrete is simply the abstract rendered familiar by usage'.[53]

Such a 'post-axiomatic' stage might also act as a contextual category in which some of the tensions between conceptualism and realism are finally rethought. The civilians have provided Europe with the idea of a system of rules logically and coherently arranged and this notion of system will continue to play an important role in understanding a law of obligations.[54] Yet law is also about values.[55] And these values might be said to be some-

---

[50] *Ibid*, at 84–6.
[51] *Ibid*, at 337.
[52] Joerges (1998).
[53] P Langevin, quoted in Blanché (1973), at 54.
[54] Van de Kerchove and Ost (1994).
[55] Stein and Shand (1974).

thing which, in a post-axiomatic world, help endow the legal model with a 'plurality of images by which today's science can be represented, because of the presence here of different epistemological conceptions'. In turn these might force one to accept 'the full legitimacy of the existence of several methodologies'.[56] This plurality of images can be found even within the class of lawyers themselves: for example the legal historian and the legal theorist may well have quite different conceptions of contract than the legal practitioner.[57] On the other hand, whatever the conceptual differences between the common law and the civil law (or between sub-groups within the legal class), all systems recognise, for example, that people are more valuable than things (see PETL art 2:102). And, more technically, all member states, together with the EU as an institution, accept, say, that consumers need more protection than *commerçants* and *professionnels*.

John Bell uses this focal point of values as a means, if not of harmonising English and French law, at least of establishing a fundamental relationship between the two traditions.[58] According to Bell the criticism that is often levelled at continental lawyers – that they are lovers of concepts for their own elegance – is misleading. For, 'there is ample evidence that, in fact, the French are as pragmatic and instrumentalist as the English, not only in public law areas such as public service, but in private law as well'.[59] French judges, in contrast to academic writers, make use of many of the same techniques as their English counterparts in arriving at their solutions. The conceptual and logical approach was simply a creation of the law faculties trying to gain respectability much in the same way as English faculties were to do 50 years later. Bell's thesis, mirroring the conclusions of Ivanier,[60] seems to be that a distinction between *ars judicandi* and *scientia iuris* was always to be found in French law. The former exists in the conclusions of the *Ministère public*, the reports of the *juge rapporteur* and even in the notes accompanying the publication of cases; the latter informs the style of the actual written decision and much of the academic writing.[61]

John Bell is of the view that the comparatist should be looking beyond legal concepts. The 'important driving force for legal thinking is not the self-perpetuating logic of the legal concepts', he writes, 'but the values

---

[56] Villa (1990), at 29.
[57] Atias (1994), at 119–20. One might compare by way of example Ibbetson (1999) with, say, Cooke and Oughton (2000).
[58] Bell (1995).
[59] *Ibid*, at 98.
[60] See also Lasser (1995).
[61] *Ibid*.

which the law is trying to enforce and lawyers to implement'.[62] Legal concepts are just building blocks to present arguments and it is values which actually determine the kind of building to be constructed. It is a matter of form rather than substance and, accordingly, the work of those comparatists who emphasise a difference of mentality between English and French law are in danger of finding that their work does not stand up to scrutiny.[63] It is a myth based on the form of academic writing rather than the substance of judicial decision. Accordingly, the comparatist, using comparative law as a tool for getting over the initial disorientation caused by the way different legal systems present themselves, should be building upon these 'fundamentally common ways of thinking as lawyers' so as to facilitate common work on a future European agenda.[64]

OBSTACLES TO HARMONISATION

The Zimmermann and Bell view of European legal culture does not go unchallenged. In contrast to these writers who see only *rapprochement* there are others who continue to perceive only *la différence*. Just as the European languages cannot be reduced to a harmonised common discourse, so language-dependent legal systems remain closed cultural traditions.[65]

One of the most articulate and sustained criticisms of the whole *corpus iuris Europaeum* movement comes from Pierre Legrand. According to this author 'there exist in Europe irreducibly distinctive modes of legal perception and thinking, that the ambition of a European *concordantia* is (and must be) a chimera, that European legal systems are not converging'.[66] Legrand is adamant that the common law *mentalité* is irreducibly different from the civil law's for a number of reasons. The common law neither thinks in terms of rules nor cares for systematics – two features essential to the continental tradition – and, in addition, it has little understanding of the notion of a 'right' in the French sense of *un droit subjectif*.[67] The English lawyer works primarily at the level of fact and uses on occasions reasoning arguments that no self-respecting civilian judge could ever find acceptable at the cognitive level.[68] Rather than harmonising these differ-

---

[62] Bell (1995), at 98.
[63] See eg Bell (1995a).
[64] Bell (1995), at 101.
[65] Weir (1995).
[66] Legrand (1996), at 81.
[67] Legrand (1999a), at 75–102.
[68] Legrand (1995), at 72.

ences, the present interrelationship between the civil and common law within the European Union serves only to exacerbate them.

Legrand does not deny that, say, French law and English law can arrive at similar conclusions with respect to a similar fact situation. What he says is that to argue that such similarity of conclusion is evidence of similarity of mentality is to miss the point.[69] Each system arrives at its conclusion using a particular legal 'frame of mind' and these frames of mind are as different as those behind two linguistic propositions expressed in two quite different European languages.[70] The legal frame of mind involves acts of cognitive internalisation which cannot be reduced to a common denominator. Furthermore, the 'existence of a common historical reservoir, such as the *jus commune*, will not help to dispel the lack of appreciation by common law lawyers of the notions of "system" or "rule", as understood by civilians, nor will it serve to efface the lack of understanding by civilians of the importance of facts or the significance of the past at common law'.[71] Legal integration is doomed to failure unless it takes these differences of *mentalité* and culture into account.[72] Indeed Legrand goes further and asserts that harmonisation projects that fail to take account of these cultural and *mentalité* differences are dangerous since they are projects aimed at suppressing difference. And difference is never something to be apprehended in a negative perspective since it is, for example, the key to comparative legal studies.[73] Just as bio-diversity is the key to the survival of the ecosystem, so difference is the fundamental challenge for comparatists.[74] In short, *extra culturam nihil datur*.[75]

Legrand has been joined by other sceptics. Tony Weir makes the point that law is language and just as there cannot conceivably be a harmonised European language so there cannot realistically be a harmonised law.[76] He makes the further important point, in answer to those who claim a harmonised law is essential for commercial and monetary union, that England and Scotland have lived happily with separate systems for more than two centuries.[77] Indeed Weir has described the whole harmonisation project as

---

[69] *Ibid*, at 74.
[70] *Ibid*, at 73.
[71] *Ibid*, at 74.
[72] *Ibid*, at 83.
[73] Legrand (1999a), at 108.
[74] *Ibid*, at 109.
[75] *Ibid*, at 103.
[76] Weir (1995).
[77] Weir (1998a).

'demented'.⁷⁸ This more extreme comment may, ultimately, prove unhelpful in understanding why the *Principles of European Contract Law* are problematic, but calmer voices, from within the civilian tradition itself, are also raising questions that deserve serious consideration. Professor Joerges, for example, sees 'private law' as a problem in as much as it has actually allowed private lawyers to isolate themselves from European law. Privatists assume that their area can be understood from the position of the internal core categories of obligations, property, succession and family law. Yet the truth is that these internal categories appear largely immune from actual European law in that 'both the Community legislature and the (otherwise activist) ECJ have proved to be extremely cautious in their approach to the traditional realms of private law.'⁷⁹ What European law is in fact doing is to constitutionalise Europe as a private law society and this is, in turn, creating a situation where the old models of law need to be abandoned. 'Private law in this perspective', Joerges observes, '*is* constitutional law'.⁸⁰

Professor Teubner also raises a question about the viability of legal integration. He thinks that a concept such as good faith could prove to be a 'legal irritant' when transplanted from one legal culture into another. The unthinking transplantation of one concept, fashioned within a set of particular economic and cultural circumstances, from one system to another could 'work as a fundamental irritation which triggers a whole series of new and unexpected events'.⁸¹ It could result not in harmonisation, but further legal fragmentation in Europe, for 'it seems that contemporary trends toward globalisation do not necessarily result in a convergence of social orders and in a uniformisation of law'.⁸² Thus if good faith is transplanted from civil to English law, says Teubner, 'and if it is supposed to play also in the new context its role of linking contracts to a variety of different discourses, then it is bound to produce results at great variance with continental legal orders'.⁸³ British economic culture is not like German economic culture and the result could be that good faith might become 'a quasi-constitutional constraint . . . on strong hierarchies of private government and a constraint on certain expansionist tendencies of competitive processes'.⁸⁴ Contract would move from being a private

---

⁷⁸ Weir (2004), at 3.
⁷⁹ Joerges (1998).
⁸⁰ *Ibid*, at 149.
⁸¹ Teubner (1998), at 12.
⁸² *Ibid*, at 13.
⁸³ *Ibid*, at 23–4.
⁸⁴ *Ibid*, at 28.

law device emphasising discretion and commercial freedom to one where it assumed a quasi-public law role setting 'low-discretionary rules that draw clearly-defined legal limits to quasi-administrative discretion'.[85] These comments might seem more low-key in some respects than the assertions of Legrand and Weir. Indeed Teubner has some reservations about Professor Legrand's thesis.[86] But the importance of both Joerges and Teubner is that they are sensing the destruction of the traditional model of law that distinguishes private from public and commercial law from civil law.

ROLE OF COMPARATIVE LAW

A critic might respond that Pierre Legrand is focusing too much on the empty form of legal architecture rather than upon the solid substance of the social values which determine the actual shape and design of the building to be constructed.[87] After all, as both Zimmermann and Bell make clear, the role of the comparatist is to facilitate a 'working together in building a common system'[88] at the level of legal education (Bell) or legal science (Zimmermann). And that 'the best comparisons focus on concrete issues, rather than on grand distinctions between legal systems'.[89] Furthermore, with respect to Legrand's cultural point, Warrington suggests that there may develop a European-wide culture that could absorb, or at least co-exist with, the more local differences.[90] These no doubt are valid points. Nevertheless two aspects of Legrand's thesis need to be emphasised here.

First, Legrand's theory must be viewed in the wider context of his own pessimistic analysis of the state of comparative law in Europe today. Comparative legal studies is 'the work of indifferent intellectuals' which, when not banal and vacuous, betrays 'an almost complete absence of theoretical insight'.[91] Thus when German authors talk of harmonisation through dogmatisation (*Dogmatisierung*) and legal science (*Rechtswissenschaft*), it in effect amounts to a form of intellectual imperialism since any sophisticated comparatist should know that the whole

---

[85] *Ibid*, at 29.
[86] *Ibid*, at 14–15.
[87] *Ibid*, at 14–15.
[88] Bell (1995), at 101.
[89] *Ibid*, at 63.
[90] M Warrington, doctoral thesis (Katholieke Universiteit, Brussels).
[91] Legrand (1995a), at 3. See also Legrand (1996b) and (1998).

tradition of the common law is distinctly *Unwissenschaftlichkeit*.[92] The inability of comparative law to engage seriously with theory has, according to Legrand, become what Bachelard would have called an 'epistemological barrier'.[93] What is needed, says Legrand, is a programme that functions 'as an act of defiance or rebellion'. An act which will dislodge 'the comforting certainties of conventional knowledge thereby affording a means of liberation' from 'ineffectual research agendas' that suppose the existence of law as some kind of non-ideological construction which exists as a perfect isomorphy of the world such-as-it-is.[94] The good comparatist should be 'continually making small erosions to the established order'.[95]

Secondly, Legrand is particularly concerned by the apparent lack of commitment on the part of any comparatist to engage with theory.[96] He argues that comparatists 'must engage in epistemological investigations, that is, ask how knowledge is constituted and how rationalities are shaped'; they 'must consider the historical background that defines the conditions of possibility of particular forms of knowledge'.[97] In other words, a central task of comparative law is to investigate the question of what it is to have knowledge of law.

This epistemological claim for comparative law is what underpins Legrand's insistence that European legal systems are not converging. If one sees, like John Bell, legal concepts simply as instrumental building blocks for a grand structure designed by social, political, economic and moral values, then harmonisation of an area like the law of obligations is only a matter of adjusting the instruments or re-arranging the building blocks so as create a common edifice. Comparative law, according to Bell, does not focus on rules, norms, systems and concepts as such; it draws attention 'to the cultural, social, religious, and economic setting of a legal system' and to the specific legal tradition 'which has a significant effect on the way functions are performed'.[98] Lawyers for Bell are social problem-solvers always in search of the 'pragmatic solution'. Thus even although the conceptual approach in France and in England to a claim by the victim of a railway or supermarket accident may well be different in the two legal systems, there is 'a presumption of similarity at least in terms of the general range

---

[92] Legrand (1995a), at 3–4.
[93] *Ibid*, 18.
[94] *Ibid*, 20.
[95] *Ibid*.
[96] See generally Legrand (1999a).
[97] *Ibid*, at 23.
[98] Bell (1994), at 31.

of outcomes achieved by each system'.[99] As far as Bell is concerned, the conceptual architecture is a superficial aspect of legal knowledge hardly, it would seem, worthy of attention from the epistemologist.

Legrand, in contrast, is of the view that differences of conceptual framework go to the heart of legal knowledge itself. Thus, for example, the differences to be found in the way that a French court and an English court handles a legal problem such as that of damage caused by a thing is not just a matter of legal form. It is very much part of the deep structure of legal knowledge. Consequently Legrand totally rejects *praesumptio similitudinis* as the method to be adopted by the comparatist. Instead comparative legal method should start out from *praesumptio differentia*.[100] Comparative legal studies must, if it is to have any epistemological value, be about difference since 'comparison requires at least two elements' and 'the comparison of two elements must logically imply difference and deny sameness'.[101] The comparatist in favour of unification and harmonisation is, in short, not a comparatist.

OBLIGATIONS AND PROPERTY

It should be evident from what has been said so far that the debate about harmonising private law in Europe is both passionate and complex. Nevertheless the debate cannot be ignored because it is of direct relevance to the question of whether or not there is a European or even transnational 'law of obligations'. Legrand argues that such structures that supposedly transcend cultures are nothing but myth.[102] In contrast, Watson and Birks have argued (or at least implied) that there is an organising system that is 'out there' so to speak. There is no right and wrong answer to this debate in the sense that one or other theory can be falsified by reference to the behaviour of an external object. In other words one cannot apply the 'Popper test'.[103] Everything depends upon the paradigm and methodological model adopted. And so while Legrand is advocating a hermeneutical approach (rules are simply signifiers of a deeper cultural mentality) within a cultural paradigm, Watson is asserting a structural approach more within a nature paradigm (the Gaian system as science).[104] To a large

---

[99] Bell (1995), at 71.
[100] Legrand (1999a), at 36–9, 108–10.
[101] *Ibid*, at 110–11.
[102] Legrand (2006).
[103] cf Pheby (1988), at 22–36.
[104] Although this is not to suggest that Watson is a natural lawyer.

extent, then, the obligations lawyer has a choice. In which paradigm does she wish to function? Of course there is more to it than this. There is a whole political context about European unification and about globalisation and this will undoubtedly be of equal influence.

This said, it might however be useful to adopt the Legrand approach with regard to the role of comparative law and the comparatist. That is to say, it may be valuable, with respect to the law of obligations, to highlight differences that could act as serious obstacles to the fashioning of a European law of obligations. The aim here is not so much to take sides in the debate, but to indicate that even if one operates within the structural scheme – to accept that there is an institutional system inherited from Roman law that transcends national cultures – the problems are by no means resolved. Indeed structuralism reveals as many problems in the path of harmonisation as the hermeneutical approach advocated by the cultural theorists.

If one recalls the law of restitution this subject reveals some of the problems with attempting to import an obligations category from the civil law tradition. Several types of claim embraced by the principle of unjust enrichment are based on ownership rather than on an *in personam* obligation (see Chapter 16). A similar situation can be found in tort where causes of action such as trespass to goods and conversion are designed to remedy interference with possessory or proprietary titles to goods.[105] In other words part of the English law of property is to be found in the English law of obligations. Indeed there is even one English case where ownership was a matter of status, that is to say part of the law of persons.[106] Consequently, in terms of the institutional system, as subsequently developed by legal scientists, this intermixing rather undermines the whole point of having a law of obligations since this is a category that is supposed to stand in stark contrast to a law of property and to the law of persons. Real rights, in other words, are supposed to be sharply distinguished from personal rights, and patrimonial rights are to be differentiated from non-patrimonial rights.[107] One might note also that the trust, which splits the enjoyment of a thing from the power of disposal, could never be reconciled with article 544 of the *Code civil*. In fact if one poses a question about the whereabouts of the English law of moveable property the answer is that it is largely to be found in the law of obligations. Whatever Professor Zimmermann may think, then, about a common history or a *ius commune*, the truth is that

---

[105] See eg *Waverley Borough Council v Fletcher* [1996] QB 334.
[106] *Stevenson v Beverley Bentinck Ltd* [1976] 1 WLR 483.
[107] Beignier (2003).

the common law simply does not accept the idea, so important to German systematics (and to the civil law as a whole), that the law of obligations is defined at the level of legal systematisation by its complete opposition to the law of property (and to the law of persons). As the remedy of tracing so clearly indicates, there is not always a sharp frontier between owning and owing.

This property problem does not stop with moveable things. The regime of real property law in England is very different from anything to be found in the Roman model of property because it is based on a feudal model. One of the main characteristics of feudalism was that it made a fundamental distinction between land and other property and this distinction is still imprinted on English legal thinking. All land was held by the king and he devolved land to his lords and barons who in turn granted interests to those lower down the political and social hierarchy. Accordingly, from the legal point of view, several persons could at one and the same time have legal relationships in the same piece of land. 'Ownership belongs to a flat world in which rights in land or other forms of wealth are dependent upon no authority except the state', observes Milsom, but feudal tenure 'belongs to a smaller world in which there is no need and no room for abstract ideas like ownership'.[108]

The central concept in this feudal English model is the notion of an 'estate' which represents the temporal aspect of land – a 'fourth dimension'[109] – capable of being divisible between various holders, often during differing time periods, but remaining, metaphysically speaking, as a single whole. As Lord Hoffmann has put it:

> ... [T]he beneficial ownership of land may be divided in terms of time as well as space, so that the right to enjoyment of the land for a limited period, such as for life or a term of years, and the right to enjoy land after the expiry of that period, can exist simultaneously as property interests in possession and in remainder or reversion. One such interest may form the subject matter of a gift while the other is retained.[110]

There is, it must be said, a Roman element in as much as the word 'estate' is derived from the Latin word *status* and once reflected the idea of a person's status in relation to a piece of land.[111] But this means, once again, that the term 'estate' is a concept that transgresses the boundary between the law of persons and the law of things. Moreover in operation it was far

---

[108] Milsom (1981), at 100.
[109] Lawson (1958), at 67.
[110] *Ingram v IRC* [2000] 1 AC 293, at 300.
[111] Graveson (1953), at 7–14; Patault (1989), at 48–50.

removed from Roman thinking in that several people can enjoy at one and the same time 'ownership' rights in the same piece of property and each of these rights is, as Lord Hoffmann indicates, separately alienable. With the disappearance of feudalism, it may be tempting to apply the Roman model of ownership, but this would be dangerous. In the civil law, ownership is the coming together of the *ius utendi, fruendi* and *abutendi*, but the 'fee simple' of the common law, the nearest thing to ownership, is 'a fragmentable quantum of interest'. And this fee simple 'has, more than any other factor, made it both impossible and superfluous to attempt to rivet what a Common Lawyer would consider the oversimplified notion of ownership on the common law system of real property law'.[112]

SPIRIT OF NON-CODIFICATION

Of course one can legitimately ask why this real property model should be an obstacle to the harmonisation of the law of obligations. The response is to be found in the idea of 'property interests' alluded to by Lord Hoffmann. The common law as a whole is not an institutional model of 'rights' since, instead, it tends always to think in terms of interests defined and protected as much by a law of actions (remedies) as by a law of substantive rights.[113] In addition, the reasoning methods employed have never been axiomatic in the sense of starting out from an abstract rule and applying deductively. The method has been in the hands of practitioners who have advanced their legal arguments casuistically on the basis of the facts of particular cases. This in turn has given rise to a particular problem when it comes to trying to re-organise the common law to conform to schematic theory. As Stephen Waddams explains:

> Legal reasoning . . . has been a complex process, neither illogical in the sense of unreasoned or badly reasoned, nor reducible to any form of logic recognized outside the law. The concepts of contract, wrongdoing, and unjust enrichment have, at the point of their operation (that is, in the context of particular legal issues), often worked concurrently and cumulatively. They have been mutually complementary in the sense that each has supplemented and filled out the meaning of the others. At higher levels of generality the same complementarity may be observed in the relations between obligations and property, and between private right and public policy.[114]

And he continues:

---

[112] Lawson (1972), at para 38.
[113] Samuel (2004).
[114] Waddams (2003), at 224–5.

Two consequences follow on these complexities: it has not been possible to explain Anglo-American private law in terms of any single concept, nor has any map, scheme, or diagram proved satisfactory in which the concepts are separated from each other, as on a two-dimensional plane. The idea of mapping cannot entirely be discarded, and it owes its attraction partly to the fact that it is understood in many different ways, some of which are essential to the organization of thought. But insofar as it implies a separation of legal concepts from each other, or the assignment of each legal issue to one concept alone, it is apt to distort an understanding of the past, and consequently also of the present . . .[115]

Perhaps another way of putting this is to say that the common law functions in more than one dimension. In one dimension there is the *actio* itself with its own particular relationships and rules, for example the rules of damages or injunctions; in another dimension, there is the law of status. In yet another – third – dimension, there are causes of action such as conversion, trespass and so on. Such a multi-dimensional model might at first sight appear unnecessarily convoluted, but it can arguably act as a means for better appreciating the internal workings of the common law. Ownership can in this scheme be a matter both of status and of remedies;[116] equally restitution can consist of an *actio in personam* based upon a relationship *in rem*.[117] Indeed even the protection of the enjoyment of property can straddle private and public interests.[118] The point to be made, then, is that the common law is not so much a 'seamless web' – a metaphor that suggests two dimensions – but more a three-dimensional flexible frame structure. The common lawyer might use the Roman institutions of *persona*, *res* and *actiones* to construct and reconstruct frameworks of social structures, but in doing so operates in a much less rigid world than that of the codes and this means that harmonisation through codification is likely to fail in as much as the common lawyer will always understand the exercise differently from those endowed with the spirit of codification. There will always be a certain conceptual anarchy in common law legal reasoning.

CONCLUSION: ABANDONING THE OBLIGATIONS CATEGORY

Indeed one could go further and argue that the whole idea of a law of obligations belongs to a past era. The new economic reality both at a

---

[115] *Ibid*, at 226.
[116] *Stevenson v Beverley Bentick Ltd* [1976] 1 WLR 483.
[117] *Lipkin Gorman v Karpnale Ltd* [1991] 2 AC 548.
[118] *Miller v Jackson* [1977] QB 966.

European and a global level is one where rigid distinctions between personality rights (supposedly non-patrimonial), property rights and obligation rights no longer make sense. Privacy and dignity can be traded like a cargo of beans[119] and debts are a major form of property. As Christian Joerges has argued (as we have seen), what is needed is a new way of thinking about law in the modern EU and this should involve the abandoning of old ways of thinking.[120]

Yet if this is unacceptable to civil lawyers, one conclusion that can still be drawn from this is that the expression 'law of obligations' must be treated with great caution by English lawyers. It might seem at first sight an attractive generic category and might even appear to make the common law more attractive in a rational sort of way to lawyers from other EU countries. However as a viable idea it is a little like Iraq's supposed Weapons of Mass Destruction; that is to say a viable idea in the abstract but illusive when one moves to ground level. That contract, tort and restitution should come together to form a generic category of obligations appears in the abstract as a rational idea; but when one gets to examine the individual causes of action all the pieces do not fit into the neat systematic pattern created by those post-16th century Romanists reworking Gaius's and Justinian's classification schemes. Moreover, as we saw in an earlier chapter, the common law has never subscribed to, or even had any notion of, a general theory of obligations (see Chapter 3). There has never ever been anything above or beyond the specific categories of contract, tort and restitution. There is, in short, no point in the common law adopting the category.

It would, perhaps, be better to say that English law is based on a spectrum between several conceptual poles. At one pole there is the law of contract and at another pole the law of real property. Yet a third pole must now be established which represents the criminal law and criminal procedure. In between these poles there is a law of various causes of action (including statutory orders and the like) and remedies – which can be loosely grouped into categories like tort, family law and so on – reflecting different facets of the individual in society. Some causes of action are patrimonial and reflect the individual as an *economic unit*; other causes of action (for example defamation, harassment, certain human rights) are framed around the individual as a *social being*. Yet other causes of action (false imprisonment, malicious prosecution, certain human rights) give expression to the idea of the individual as a *political (constitutional) unit*.

---

[119] *Douglas v Hello! Ltd (No 3)* [2008] 1 AC 1.
[120] Joerges (1998).

In addition there are now statutory restitution claims that intermix all of these facets. Such facets give rise to a categorisation that is too weak, of course, to found an inference model from which solutions to cases can be deduced through syllogistic logic. Also, some sets of facts raise at one and the same time social and patrimonial interests; other sets of facts intermix the social and the constitutional or the constitutional and the patrimonial.[121]

Understanding contractual and non-contractual 'obligations', in English law at least, requires a subtle and flexible mind that comprehends both legal taxonomy, together with the logic that flows from it, and the limits of such taxonomy in the face of a complex social reality. Categories are the respected employees of legal reasoning, but they are not the masters. There is no scientific reason why the world needs to be divided into contract, tort and restitution; there is only assertion based on conceptual coherence and consensual acceptance by those operating within the discipline of law. Given that the common law is a system that functions more at the level of fact and argumentation than abstract rule regime, the idea of a law of obligations defined within a highly coherent system is alien to its historical and epistemological (knowledge and method) tradition. The common law, in other words, is not an area capable of being reduced to a concise 'map'.[122] This is a lesson that those learning the law ought never to forget and, perhaps, those attempting, in good faith, to harmonise private law, should also not forget. But even if the lesson is lost on Europe's codifiers, their end result will probably be meaningless. A transnational code of obligations law will, for the common lawyer, simply not represent legal knowledge, something that the Roman jurists specifically and clearly understood (D.50.17.1). Rather than a law of obligations it might be better to see in England a law of debt and a law of liability in which ideas of status, property, misstatement, duty, fault, damage, causation, interests and the like all tend to intermix in the multi-faceted arguments, often based on analogy rather than the syllogism, presented by practitioners to judges. Anything more is merely a form of legal astrology.

---

[121] See eg *Watkins v Home Office* [2006] 2 AC 395.
[122] See further Samuel (2005).

Bibliography

Alland, D and Rials, S (eds) (2003), *Dictionnaire de la culture juridique* (Presses Universitaires de France, 2003).
Allison, JWF (1996), *A Continental Distinction in the Common Law: A Historical and Comparative Perspective on English Public Law* (Oxford University Press, 1996).
Ashton (Baroness) (2006), Harmonisation of European Contract Law – the United Kingdom Government's Thinking, in Vogenauer and Weatherill (2006), 245.
Atias, C (1994), *Épistémologie du droit* (Presses Universitaires de France, 1994).
Atiyah, P (1979), *The Rise and Fall of Freedom of Contract* (Oxford University Press, 1979).
Baker, J (2002), *An Introduction to English Legal History* (Butterworths, 4th ed., 2002).
Baker, J (2003), *The Oxford History of the Laws of England: Volume VI 1483–1558* (Oxford University Press, 2003).
Beignier, B (2003), Droits, in Alland and Rials (2003), 533.
Bell, J (1989), The Effects of Changes in Circumstances on Long-term Contracts: English Report, in Harris and Tallon (1989), 195.
Bell, J (1994), Comparative Law and Legal Theory, in Krawietz, MacCormick and von Wright (1994), 19.
Bell, J (1995), English Law and French Law – Not So Different? (1995) 48 *Current Legal Problems* 63.
Bell, J (1995a), Book review of Samuel (1994) 15 *Legal Studies* 461.
Bell, J (2006), *Judiciaries within Europe: A Comparative Review* (Cambridge University Press, 2006).
Bengoetxea, J (1993), *The Legal Reasoning of the European Court of Justice* (Oxford University Press, 1993).
Bergel, J-L (2003), *Théorie générale du droit* (Dalloz, 4th ed., 2003).
Berger, KP (2004), European Private Law, Lex Mercatoria and Globalisation, in Hartkamp *et al* (2004).
Birks, P (1996), Equity in the Modern Law: An Exercise in Taxonomy (1996), 26 *University of Western Australia Law Review* 1.
Birks, P (2000), Introduction, Birks, P (ed), *English Private Law* (two volumes) (Oxford University Press, 2000).

Blanché, R (1973), *La science actuelle et le rationalisme* (Presses Universitaires de France, 2nd ed, 1973).
Blanché, R (1983), *L'épistémologie* (Presses Universitaires de France, 3rd ed., 1983).
Bower, G (1848), *Commentaries on the Modern Civil Law* (Stevens and Norton, 1848).
Burrows, A (1995), Swaps and the Friction between Common Law and Equity [1995] *Restitution Law Review* 15.
Cairns, J (1984), Blackstone, An English Institutist: Legal Literature and the Rise of the Nation State (1984) 4 *Oxford Journal of Legal Studies* 318.
Cane, P (1997), *The Anatomy of Tort Law* (Hart Publishing, 1997).
Canivet, G, Andenas, M and Fairgrieve, D (eds) (2004), *Comparative Law Before the Courts* (British Institute of International and Comparative Law, 2004).
Cohen, F (1935), Transcendental Nonsense and the Functional Approach (1935) 35 *Columbia Law Review* 809.
Cooke, J and Oughton, D (2000), *Common Law of Obligations* (Butterworths, 3rd ed., 2000).
Cownie, F (2004), *Legal Academics* (Hart, 2004).
Deroussin, D (2007), *Histoire du droit des obligations* (Economica, 2007).
Dubouchet, P (1991), *La pensée juridique avant et après le Code civil* (L'Hermès, 2e.éd., 1991).
Fleming, J (1985), *An Introduction to the Law of Torts* (Oxford University Press, 2nd ed., 1985).
Gazzaniga, J-L (1992), *Introduction historique au droit des obligations* (Presses Universitaires de France, 1992).
Giliker, P (2000), A 'New' Head of Damages: damages for mental distress in the English law of Torts (2000) 20 *Legal Studies* 19.
Graveson, R (1953), *Status in the Common Law* (Athlone, 1953).
Gray, K and Gray, S (2003), The Rhetoric of Reality, in J Getzler (ed), *Rationalizing Property, Equity and Trusts* (Butterworths, 2003), 204.
Haanappel, PPC and Mackaay, E (1990), *New Netherlands Civil Code* (Deventer, 1990).
Harris, D and Tallon, D (eds) (1989), *Contract Law Today: Anglo-French Comparisons* (Oxford University Press, 1989).
Hartkamp, A, *et al* (eds) (2004), *Towards a European Civil Code* (Kluwer/Ara Aequi Libri, 3rd ed., 2004).
Hedley, S (1999), How has the Common Law Survived the 20th Century? (1999) 50 *Northern Ireland Legal Quarterly* 283.
Hondius, E (2004), Towards a European Civil Code, in Hartkamp *et al* (2004), 3.

Honoré, A (1969), Causation and Remoteness of Damage, *International Encyclopedia of Comparative Law*, volume XI, chapter 7 (JCB Mohr) (completed 1969).

Ibbetson, D (1999), *A Historical Introduction to the Law of Obligations* (Oxford University Press, 1999).

Ivainer, T (1988), *L'interprétation des faits en droit* (Librairie générale de droit et de jurisprudence, 1988).

Jacob, J (1987), *The Fabric of English Civil Justice* (Stevens, 1987).

Jagtenberg, R, Orücü, E and de Roo, AJ (eds) (1995), *Transfrontier Mobility of Law* (Kluwer, 1995).

Jestaz, P, and Jamin, C (2004), *La doctrine* (Dalloz, 2004).

Jolowicz, H (1957), *Roman Foundations of Modern Law* (Oxford University Press, 1957).

Jones, J (1940), *Historical Introduction to the Theory of Law* (Oxford University Press, 1940).

Joerges, C (1998), European Challenges to Private Law: On False Dichotomies, True Conflicts and the Need for a Constitutional Perspective (1998) 18 *Legal Studies* 121.

Jouanjan, O (2005), *Une histoire de la pensée juridique en Allemagne (1800–1918)* (Presses Universitaires de France, 2005).

Kötz, H and Flessner, A (1997), *European Contract Law: Volume One: Formation, Validity, and Content of Contracts; Contract and Third Parties* (Oxford University Press, 1997; trans T Weir).

Krawietz, W, MacCormick, N and von Wright, GH (eds) (1994), *Prescriptive Formality and Normative Rationality in Modern Legal Systems: Festschrift for Robert Summers* (Dunker and Humblot, 1994).

Lasser, M (1995), Judicial (Self-) Portraits: Judicial Discourse in the French Legal System (1995) 104 *Yale Law Journal* 1325.

Lawson, FH (1951), *The Rational Strength of English Law* (Stevens, 1951).

Lawson, FH (1955), *Negligence in the Civil Law* (Oxford University Press, 1955).

Lawson, FH (1958), *Introduction to the Law of Property* (Oxford University Press, 1958).

Lawson, FH (1972), Common Law, *International Encyclopedia of Comparative Law*, volume VI, chapter 2, part II (JCB Mohr), para. 38 (completed 1972).

Lawson, FH (1980), *Remedies of English Law* (Butterworths, 2nd ed., 1980).

Legrand, P (1995), Legal Traditions in Western Europe: The Limits of Commonality, in Jagtenberg, Orücü and de Roo (1995), 63.

Legrand, P (1995a), *Comparatists-at-Law and the Contrarian Challenge* (Inaugural Lecture, Tilburg University, 1995).

Legrand, P (1996), European Legal Systems are not Converging (1996) 45 *International and Comparative Law Quarterly* 52.

Legrand, P (1996a), *Sens et non-sens d'un code civil européen* [1996] *Revue Internationale de Droit Comparé* 779.

Legrand, P (1996b), How to Compare Now (1996) 16 *Legal Studies* 232.

Legrand, P (1997), Against a European Civil Code (1997) 60 *Modern Law Review* 44.

Legrand, P (1998), Are Civilians Educable? (1998) 18 *Legal Studies* 216.

Legrand, P (1999), John Henry Merryman and Comparative Legal Studies: A Dialogue (1999) 47 *American Journal of Comparative Law* 3.

Legrand, P (1999a), *Le droit comparé* (Presses Universitaires de France, 1999).

Legrand, P (2006), Comparative Legal Studies and the Matter of Authenticity (2006) 2 *The Journal of Comparative Law* 365.

Legrand, P (2009), *Le droit comparé* (Presses Universitaires de France, 3rd ed., 2009).

Legrand, P and Samuel, G (2005), Brèves épistémologiques sur le droit anglais tel qu'en lui-même [2005.54] *Revue Interdisciplinaire d'Études Juridiques* 1.

Legrand, P and Samuel, G (2008), *Introduction au* common law (*Repères nº 514*) (La Découverte, Paris, 2008).

Lévy, J-P, and Castaldo, A (2002), *Histoire du droit civil* (Dalloz, 2002).

Lewis, R (2005), Insurance and the Tort System (2005) 25 *Legal Studies* 85.

Lewis, R (2009), The Politics and Economics of Tort Law: Judicially Imposed Periodical Payments of Damages (2009) 69 *Modern Law Review*.

Liard, L (1894), *L'enseignement supérieur* (1894).

Lobban, M (1991), *The Common Law and English Jurisprudence 1760–1850* (Oxford University Press, 1991).

Maine, H (Sir) (1890), *Early Law and Custom* (John Murray, 1890 edition).

Markesinis, B, Auby, J-B, Coester-Waltjen, D and Deakin, S (1999), *Tortious Liability of Statutory Bodies: A Comparative and Economic Analysis of Five English Cases* (Hart, 1999).

Mathieu-Izorche, M-L (2001), *Le raisonnement juridique* (Presses Universitaires de France, 2001).

McCrudden, C (2006), Legal Research and the Social Sciences (2006) 122 *Law Quarterly Review* 632.

Mestre, J-L (1985), *Introduction historique au droit administratif français* (Presses Universitaires de France, 1985).

Milsom, S (1981), *Historical Foundations of the Common Law* (Butterworths, 2nd ed., 1981).

Mincke, W (1992), Practical and propositional knowledge as the basis of European legal education, in De Witte, B and Forder, C (eds), *The Common Law of Europe and the Future of Legal Education* (Kluwer, 1992), 285.

Ourliac, P and De Malafosse, J (1969), *Histoire du droit privé 1/Les Obligations* (Presses Universitaires de France, 2nd ed., 1969).

Patault, A-M (1989), *Introduction historique au droit des biens* (Presses Universitaires de France, 1989).

Perelman, Ch (1979), *Logique juridique: Nouvelle rhétorique* (Dalloz, 2nd ed., 1979).

Pheby, J (1988), *Methodology and Economics: A Critical Introduction* (Macmillan, 1988).

Pringsheim, F (1935), The Inner Relationship Between English and Roman Law [1935] *Cambridge Law Journal* 347.

Rampelberg, R-M (2005), *Repères romains pour le droit européen des contrats* (LGDJ, 2005).

Reimann, M and Zimmermann, R (eds) (2006), *The Oxford Handbook of Comparative Law* (Oxford University Press, 2006).

Robin-Olivier, S and Fasquelle, D (eds) (2008), *Les échanges entre les droits, l'expérience communautaire* (Bruyland, 2008).

Rudden, B (1989), The Domain of Contract: English Report, in Harris and Tallon (1989), 81.

Rudden, B (1991–92), Torticles (1991–92) 6/7 *Tulane Civil Law Forum* 105.

Salter, M (1992), Towards a Phenomenology of Legal Thinking (1992) 23 *Journal of the British Society for Phenomenology* 167.

Samuel, G (1994), *The Foundations of Legal Reasoning* (Maklu, Antwerp, 1994).

Samuel, G (2000), Can Gaius Really be Compared to Darwin? (2000) 49 *International and Comparative Law Quarterly* 297.

Samuel, G (2003), *Epistemology and Method in Law* (Ashgate, 2003).

Samuel, G (2004), The Notion of an Interest as a Formal Concept in English and in Comparative Law, in Canivet, Andenas and Fairgrieve (2004), 263.

Samuel, G (2005), Can the Common Law be Mapped? (2005) 55 *University of Toronto Law Journal* 271.

Samuel, G (2007), Civil Codes and the Restructuring of the Common Law, in Fairgrieve, D (ed), *The Influence of the French Civil Code on the Common Law and Beyond* (British Institute of International and Comparative Law, 2007).

Samuel, G (2009), Can Legal Reasoning be Demystified? (2009) 29 *Legal Studies* 181.
Simpson, A (1975), Innovation in Nineteenth Century Contract Law (1975) 91 *Law Quarterly Review* 247.
Stein, P (1980), *Legal Evolution: The Story of an Idea* (Cambridge University Press, 1980).
Stein, P (1984), *Legal Institutions: The Development of Dispute Settlement* (Butterworths, 1984).
Stein, P (1988), Continental Influences on English Legal Thought 1600–1900, in P Stein, *The Character and Influence of the Roman Civil Law* (Hambledon, 1988) 224.
Stein, P (1999), *Roman Law in European History* (Cambridge, 1999).
Stein, P and Shand, J (1974), *Legal Values in Western Society* (Edinburgh University Press, 1974).
Sutton, R (1929), *Personal Actions at Common Law* (Butterworth and Co, 1929).
Terré, F, Simler, P and Lequette, Y (2002), *Droit civil: Les Obligations* (Dalloz, 8th ed., 2002).
Teubner, G (1998), Legal Irritants: Good Faith in British Law or How Unifying Law Ends Up in New Divergences (1998) 61 *Modern Law Review* 11.
Treitel, G (1988), *Remedies for Breach of Contract* (Oxford University Press, 1988).
Turpin, T and Tomkins, A (2007), *British Government and the Constitution: Text and Materials* (Cambridge University Press, 6th ed., 2007).
Van de Kerchove, M and Ost, F (1994), *Legal System Between Order and Disorder* (Oxford University Press, 1994; trans I Stewart).
Vigneron, S (2008), *Le rejet de la bonne foi en droit anglais*, in Robin-Olivier and Fasquelle (2008), 307.
Villa, V (1990), *La science du droit* (Librairie Générale de Droit et de Jurisprudence *et* Story-Scientia, 1990; trans. Nerhot, O and Nerhot, P).
Villey, M (2006), *La formation de la pensée juridique moderne* (Quadrige/Presses Universitaires de France, 2006; edited and republication of 1975 edition).
Vogenauer, S and Weatherill, S (eds) (2006), *The Harmonisation of European Contract Law: Implications for European Private Laws, Business and Legal Practice* (Hart, 2006).
Waddams, S (2000), Breach of Contract and the Concept of Wrongdoing (2000) 12 *Supreme Court Law Review* 1.
Waddams, S (2003), *Dimensions of Private Law: Categories and Concepts in Anglo-American Legal Reasoning* (Cambridge University Press, 2003).

Watson, A (1981), *The Making of the Civil Law* (Harvard University Press, 1981).

Watson, A (1994), The Importance of 'Nutshells' (1994) 42 *American Journal of Comparative Law* 1.

Weir, T (1992), Contracts in Rome and England (1992) 66 *Tulane Law Review* 1615.

Weir, T (1995), *Die Sprachen des europäischen Rechts* [1995] *Zeitschrift für Europäisches Privatrecht* 368.

Weir, T (1998), The Staggering March of Negligence, in Cane, P and Stapleton, J (eds), *The Law of Obligations: Essays in Celebration of John Fleming* (Oxford University Press, 1998), 97.

Weir, T (1998a), Divergent Legal Systems in a Single Member State [1998] *Zeitschrift für Europäisches Privatrecht* 564.

Weir, T (1999), Non-Performance of a Contractual Obligation and its Consequences, in English Law, in L Vacca (ed), *Il contratto inadempiuto: Realtà e tradizione del diritto contrattuale europeo* (G Giappichelli, 1999).

Weir, T (2004), *A Casebook on Tort* (Sweet and Maxwell, 10th ed., 2004).

Weir, T (2006), *Introduction to Tort Law* (Oxford University Press, 2nd ed., 2006).

Wieacker, F (1995), *A History of Private Law in Europe* (Oxford University Press, 1995; trans T Weir).

Williams, G (1951), The Aims of the Law of Tort (1951) 4 *Current Legal Problems* 137.

Williams, G and Hepple, B (1984), *Foundations of the Law of Tort* (Butterworths, 2nd ed., 1984).

Winfield, PH (1931), *The Province of the Law of Tort* (Cambridge University Press, 1931).

Zakrzewski, R (2005), *Remedies Reclassified* (Oxford University Press, 2005).

Zenati, F and Revet, T (1997) *Les biens* (Presses Universitaires de France, 2nd ed., 1997).

Zimmermann, R (1996), *The Law of Obligations* (Oxford, 1996).

Zimmermann, R (1996a), Savigny's Legacy: Legal History, Comparative Law, and the Emergence of a European Legal Science (1996a) 112 LQR 576.

Zimmermann, R (2004), Roman Law and the Harmonisation of Private Law in Europe, in Hartkamp *et al* (2004), 21.

Zimmermann, R (2006), Comparative Law and the Europeanization of Private Law, in Reimann and Zimmermann (2006), 539.

Zweigert, K, and Kötz, H (1998), *An Introduction to Comparative Law* (Oxford, 3rd ed., 1998; trans T Weir).

Index

abatement 231
abuse
  child 213
  of contract 86
  of legal process 180, 182
  of position 290
  of power 84, 141, 178, 183
  of public office *see* misfeasance in public office
  of rights 41–4, 58, 64, 86, 108, 113
  sex 211
acceptance
  free 303
  generally 27, 54, 91, 96, 98, 99–104, 105, 106, 108–10, 118–19, 131
accessio 29
accidents
  cost of 158
  traffic 3, 14, 23, 39, 159, 176, 195, 219, 223, 224–5, 246
  work 3, 14, 23, 39, 159, 176, 207, 217–18, 222–3
account of profits 49, 58, 64–5, 75, 76, 128, 160, 256, 257, 296, 299, 301, 302, 305, 306, 307
accountant 258–9
act
  acts and activities xvi, 39
  extra-hazardous 244
  of God 34, 235, 272, 280
    see also force majeure; impediment
  individual 152
  negligent 277
  legal 26, 27, 93
  reasonable 289
  unlawful 216–18, 302
actio
  de in rem verso 24
  generally 2, 11, 16, 27, 42, 47, 67, 94, 174, 296

  in personam *see* action
  in rem *see* action; vindicatio
  negotiorum gestorum 24, 302–3
  see also ex turpi causa non oritur actio
action
  causes of 51–3, 54–5, 57, 67, 154–7, 158, 174, 175, 179, 193, 199, 204, 234, 236, 257, 296, 310–11
  ex contractu 16
  damages 159–60, 249–51
  forms of 5, 8, 9, 17, 45, 48, 51, 52, 53, 155–7, 158, 178, 179, 193, 238, 249, 270, 311
  generally 2
  in personam 10–12, 24, 28, 40, 301, 308, 310
  in rem 10–12, 24, 28, 37, 40, 41, 49, 301, 307, 308, 310
  money had and received 301, 302, 308, 309, 310
  money paid 301, 302–3
  on the case 50, 156, 269
  personal 48, 51, 309
  quantum meruit 301, 303–4
  quantum valebat 303
  real 48, 309
  striking out 182, 197, 199–200, 212–13, 245
  see also remedies; vindicatio
activity
  and acts *see* acts and activities
  anti-social 230, 272
  dangerous 23, 179
  illegal 272
actor 284–7, 290
agency 243, 247, 303
agreement
  generally 47, 54, 70, 94–5, 136, 150–51
  implied 47
  lock out 104–5

sufficient 17, 98
  see also contract; conventio
analogy 19, 53, 165–6, 171, 182, 202, 318
  see also reasoning
animals xiv, 22, 23, 219, 223–4, 231, 235
argumentation 169–70, 319
ars judicandi 318, 319–20, 321
  see also methodology
assault *see* trespass (to the person)
assent 54
assignment 46, 47
assumpsit 5, 49, 50, 56, 96, 155, 309
  see also indebitatus assumpsit
attorney-general 233
auction *see* sale
Austin, John 9
auxiliaries 23, 179
axiology 157–8, 169–70, 275, 282, 320
axiom 18, 20, 34, 266, 269, 280, 317, 320
  see also system and systematics

Bachelard, Gaston 326
bad faith 183, 304
bailment 80, 82–3, 94, 100, 242, 244, 285–6, 303, 308, 310
balance of probabilities 275
bargaining power 84
battery *see* trespass (to the person)
battle of forms 103
Bell, John 321–2, 325, 326–7
behaviour
  abusive 44, 84, 179–92
    see also malice
  criminal 299
  idealised 195
  illegal 181
  unlawful 216–18
Bentham, Jeremy 9
bereavement 206, 209, 293
Birks, Peter 254, 255, 315, 327
Blackstone, Sir William 5, 26
Blanché, Robert 317
blood 221
boat 245–6, 285, 288
body
  governmental *see* public (body)
  ownership of 19
  public *see* public (body)
bona fides 31, 86–8
  see also good faith
breach
  anticipatory 150
  fundamental 139, 146
  of confidence 257
  of implied term 260
  of promise 143
  of statutory duty 156, 176, 179, 183, 193, 215, 216–18, 220, 222, 237, 240, 263, 273, 302
  serious 75, 76, 149–50
  see also duty (breach of); inducing a breach of contract
brothel 190
builders 100
buildings
  dangerous 233
  generally 23
  inspector of 211
  see also land; liability
burden of proof 197, 224, 240
bus 91, 100
business
  efficacy test 140
  interest *see* interest
  reputation 256

Cane, Peter 158
capacity 128–9, 132
carriage 71, 82, 94, 115
categories, legal xiv
cases
  awkward 7
  difficult 101–3
cas fortuit 144
causa 16, 18, 29, 93, 94, 312
causa causans 266
causa sine qua non 266, 267
causation
  actionability (and) 265, 269–72, 293
  but for test 267, 273, 277
  common sense approach to 179, 266
  directness (and) 266, 269
  factual 264, 265, 267, 272–83, 289
  generally 19, 72, 73, 92, 176, 179, 193, 194, 260, 263–94
  last opportunity (and) 266

legal 206, 264, 265, 267, 283–8, 289
levels of operation 266, 269–90
nominalist approach to 268–9, 287–8
overlapping causes 278–80
theories of 179, 265–9
see also damage; damages; causa causans; causa sine qua non; novus actus interveniens
cause
  generally 17
  sans 25, 27, 37, 38, 40, 300–301
certainty 104, 107, 202
certum est quod certum reddi potest 104
Chancery 6, 12, 49, 60, 62, 64, 74, 119, 120, 126, 305, 307
  see also equity
change of circumstances 81
  see also hardship
chaos 7
  see also order
charity 160
charterparty contracts 80, 135
child 226, 227
civil law xv, 3, 4, 8, 9, 84, 276, 322–3
  see also Roman law
claim
  and action *see* action
  and remedy 309
claimant
  incapable 128–9
  unforeseeable 207
clause
  abusive 84
  adjudication 83
  exclusion 73, 136, 137, 141–2, 145–8, 149, 271
  incorporation of 100, 145
  limitation 73, 136, 141–2, 145–8, 271, 286
  liquidated damages 142
  penalty 86, 96, 141–2
  reasonable 142
  unfair 84, 141–2
clausula rebus sic stantibus 30, 34, 145
clean hands 113, 130, 151
codes
  European 69
  and method 2–3
codification 314–15

coherence 3, 6, 7
common
  law 322–3
  sense 136, 279
  ways of thinking 322
Common Frame of Reference 312
communication
  of acceptance 102
  of intention 105–6
comparative
  dimension xv
  law 211
comparison xvi
compensation *see* damages
compulsion 302–3
concept
  fuzzy 320
  legal 321–2, 326
  quasi-normative 255
condictio 24, 26, 37, 38, 41, 47, 49, 302
condition
  as term 54, 132, 134, 137–9, 143, 150
  contingent 137–8
  implied 31, 34, 121, 122–3, 144
  in modern law 30
  in Roman law 29
  meaning of 138
  resolutive 30
  suspensive 30
conduct *see* behaviour
confidential information *see* information
Conseil d'État 15, 30, 213–14
consensus
  absence of 105–6, 296
  ad idem 27, 105–6, 109, 117
  generally 16, 24, 25, 93, 95, 97, 107
consent 105–6, 117–18, 120, 191, 260, 263, 270–71, 277, 318
consequence
  foreseeable *see* foreseeability
  natural 280
  see also volenti non fit injuria
consideration
  in contract 18, 54, 80, 89, 91, 94, 99, 101, 106, 107, 110–16, 150–51, 249, 313
  total failure of 137, 302

conspiracy 183–4, 187
consumer 91, 92, 132, 141, 146, 198, 221, 251, 321
contemplation 77
contempt of court 61
contra proferentem 86, 136, 145–6
contract
  administrative 83
  advantageous 79
  aléatoire 79
  and constitutionalisation 324–5
  and contracts 78–9, 94
  and conveyance 82
  and methodology 90–93
  and quasi-contract 309–10
  and third parties 114–16
    see also privity of contract
  and tort 53–5, 90, 91, 155, 159, 249, 250, 251, 258–62, 301
  as if 296
  banking 79, 94
  bilateral 31, 79, 80, 149–50
  breach of xiv, 54, 61, 75, 97, 132, 138–9, 154, 263, 286–7
    see also breach
  cancelled 131–2
  classical model of 70, 117
  classification of 78–2
  collateral 102, 105, 130, 138, 146
  commercial 84–5, 106–7
  commutatif 79
  consensual 94
  consumer 84–5, 146–7
  defective 117–22
  definition of 70–72
  different conceptions of 321
  discharge of 54, 143, 144, 151
  dissolution of 90
  distant selling 131
  efficient breach of 61, 63–4
  energy 107
  estate agent 80, 108
  family 107, 112
  fictitious 56
  formation of 54, 90, 91, 93–111, 125
  freedom of 54, 85–6, 141
  frustration of 54, 56, 75, 88, 132, 144–5, 263, 297
  gambling 131
  generally xiv, 9, 13–14, 28–9, 36–8, 157, 201, 205, 220, 235, 245, 249, 260–61, 281, 289, 308, 324–5
  gratuitous 79, 80
  history of 15–18, 53–5
  illegal 56, 129–31, 304
  implied 56, 307–8, 309
  in civil law 15–18, 28–9
  in common law 53–5
  innominate 16, 17, 79, 94
  instantaneous 80–81
  interpretation of 72, 84, 122–3, 133–6, 145
  long-term 80–81
  named 17, 79
  non-performance of *see* non-performance
  onerous 30
  pension 79
  performance of *see* performance
  private law 83–4
  privity of *see* privity of contract
  province of 88–9
  public law 83–4
  public works 84
  publishing 79
  purpose of 61
  real 94
  renegotiation of 30, 145
  service 81–2, 104, 241
  services 241
  standard form 102–3, 146
  supply 81–2
  synallagmatic 16, 31, 79
  termination of 67, 138–9, 149–50
  theory of 15–16, 26, 50, 55, 69, 78–9, 90, 91, 96, 141
  to contract 104
  types of 78–2
  unenforceable 119–20, 128, 129, 131, 272, 304
  unilateral 79, 80, 107–8
  unreasonable 84
  validity of 123
  variation of 112–14, 151
  void 56, 67, 118–19, 121, 123–5, 128, 129, 131, 272, 302, 304, 307
  voidable 119, 123–9, 128–9
  waiver of 151

see also consideration; inducing a breach of contract; liability
contractor
  independent 236, 241, 244
  reasonable 88
contribution 243, 269, 280, 306
control
  device 194, 282
  exercise of 241
conventio 16, 24, 25, 93, 94–5, 97, 98, 313
conversion 50, 56, 68, 75, 83, 124, 130, 156, 161, 162, 184–5, 240, 264, 308, 328
  see also trover
conveyance 82
corpus iuris Europaeum 322
corruption 254
counter-offer 103
cour de cassation 30
course of a business 85
course of dealing 100
course of employment *see* employment
court
  Chancery *see* Chancery
  Common Pleas 48
covenant 5, 96, 116
cricket 178
crime 190
criminal injuries compensation 160
Crown
  generally 83
  Prosecution Service 215–16
culpa
  generally 19, 22, 37, 39, 42, 152–3, 174
  in custodiendo 23
  in vigilando 23
  lata 32
  levis 32
  levissima 32
  liability 200
  see also fault
culture 4, 323, 324–5, 327, 328
custom 69

damage
  and damages 159, 177
  contemplated 286–7
  delictual 18
  direct 156, 283–4
  economic *see* loss
  financial *see* loss
  foreseeable *see* foreseeability
  generally 21, 47, 63, 72, 77, 156, 176–7, 192, 280, 298, 320
  humiliation 257–8
  indirect 156
  intangible 177, 232, 237
  intentional 179–92
  lost years 293
  nature of 156, 237
  necessity
  noise 180
  overlapping 278–80
  pain and suffering 293
  personal injury 159, 175, 198, 207, 221, 225, 229, 235, 237, 279, 291–3
  physical 177, 180, 192, 203, 221, 259, 287
  psychological 177, 180, 201, 206–9, 262, 268–9, 270, 281, 293
  remoteness of 264, 283–8, 293
  restitutionary 65–6, 75
  risk of 268
    see also risk
  special 190, 232
  tangible 177, 232
  to land 231
  to property 198, 207, 293
  unconsciousness 292
  untypical 287–8
  wrongful 18–23, 38–9, 313
  see also loss; mental distress
damages
  aggravated 293
  causation and 264–5
  compensatory nature of 291
  consistency in award of 292
  contractual 261, 286–7
  defamation 252
  equitable 160, 305
  exemplary 161, 177, 291
  generally 36–8, 58, 61–3, 73, 74, 99, 109, 128, 132, 159–60, 232, 250, 256, 288–94, 312
  liquidated 142
  measure of 264, 290–4
  nominal 305

non-pecuniary 203
parasitic 167, 170
pecuniary 203
restitutionary 296, 301
tortious 261
unliquidated 157
damnum emergens 203
dangerous
  animal *see* animal
  premises *see* occupier; premises
  product *see* product
  thing xvi
debt
  and damages 36–8, 49, 73–4, 76–7, 91, 92, 155, 160
  and property 310
  and tort 305–6
  and trespass xiv, 53–4, 309
  and unjust enrichment 53–7, 295, 301, 308
    see also quasi-contract; Restitution
  enforceability of 112–14
  equitable 296, 305
  generally 5, 26, 36–8, 46, 49, 56, 58, 63–4, 66, 73–4, 75, 78, 96, 106, 142, 288–9, 297, 309–10, 312
deceit 5, 49, 120, 156, 169, 178, 185, 189, 201, 204, 249–50
declaration 67
deduction 18, 166, 317, 318
deed 116
defamation 55, 155, 157, 162, 177, 179, 185–6, 189, 204, 240, 249, 251–5, 257, 258, 310
  see also libel; slander
defective
  equipment 222–3
  premises 228–9
  product *see* product
defence
  act of a stranger 234–5, 272
  act of God *see* act
  best practicable means 231
  change of position 304, 307
  consent *see* consent; volenti non fit injuria
  contributory negligence 264–5, 281, 289

  defamation (to) 252–3
  estoppel *see* estoppel
  ex turpi causa *see* ex turpi causa non oritur actio
  fair comment 185, 252
  justification 233
  locality 177, 237
  mitigation *see* mitigation
  necessity 191, 214, 271–2
  privilege 252, 253, 257
  state of scientific knowledge 221–2
  statutory authorisation 232
  truth 252
  volenti *see* volenti non fit injuria
delict
  generally xv, 18–21
  theory of 18
deposit 79
deterrence 160, 161, 175
detinue 5, 26, 49–50, 53, 54, 156
dialectics 4, 170
dies 29
Digest of Justinian 3
dignity 12–13, 21, 257, 258, 277–8
Director of Fair Trading 147
discount rate 292
discretion 60, 62
dog 223–4, 231
dogmatisierung 325
dol 32
dolus 42, 120
  see also fraud
Domat, Jean 20, 95
dominium 11, 15
  see also ownership
droit subjectif *see* Right
Dumoulin, Charles 31
duress
  economic 126–8
  generally 56, 66, 98, 99, 117, 118, 119, 120, 123, 125–8, 199
  to goods 126
  to the person 126
duty
  breach of 157, 189, 194–7, 259, 260, 281–2, 285
  common 226
  implied 258
  level of 32–3
  non-delegable 244–8

occupier's 225–38
of care 156, 166, 168, 177, 189, 193, 194, 197–213, 217, 226–9, 245–6, 247, 254, 259, 260, 270, 293
of co-operation 87
of loyalty 87
statutory 107, 156, 179
to mitigate 290
to negotiate in good faith 88, 104
to a patient 278
to renegotiate 81
see also breach; liability; omission

economics 285
education 325
elephant 171
emergency
    generally 303
    legal 5, 6, 8
employees 23, 240–42
employers 217, 255
employment
    contract 90
    course of 148, 240, 241–2
    reference 253–4
enrichment 297–9
    see also unjust enrichment
environment 23, 238
epistemology 1, 315, 317, 320, 326–7
equity 46, 58–9, 64, 65, 67, 74, 75, 76, 86, 88, 89, 108, 113, 118, 142, 150–51, 187, 250, 256, 296, 301, 305–9, 310
    see also Chancery
error *see* mistake
error in negotio 125
error in persona 124
escape
    borstal boys 245–6
    rule 233–5
    see also Rylands v Fletcher rule
estate 329–30
estoppel 80, 88, 106, 108, 109–10, 113–14, 127–8, 150–51
European Commission Action Plan 312
ex facto ius oritur 316
ex turpi causa non oritur actio 129–30, 272

exceptio non adimpleti contractus 31
expense
    increase in 145
    of another 299
experience 4
extra culturam nihil datur 323

facts
    and law 194
    construction of 276
    hidden 319
    importance of 323
    interpretation of 319–21
    legal 25, 27, 93
    material 164–6
    pleading of 51–2
fairness 146, 202, 203, 205, 210–11, 243–4, 248, 276, 282, 292
    see also justice
false imprisonment *see* trespass (to the person)
family 160, 206, 292
fault 19–21, 22, 23, 27, 29, 32–6, 39–40, 42, 44, 73, 91, 92, 109–10, 152–3, 155, 156, 163, 174–5, 176, 177–9, 215, 223, 254, 255, 259, 281, 320
favor contractus 104
fee simple 330
feudal model 45, 68, 329
fiction 49, 309–10
financial regulator 211
fire 235, 288
Fleming, John 158
force majeure 34–5, 38, 47, 144, 145, 246, 272
forgery 125
formalism 1, 157, 216, 319
forms of action *see* action
forseeability 19, 36, 234, 259, 264, 266, 272, 284–8
    see also damage (remoteness of)
frangenti fidem non est fides servanda 31
fraud 32, 39–40, 66, 98, 99, 111, 117, 118, 119, 123–6, 130–31, 169, 178, 185, 249–50, 254–5
    see also dol
freedom
    of contract *see* contract
    of speech 192, 252, 256

of the press 192, 256
    to act 175
frustration *see* contract
function and functionalism 1, 7, 70, 158, 166–8, 169, 171, 211, 216, 243, 285

Gaius 12, 18, 24, 44, 56, 295, 314–15
genera non pereunt 11, 38
genus and species 287–8
gift 110, 111
Glossators 19
good faith 42, 43, 86–8, 119, 123, 136, 140, 147–8, 320, 324–5
    see also bad faith; bona fides
Good Samaritan 209
goods
    and services 81–2
    defective 220
    quality of 81, 82, 140–41
    sale of *see* sale
Grotius, Hugo 20

harassment 159, 168, 186, 240
hardship 81
    see also change of circumstances
harm *see* damage; loss
harmonisation
    obstacles to 322–5
    of obligations *see* obligation
    of private law xiii, xiv, 124, 312–33
    theory of 312
Hepple, Bob 162
hermeneutics 19, 171, 319–20, 327, 328
highway 230, 232, 233
Hillsborough stadium tragedy 207–9
hire 54, 79, 82, 90, 92–3, 94, 95
hire purchase 146, 162
history 4, 285
Honoré, Anthony 265, 266
horseplay 270
humanist jurists 2, 40

Ibbetson, David 50
identity 123–5
ideology 85
impediment 33, 144
    see also force majeure
imperialism 325–6
imperium 15

imprévision 30, 34–5, 145
indebitatus assumpsit 49
individualism 154, 174, 175
inducing a breach of contract 187, 270
induction 18, 19, 166, 317, 318, 320
inexperience 177–8
information
    confidential 59, 256, 257
    misleading *see* misreprepresentation; misstatement
injunction 58, 59–60, 68, 74, 147, 159, 168–9, 181, 186, 231, 232, 237, 256, 257, 305
injuria 174
injury *see* damage
innkeepers 21
innuendo 252
in pari delicto potior est conditio defendentis 130–31
institutes
    generally 4, 5, 13, 25
    of Gaius 2, 10, 40, 327
    of Justinian 2, 4, 13, 23, 314
institution 12
institutiones *see* institutes
institutional scheme 2–3, 5, 8, 10, 12, 14, 15, 40, 48, 314–15, 327, 328
insult 18, 249, 257
insurance
    company 298, 306
    contracts 79, 94, 138
    fire 235
    generally 175, 292, 306
    motor 247
    position 149, 204, 209, 236, 242–3, 251, 272, 276
    liability xiv, 39, 211
    risk 298–9
    see also subrogation
intention
    generally 32, 105–7, 110, 178, 179–92
    to create legal relations 54, 91, 99, 106–7
    of words 251
    statutory 170–72
interest
    best 260, 271, 290
    business 188, 189, 256
    car journey (in) 239, 247
    commercial 181, 189, 258

community 214, 216, 237
constitutional 277
consumer 251
dignity 278
environmental 238
economic 42–4, 159, 189, 201, 203, 204, 225, 230, 253, 254–5, 258
expectation 62, 63, 77, 161, 286–7, 291
feudal 329
fragmented 330
future generation (of) 238
generally 20–21, 32, 36, 43, 58, 59, 63, 87, 127, 157, 159–60, 168–9, 179, 192, 200, 253, 254, 255, 277, 278, 283, 285, 288, 290, 320
health 199, 200, 277
receiving information (in) 252
individual 214, 225
intangible 254
land (in) 232
legitimate 41, 42, 181
liberty 168, 200
local 238
mental 206, 293
national 238
party's 135
personal injury 159, 168
privacy 256–8
private 10, 60, 130, 230, 232, 252, 257
professional 189
property 168, 200, 329
protected in tort 153, 157, 177, 199, 201, 282
public 15, 21, 60, 130, 145, 152, 186, 211, 212, 215, 225, 230, 232, 233, 238, 252, 257, 260
reliance 161
reputation 162, 188, 204–5, 251, 253, 254–5, 258, 291
restitutionary 65–6, 305
restoration 77, 161, 291
state 15
sufficient 183
third party 78, 252
interference
with contract 187
with goods 168, 184–5
with liberty 168

interpretation
generally *see* contract
intention of parties 135–6
literal 135
statutory *see* legislation
intimidation 128, 187–8
invitation
to tender 104–5
to treat 91
ius
abutendi 330
commune 20, 35, 45, 313, 314–16, 323, 328
fruendi 330
generally 42
incorporalis 45
in personam 11, 82
in re aliena 41
in rem 11, 82, 307
naturale 314
publicum 15
rerum 40, 44
utendi 330
Ivanier, Théodore 319–20, 321

Joerges, Christian 324, 325
Jolowicz, Herbert Felix 40
judges 321
judicial review 84, 216
juge rapporteur 321
jurisprudentia rationalis 318
jury 4, 6, 121, 194, 195, 252, 272, 283, 294, 314
jus *see* ius
justice 162–3, 169, 170, 172, 173, 202, 205, 210–11, 275–6, 282, 295, 296, 299, 303, 306
see also fairness
justification 185

knowledge
of law 326–7
of risk 271
Kötz, Hein 316

land 82, 225–34, 236, 245
Lando Commission 79
law
administrative 89, 145, 159, 244, 260, 262, 294

and economics 163
and equity 305
and fact 12, 194
black-letter 7
books 3–4
canon 16, 313
civil *see* civil law
commercial 69, 84, 325
　see also lex mercatoria
Commission 148
comparative 211, 314, 321–7
constitutional 159, 252, 253, 256, 294, 324
criminal 161, 190
customary 16
doctrinal 7
faculty 314
harmonisation of *see* harmonisation
map of *see* map
medical 271
mercantile 16, 30
　see also lex mercatoria
of actions 2, 304, 309
of obligations *see* obligations
of persons 12–13, 186, 278, 328, 329
of procedure *see* procedure
of property 10, 308, 328–9
of restitution *see* restitution
of things 2, 44, 329
　see also ius (rerum)
private 10, 107, 216, 257, 321, 324, 325
public xiv, 10, 14–15, 71, 107, 216, 230, 252, 257, 258, 260, 262, 321, 325
quasi-public 325
rationalisation of 172
Roman *see* Roman law
syllabus 6
lawyers
　canon 16, 30, 31
　civil 18
　private 324
　problem solver 326
legislation
　generally 26
　interpretation of 72, 134, 170–72
　private 17, 54, 70–72
　style of 164
Legrand, Pierre 322–3, 325–7, 328

Lex Aquilia 18–20, 38–9, 152
lex mercatoria 30, 31, 46, 313, 315
liability
　administrative 15, 158, 210, 213–16
　business 229
　civil 158–9, 210
　conditions of 282–3
　contractual 26, 72
　　see also non-performance
　delictual 295
　employers' 22, 239–47
　escaping 263–94
　ex contractu 53
　ex delicto 25, 53
　extra-contractual 13–14, 38–40
　extra-hazardous 234, 244
　fault *see* culpa; fault
　for aircraft 225
　for animals *see* animal
　for children 246–7
　for gain 295–7
　for motor vehicles 224–5, 239, 247–8
　for people 239–48
　for things 154, 218, 219–38
　for words 200–201, 249–62
　forced on people 301, 303
　group 154
　landlords' 228–9
　no fault 21–3, 39, 55, 163, 215, 219
　non-contractual 26
　notion of 174
　occupiers' 21, 171, 226–38
　personal injury 141
　product 220–22
　professional 204, 249, 258–62
　publisher 248–9
　quasi ex contractu 25
　quasi-contractual 295, 301–4
　strict 179, 214, 237, 252, 263, 271
　vicarious 52, 154, 179, 212, 219, 239–44, 245, 246, 298
libel 186, 249, 251
liberty 21
licensee 226
lien juridique 10
livestock 223–4
loan 54
local authority 84, 201–2, 206, 210–13, 237, 262

logic 4, 7, 57, 165, 167, 172, 277, 279, 282, 317, 319, 321
  see also syllogism
loss
  amenity (of) 293
  chance (of a) 177, 273–8
  consequential 203
  economic 21, 167–8, 170, 177, 178, 180–81, 189, 190, 199, 201, 203–5, 206, 220–21, 233, 262, 287, 289
  future economic 291
  lies where it falls 153, 174
  notion of 66, 203
  outcome (of an) 275
  profit (of) 286
  spreading 168, 243, 298
lucrum cessans 203

Maine, Sir Henry 3
malice 42–3, 179–92, 254
malicious
  falsehood 180, 188, 189, 255
  prosecution 162, 180, 182, 188, 270
  procurement of a search warrant 182
mandate 94
map and mapping 5, 12, 163, 164–5, 315
maxims 9
  see also regulae iuris
mental distress 62, 160, 171, 186, 206, 257, 287, 293
mentality
  difference of 8, 318, 322–3
  English 4–7, 310
  political and social 164
  reasoning 319
mesothelioma 275
metaphor 170
method and methodology xv, 4, 6, 19, 69, 90–93, 163–6, 169–73, 191–2, 201–2, 236–8, 284, 310, 316, 317–22, 327
Milsom, SFC 329
ministère public 321
minor 128–9
misfeasance in public office 55, 182–3, 217
misrepresentation 56, 64, 66, 67, 88, 99, 119, 120, 121, 123, 124, 125–6, 146, 185, 200, 249–50, 305
misstatement 75, 200–201, 204–5, 249–51, 258–9, 260
mistake
  fact (of) 302
  generally 66, 75, 98, 99, 117, 118, 119, 120–25, 144
misuse of confidential information 256
mitigation 73, 264, 265, 289–90
model
  feudal *see* feudal model
  multi-dimensional 331
  Roman 68, 329
  rule 7
modus 29
morality xv, 169–70
mos geometricus 44, 317–18
motive 41–4

National Health Service 160, 210, 260
nature 315
necessity 302
  see also defence
negligence
  contributory *see* defence
  exclusion of 141–2, 146
  generally 19, 32, 35, 50, 52, 55, 68, 141–2, 154, 156–7, 168, 177–9, 184, 185, 193, 226, 277, 310
  medical 71, 267, 274, 277–8
  professional 71, 258–62
  tort of 188–9, 193–209, 210, 217, 220, 221, 222, 230, 235, 236, 238, 240, 254, 258–62, 263, 265
  see also duty
nervous shock *see* damage (psychological)
non cumul 205
non natural use 234
non-performance xiv, 33–6, 73, 76, 90, 97, 123, 132, 133–51, 154
non est factum 125
non videntur qui errant consentire 118
notice 100, 229, 271
novus actus interveniens 266, 280–83, 289
nudum pactum 16

nuisance
  generally 41, 49, 154–5, 156, 179, 181, 193, 210, 215, 217, 237, 238, 245, 246, 310
  private 52, 55, 59–60, 162, 177, 179, 186, 190, 220, 225, 229, 230, 231–2, 233, 235, 236, 237, 238
  public 50, 52, 53, 55, 179, 186, 190–91, 220, 225, 229, 230, 232–3, 236, 237, 238, 244, 245, 264
  statutory 231

object
  and cause 96
  in Roman law 29
obligation(s)
  and actions 27, 154, 309
  and liability 72
  and property *see* property
  civil 47
  code of 2
  common law and 48–68, 68
  contractual 72, 147
  definition 1
  discharge of 117
  extinction of 46–7, 117
  harmonisation of 312–33
  in personam 328
  landlords' 226, 228–9
  law of xvi, 9, 328–9
  performance of *see* performance
  pre-existing 156
  primary 76–7
  natural 28–9, 47, 300
  non-performance of *see* non-performance
  of ends 32–3, 35, 81, 141
  of means 32–3, 81, 141
  secondary 76–7
  structure of 250–51
  theory of 27–7
  transnational 312–33
  to inform 123
occupier xvi, 21, 220, 225–34, 245
offer
  cross 105
  generally 27, 54, 91, 96, 97–104, 106, 108–10, 118–19, 131

  of amends 253
  revocation of 107–8
omission 202, 206, 209, 210, 226, 232, 249, 262, 270
ontology 276
order 7
owing 11, 301, 308, 329
ownership 10–14, 38, 44, 45, 54, 82, 301, 308, 328, 329, 330
  see also dominium
owing 11, 301, 308, 329

pact 16, 94, 95
pacta sunt servanda 16
pandectists 9, 20
paradigm 327–8
parliamentary commission 6
party
  three-party situations 206, 207, 208
  two-party situations 206, 208
partnership 79, 94, 95
passing off 189, 255–6
payment
  owing *see* debt
  voluntary 300
penalty 86
  see also clause
performance
  and third parties 148–9
  defective 142–4, 149–50, 154
  enforced 37, 47
  generally 46–7, 54, 111, 132, 142–51
  onerous 144–5
  part 301
  quality of 36
  specific 58, 60–61, 64, 74, 82, 97–8, 305
  substantial 143–4, 301
  withholding 31
  see also contract; exceptio non adimpleti contractus; non-performance
person(s)
  and action
  and thing 12
  law of *see* law
  legal 239, 245
  natural 147

persona 11, 37, 46, 62
personne morale 239
philosophy
　armchair 211
　contract *see* contract
　moral 295
　tort *see* tort
　see also epistemology; theory
planning permission 232
police 201, 206, 207–9, 210, 211, 212–13, 216, 260, 271, 281, 294
policy xv, 129, 131, 154, 163, 166–8, 169, 172, 173, 202, 203–4, 205, 210–13, 228, 243–4, 260, 262, 267, 271, 272, 273, 275, 283, 298, 300, 304
pollution 53
pork 221
possession 41, 54, 82–3, 124, 308, 318, 328
post-axiomatic 320–21
　see also axiom
postal rule 101, 109
Post-Glossators 15, 16, 19, 30, 31
Pothier, Robert 22, 31, 51, 95, 118
practitioner 318
precedent 7, 55, 164–6, 195–6, 202, 216, 234
pre-contractual
　domain 88
　liability 104–5
premises
　dangerous xiv, 227–34
　defective *see* defective
　harm off 229–34
　harm on 225–9
　see also liability
pressure
　amounting to a threat 187–8
　causing annoyance 190
　causing anxiety 186
　improper 113
presumption
　of difference 327
　of fault 178
　of similarity 326
price
　none 104
　non payment *see* debt
　reasonable 104

principle
　abstract 282
　causal 282
　contemplation *see* damage
　directness *see* damage
　equality 214
　ethical 158
　fault *see* fault
　foreseeability *see* foreseeability
　generally 155–6, 182
　neighbour 156, 198–9, 202
　unjust enrichment *see* unjust enrichment
Pringsheim, Franz 316, 319
privacy 12–13, 159, 162, 186, 192, 216, 256–8
privilege 185
privity of contract 89, 114–16, 251
proceeding in personam 56
procedure 2, 8, 199–200, 270
products
　dangerous
　defective 146, 198
　generally xiv, 23,
Promise
　breach of 96
　contractual 245, 249, 271
　　see also contract
　enforceable 99–101, 112–16, 118
　exchange of 96
　fundamental 138
　generally 54, 70, 71, 93, 95–105, 114, 136–7, 249, 313
　gratuitous 150
　implied 71
　non-serious 101–2
　unilateral 96
promissio *see* promise
property
　and obligation 10–14, 37–8, 44–6, 82, 159, 242, 305, 308
　consumable 12, 24, 37
　　see also res (fungibilis)
　generally 13, 57, 58–9, 89, 129
　incorporeal 40, 41, 44
　　see also res incorporalis
　intangible 44
　intellectual 255–6
　moveable 329
　personal 82

real 329, 330
title 328
see also right
proximity 21, 198–9, 202, 208, 259
public
authority 186, 257
see also local authority
body 201–2, 206, 209, 210–12, 252, 260, 262
interest *see* interest
law *see* law
nuisance *see* nuisance
official 252
publication 251
publisher 248
punishment 161

quality 140
quantum meruit *see* action
quantum valebat *see* action
quasi-contract 13, 23–5, 56–7, 130, 295, 301–4, 306, 307–8, 309–10
see also restitution; unjust enrichment
quasi-criminal 61
quasi-delict 13, 21–3, 152–3, 295
quasi ex delcito 152
quasi ex maleficio 21
qui facit per alium facit per se 243, 247
quid enim si 316

railways 23
Rampelberg, René-Marie 17–18
ratio decidendi 72, 164–6, 202
rationalisation 5, 172, 304
rationality 4, 254
realism
American 6
generally 7
reasonable
businessman 290
journalist 186, 253, 257
man 194, 195, 284
reasonableness 63, 72, 123, 140, 146, 173, 193, 202, 210–11, 281–2,
reasoning
analogical 19, 53, 165–6, 171, 202
casuistic 34
causal 19
dialectical 319

judicial 7, 165–6, 169–72, 211, 241, 269, 322
legal 9, 89, 211, 255, 310, 319, 322
reception of Roman law 9
Rechtswissenschaft 325
rectification 122, 305
reference *see* employment
reform
generally 6
of law books 3
of legal education 5, 6
register of writs 50
regulae iuris 9
see also maxims
regulation 72
relationship
close to contract 204
contractual 209, 244, 249, 250, 281
fiduciary 64, 249, 250, 307
inner 316
pre-existing 303
special 201, 204, 250
reliance 106, 201, 205
remedies 6, 10, 26, 29, 36–8, 46, 49, 57–68, 70, 72, 73–7, 87, 92, 120–22, 187, 216, 231, 256, 288–94, 301–11, 316
see also account of profits; actio; action; damages; debt; injunction; performance (specific); self-help; rectification; rescission
remoteness *see* damage
replevin 5
representation 113, 120, 134, 138
request 300
res
corporalis 38, 46
fungibilis 37
generally 11, 37, 44, 62, 66
incorporalis 38, 45
ipsa loquitur 197, 215, 240, 259
see also thing
rescission
generally 31, 58, 75, 76, 119
in common law 66
in equity 66–8, 74–5, 88, 99, 119, 120, 121–2, 125–9, 132, 305
rescuer 207, 208–9, 281

responsibility
  assumption of 201, 204–5
  individual 163
restitutio in integrum 62, 67
restitution
  claim in 38, 40, 49, 66, 75–6, 126, 128, 160
  generally 55–7, 65–6, 130, 160, 177, 295–311
  law of xv, 126, 157, 161, 295–311, 328
    see also unjust enrichment; quasi contract
restraint of trade 131
revolution
  industrial 6, 13–14, 39, 51
  knowledge 326
reward cases 80, 109
rhetoric 319
right
  abuse of see abuse
  and remedies 41, 87, 119–20, 296, 316
  by ricochet 5, 78, 292
  commercial 258
  constitutional 162, 177, 258, 294
  contractual 67, 77–8, 147
  generally 41, 44–5, 58, 59, 66, 153, 257, 322
  human 12–13, 15, 55, 159, 162, 171–2, 185, 186–7, 200, 212–13, 215, 216, 230, 238, 252–3, 256–8, 272
  in land 162
  in personam 2, 13–14, 82, 114, 307
  in rem 2, 13–14, 82, 114, 301, 307
  in tort 157, 161–2, 168–9
  intellectual property 255–6
  legal 10
  non-patrimonial 12–13, 162, 328
  obligational 40–41
  patrimonial 13–14, 159, 328
  personal 11, 41, 44, 77, 328
  personality 12–13, 159, 162, 186
  private 217
  property 58–9, 77–8, 130–31, 159, 162, 181, 189, 256, 257, 308–9, 310
  protection of 161–2
  real 11, 44, 77, 328
  reputation 251
  restitutionary 304
  social function of 42
  subjective 2, 41–2, 44
  to a fair trial 200
  to choose 277–8
  to enjoyment 329
  to know 277
  to possession 45, 308
  to roam 227
  to use highway 168
  transfer of 45, 46
  underlying 57–8
risk 72, 149, 153, 155, 174, 178, 195, 214, 215, 226, 227, 228, 236, 259–60, 268, 271, 272, 274–8, 281, 287, 298–9, 300
robbery 18
Roman
  law xvi, 1–3, 4, 5, 6, 8, 10–14, 15–16, 18–19, 21–2, 23–4, 28–9, 31, 34, 35–6, 38–9, 40, 41–2, 78–9, 86–7, 93, 94, 95, 104, 120, 152, 154, 161, 174, 177–8, 179, 265–6, 295, 296, 302–3, 313, 314–17
    see also reception of Roman law
  model see model (Roman)
Rudden, Bernard 83
rule model 7
rules
  application of 165–6, 173
  moral 87, 158
  postal see postal rule
  see also axiom; principle
Rylands v Fletcher rule 179, 190, 220, 230, 233–4, 235, 236, 237, 238, 272

safe system 221, 236–7, 246
sale
  auction 102
  car boot 85
  generally 31, 36, 54, 71, 79, 80, 90, 94, 95, 137, 146
salvage 304
sans cause 25, 27, 37, 38, 40, 300–301
science
  German legal 6, 7
  of law 3, 6, 313, 314–18
  social 7
    see also scientia iuris

scientia iuris 2, 313, 314–16, 318, 319, 321
self-help 31, 76, 134, 231
servant *see* employee
shop 100
silence 109
slander 186, 249, 251
social security 160
sociology 7
solicitor 101
solidarity 23, 87–8
sport 191, 270
statistics 39, 163, 174, 225
status 13, 72, 84–5, 132, 140, 156, 162, 209, 226, 237, 238, 329
statute *see* legislation
Stein, Peter 2, 12
stipulation 16, 95, 116, 121, 148
structure and structuralism 3, 19, 314–15, 327, 328
subrogation 243, 298, 301, 306, 310
suicide 281–2
supermarket 99–100, 236–7
surveyor
  professional *see* liability (professional)
  ship 211
syllogism 165–6, 167, 318, 319
  see also logic
system and systematics 1, 5, 7, 9, 53–4, 314–15, 317–18, 320, 323, 327, 329

taxi 100, 247–8
taxonomy 2, 5, 12, 26, 44, 45, 55–7, 68, 255
term
  abusive 86
  and representation 134
  express 134, 137
  fundamental 86, 137, 143, 146
  generally 72, 136–42
  implied 54, 122–3, 134, 137, 139–41, 144, 184, 260
  in modern law 30
  in Roman law 29
  innominate 139, 150
  onerous 106
  unfair 141–2, 146–8
test
  connection 242

directness *see* damage
foreseeability *see* foreseeability
textbooks 6, 51, 54
Teubner, Gunter 324–5
theory
  contract *see* contract
  obligation 27–47
  tort *see* tort
  vicarious liability 242–4
title 82, 184, 328
  see also conveyance
theft 18
thing
  dangerous 220, 233–5, 244, 272
  escape of 233–5, 272
  generic 92
  moveable 329
  nature of 315
  transfer of 81–2, 94
  specific 92
  see also goods; res
threat 181, 187–8, 249
  see also harassment
tobacco 221
tort
  administrative 182
  aims of 160–63, 175, 195, 285
  and contract *see* contract (and tort)
  and method 163–6, 191–2
  and property 65–6, 308–9
  and unjust enrichment 309–11
  definition 156–8
  economic 180–81, 184, 187, 189
  existence of 240
  fragmented nature of 158–9
  generally xiv, 13, 53–5, 130, 148, 154–76, 289, 294, 306, 309
  intentional 184–91
  or torts 155
  philosophy of 162–3
  policy of 158–9, 285
  purpose of 158–9, 174–6, 285, 294
  statutory 162
  theory of 162–3, 174–6, 244
  see also abuse; breach (of statutory duty); conspiracy; conversion; defamation; deceit; detinue; harassment; inducing a breach of contract; intimidation;

liability; malicious; misfeasance in public office; misuse of confidential information; negligence; nuisance; passing off; privacy; *Rylands v Fletcher* rule; trespass
tracing 301, 307–9, 310, 329
trade libel *see* malicious (falsehood)
transaction
  nature of 84–5, 94
  vague 104–5
transplant 315
trespass
  generally 5, 49, 50, 53, 54, 55, 66, 68, 75, 76, 96, 155, 156, 161, 168, 177, 178, 179, 191, 193, 210, 225, 230, 238, 240, 257, 310
  on the case 50, 156, 193
    see also action
  to goods 50, 56, 66, 162, 168, 184, 185, 191, 328
  to land 50, 52, 66, 162, 191, 225, 270
  to the person 50, 76, 162, 177, 180, 186, 191, 269, 271, 277, 294
trespasser 227–9, 235, 236, 237
trover 5, 50
  see also conversion
trust xiii, 57, 292, 300, 307, 308, 328
trustees xiii
truth 185

ubi emolumentum ibi onus 23
ubi remedium ibi ius 316
ultra vires 56, 128, 307
unconscionability 74
undue influence 66, 111, 119, 120, 127, 305
university law faculties 5
unjust 300–301
unjust enrichment 12, 24–5, 38, 39–40, 56–7, 58, 61, 64, 66, 75, 88–9, 126, 130–31, 155, 161, 256, 295–311, 312, 328
  see also restitution; quasi contract
unlawfulness 180–81
unreasonable
  behaviour *see* duty (breach of)
  generally 237
  intervening act 281–2

risk 281
use of land 180, 190, 220, 231–2, 233, 237
unwissenschaftlichkeit 326
usage 69
user principle 65

value 192, 321–2, 326
vengeance 28
vicarious liability *see* liability
victim
  family of 292
  primary 207
  secondary 207
  take your victim as you find him 268, 288
Villey, Michel 316
vinculum
  aequitatis 28
  iuris 10, 15, 28, 29, 46, 114, 117, 134, 136, 152, 156, 174, 313
  see also lien juridique
vindicatio 37, 41
  see also action (in rem); ownership
visitor 226, 236
vitiating factor 88, 90, 98, 117–22
volenti non fit injuria 73, 266, 271
Volksgeist 316
volonté 26

Waddams, Stephen 7, 163, 164, 173
warn
  failure to 277–8
  product (about) 221
warranty 54, 121, 134, 137–9, 143
Warrington, Mark 325
Watson, Alan 314–15, 327
Wegfall der Geschäftsgrundlage 35
Weir, Tony 133, 157, 203, 265, 323–4, 325
Wieacker, Franz 317
Willenserklärungen 95
Williams, Glanville 160, 162
window cleaner 101
Winfield, Percy 157
writ
  generally 48–50
  of debt 26, 53–4
  of trespass 53–4
    see also trespass

worker
  factory 222–3
  social 211

Zimmermann, Reinhard 20, 313–14,
  322, 325, 328
Zweigert, Konrad 316